Chomoran

Sachi's MONSTROUS Appetite

1

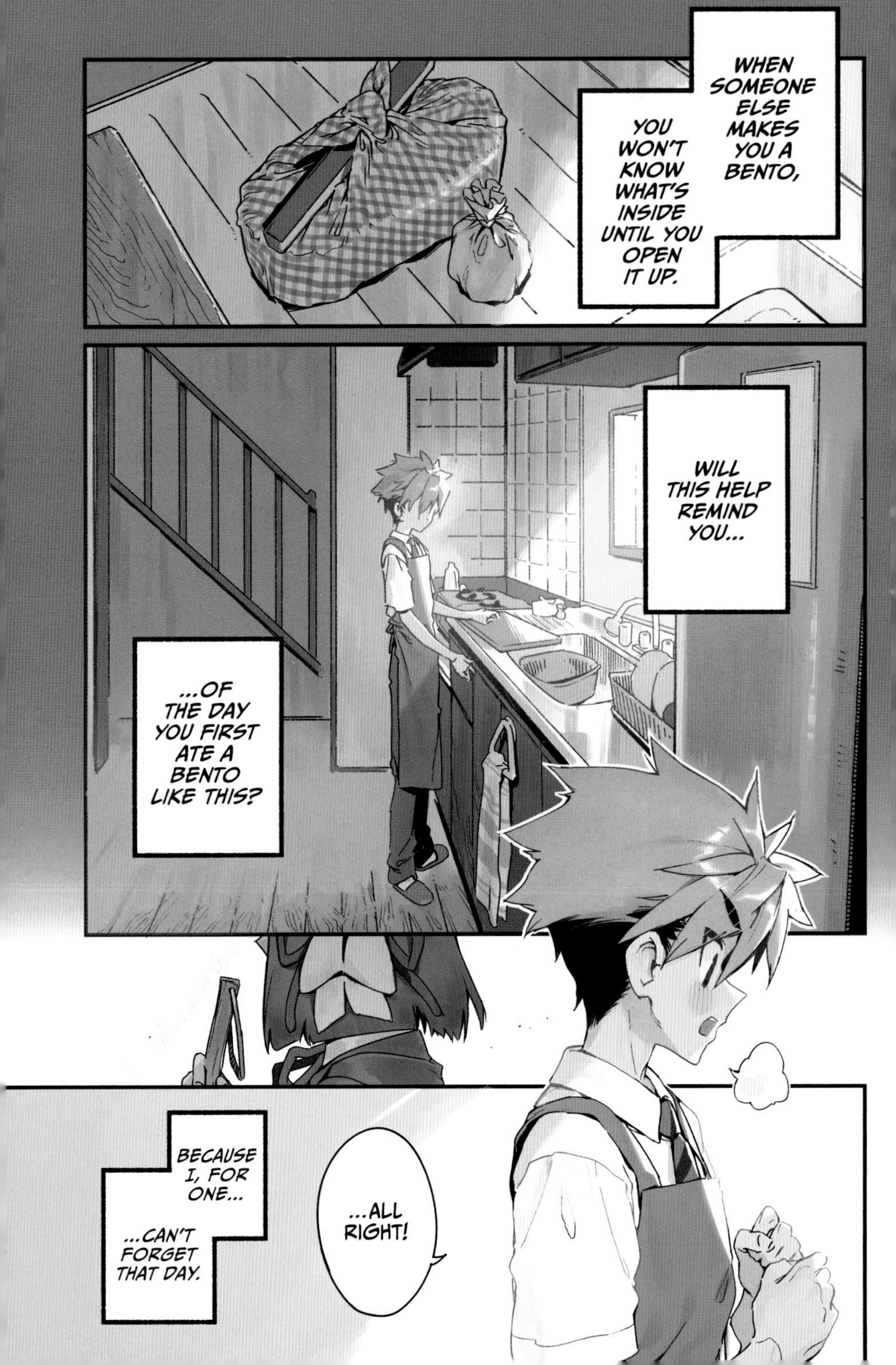
WHEN SOMEONE ELSE MAKES YOU A BENTO,
YOU WON'T KNOW WHAT'S INSIDE UNTIL YOU OPEN IT UP.
WILL THIS HELP REMIND YOU...
...OF THE DAY YOU FIRST ATE A BENTO LIKE THIS?
BECAUSE I, FOR ONE...
...CAN'T FORGET THAT DAY.
...ALL RIGHT!

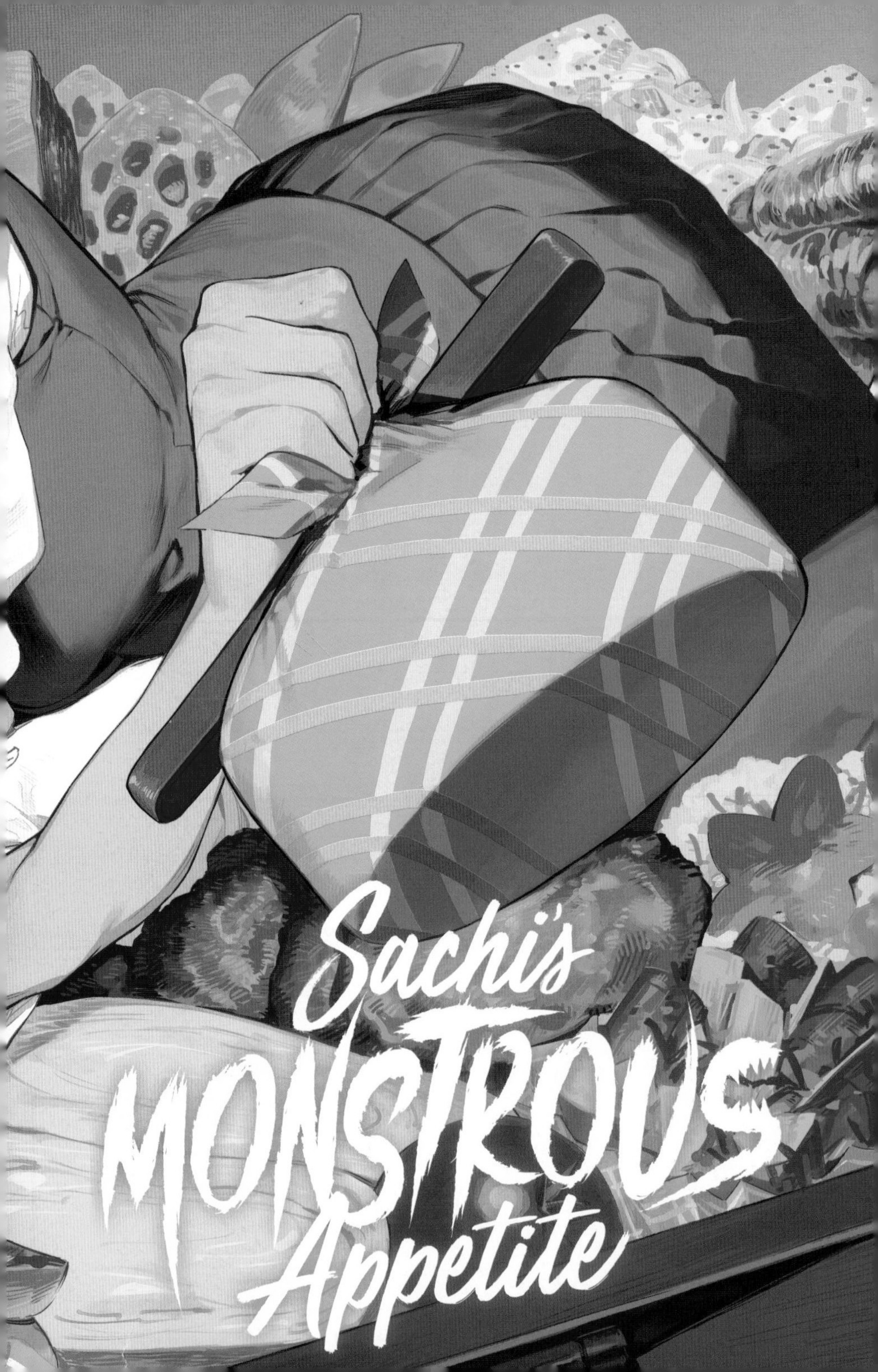
Sachi's
MONSTROUS
Appetite

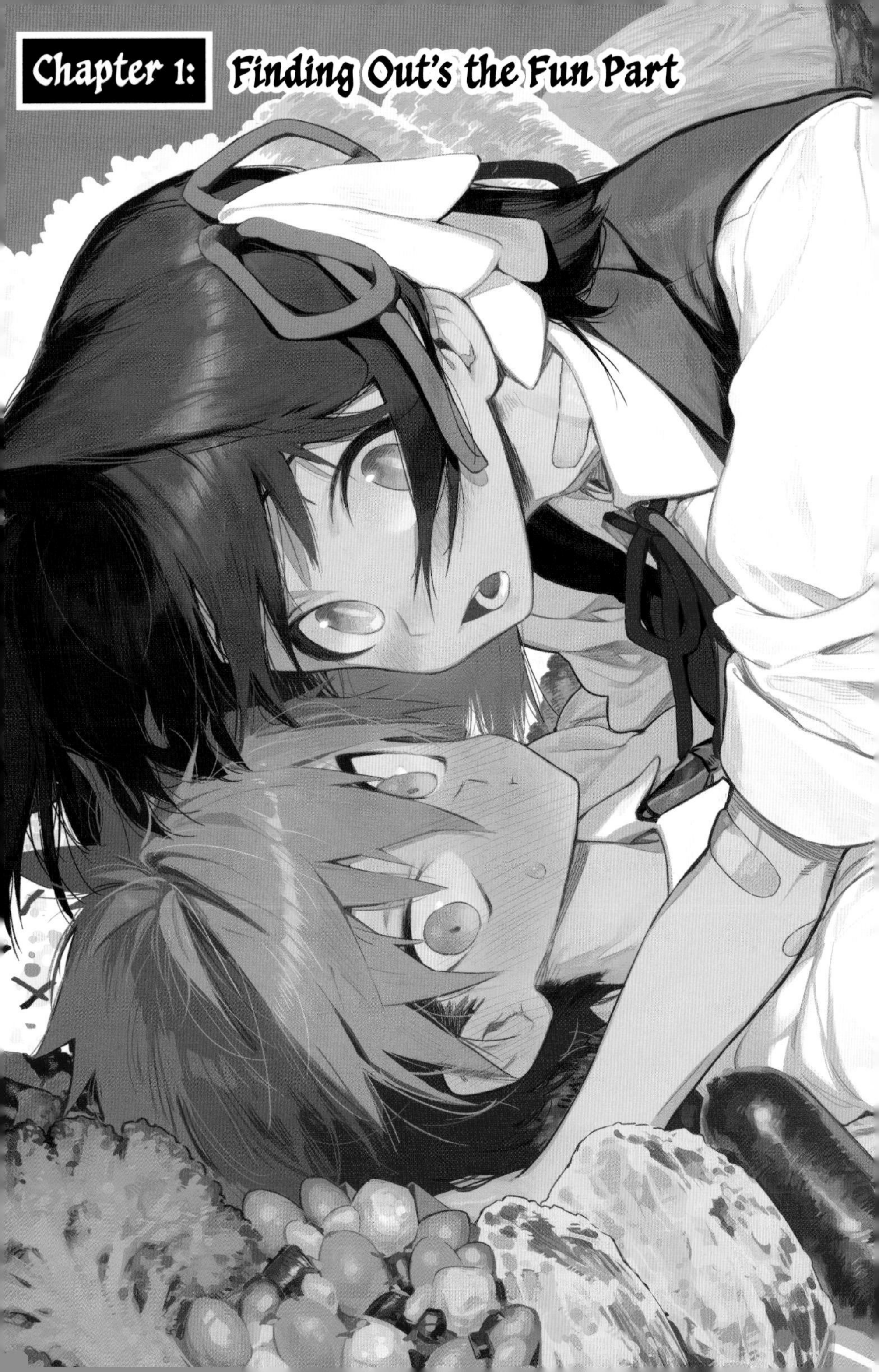
Chapter 1:
Finding Out's the Fun Part

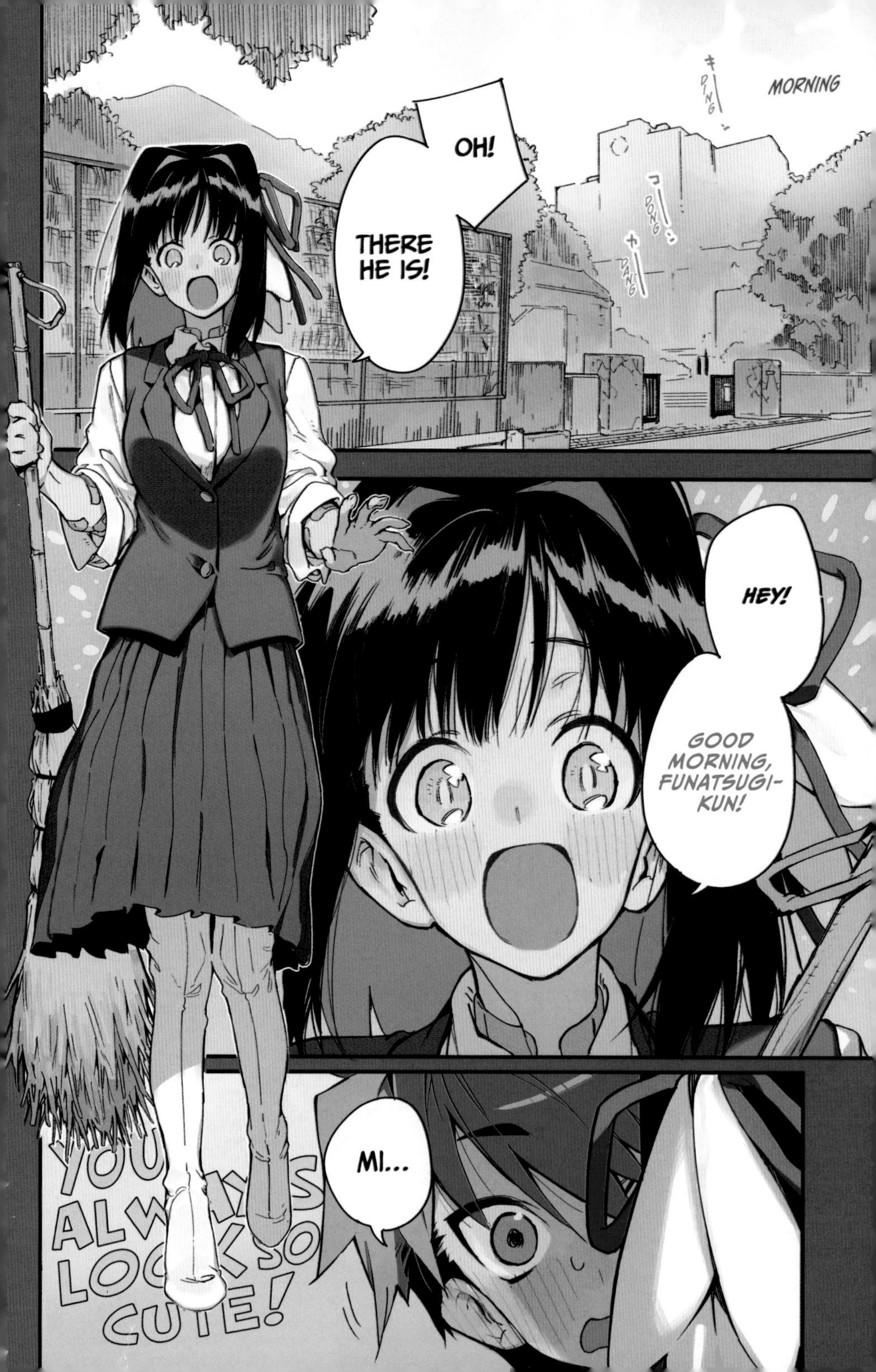
MORNING
DING
DONG
DANG
OH!
THERE HE IS!
HEY!
GOOD MORNING, FUNATSUGI-KUN!
MI...
YOU ALWAYS LOOK SO CUTE!

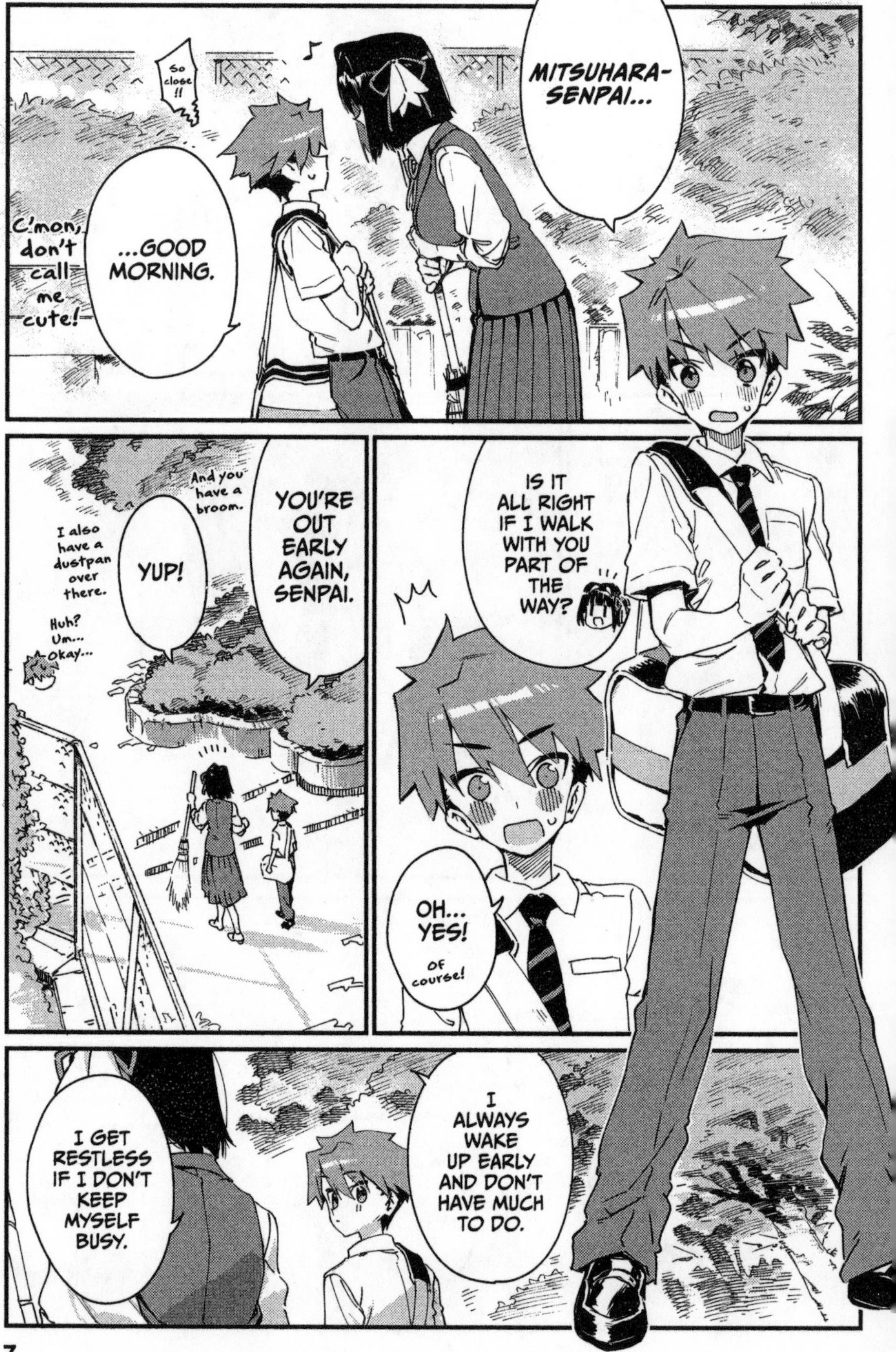
MITSUHARA-SENPAI...
So close!!
...GOOD MORNING.
C'mon, don't call me cute!
IS IT ALL RIGHT IF I WALK WITH YOU PART OF THE WAY?
OH... YES!
Of course!
YOU'RE OUT EARLY AGAIN, SENPAI.
And you have a broom.
YUP!
I also have a dustpan over there.
Huh? Um... okay...
I ALWAYS WAKE UP EARLY AND DON'T HAVE MUCH TO DO.
I GET RESTLESS IF I DON'T KEEP MYSELF BUSY.

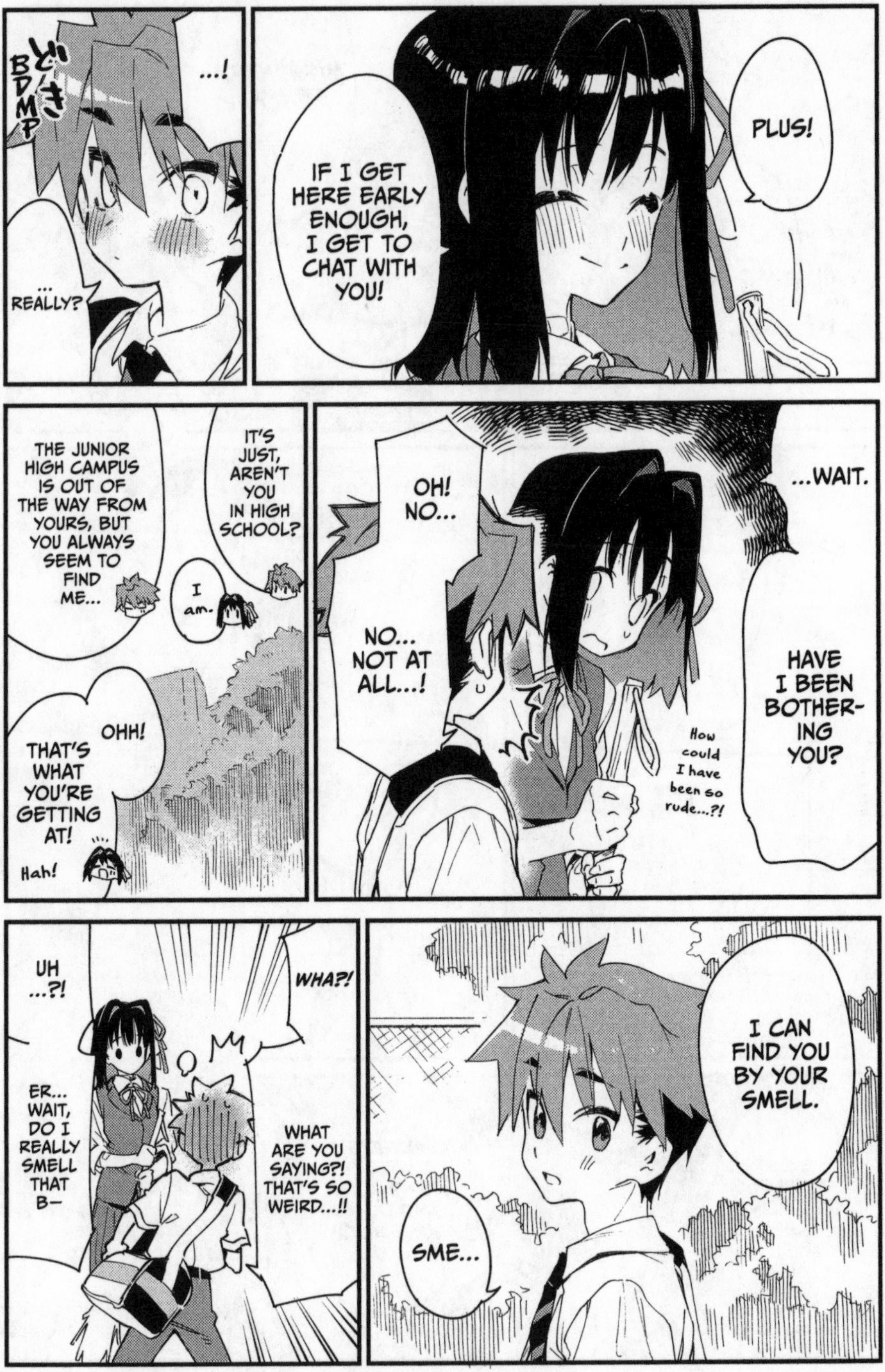
PLUS!
IF I GET HERE EARLY ENOUGH, I GET TO CHAT WITH YOU!
どき
BDMP
...!
... REALLY?
...WAIT.
HAVE I BEEN BOTHERING YOU?
How could I have been so rude...?!
OH! NO...
NO... NOT AT ALL...!
IT'S JUST, AREN'T YOU IN HIGH SCHOOL?
THE JUNIOR HIGH CAMPUS IS OUT OF THE WAY FROM YOURS, BUT YOU ALWAYS SEEM TO FIND ME...
I am.
OHH! THAT'S WHAT YOU'RE GETTING AT!
Hah!
I CAN FIND YOU BY YOUR SMELL.
SME...
WHA?!
UH ...?!
WHAT ARE YOU SAYING?! THAT'S SO WEIRD...!!
ER... WAIT, DO I REALLY SMELL THAT B—

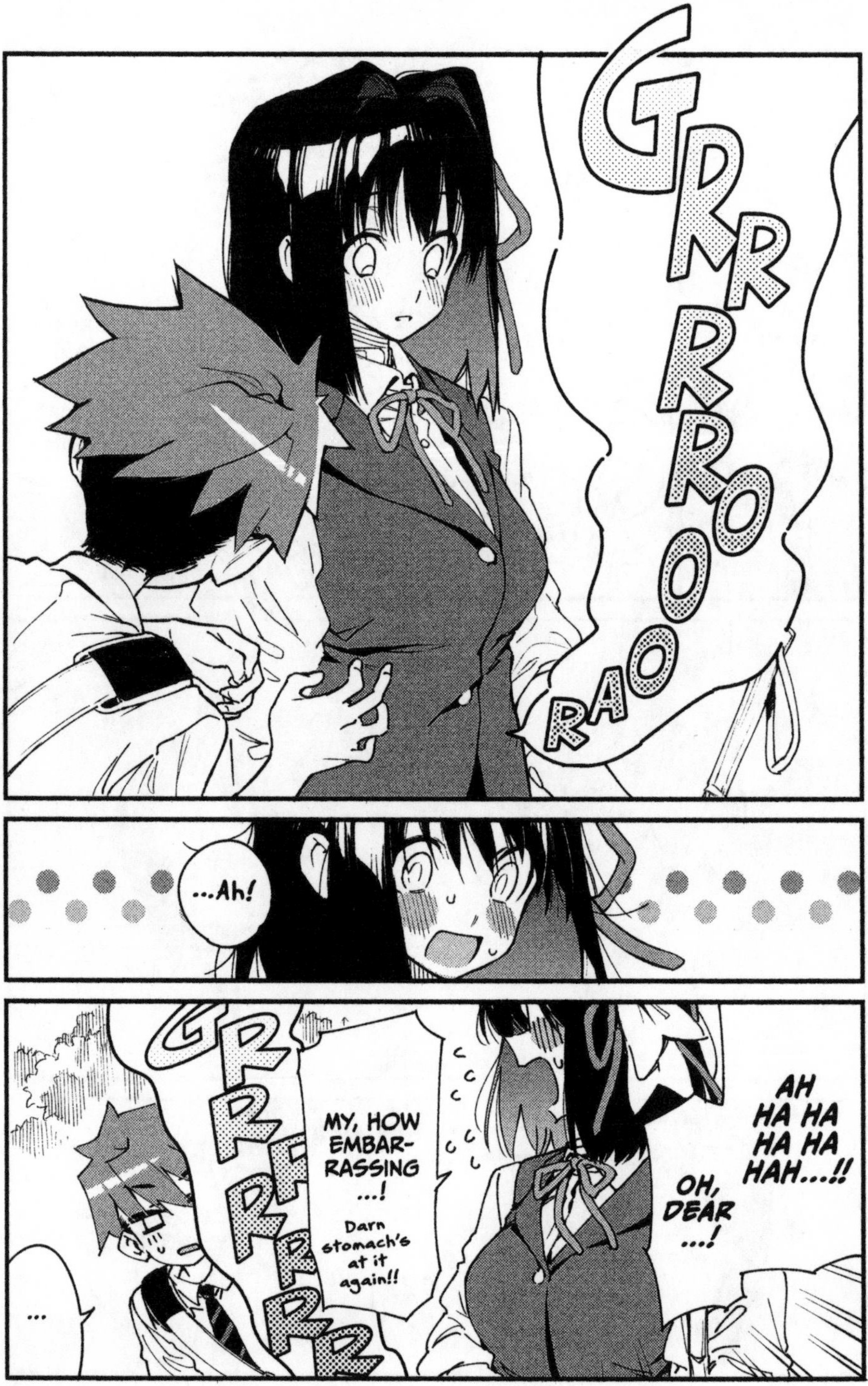
GRRRRROOOORAO
...Ah!
AH HA HA HA HA HAH...!!
OH, DEAR...!
MY, HOW EMBARRASSING...!
Darn stomach's at it again!!
GRRRRRRR
...

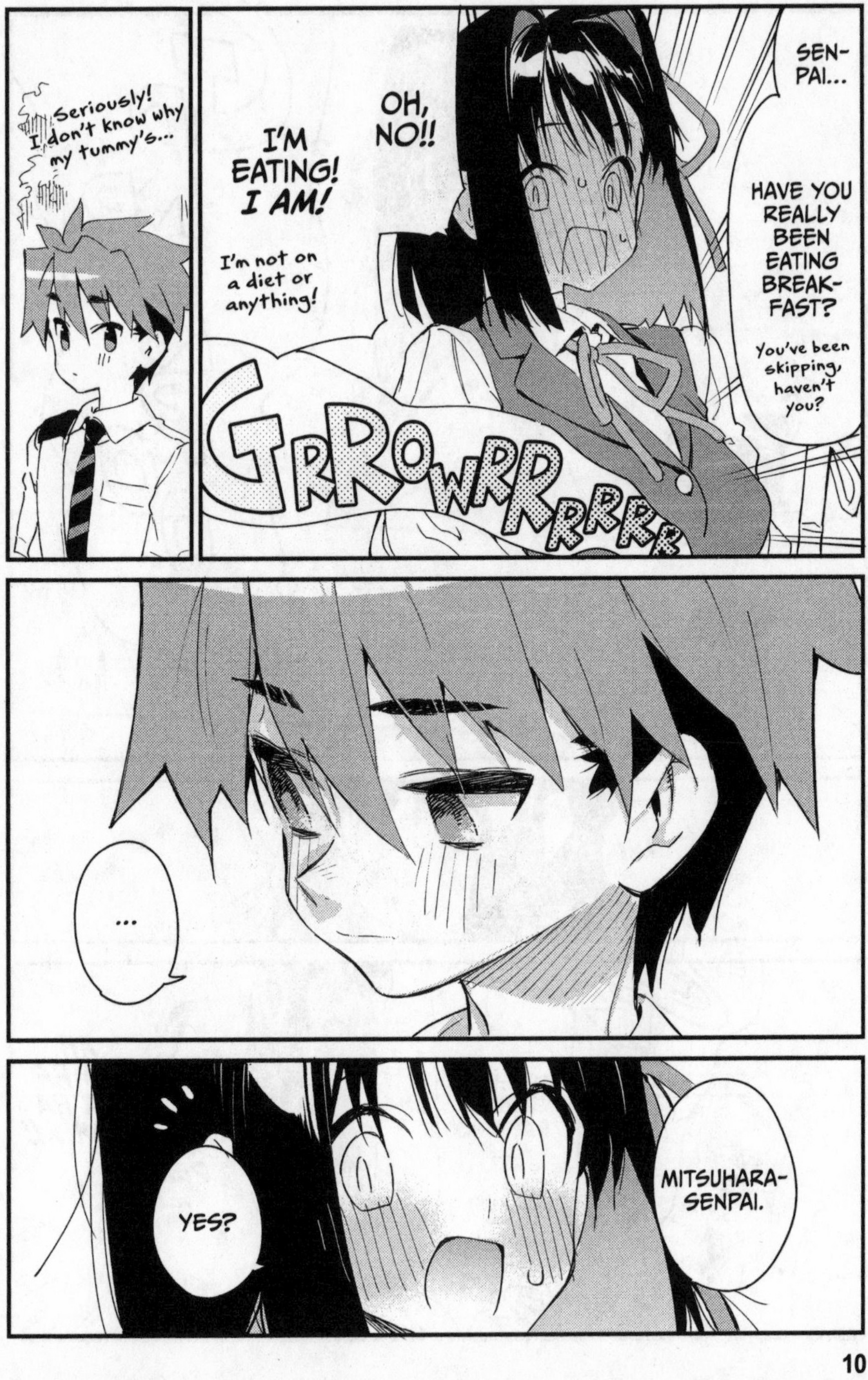
SEN-PAI...
HAVE YOU REALLY BEEN EATING BREAK-FAST?
You've been skipping, haven't you?
OH, NO!!
I'M EATING! I AM!
I'm not on a diet or anything!
GRROWRRRRRR
Seriously! I don't know why my tummy's...
...
MITSUHARA-SENPAI.
YES?

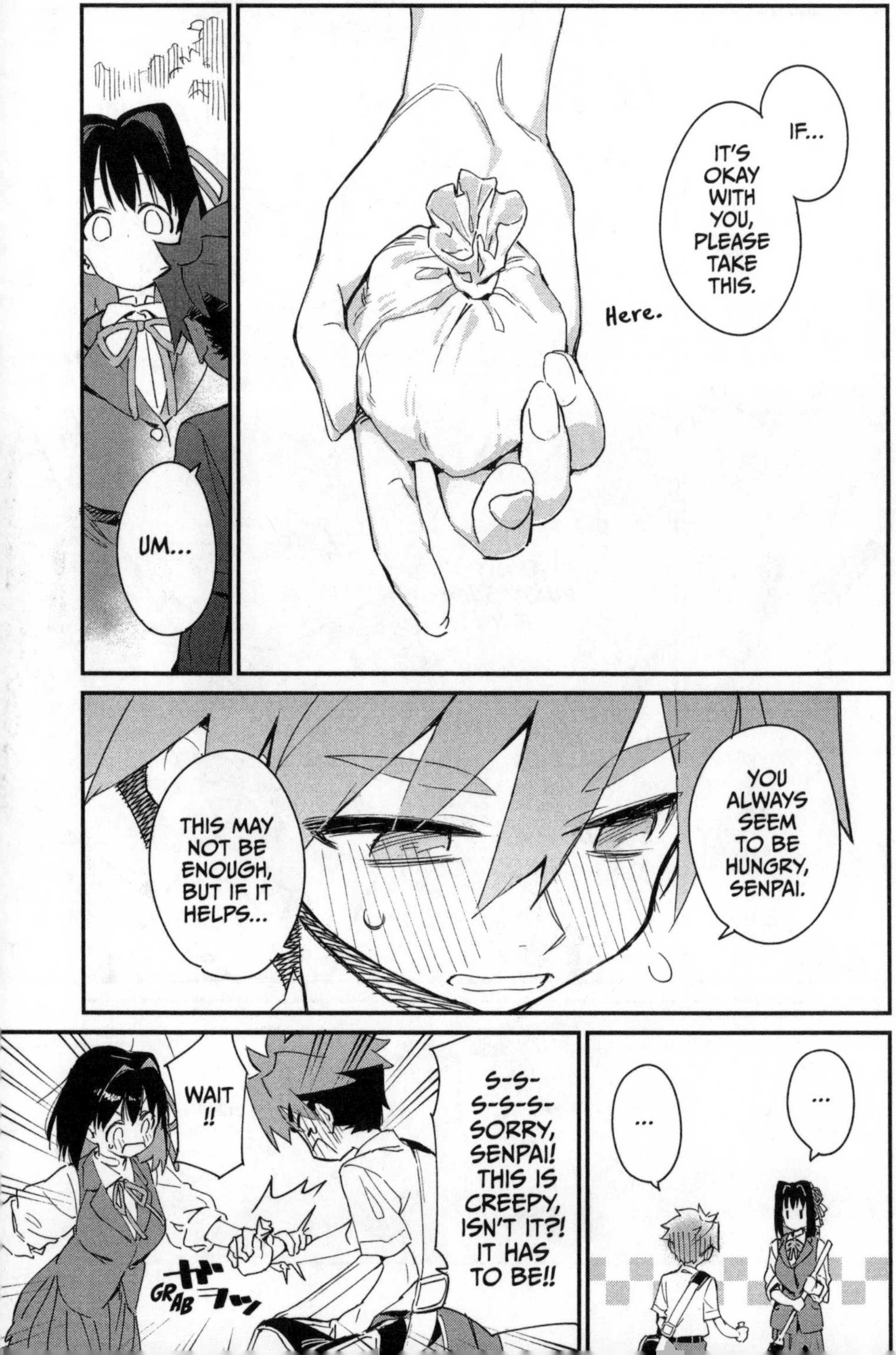
IF... IT'S OKAY WITH YOU, PLEASE TAKE THIS.
Here.
UM...
YOU ALWAYS SEEM TO BE HUNGRY, SENPAI.
THIS MAY NOT BE ENOUGH, BUT IF IT HELPS...
...
...
S-S-S-S-S-S-SORRY, SENPAI! THIS IS CREEPY, ISN'T IT?! IT HAS TO BE!!
WAIT !!
GRAB

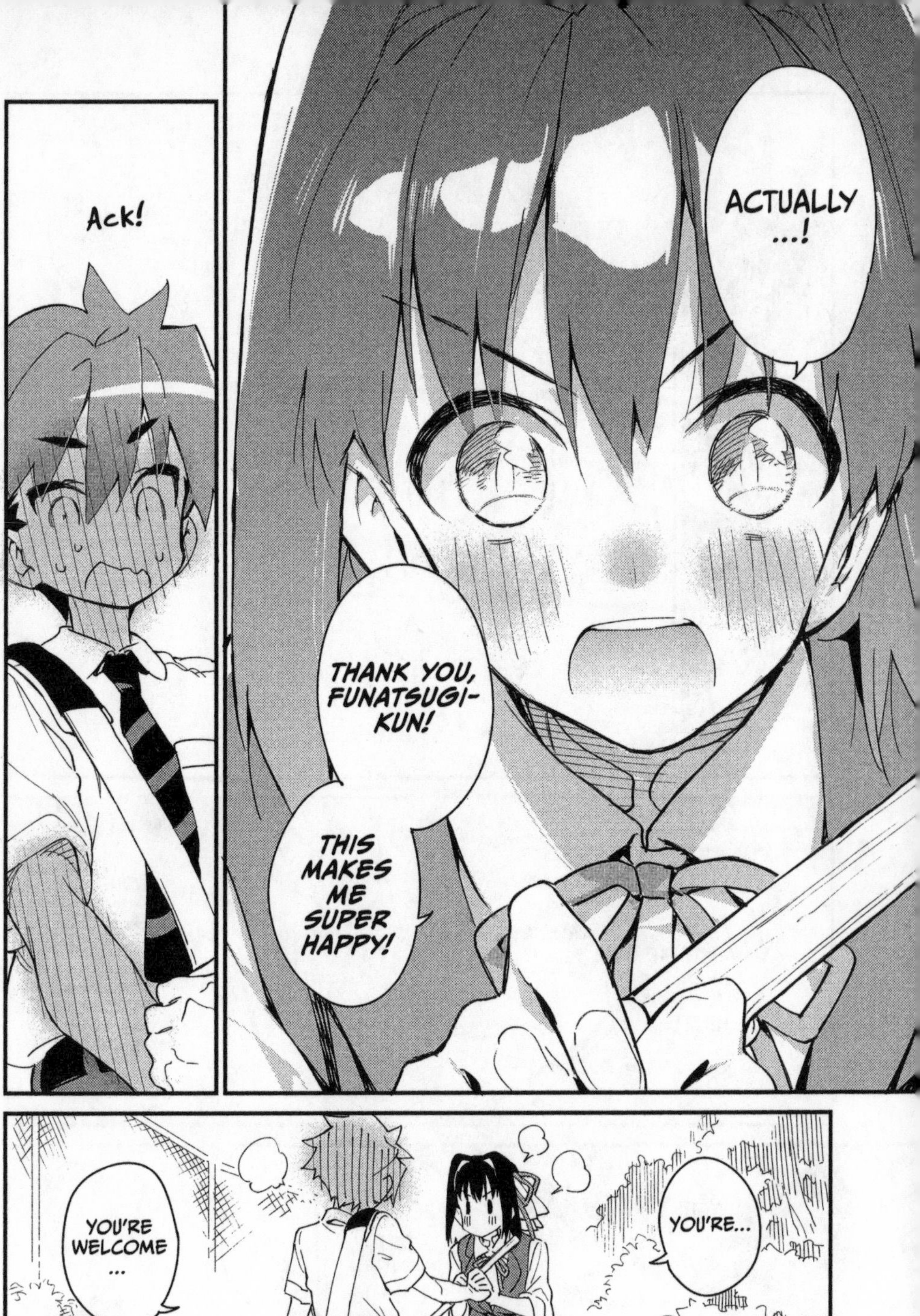
ACTUALLY ...!
THANK YOU, FUNATSUGI-KUN!
THIS MAKES ME SUPER HAPPY!
Ack!
YOU'RE...
YOU'RE WELCOME ...

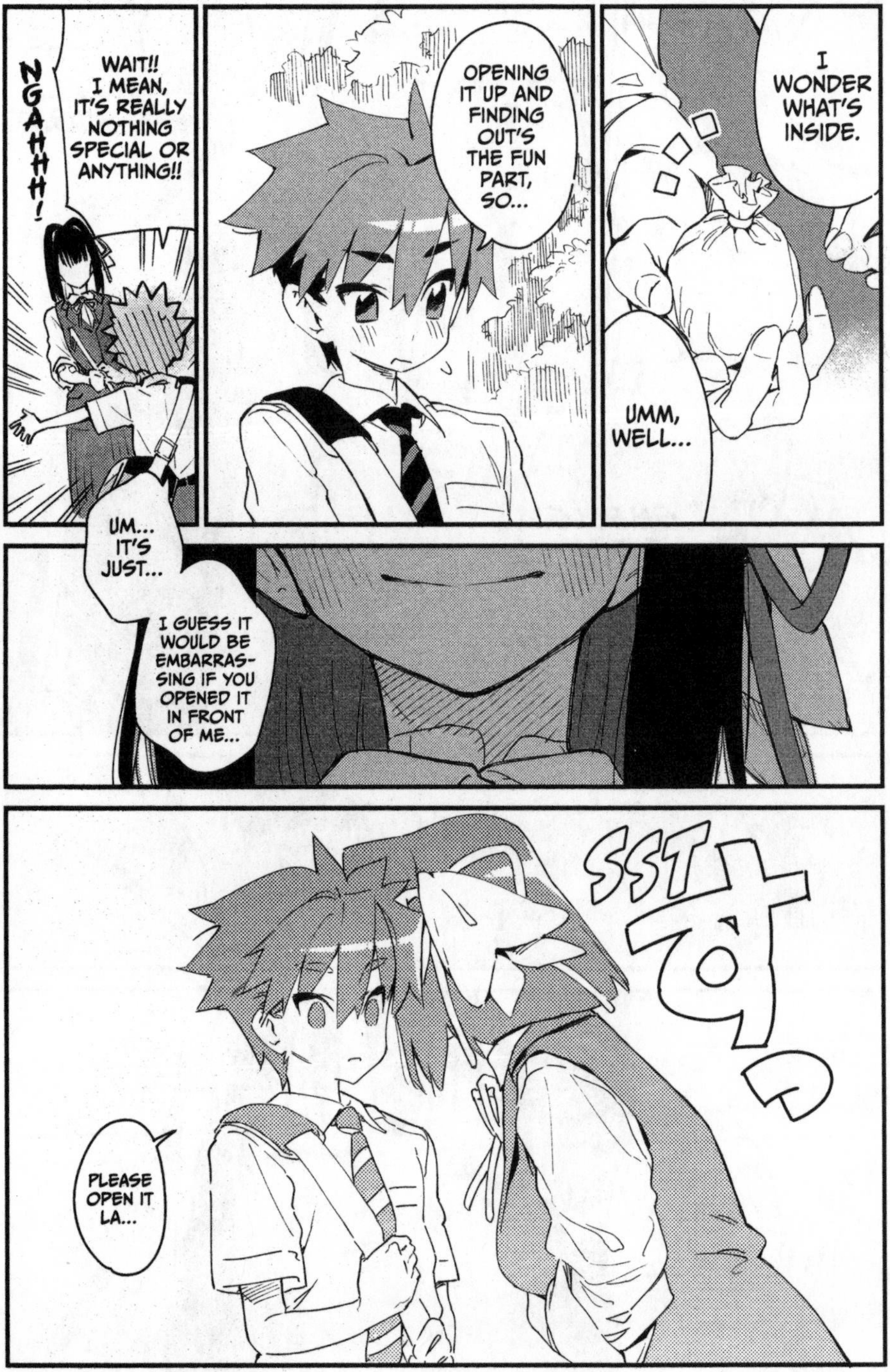
I WONDER WHAT'S INSIDE.
UMM, WELL...
OPENING IT UP AND FINDING OUT'S THE FUN PART, SO...
WAIT!! I MEAN, IT'S REALLY NOTHING SPECIAL OR ANYTHING!!
NGAHHH!
UM... IT'S JUST...
I GUESS IT WOULD BE EMBARRAS-SING IF YOU OPENED IT IN FRONT OF ME...
SST すっ
PLEASE OPEN IT LA...

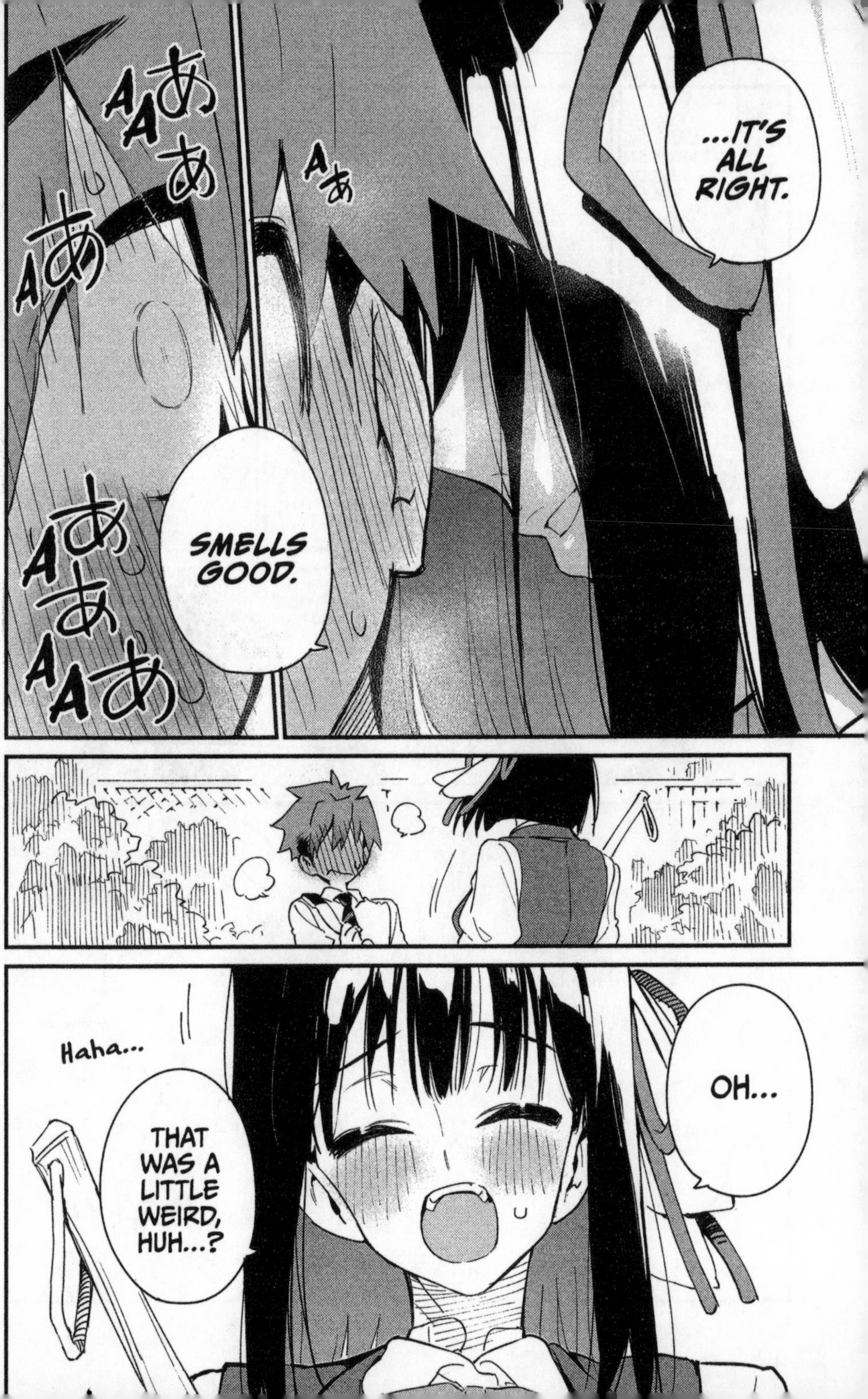
...IT'S ALL RIGHT.
Aあ
SMELLS GOOD.
AAああ
Aあ
AあAあAAあ
OH...
Haha...
THAT WAS A LITTLE WEIRD, HUH...?

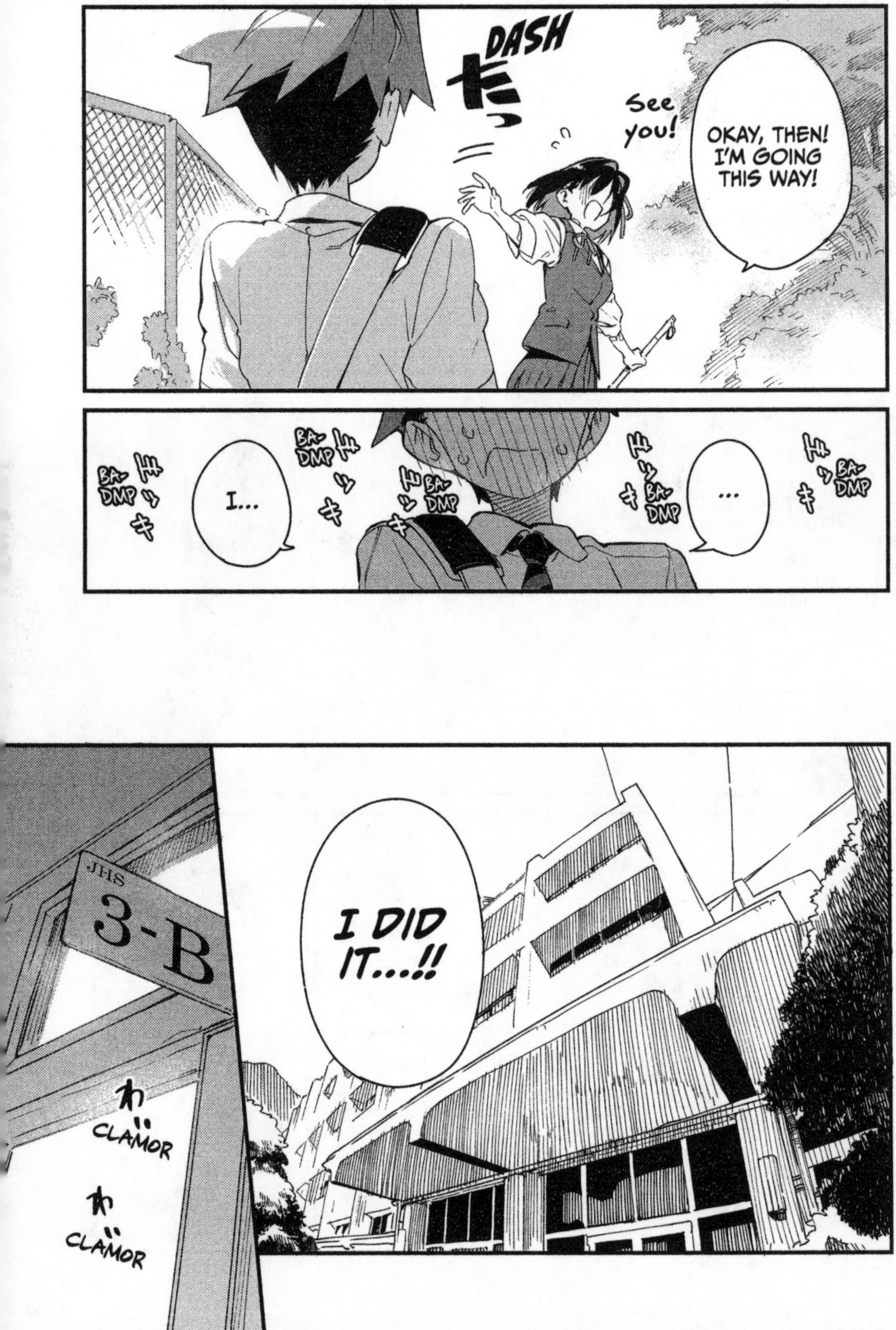
OKAY, THEN! I'M GOING THIS WAY!
See you!
DASH
BA-DMP
...
BA-DMP
BA-DMP
BA-DMP
I...
BA-DMP
I DID IT...!!
JHS
3-B
CLAMOR
CLAMOR

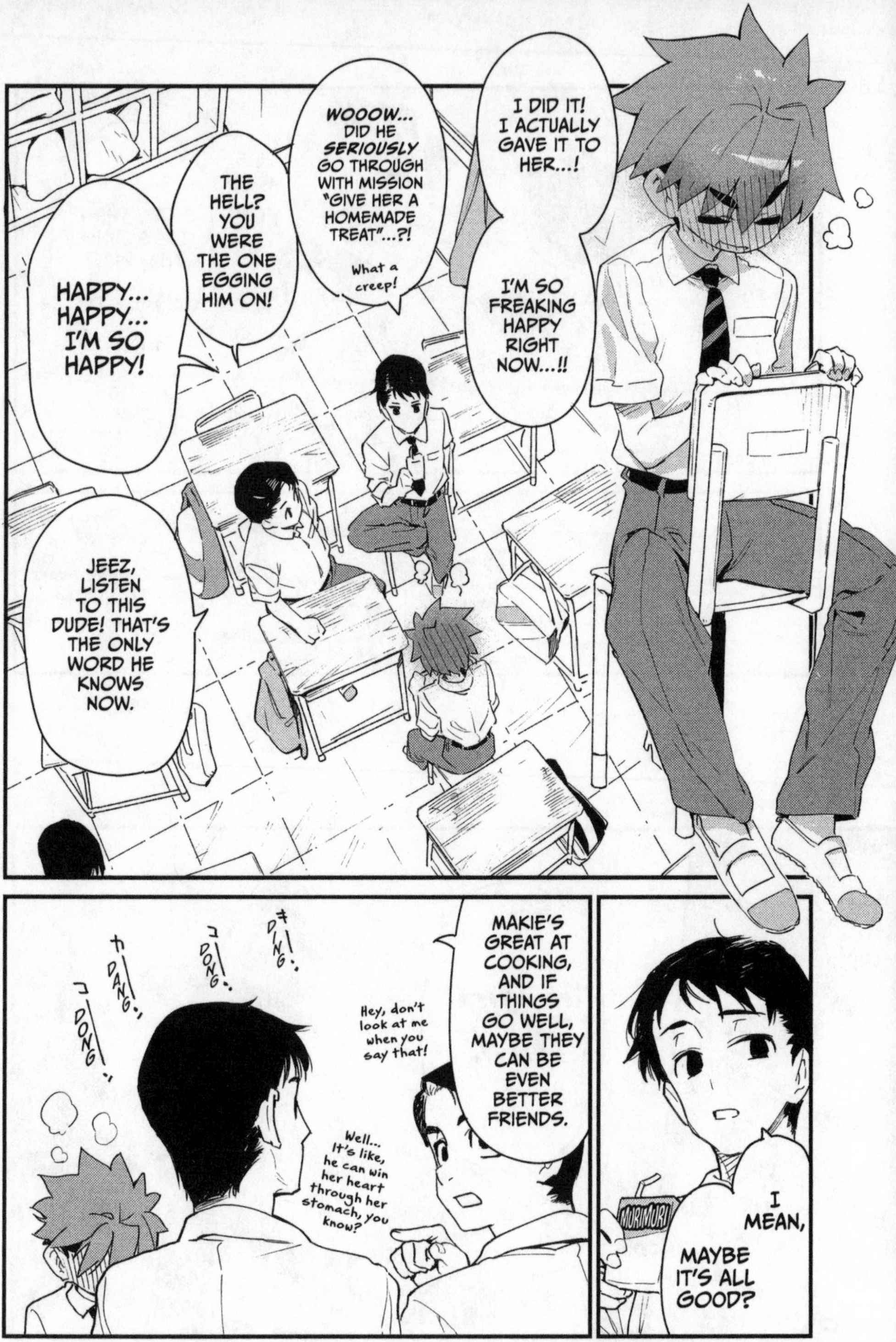
I DID IT! I ACTUALLY GAVE IT TO HER...!
I'M SO FREAKING HAPPY RIGHT NOW...!!
WOOOW... DID HE SERIOUSLY GO THROUGH WITH MISSION "GIVE HER A HOMEMADE TREAT"...?!
What a creep!
THE HELL? YOU WERE THE ONE EGGING HIM ON!
HAPPY... HAPPY... I'M SO HAPPY!
JEEZ, LISTEN TO THIS DUDE! THAT'S THE ONLY WORD HE KNOWS NOW.
I MEAN,
MAYBE IT'S ALL GOOD?
MURIMURI
キ DING..
コ DONG..
カ DANG..
コ DONG..
MAKIE'S GREAT AT COOKING, AND IF THINGS GO WELL, MAYBE THEY CAN BE EVEN BETTER FRIENDS.
Hey, don't look at me when you say that!
Well... It's like, he can win her heart through her stomach, you know?

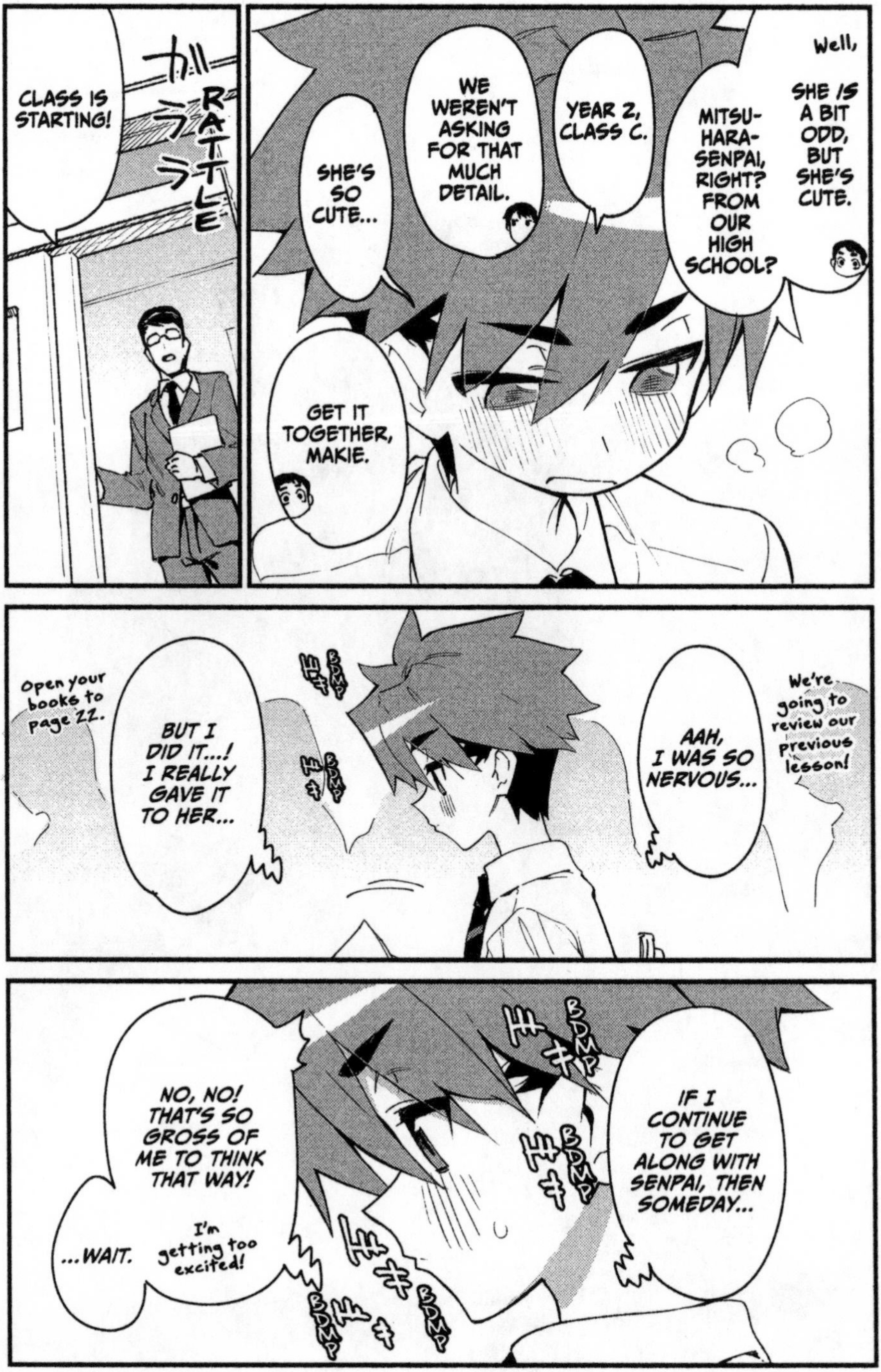
Well,
SHE IS A BIT ODD, BUT SHE'S CUTE.
MITSUHARA-SENPAI, RIGHT? FROM OUR HIGH SCHOOL?
YEAR 2, CLASS C.
WE WEREN'T ASKING FOR THAT MUCH DETAIL.
SHE'S SO CUTE...
GET IT TOGETHER, MAKIE.
RATTLE
CLASS IS STARTING!
We're going to review our previous lesson!
AAH, I WAS SO NERVOUS...
BDMP
BDMP
BUT I DID IT...! I REALLY GAVE IT TO HER...
Open your books to page 22.
IF I CONTINUE TO GET ALONG WITH SENPAI, THEN SOMEDAY...
BDMP
BDMP
NO, NO! THAT'S SO GROSS OF ME TO THINK THAT WAY!
BDMP
BDMP
I'm getting too excited!
...WAIT.

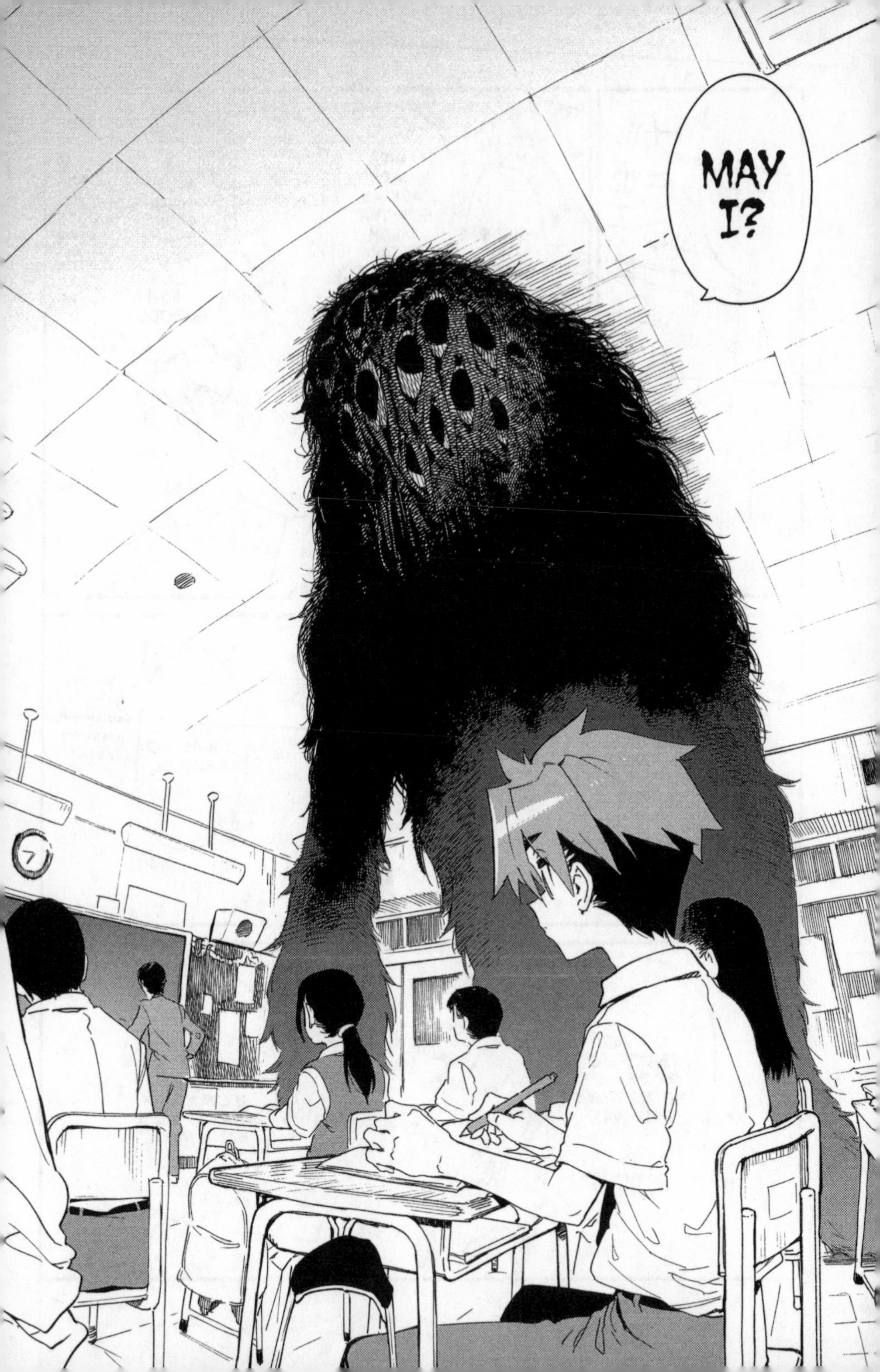
MAY I?

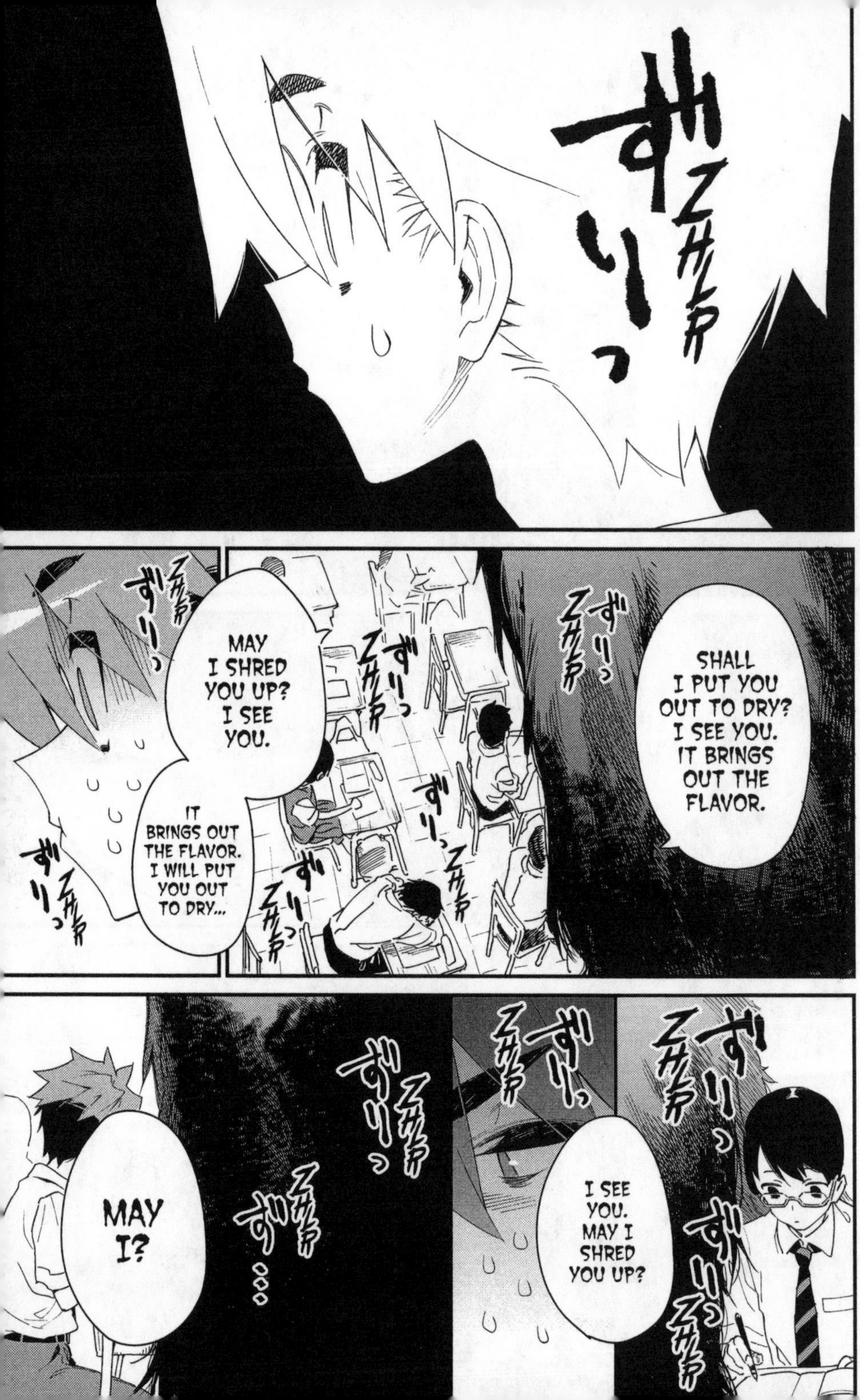
ずりっ
ZUHR
ずりっ
ZUHR
SHALL I PUT YOU OUT TO DRY? I SEE YOU. IT BRINGS OUT THE FLAVOR.
ずりっ
ZUHR
ずりっ
ZUHR
ずりっ
ZUHR
MAY I SHRED YOU UP? I SEE YOU.
IT BRINGS OUT THE FLAVOR. I WILL PUT YOU OUT TO DRY...
ずりっ
ZUHR
ずりっ
ZUHR
ずりっ
ZUHR
ずりっ
ZUHR
ずりっ
ZUHR
I SEE YOU. MAY I SHRED YOU UP?
ずりっ
ZUHR
ず…
ZUHR
MAY I?

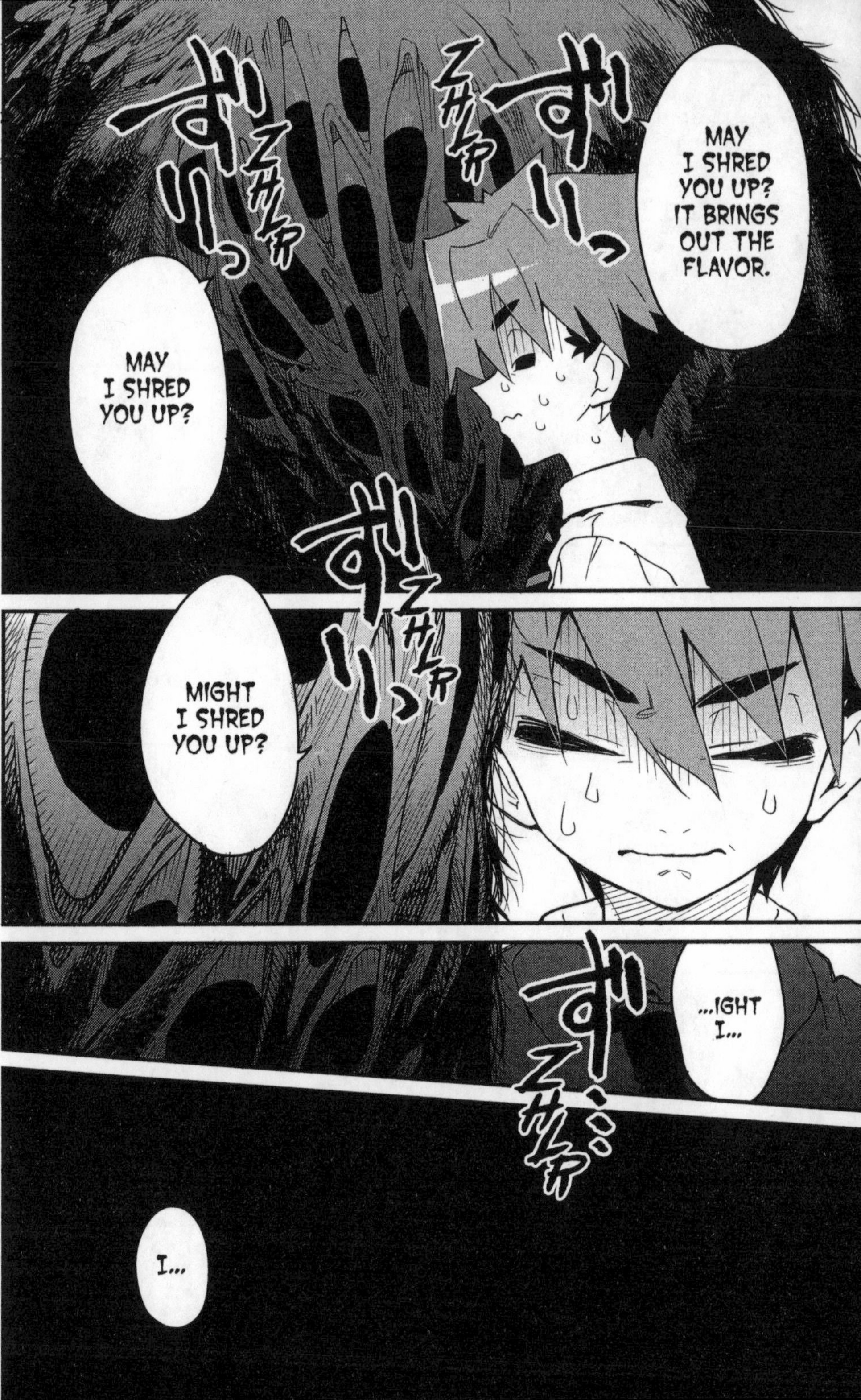
MAY I SHRED YOU UP? IT BRINGS OUT THE FLAVOR.
ZHLR
ZHLR
MAY I SHRED YOU UP?
ZHLR
MIGHT I SHRED YOU UP?
...IGHT I...
ZHLR
I...

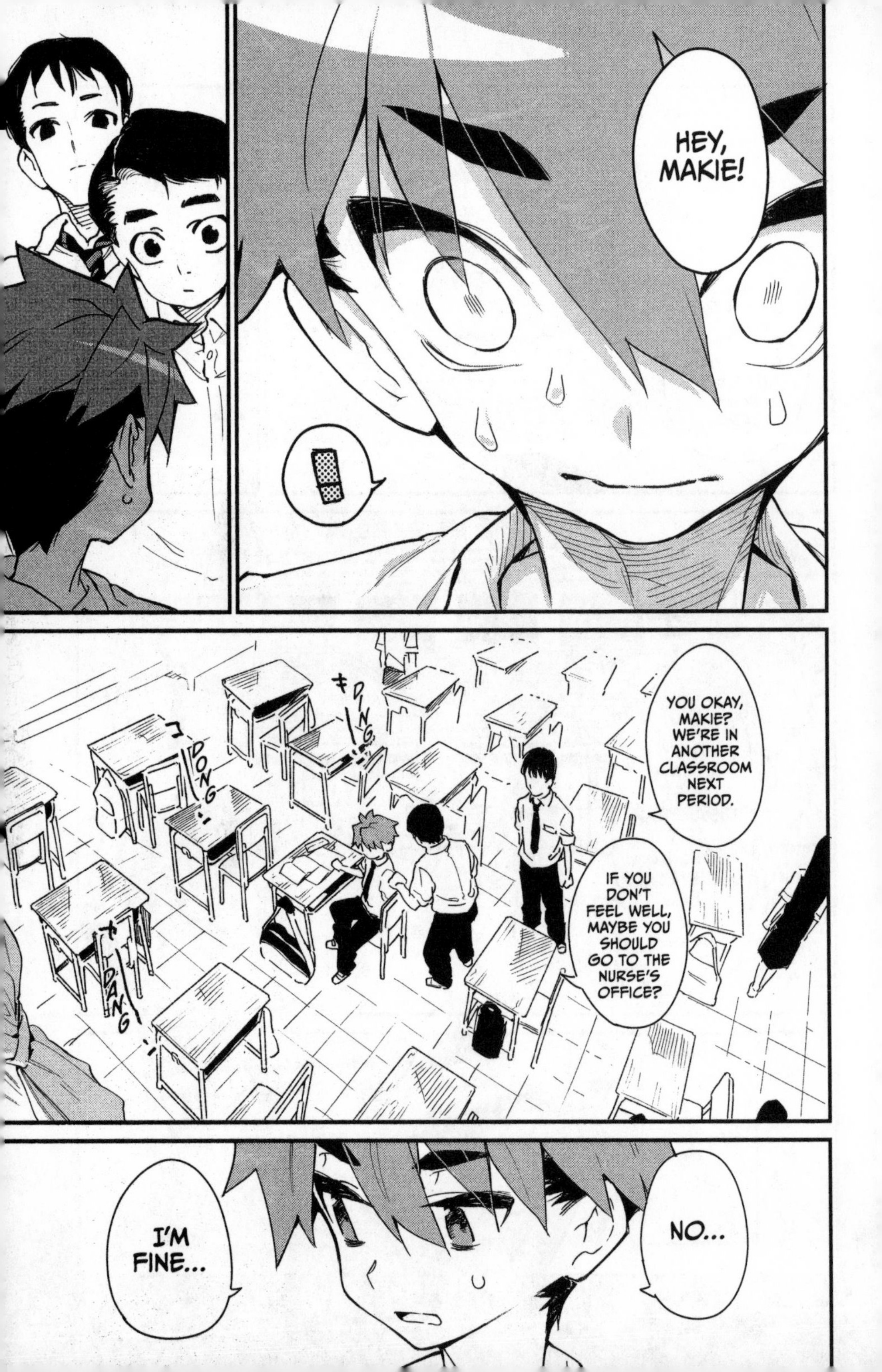
HEY, MAKIE!
YOU OKAY, MAKIE? WE'RE IN ANOTHER CLASSROOM NEXT PERIOD.
DING
IF YOU DON'T FEEL WELL, MAYBE YOU SHOULD GO TO THE NURSE'S OFFICE?
DONG
DANG
NO...
I'M FINE...

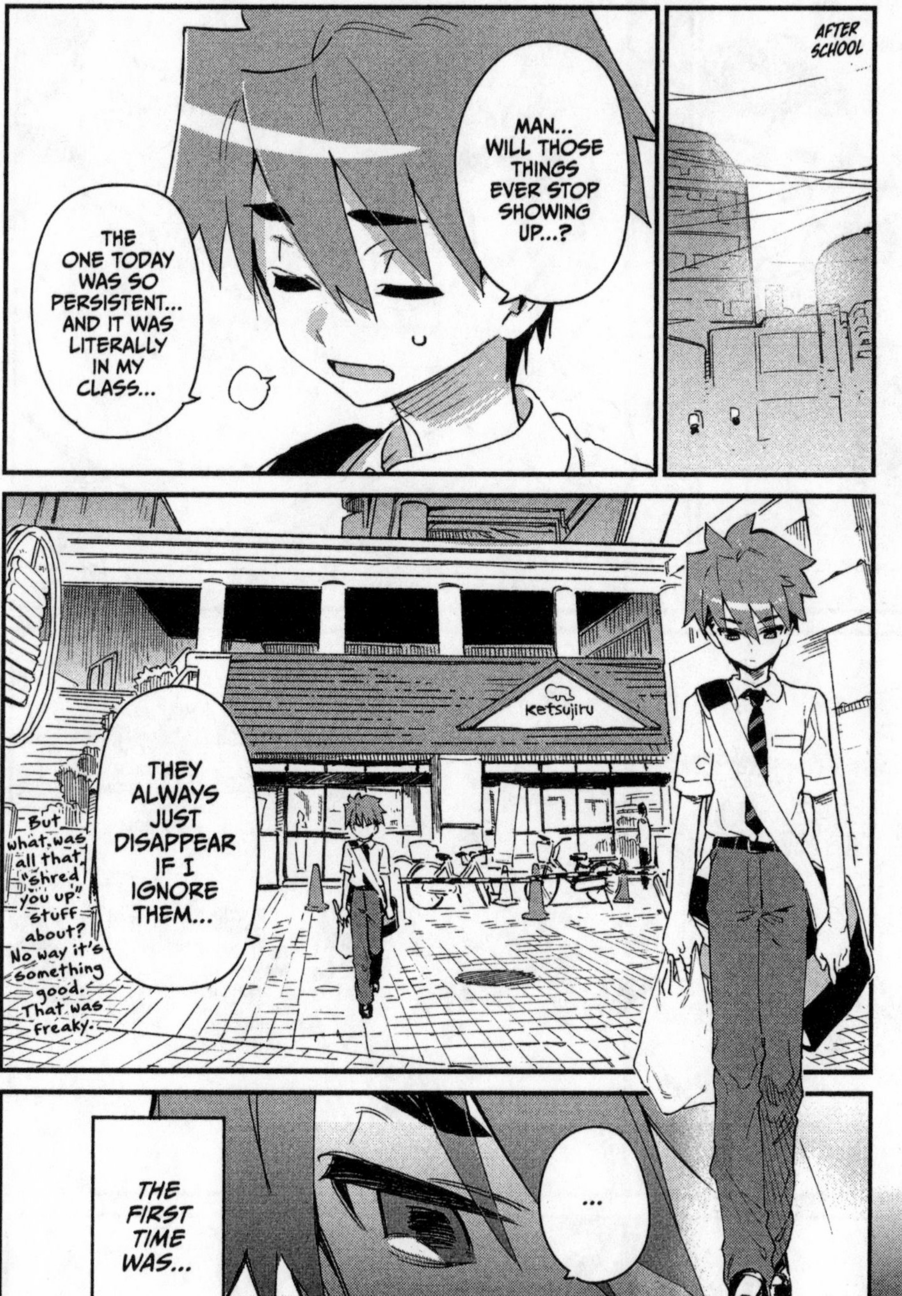
AFTER SCHOOL
MAN... WILL THOSE THINGS EVER STOP SHOWING UP...?
THE ONE TODAY WAS SO PERSISTENT... AND IT WAS LITERALLY IN MY CLASS...
Ketsujiru
THEY ALWAYS JUST DISAPPEAR IF I IGNORE THEM...
But what was all that "shred you up" stuff about? No way it's something good. That was freaky.
...
THE FIRST TIME WAS...

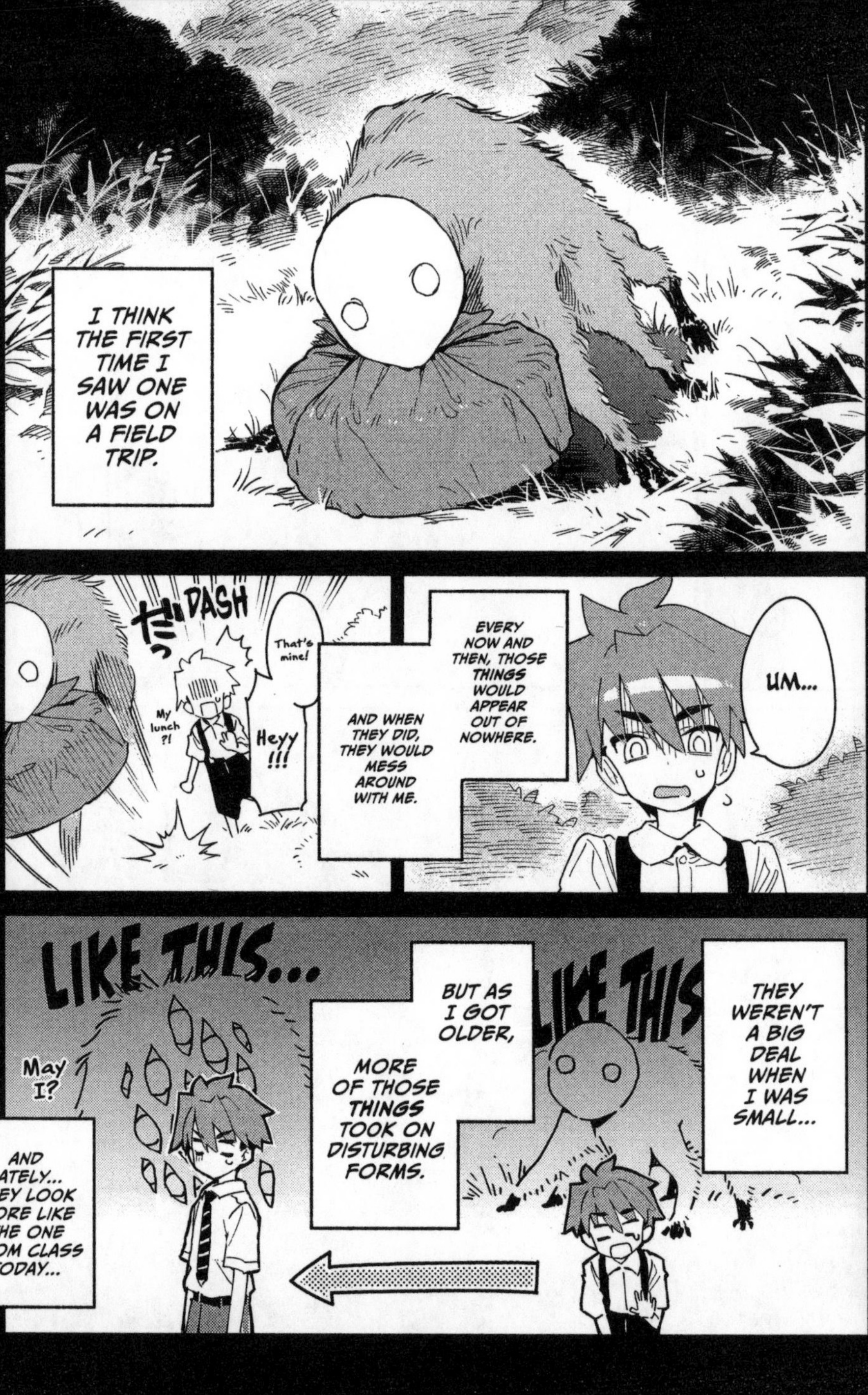
I THINK THE FIRST TIME I SAW ONE WAS ON A FIELD TRIP.
UM...
EVERY NOW AND THEN, THOSE THINGS WOULD APPEAR OUT OF NOWHERE.
AND WHEN THEY DID, THEY WOULD MESS AROUND WITH ME.
That's mine!
DASH
Heyy !!!
My lunch ?!
THEY WEREN'T A BIG DEAL WHEN I WAS SMALL...
LIKE THIS
BUT AS I GOT OLDER,
MORE OF THOSE THINGS TOOK ON DISTURBING FORMS.
LIKE THIS...
May I?
AND LATELY... THEY LOOK MORE LIKE THE ONE FROM CLASS TODAY...

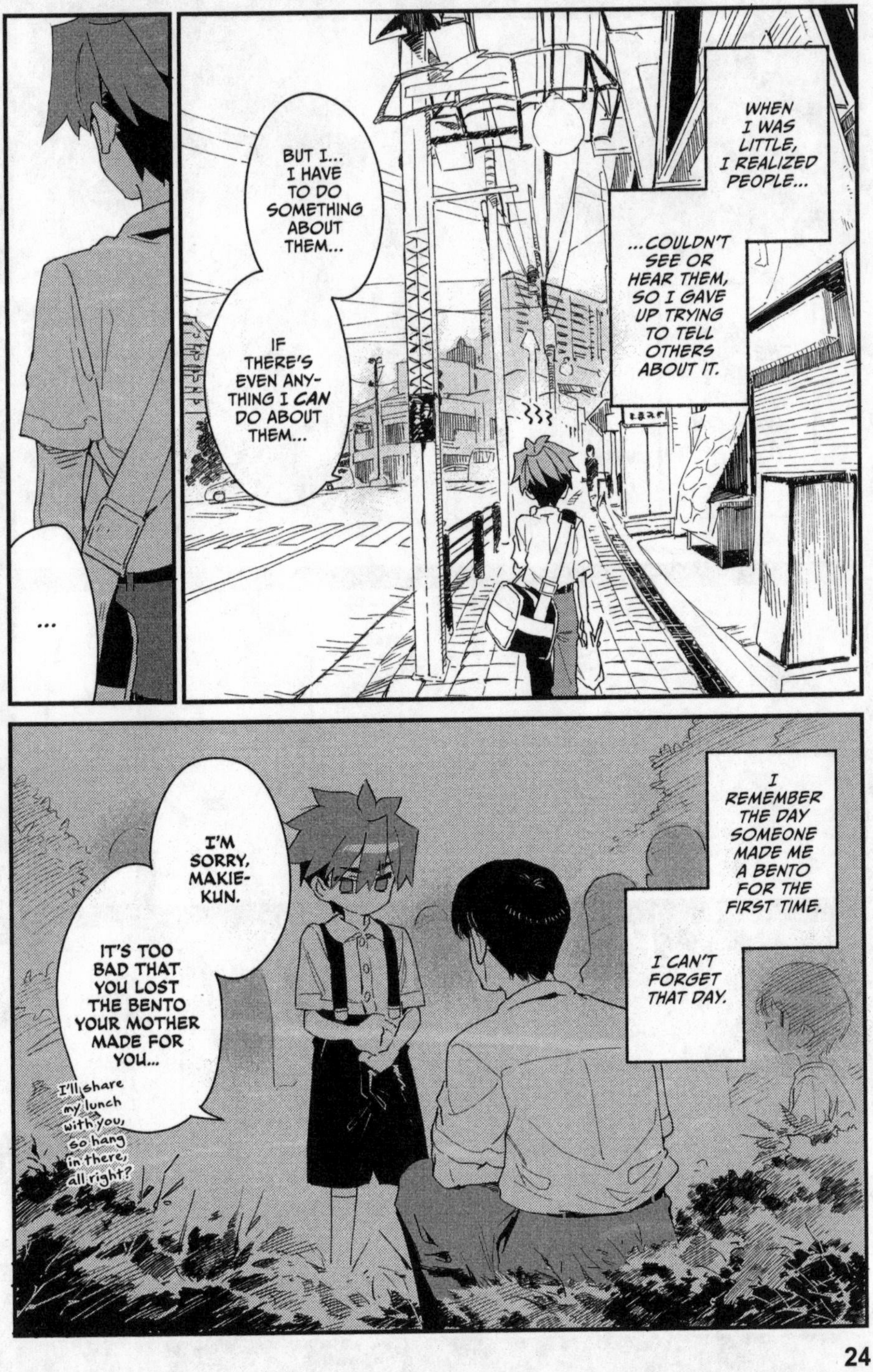
WHEN I WAS LITTLE, I REALIZED PEOPLE...
...COULDN'T SEE OR HEAR THEM, SO I GAVE UP TRYING TO TELL OTHERS ABOUT IT.
BUT I... I HAVE TO DO SOMETHING ABOUT THEM...
IF THERE'S EVEN ANYTHING I *CAN* DO ABOUT THEM...
...
I REMEMBER THE DAY SOMEONE MADE ME A BENTO FOR THE FIRST TIME.
I CAN'T FORGET THAT DAY.
I'M SORRY, MAKIE-KUN.
IT'S TOO BAD THAT YOU LOST THE BENTO YOUR MOTHER MADE FOR YOU...
I'll share my lunch with you, so hang in there, all right?

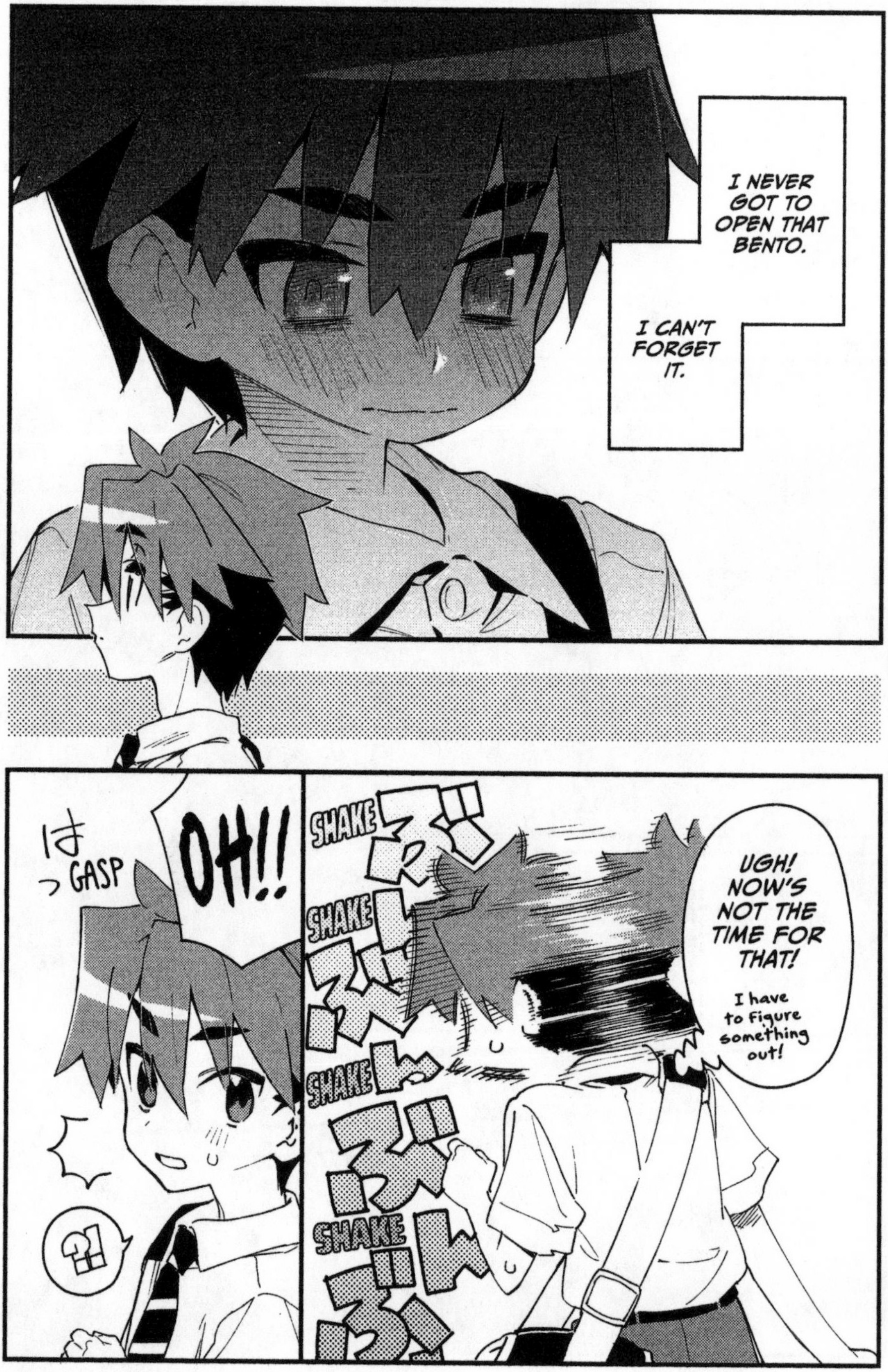
I NEVER GOT TO OPEN THAT BENTO.
I CAN'T FORGET IT.
UGH! NOW'S NOT THE TIME FOR THAT!
I have to figure something out!
SHAKE
SHAKE
SHAKE
SHAKE
OH!!
はっ GASP
?!

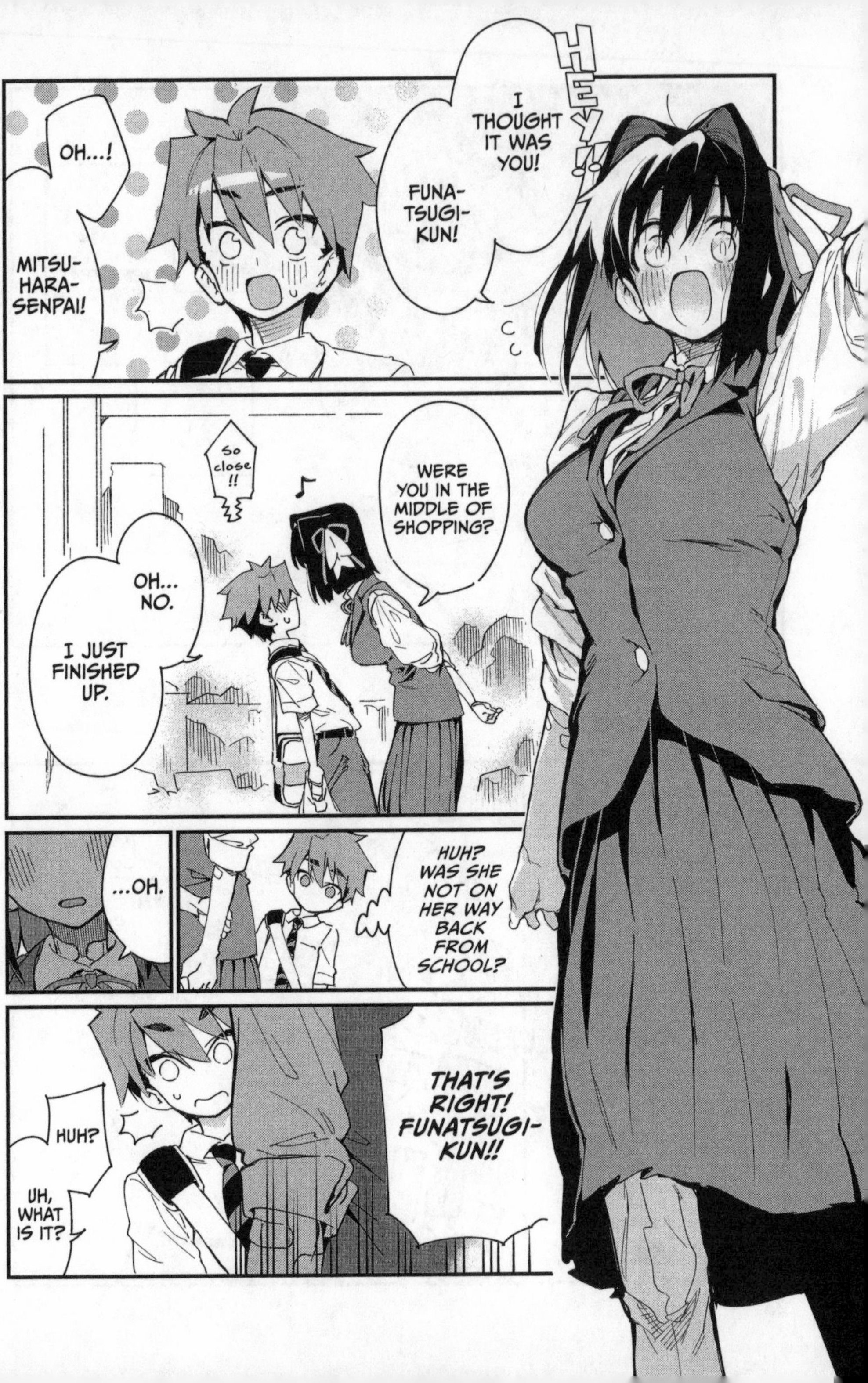
HEY!!
I THOUGHT IT WAS YOU!
FUNA-TSUGI-KUN!
OH...!
MITSU-HARA-SENPAI!
WERE YOU IN THE MIDDLE OF SHOPPING?
So close!!
OH... NO.
I JUST FINISHED UP.
HUH? WAS SHE NOT ON HER WAY BACK FROM SCHOOL?
...OH.
THAT'S RIGHT! FUNATSUGI-KUN!!
HUH?
UH, WHAT IS IT?

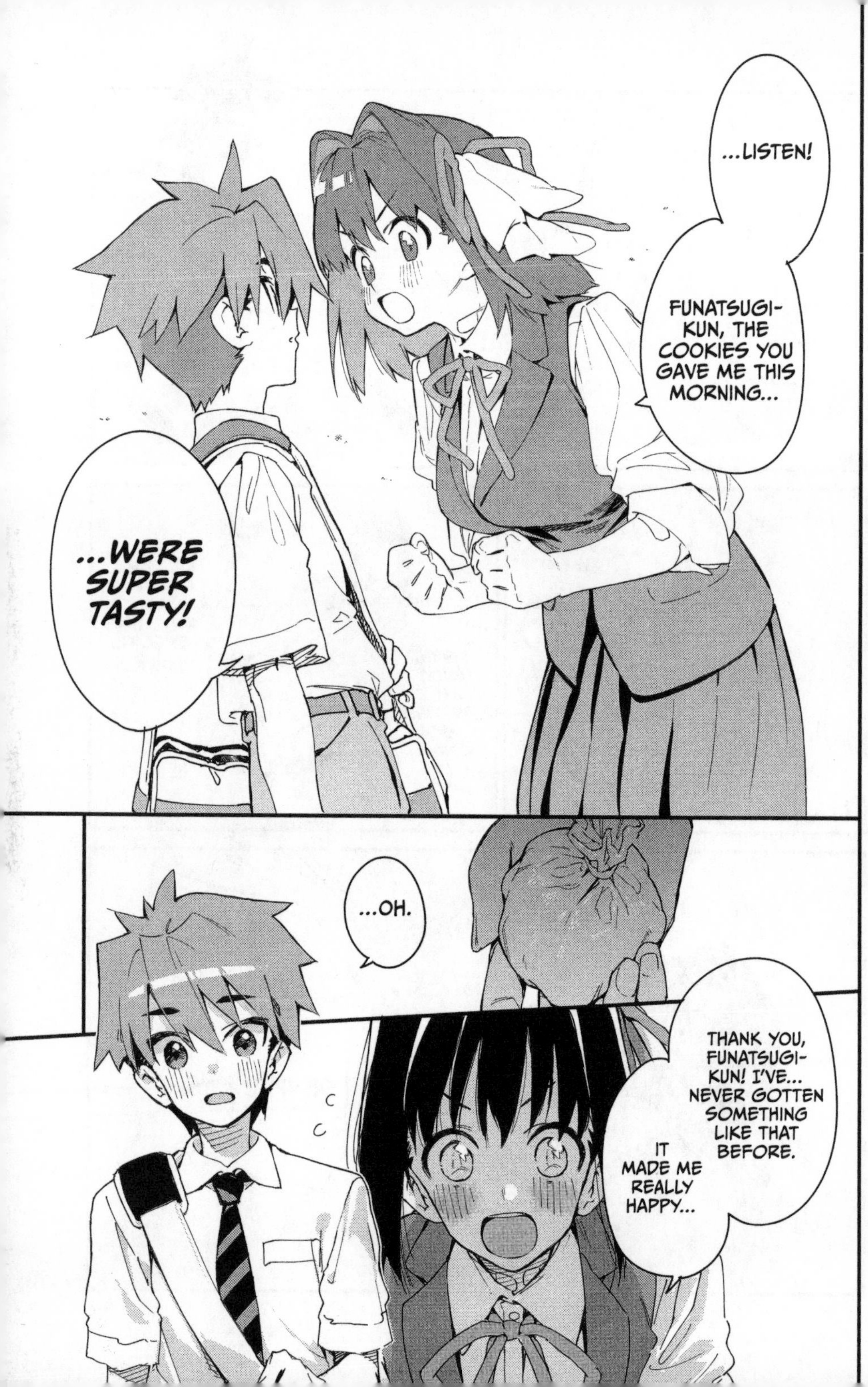
...LISTEN!
FUNATSUGI-KUN, THE COOKIES YOU GAVE ME THIS MORNING...
...WERE SUPER TASTY!
...OH.
THANK YOU, FUNATSUGI-KUN! I'VE... NEVER GOTTEN SOMETHING LIKE THAT BEFORE.
IT MADE ME REALLY HAPPY...

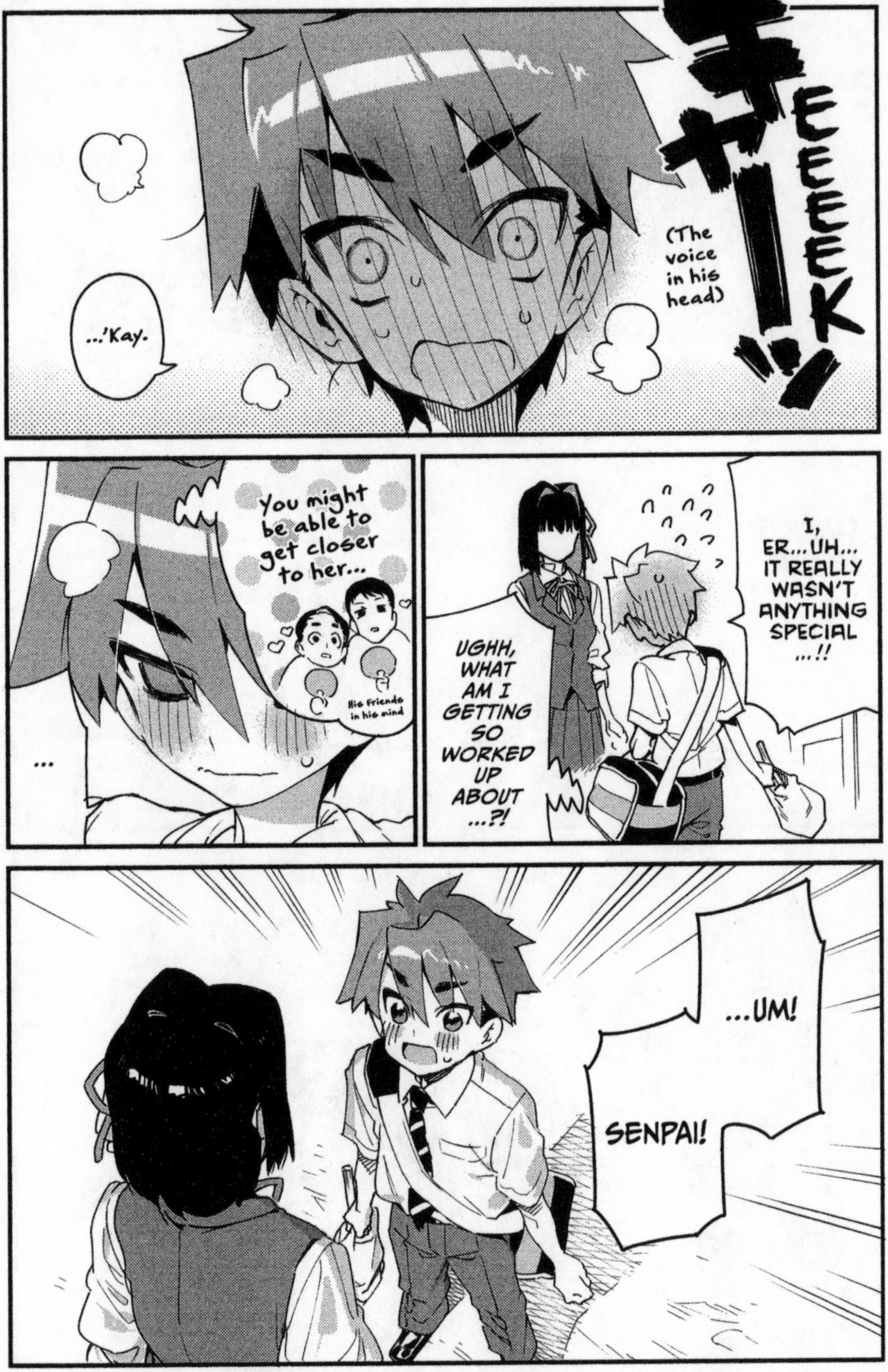

EEEEEK
(The voice in his head)
...'Kay.
I, ER...UH... IT REALLY WASN'T ANYTHING SPECIAL ...!!
UGHH, WHAT AM I GETTING SO WORKED UP ABOUT ...?!
You might be able to get closer to her...
His friends in his mind
...
...UM!
SENPAI!

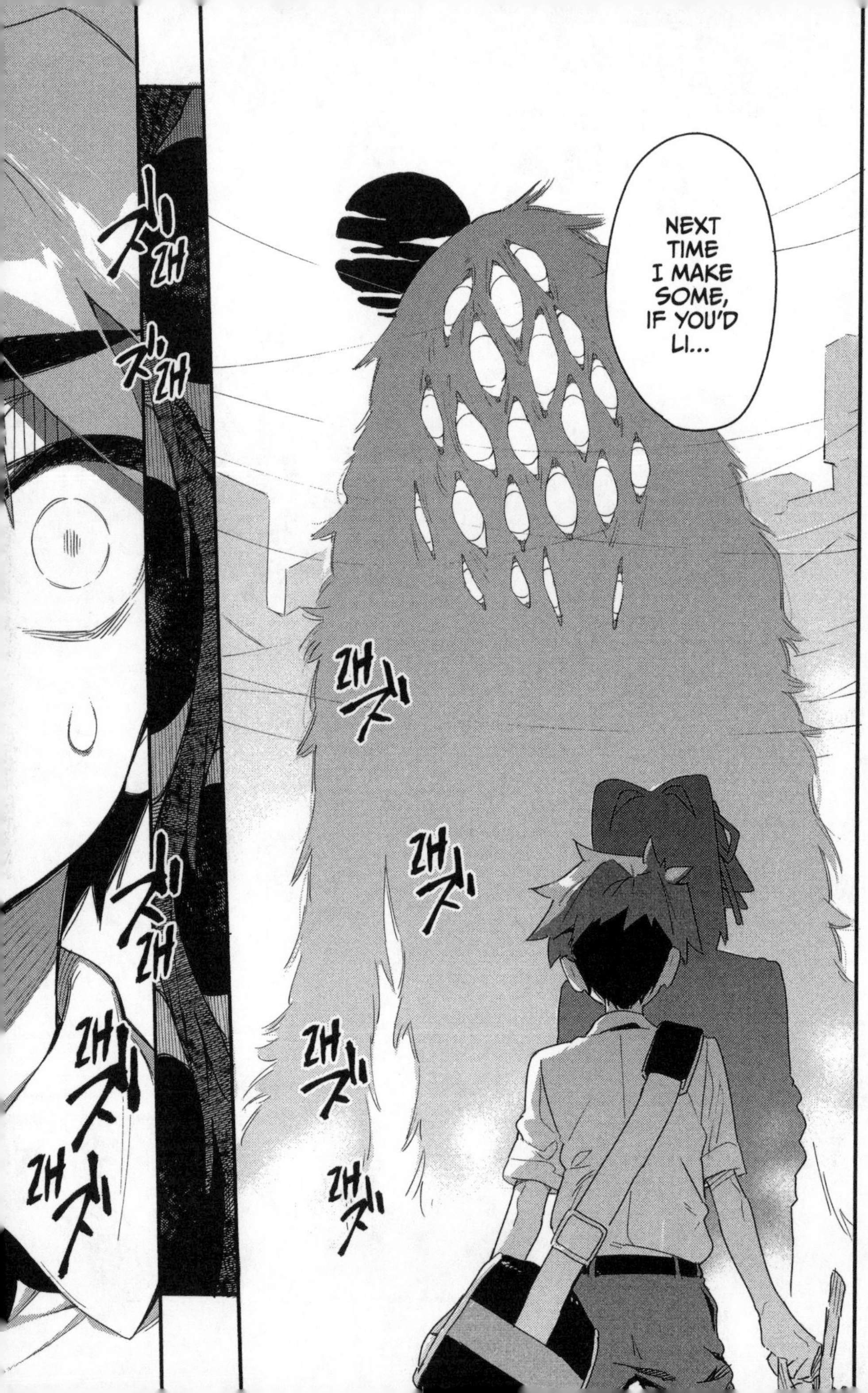
NEXT TIME I MAKE SOME, IF YOU'D LI...

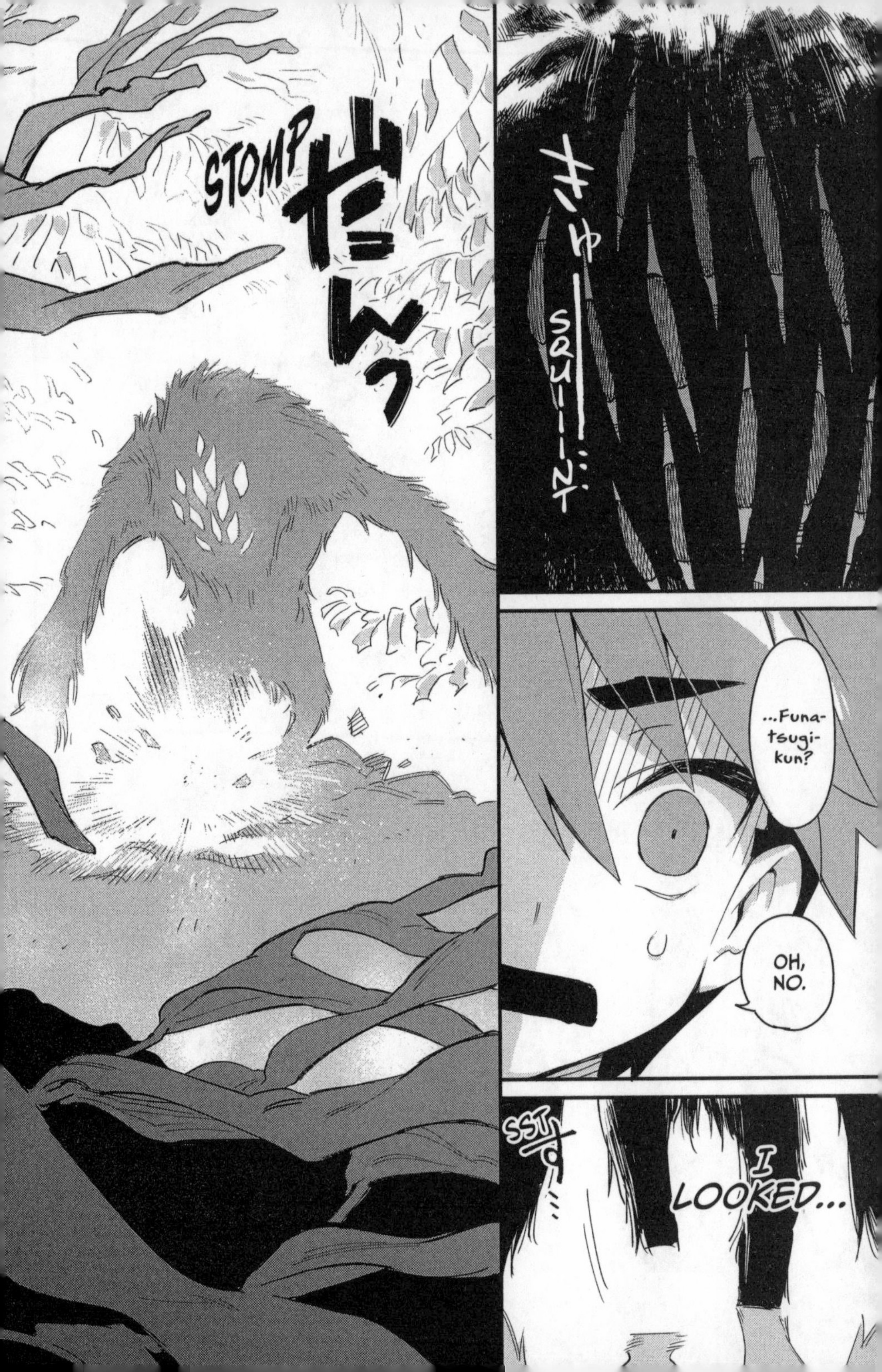
SQUIIINT
...Funa-tsugi-kun?
OH, NO.
SST
I LOOKED...
STOMP

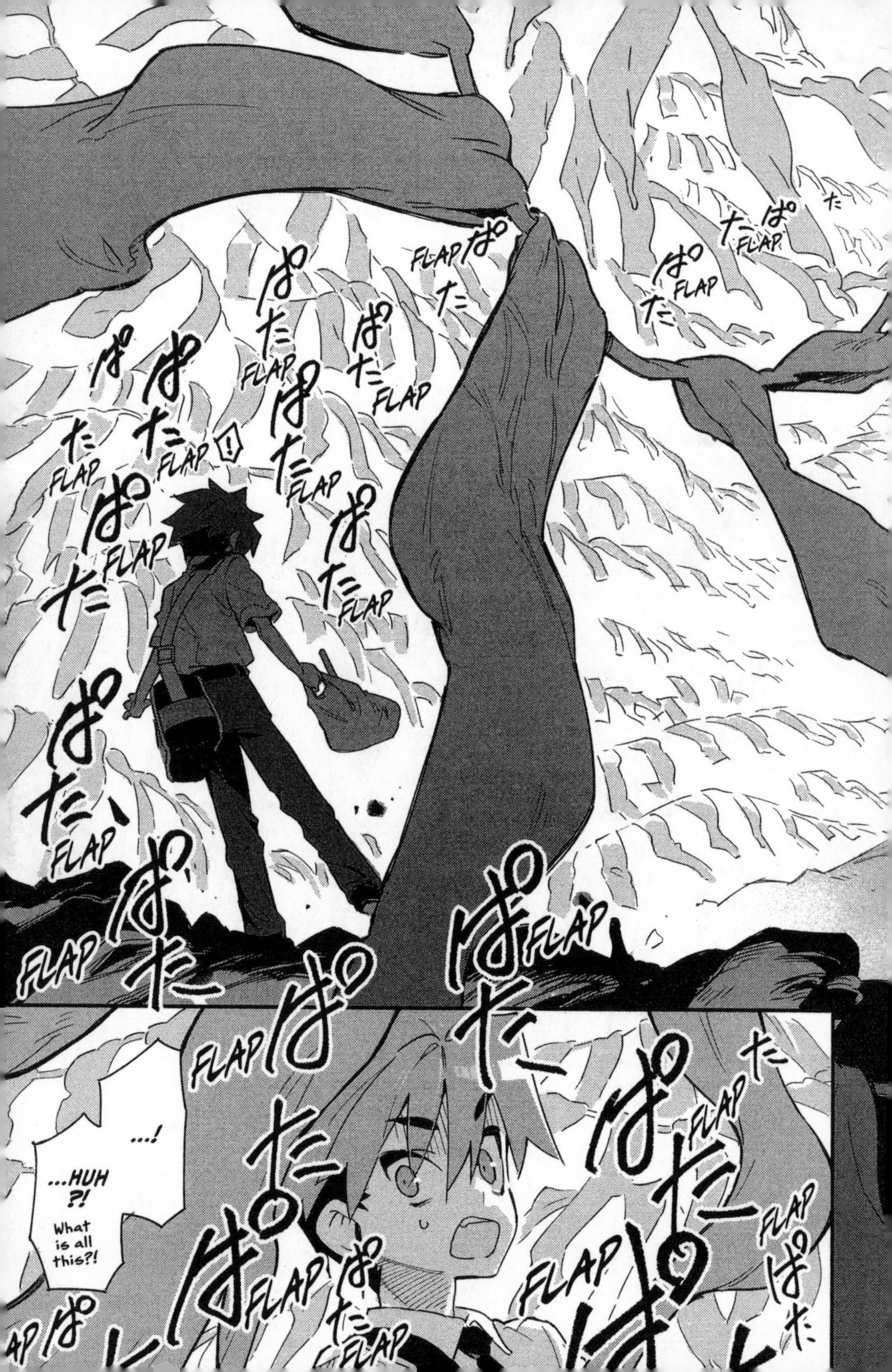

ぱた FLAP
ぱた FLAP
ぱた FLAP
ぱた FLAP
ぱた FLAP
ぱた FLAP
ぱた FLAP
ぱた FLAP
!
ぱた FLAP
ぱた、FLAP
ぱた FLAP
ぱた FLAP
ぱた FLAP
ぱた FLAP
ぱた FLAP
...!
...HUH ?!
What is all this?!
ぱた FLAP
ぱた FLAP
ぱ FLAP

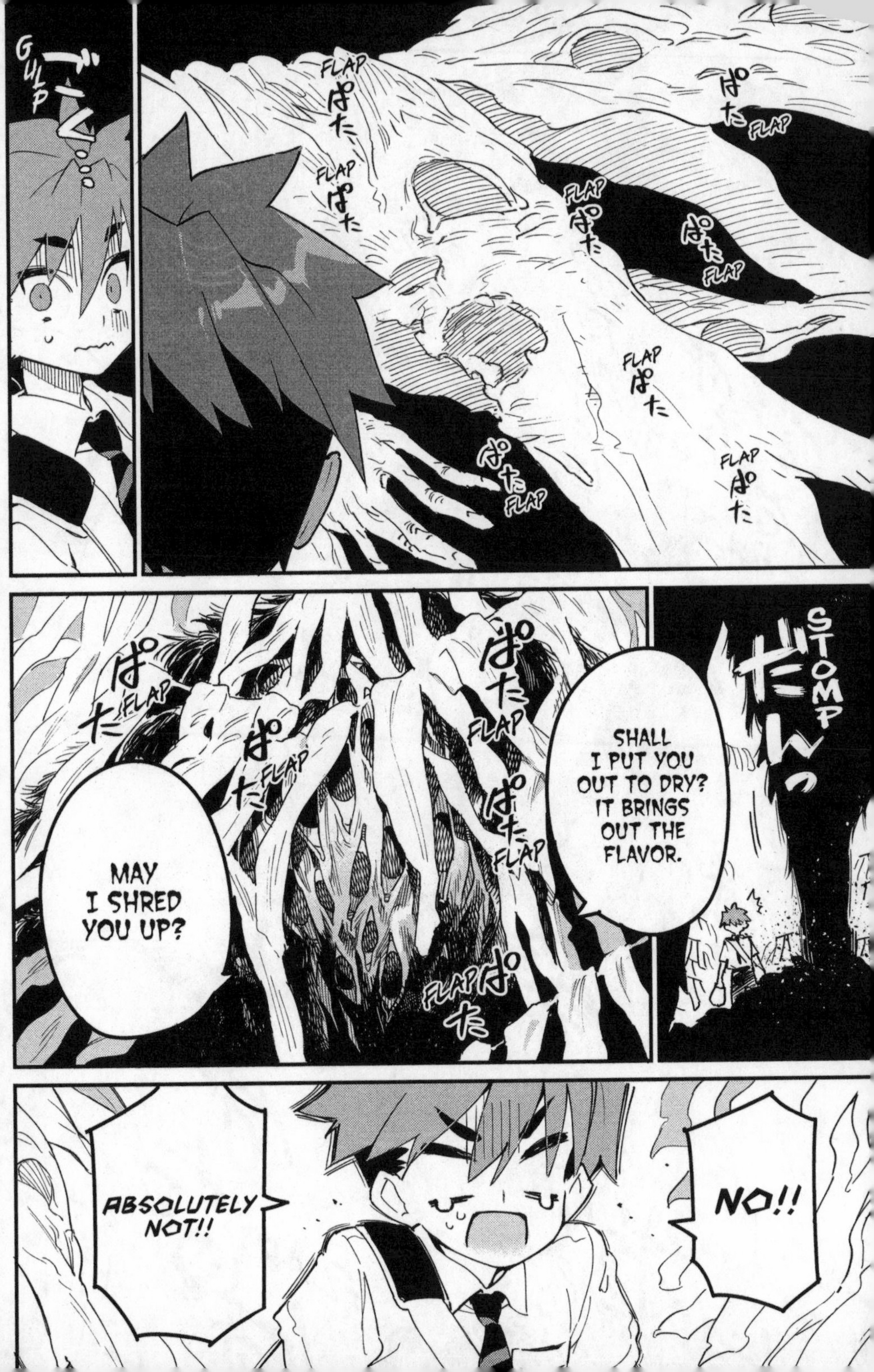

ぱた FLAP
FLAP ぱた
FLAP ぱた
ぱた FLAP
ぱた FLAP
FLAP ぱた
FLAP ぱた
ぱた FLAP
GULP
ごくっ…
STOMP
だんっ
SHALL I PUT YOU OUT TO DRY? IT BRINGS OUT THE FLAVOR.
ぱた FLAP
ぱた FLAP
ぱた FLAP
ぱた FLAP
ぱた FLAP
ぱた FLAP
MAY I SHRED YOU UP?
NO!!
ABSOLUTELY NOT!!

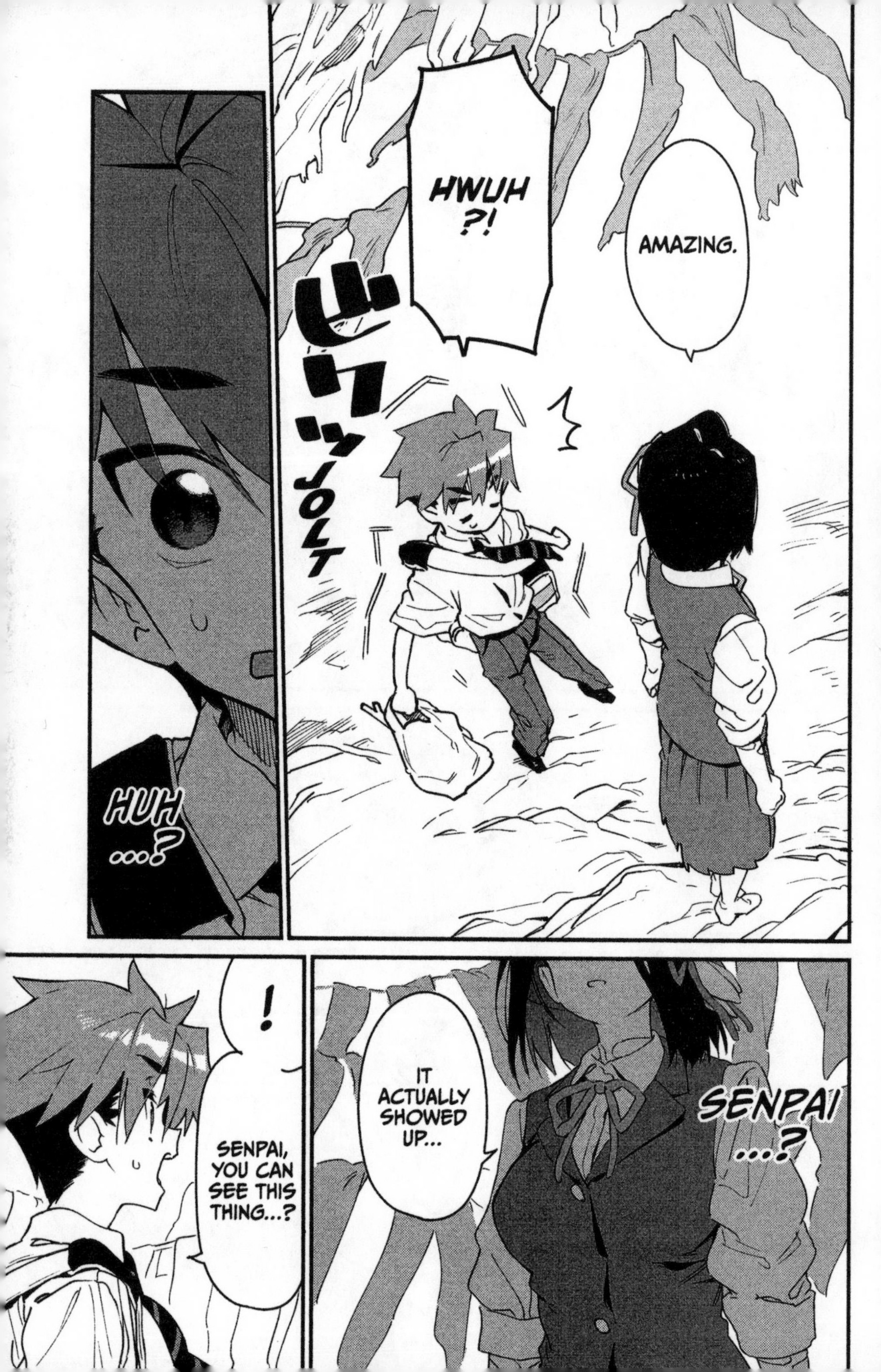
AMAZING.
HWUH ?!
JOLT
HUH ...?
SENPAI ...?
IT ACTUALLY SHOWED UP...
!
SENPAI, YOU CAN SEE THIS THING...?

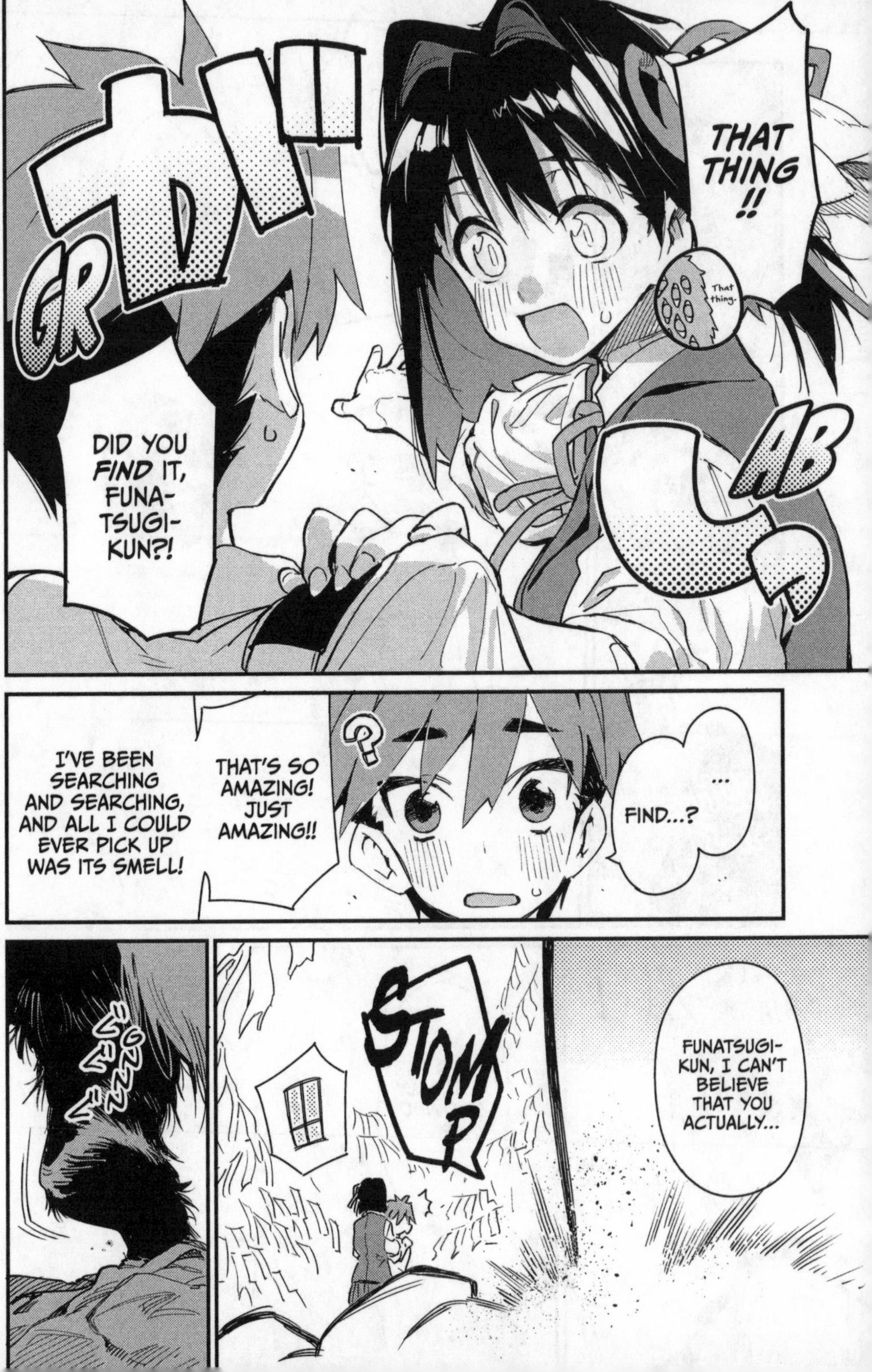
THAT THING!!
That thing.
GRAB
DID YOU FIND IT, FUNATSUGI-KUN?!
... FIND...?
THAT'S SO AMAZING! JUST AMAZING!!
I'VE BEEN SEARCHING AND SEARCHING, AND ALL I COULD EVER PICK UP WAS ITS SMELL!
FUNATSUGI-KUN, I CAN'T BELIEVE THAT YOU ACTUALLY...
STOMP

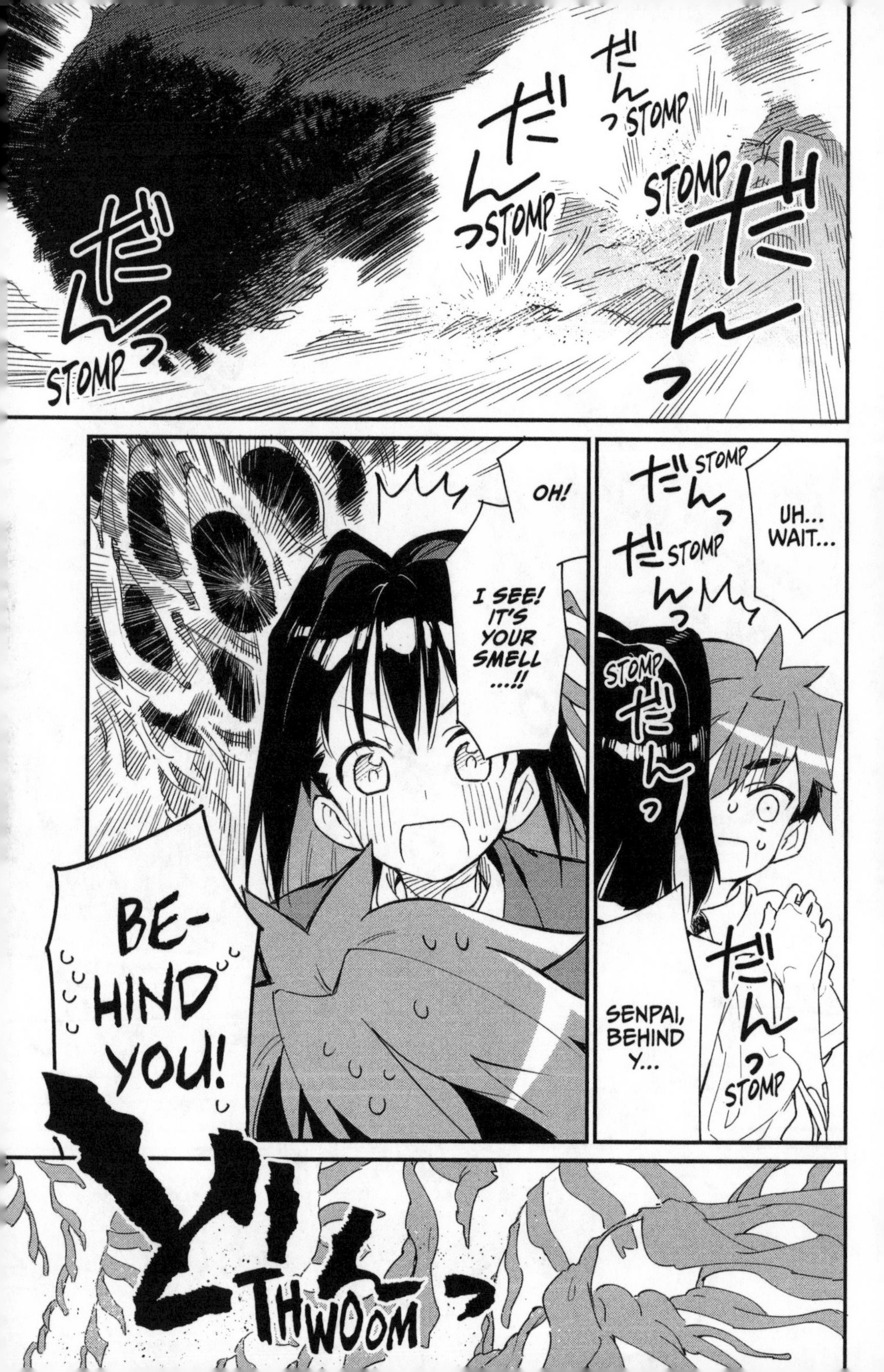

だんっ STOMP
だんっ STOMP
STOMP だんっ
だんっ STOMP
だんっ STOMP
だんっ STOMP
UH... WAIT...
STOMP だんっ
SENPAI, BEHIND Y...
だんっ STOMP
OH!
I SEE! IT'S YOUR SMELL ...!!
BE-HIND YOU!
THWOOM

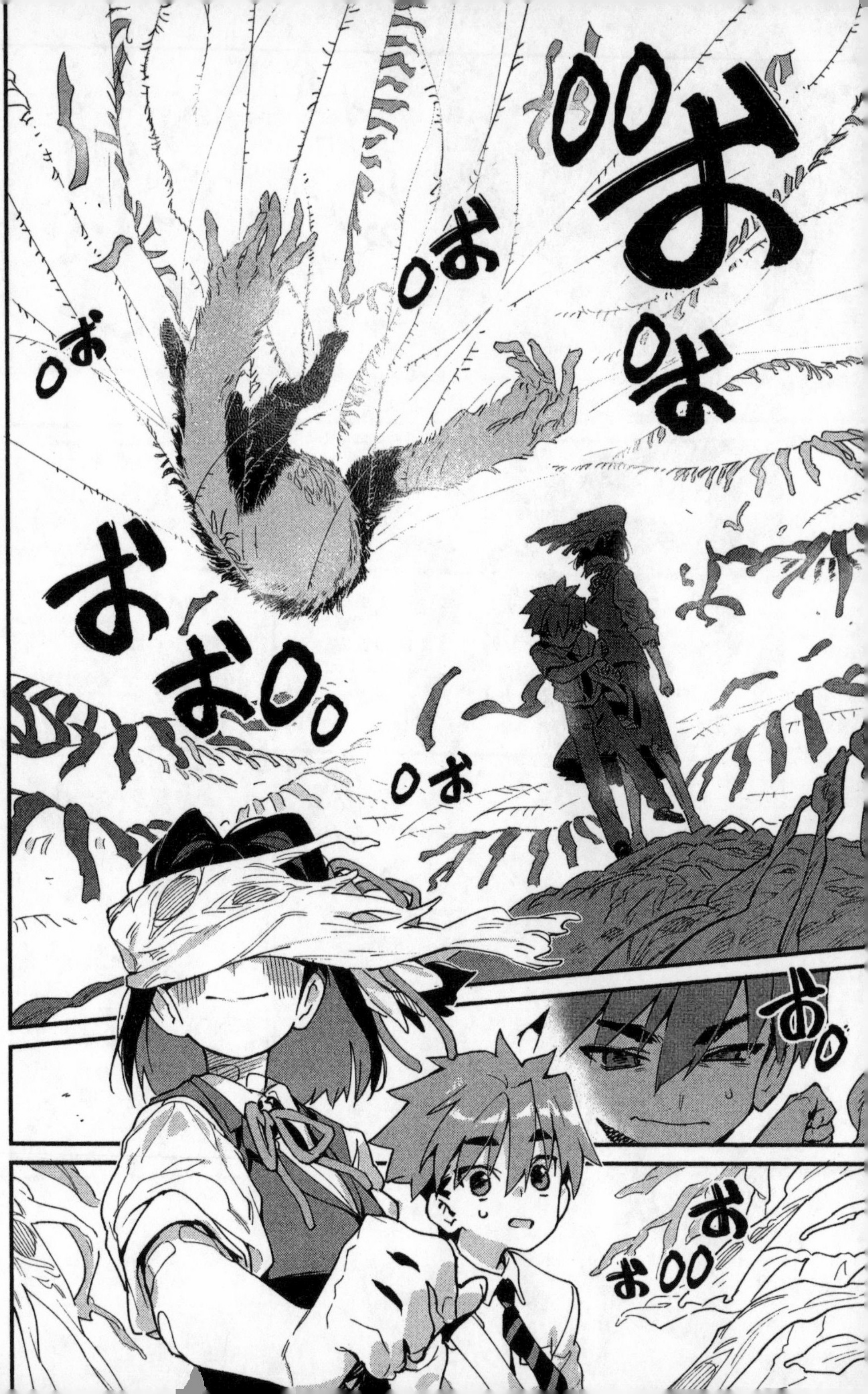
おおお
おお
おお
おお
おお
お
おお

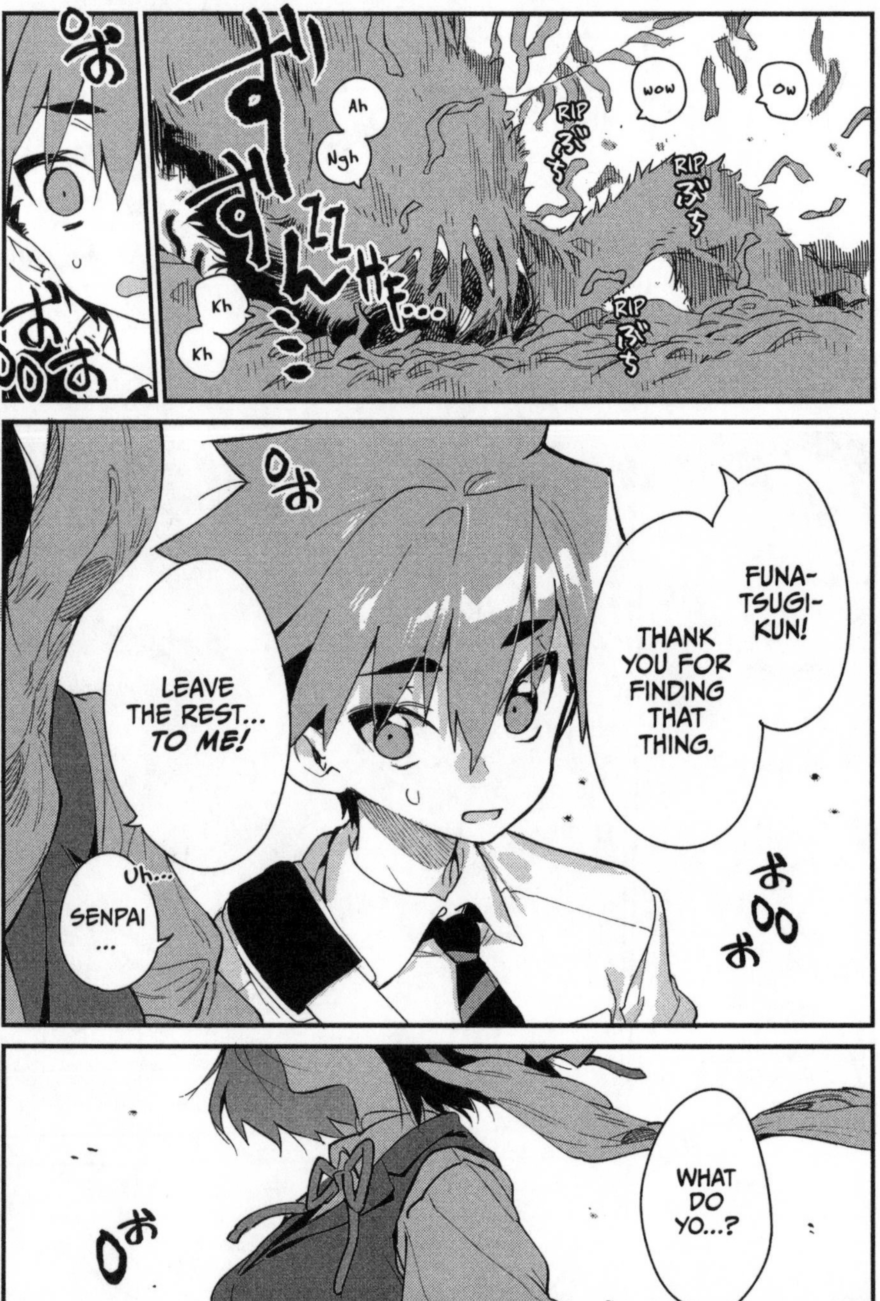
ow
wow
RIP ぶち
RIP ぶち
Ah
Ngh
Kh
Kh
RIP ぶち
FUNA-TSUGI-KUN!
THANK YOU FOR FINDING THAT THING.
LEAVE THE REST... TO ME!
Uh...
SENPAI...
WHAT DO YO...?

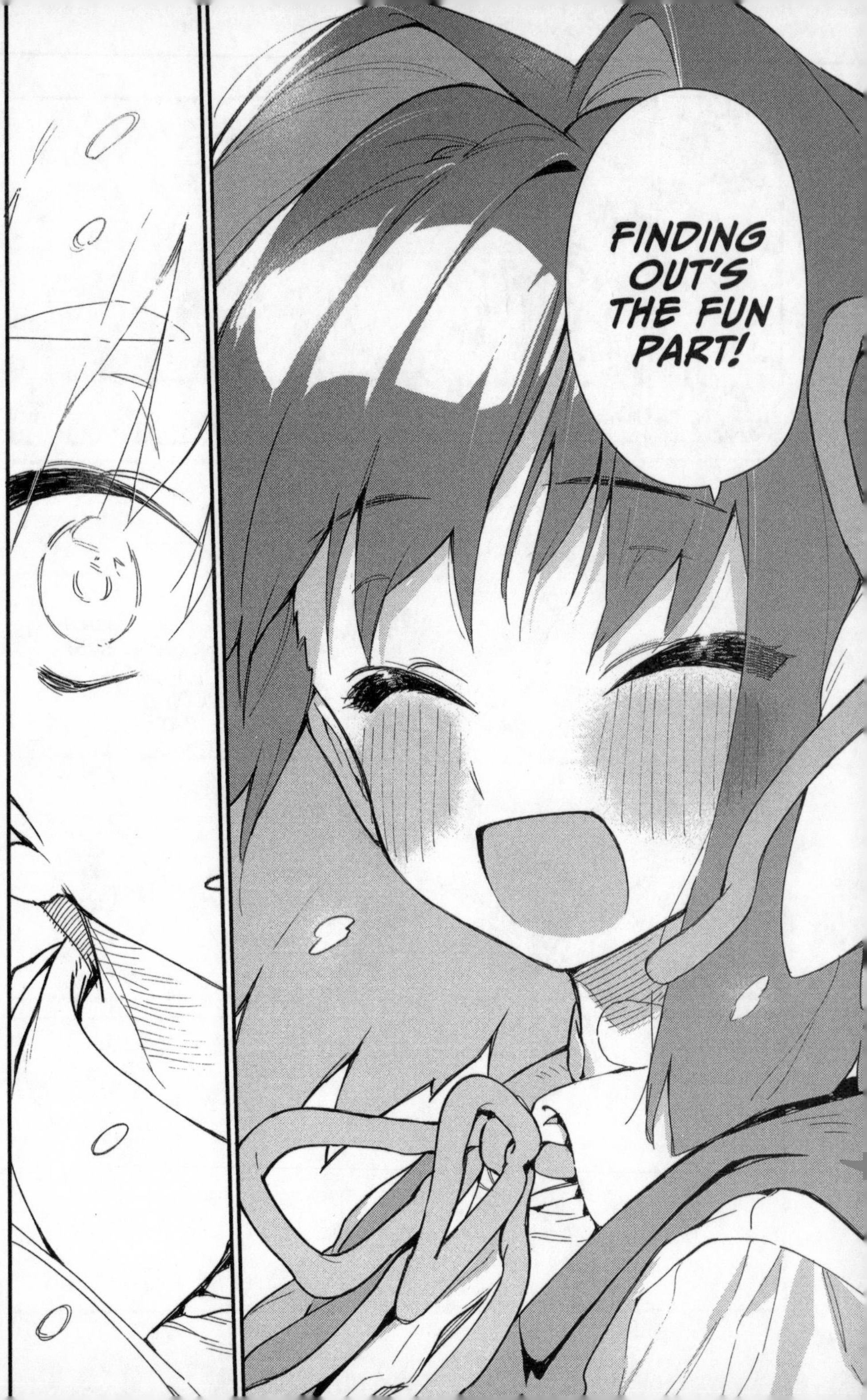
FINDING OUT'S THE FUN PART!

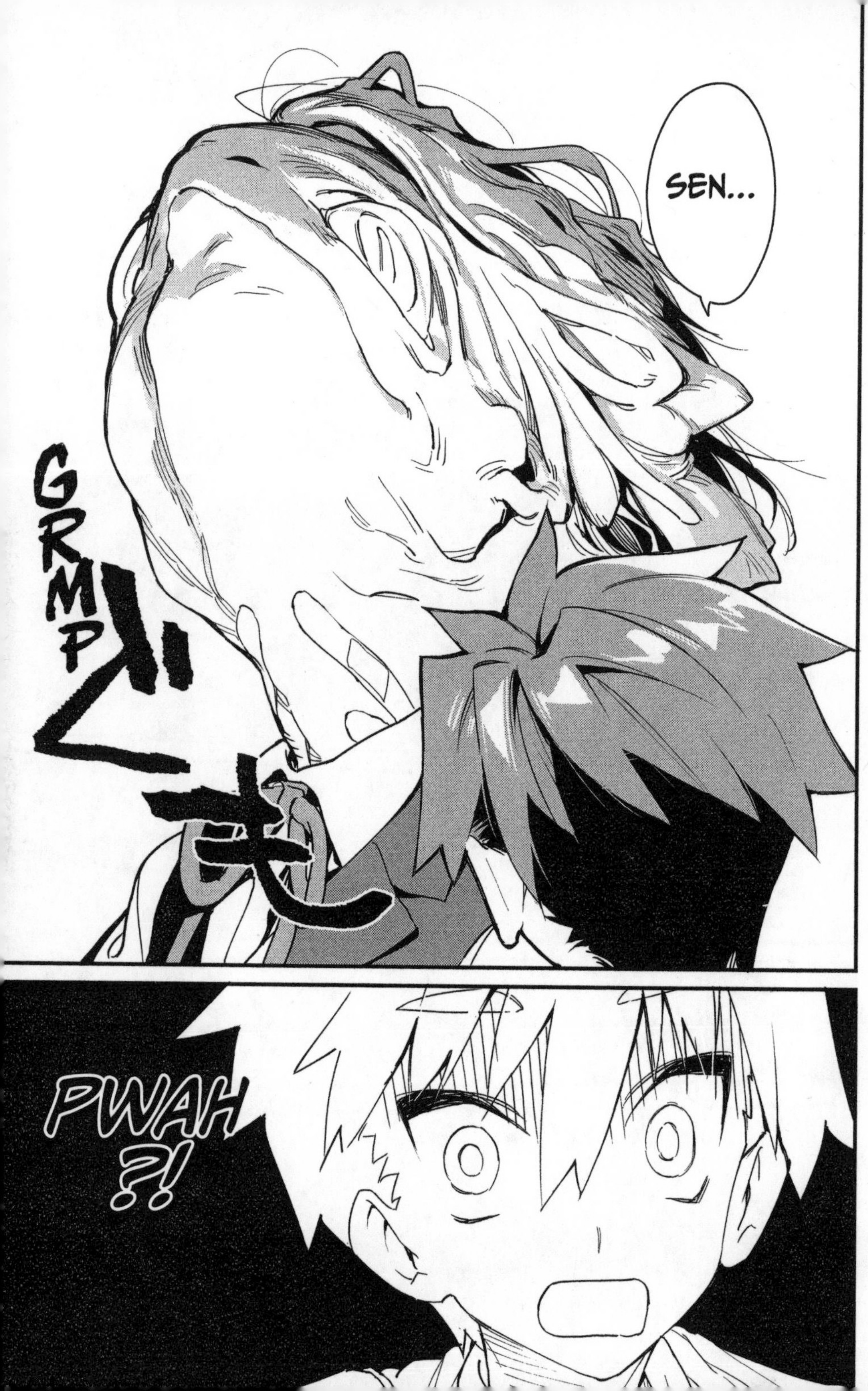
SEN...
GRMP
PWAH ?!

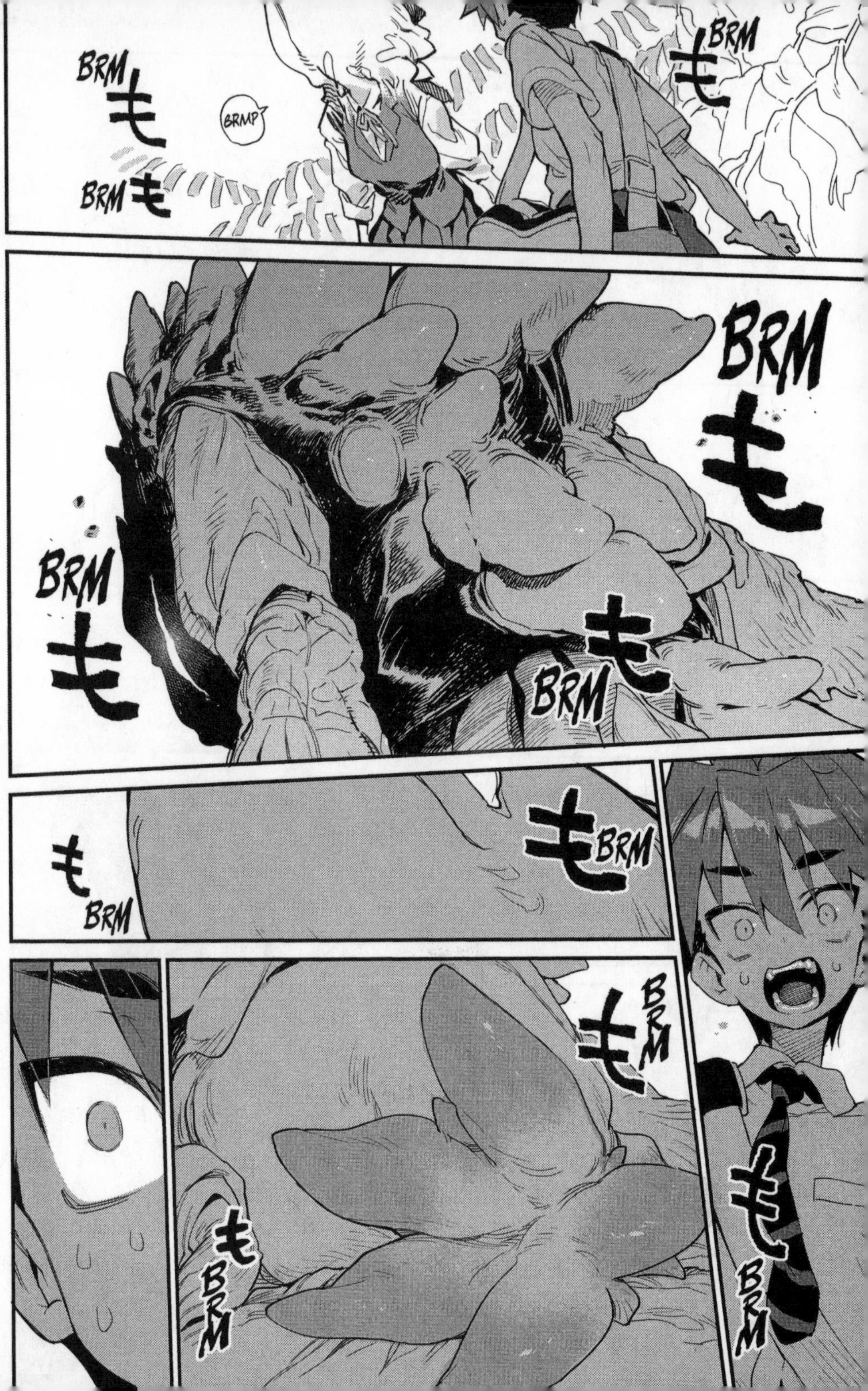

BRM も
BRMP
BRM も
BRM も
BRM も
も BRM
BRM も
も BRM
も BRM
も BRM
も BRM
も BRM
も BRM

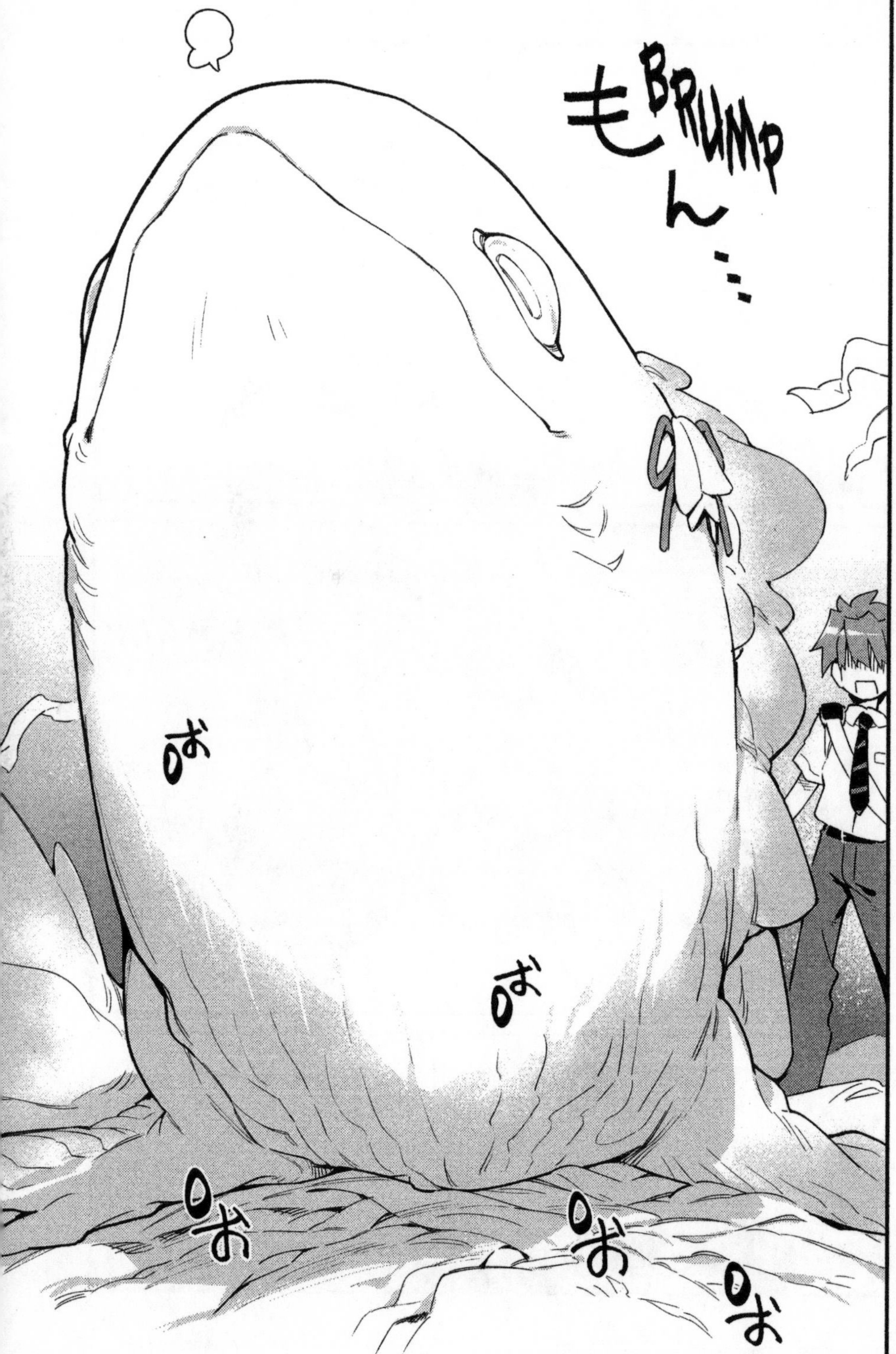
もん…
BRUMP
ぼ
ぼ
ぼ
ぼ
ぼ

WH... WHAA...
WHAAAAAT ...?!
Se...
WHAT...
Sen-pai ...?
WHAT THE HECK...
...IS GOING ON?

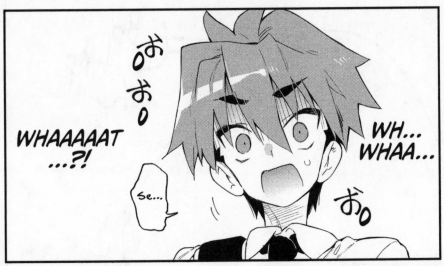

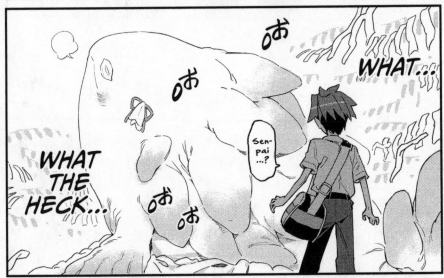

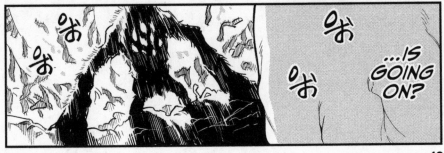

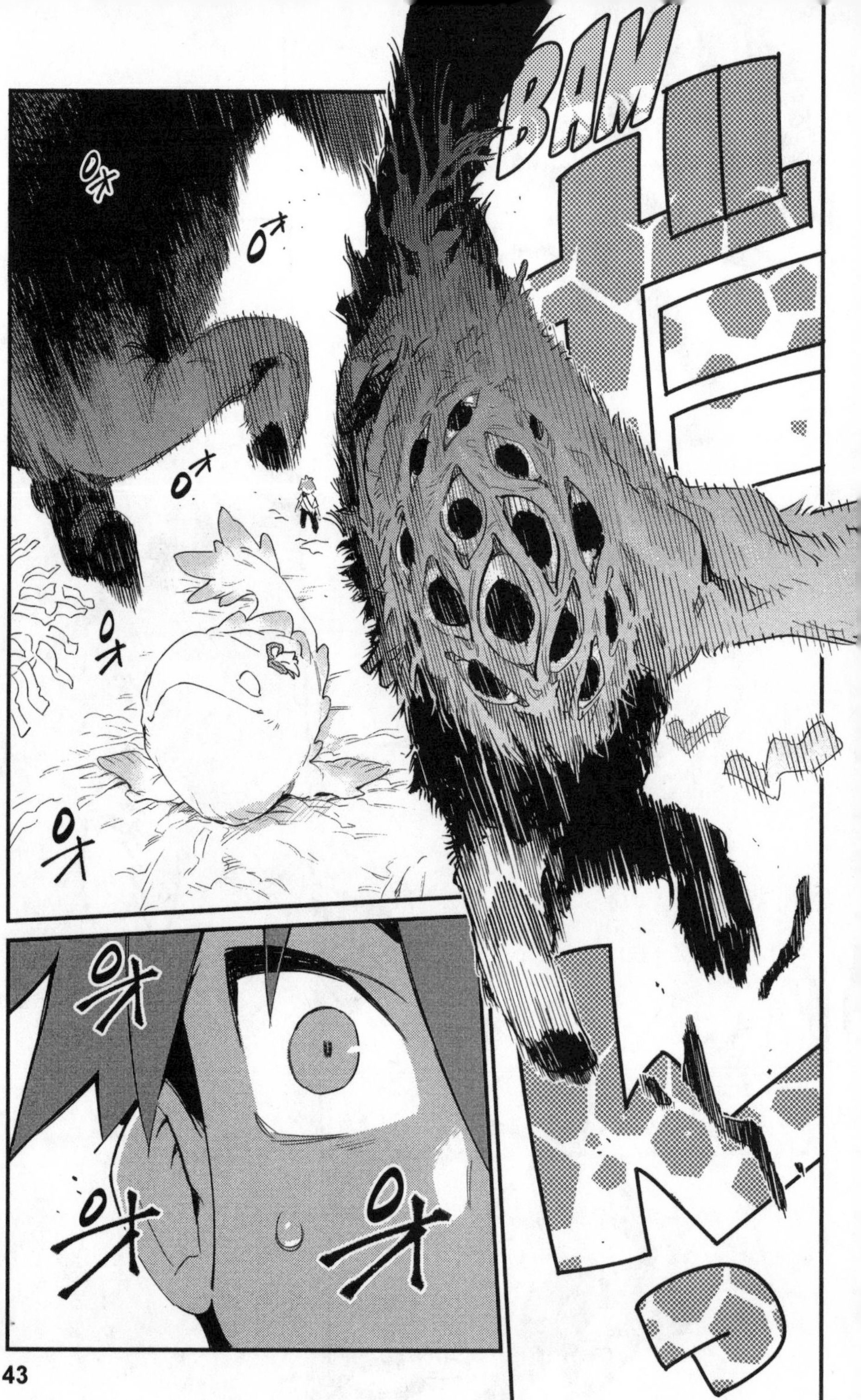
BAM

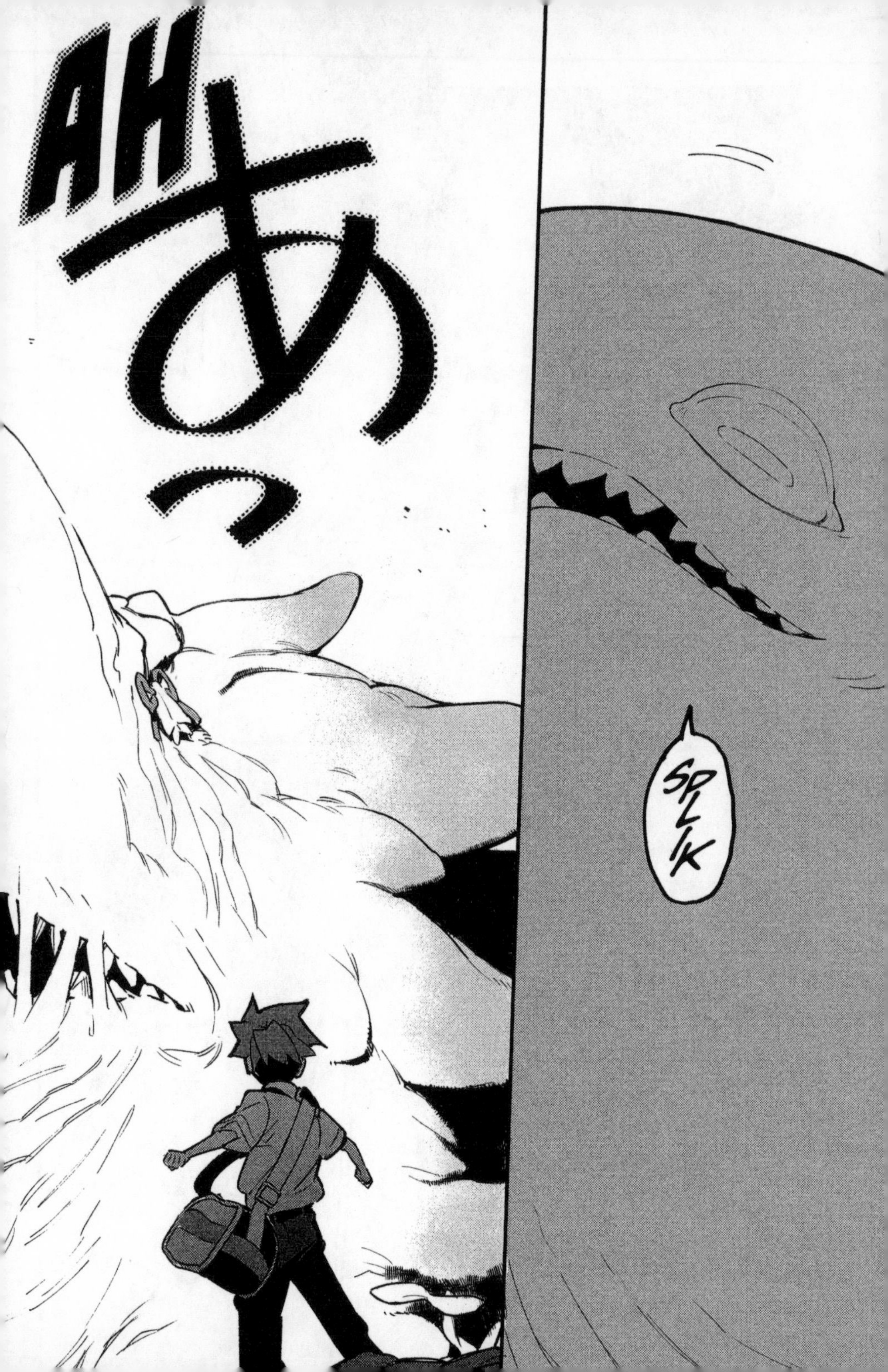
SPLIK
あっ
AH

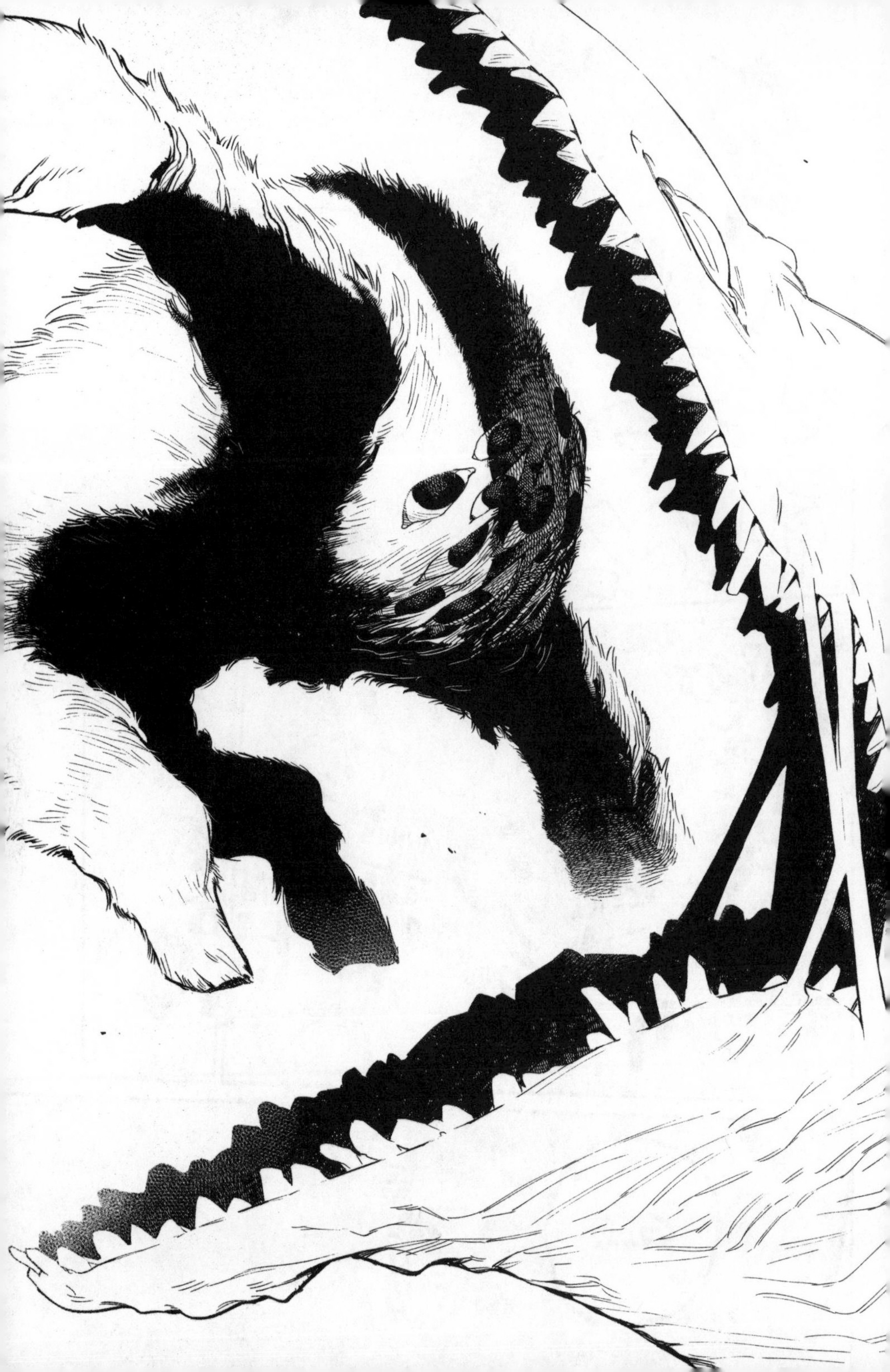

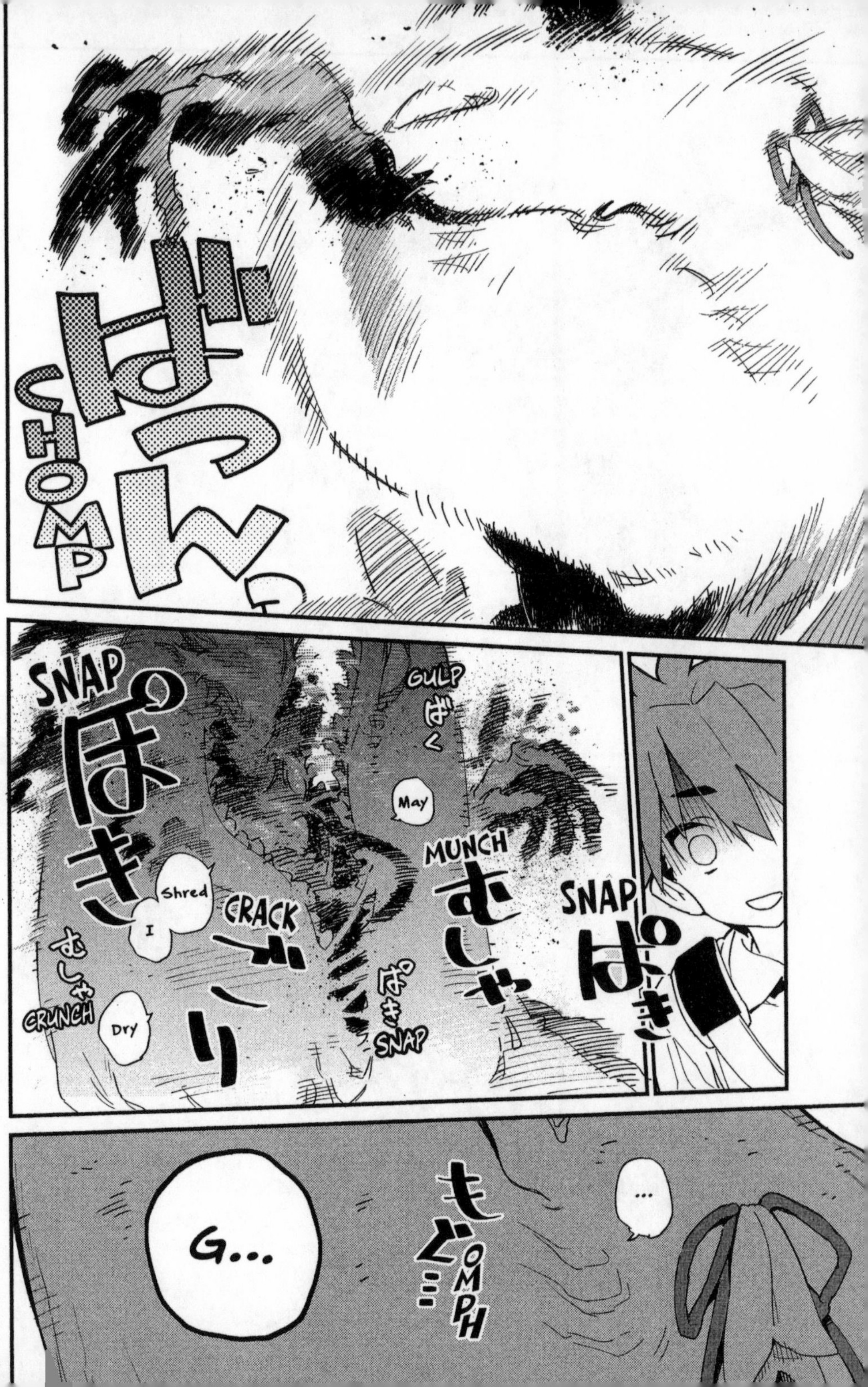
ぱっくんっ
CHOMP
SNAP
ぱきっ
GULP
ばく
May
MUNCH
むしゃ
CRACK
ごり
ぱき
SNAP
SNAP
ぽき
Shred
I
むしゃ
CRUNCH
Dry
...
もぞ
OMPH
G...

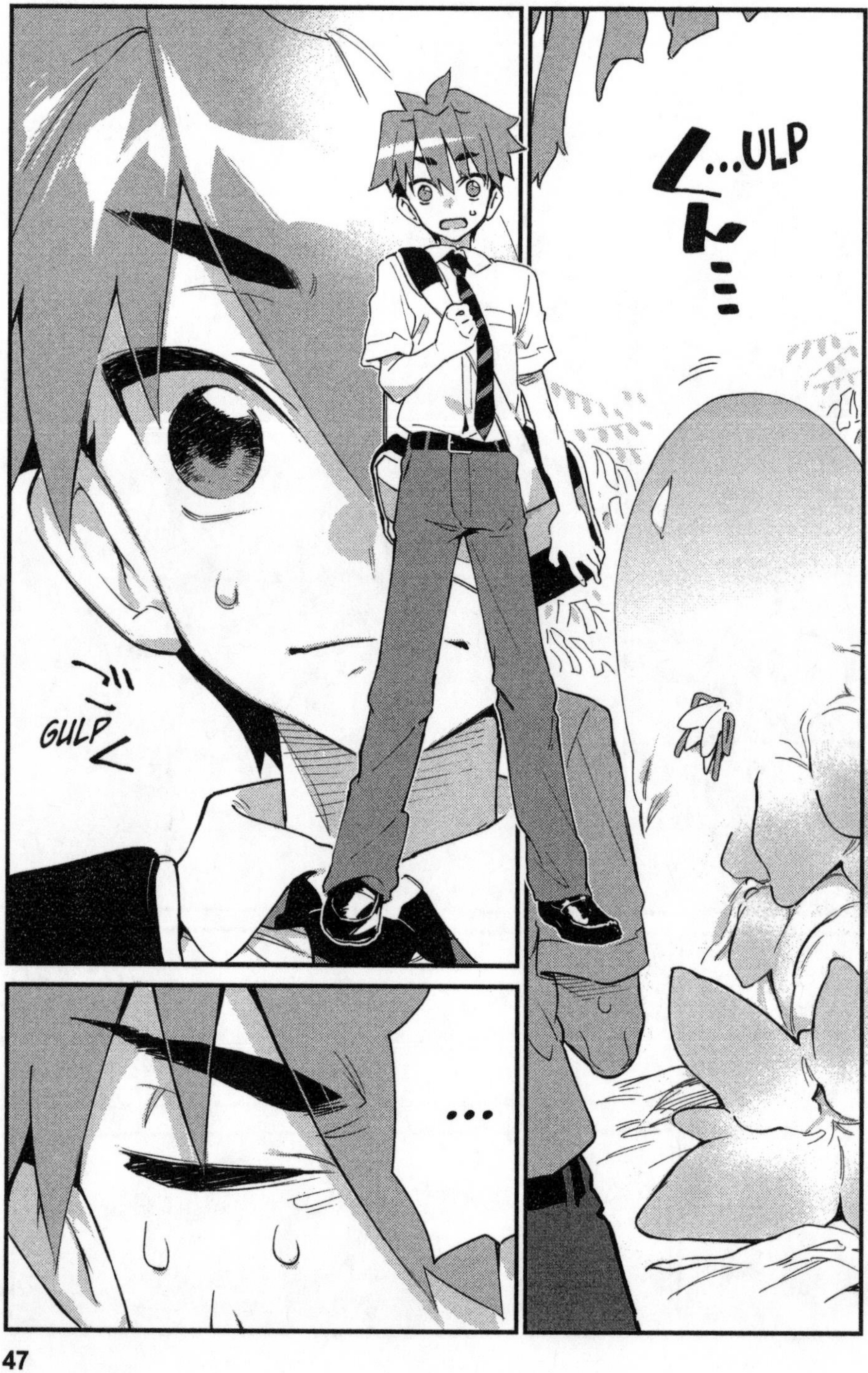
...ULP
GULP
...

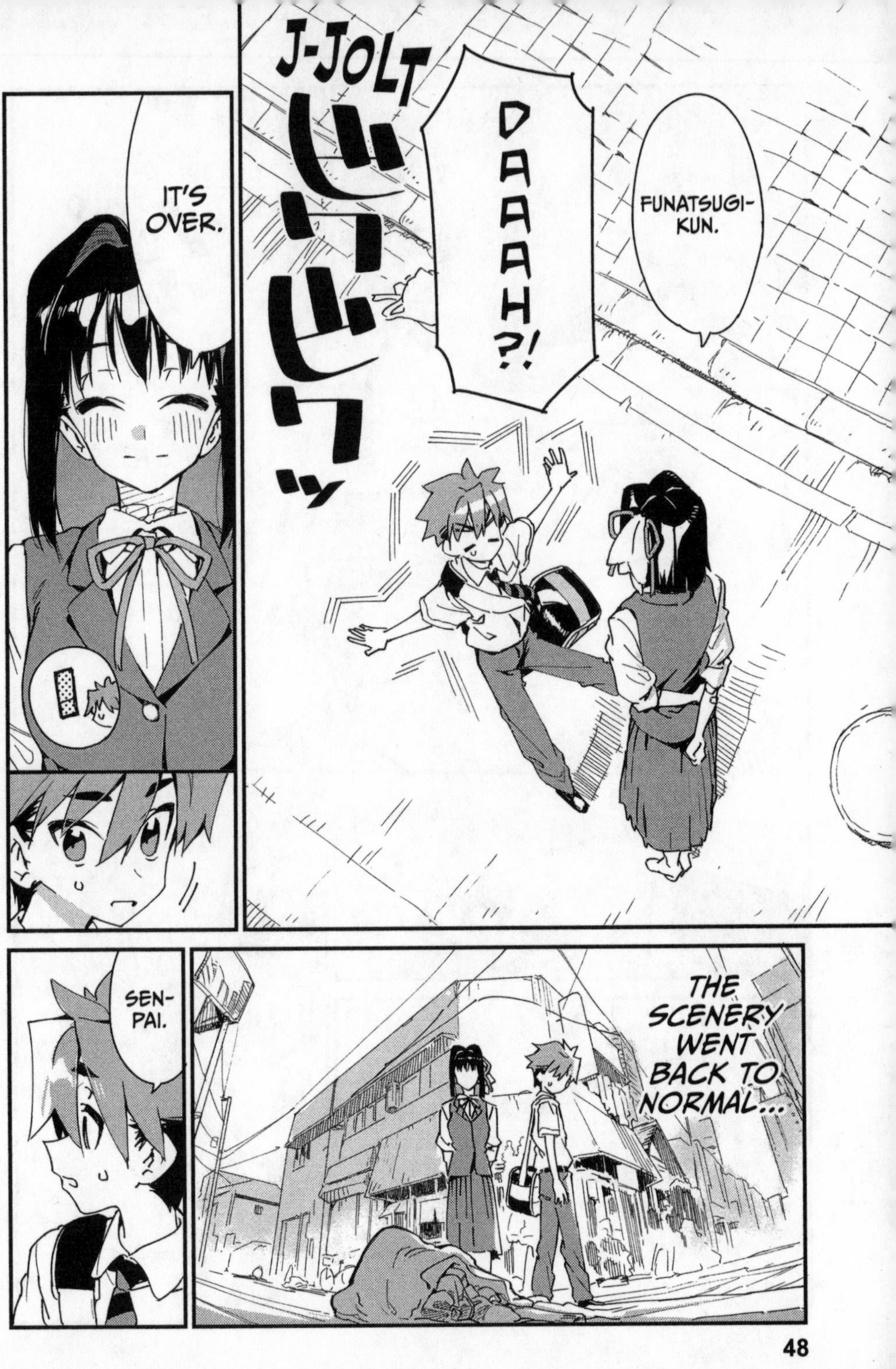
FUNATSUGI-KUN.
DAAAH?!
J-JOLT
IT'S OVER.
THE SCENERY WENT BACK TO NORMAL...
SEN-PAI.

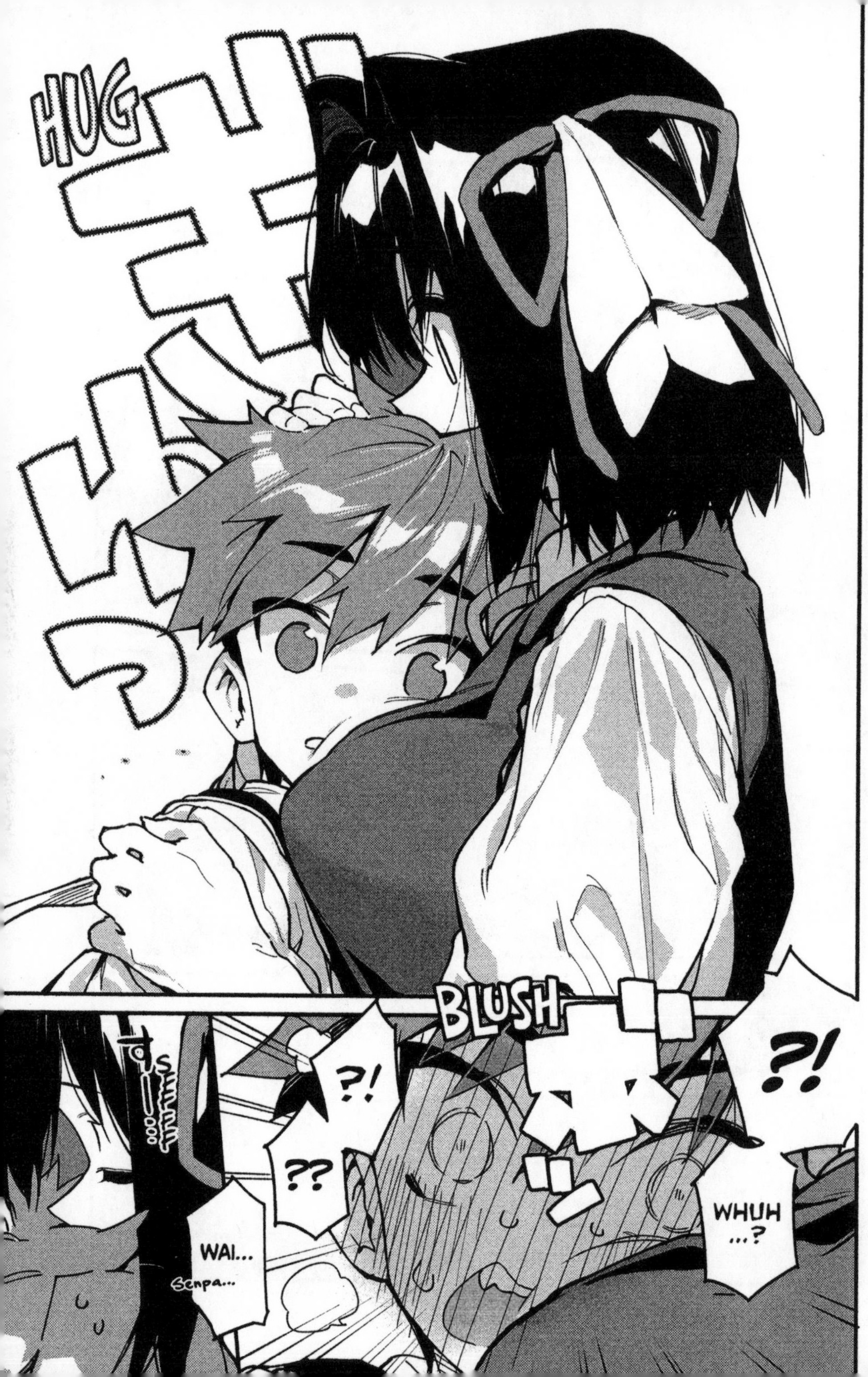
HUG
BLUSH
?!
WHUH ...?
?!
??
Shhhh
WAI...
Senpa...

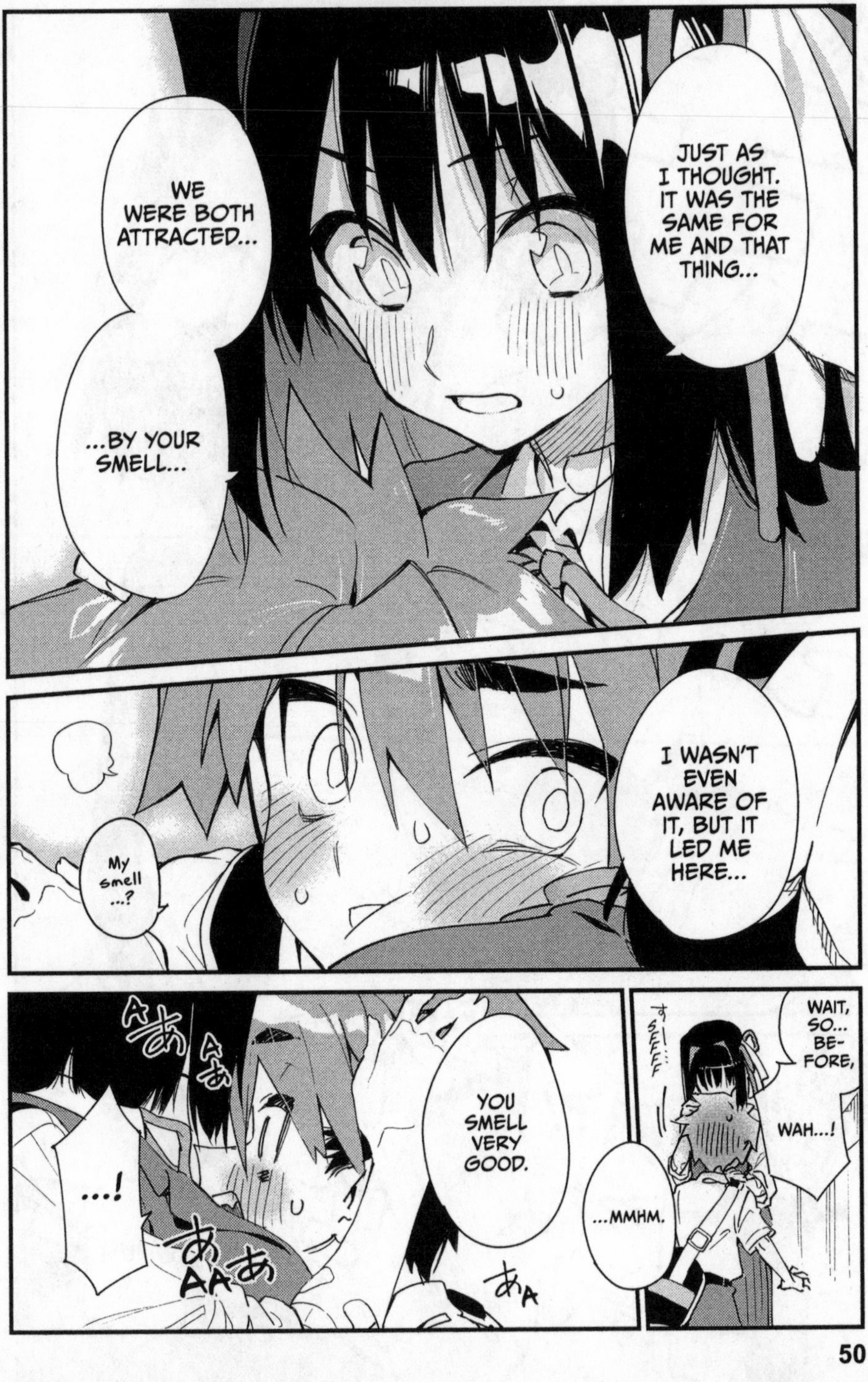
JUST AS I THOUGHT. IT WAS THE SAME FOR ME AND THAT THING...
WE WERE BOTH ATTRACTED...
...BY YOUR SMELL...
I WASN'T EVEN AWARE OF IT, BUT IT LED ME HERE...
My smell ...?
WAIT, SO... BE-FORE,
すー SFFF
WAH...!
...MMHM.
YOU SMELL VERY GOOD.
あ A
あ A
...!
ああ AA
あ A

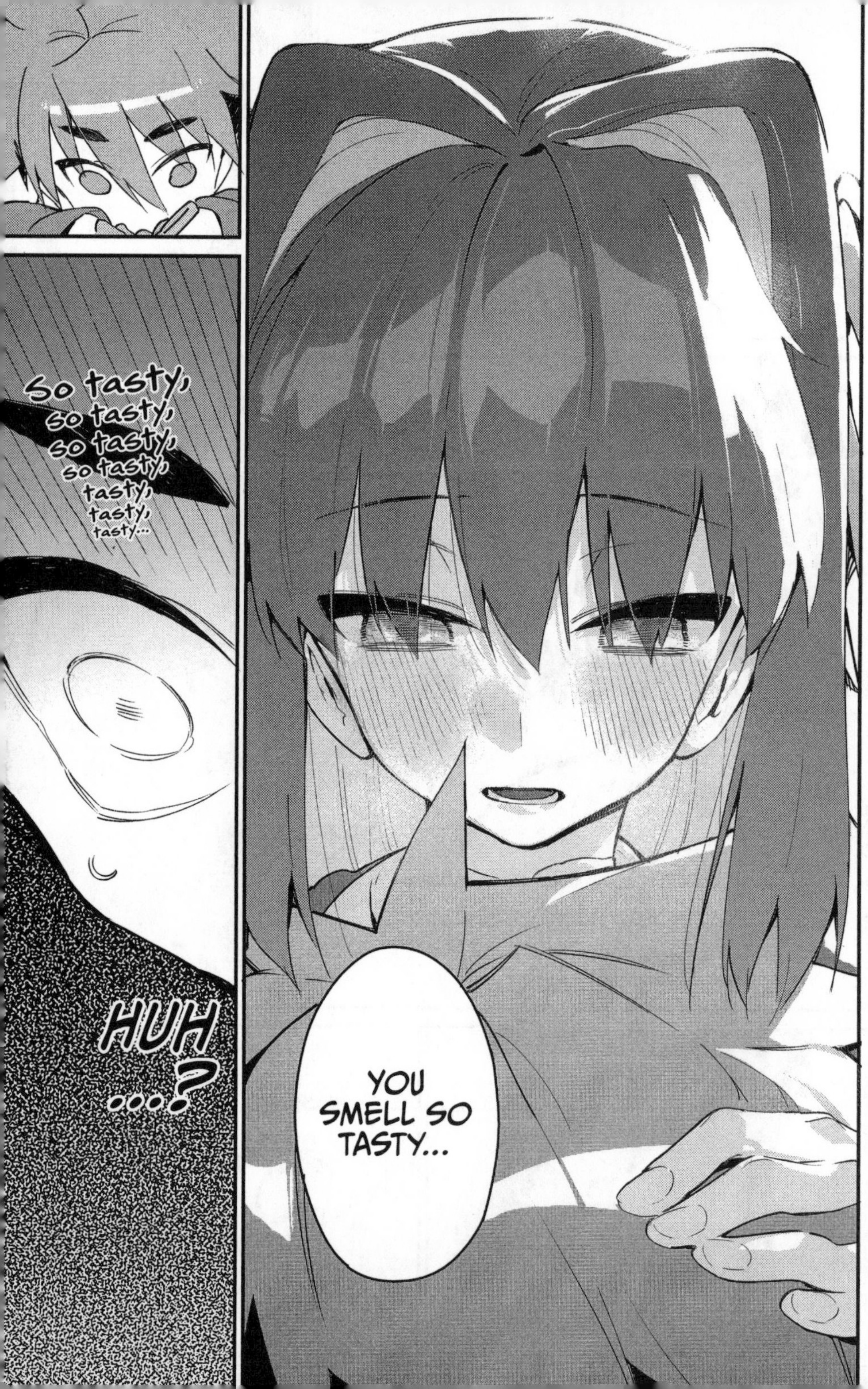
YOU SMELL SO TASTY...
So tasty, so tasty, so tasty, so tasty, tasty, tasty, tasty...
HUH ...?

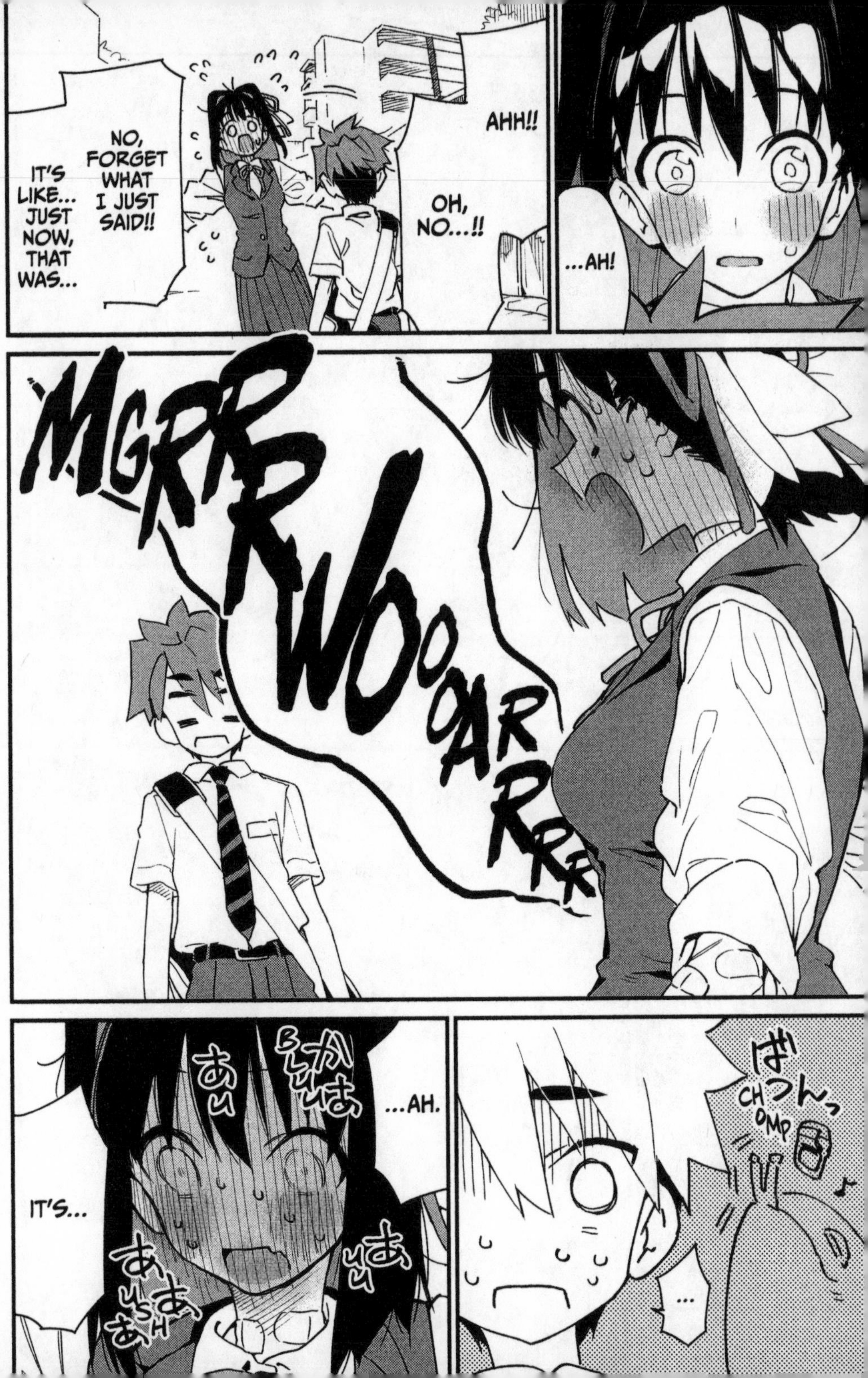

...AH!
AHH!!
OH, NO...!!
NO, FORGET WHAT I JUST SAID!!
IT'S LIKE... JUST NOW, THAT WAS...
MGRRRWOOOARRRR
ばつんっ
CHOMP
...
...AH.
BLUH
IT'S...

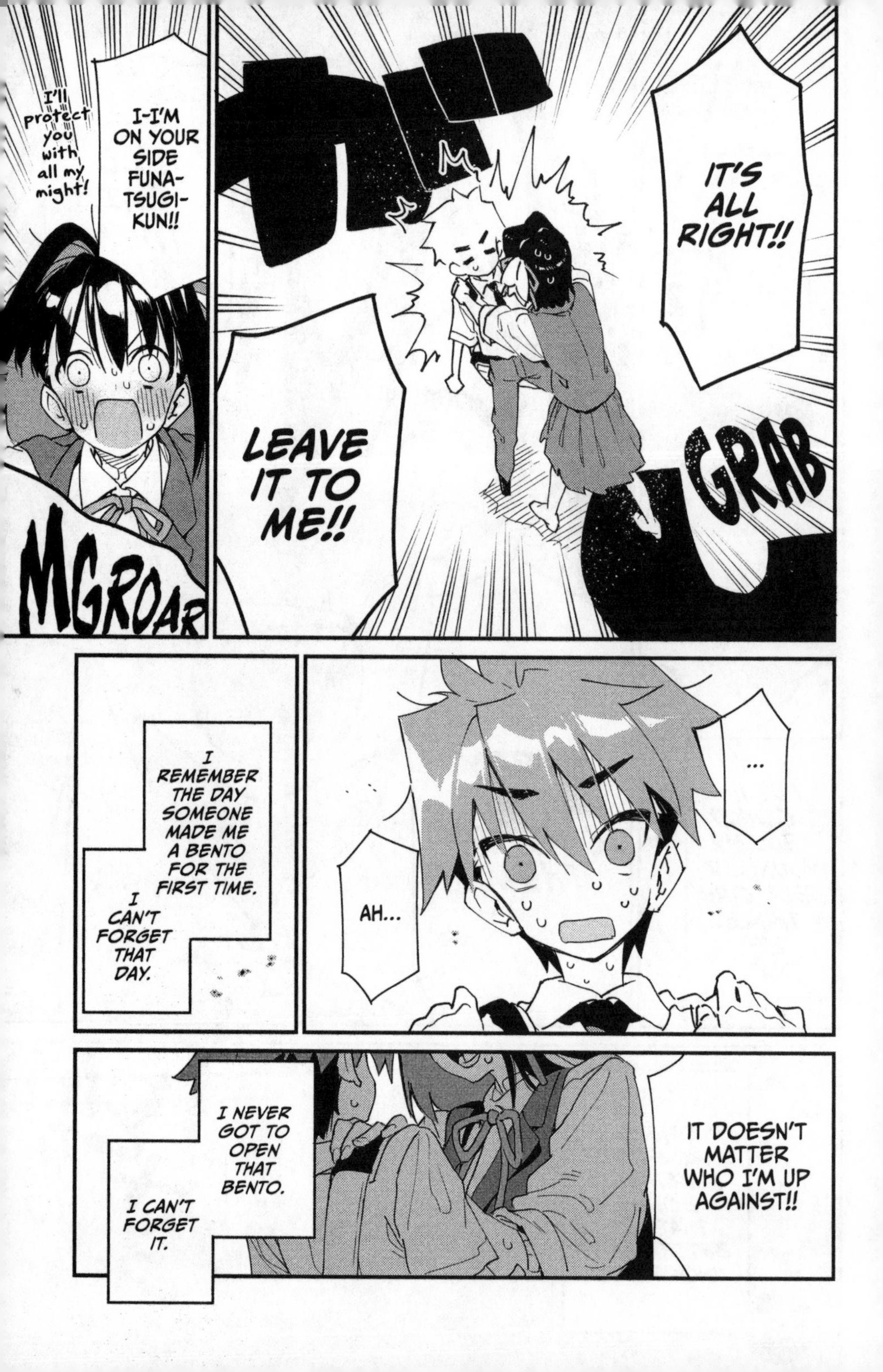
IT'S ALL RIGHT!!
GRAB
LEAVE IT TO ME!!
I-I'M ON YOUR SIDE FUNA-TSUGI-KUN!!
I'll protect you with all my might!
MGROAR
...
AH...
I REMEMBER THE DAY SOMEONE MADE ME A BENTO FOR THE FIRST TIME.
I CAN'T FORGET THAT DAY.
IT DOESN'T MATTER WHO I'M UP AGAINST!!
I NEVER GOT TO OPEN THAT BENTO.
I CAN'T FORGET IT.

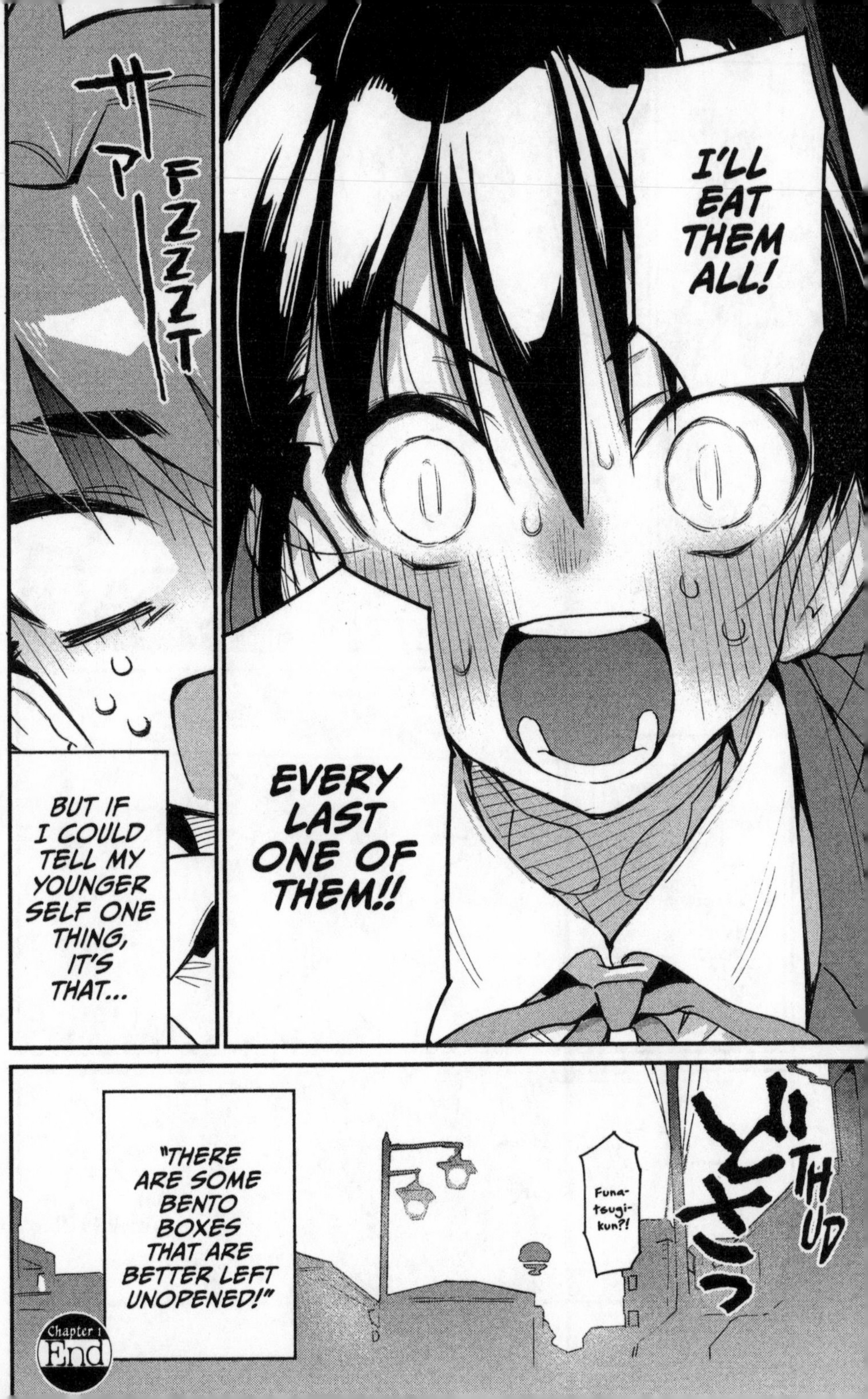
I'LL EAT THEM ALL!
EVERY LAST ONE OF THEM!!
サァー
FZZZT
BUT IF I COULD TELL MY YOUNGER SELF ONE THING, IT'S THAT...
どさっ
THUD
Funa-tsugi-kun?!
"THERE ARE SOME BENTO BOXES THAT ARE BETTER LEFT UNOPENED!"
Chapter 1
End

Chapter 2: Invitation

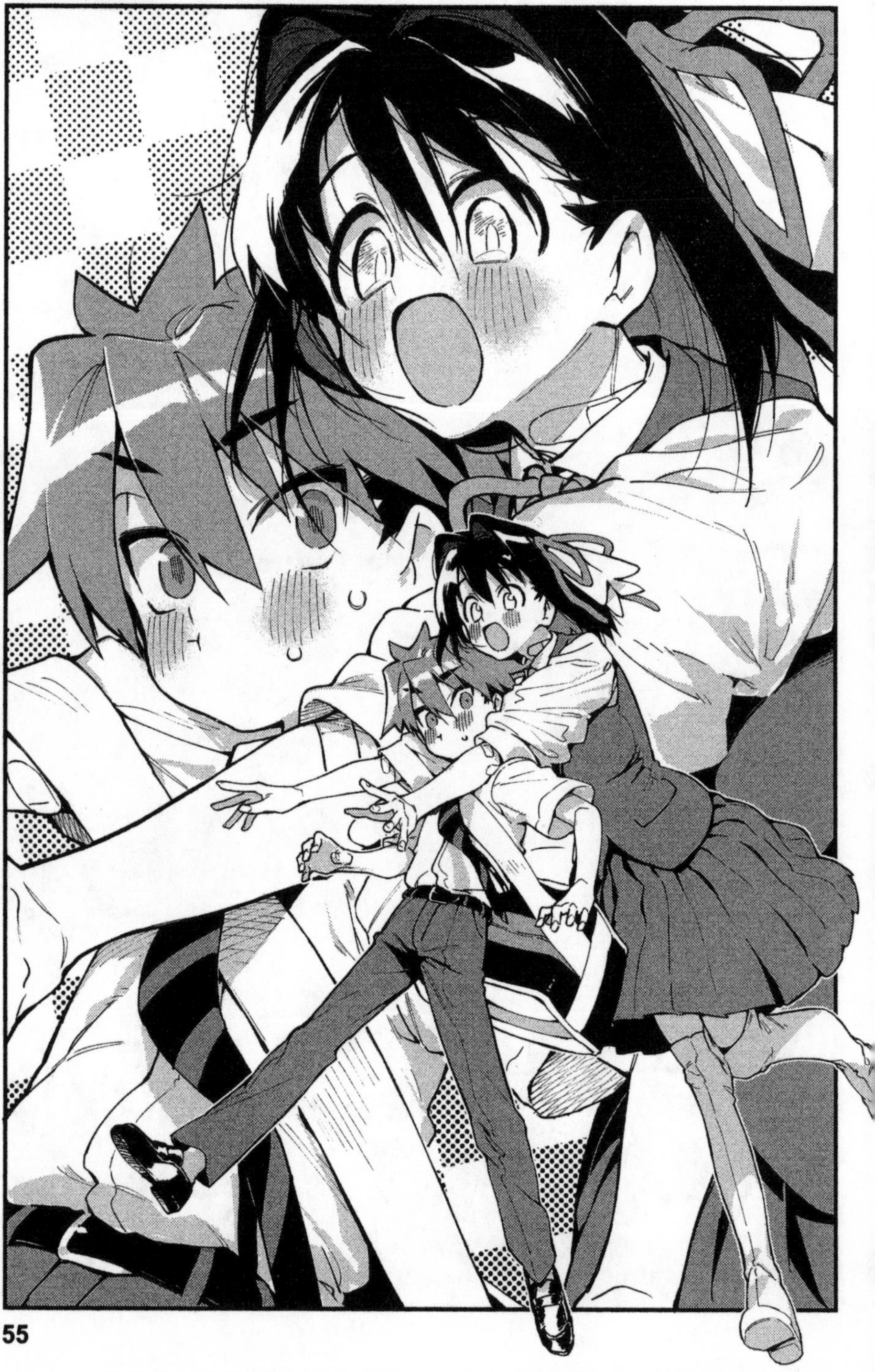

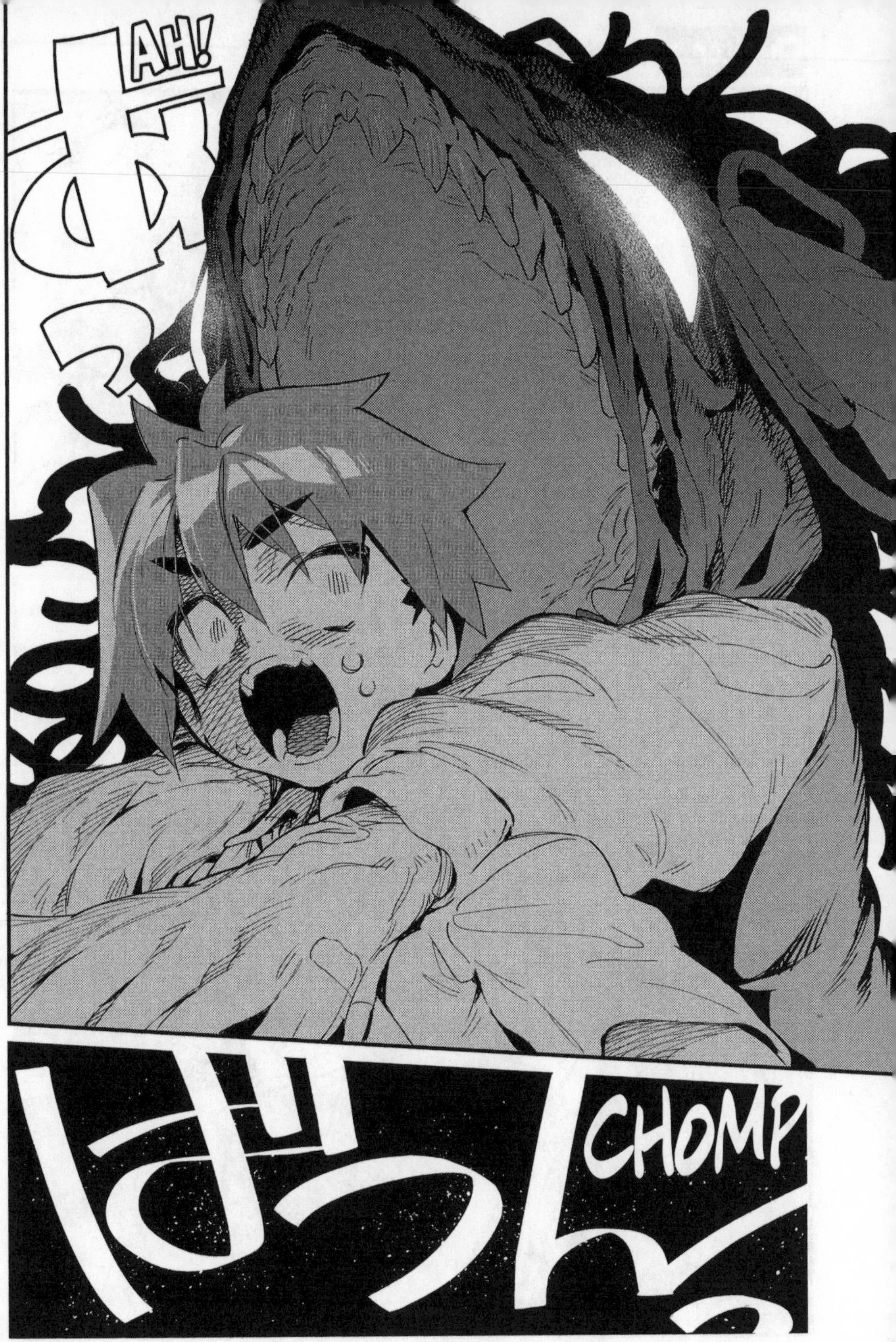
AH!
CHOMP

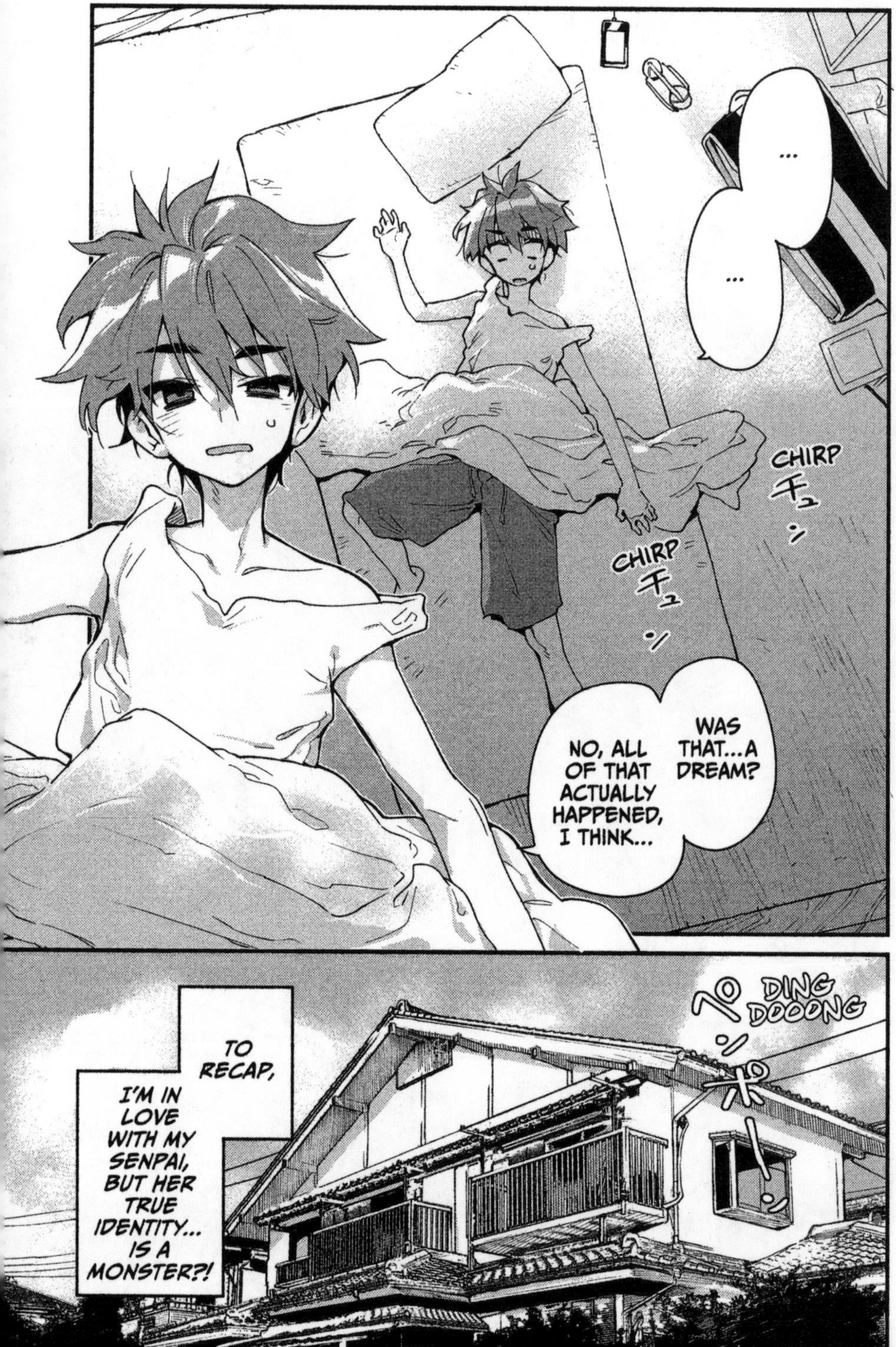
...
...
CHIRP
チュン
CHIRP
チュン
WAS THAT...A DREAM?
NO, ALL OF THAT ACTUALLY HAPPENED, I THINK...
DING DOOONG
TO RECAP,
I'M IN LOVE WITH MY SENPAI, BUT HER TRUE IDENTITY... IS A MONSTER?!

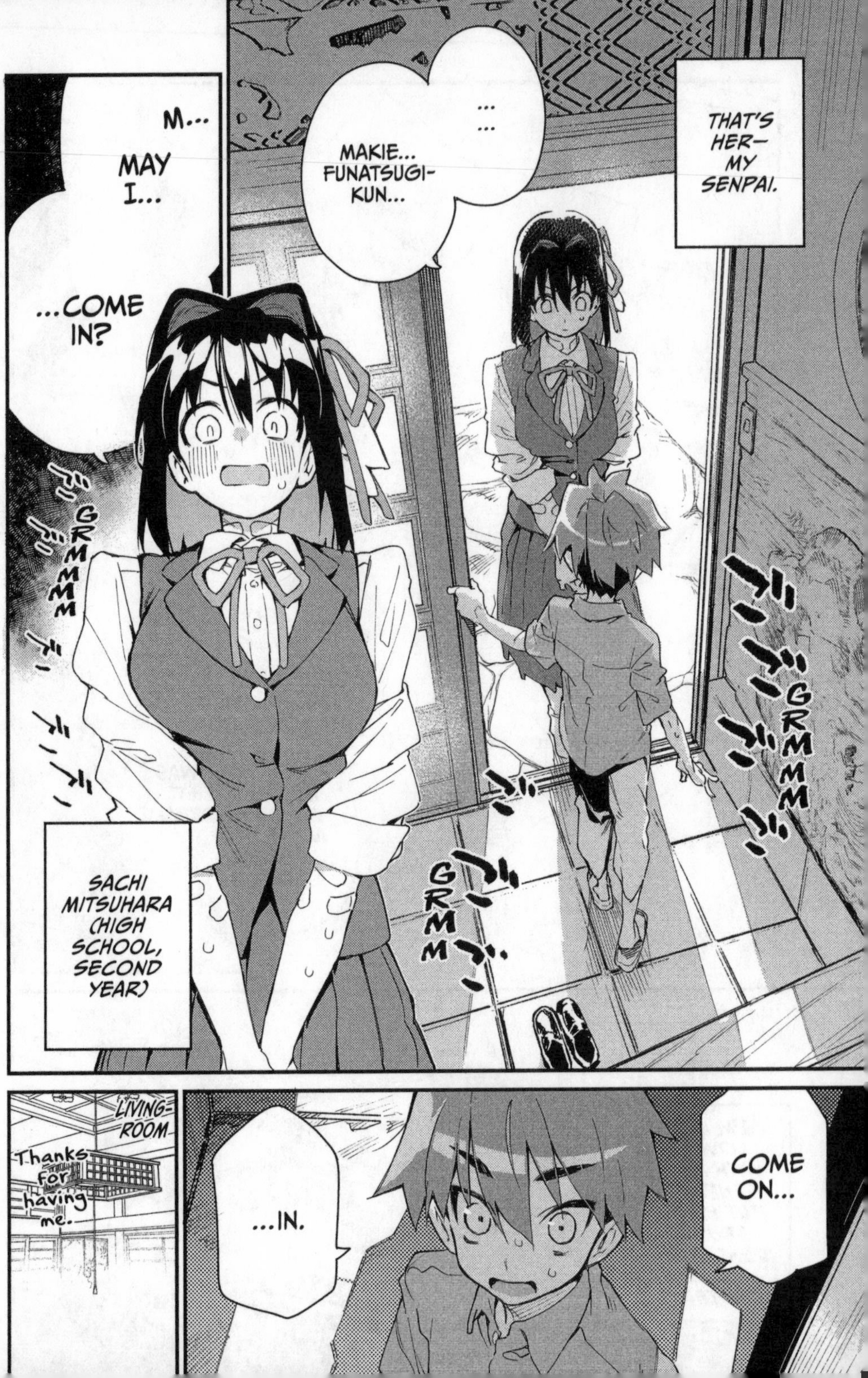
THAT'S HER—MY SENPAI.
... ... MAKIE... FUNATSUGI-KUN...
M... MAY I... ...COME IN?
GRMMM
GRMM
GRMMM
SACHI MITSUHARA (HIGH SCHOOL, SECOND YEAR)
COME ON...
...IN.
LIVING-ROOM
Thanks for having me.

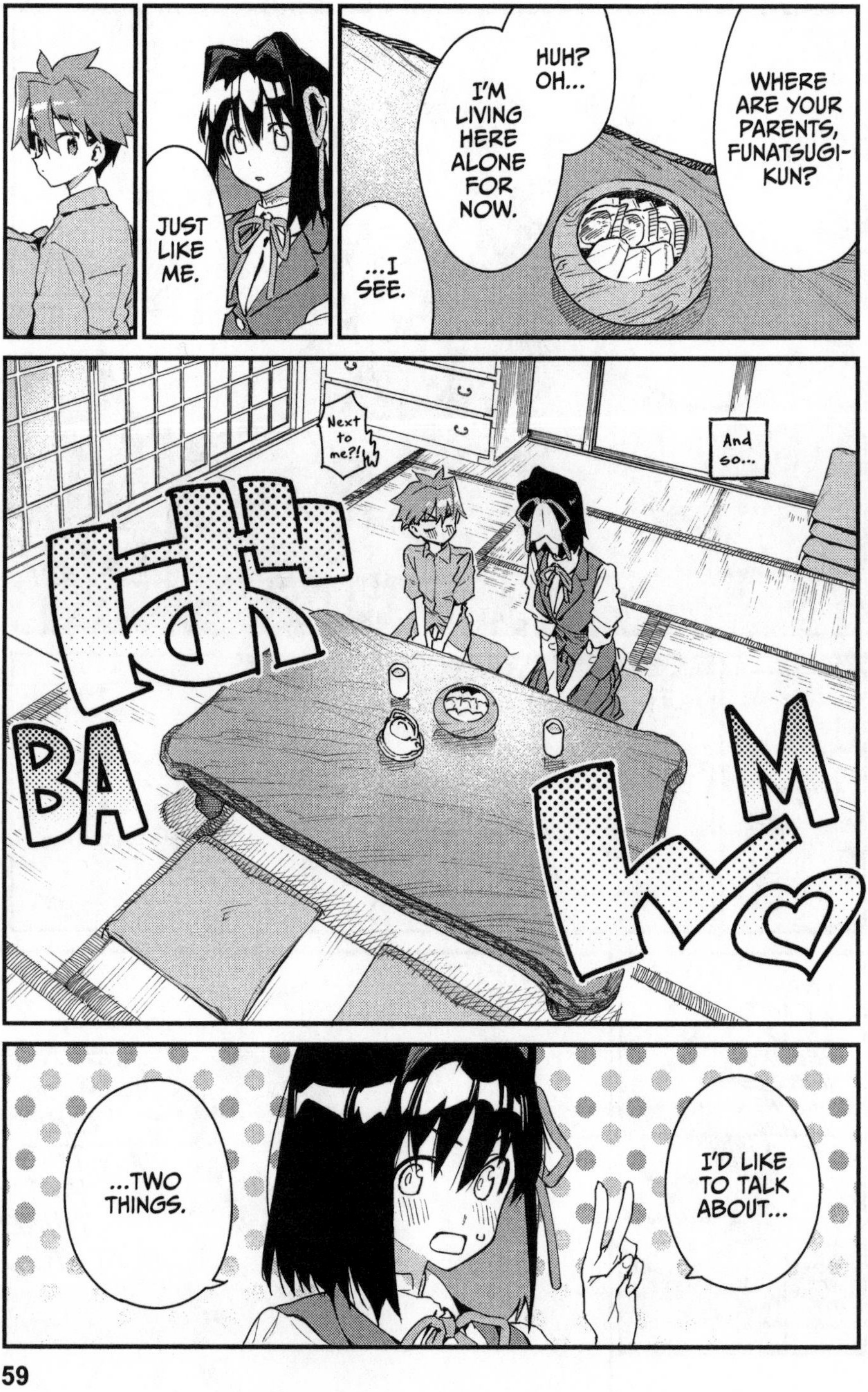
WHERE ARE YOUR PARENTS, FUNATSUGI-KUN?
HUH? OH... I'M LIVING HERE ALONE FOR NOW.
...I SEE.
JUST LIKE ME.
And so...
Next to me?!
BAM
I'D LIKE TO TALK ABOUT...
...TWO THINGS.

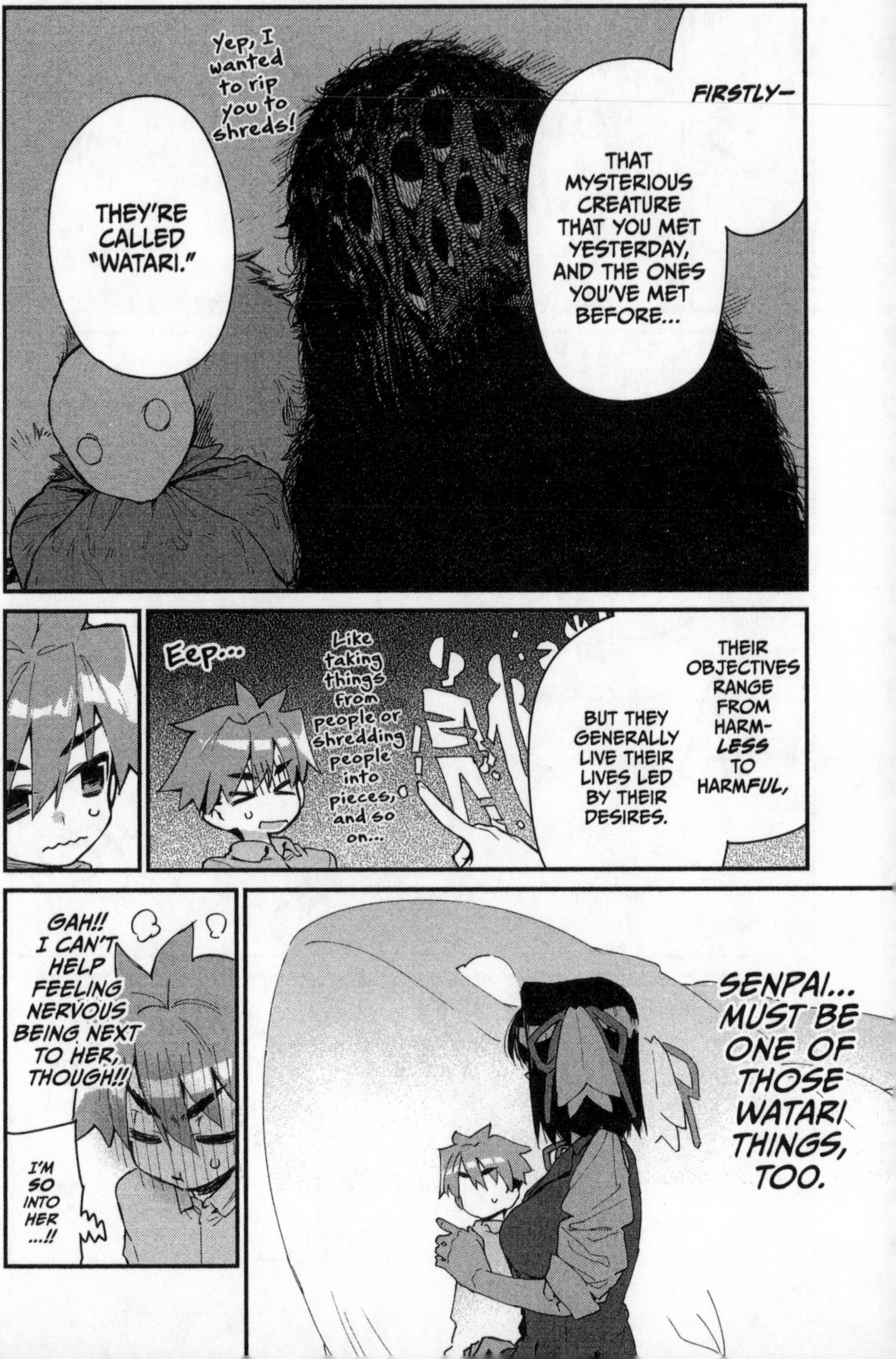
FIRSTLY—
THAT MYSTERIOUS CREATURE THAT YOU MET YESTERDAY, AND THE ONES YOU'VE MET BEFORE...
THEY'RE CALLED "WATARI."
Yep, I wanted to rip you to shreds!
THEIR OBJECTIVES RANGE FROM HARM-LESS TO HARMFUL,
BUT THEY GENERALLY LIVE THEIR LIVES LED BY THEIR DESIRES.
Like taking things from people or shredding people into pieces, and so on...
Eep...
SENPAI... MUST BE ONE OF THOSE WATARI THINGS, TOO.
GAH!! I CAN'T HELP FEELING NERVOUS BEING NEXT TO HER, THOUGH!!
I'M SO INTO HER ...!!

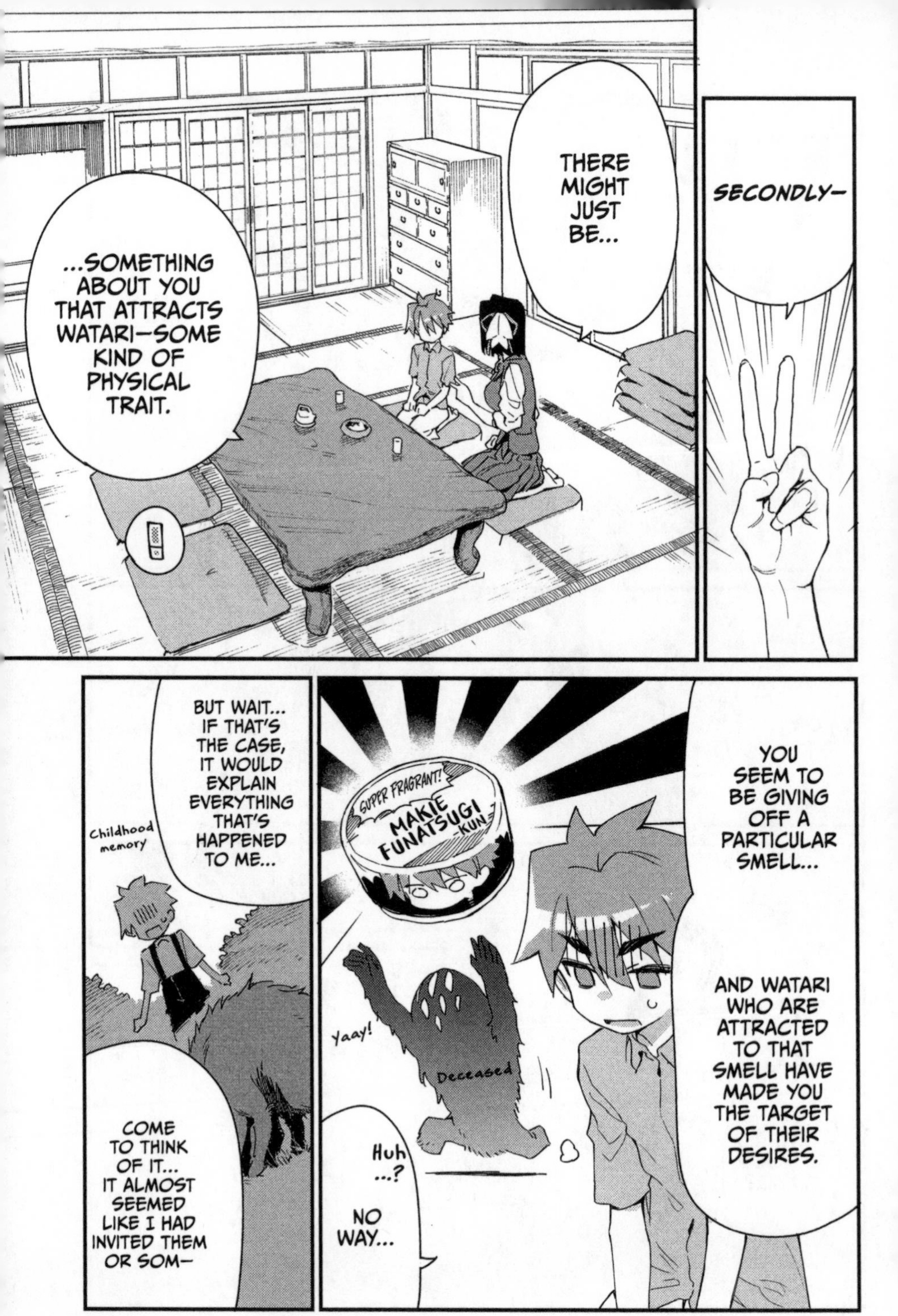
SECONDLY—
THERE MIGHT JUST BE...
...SOMETHING ABOUT YOU THAT ATTRACTS WATARI—SOME KIND OF PHYSICAL TRAIT.
YOU SEEM TO BE GIVING OFF A PARTICULAR SMELL...
AND WATARI WHO ARE ATTRACTED TO THAT SMELL HAVE MADE YOU THE TARGET OF THEIR DESIRES.
SUPER FRAGRANT!
MAKIE FUNATSUGI -KUN
Yaay!
Deceased
Huh ...?
NO WAY...
BUT WAIT... IF THAT'S THE CASE, IT WOULD EXPLAIN EVERYTHING THAT'S HAPPENED TO ME...
Childhood memory
COME TO THINK OF IT... IT ALMOST SEEMED LIKE I HAD INVITED THEM OR SOM—

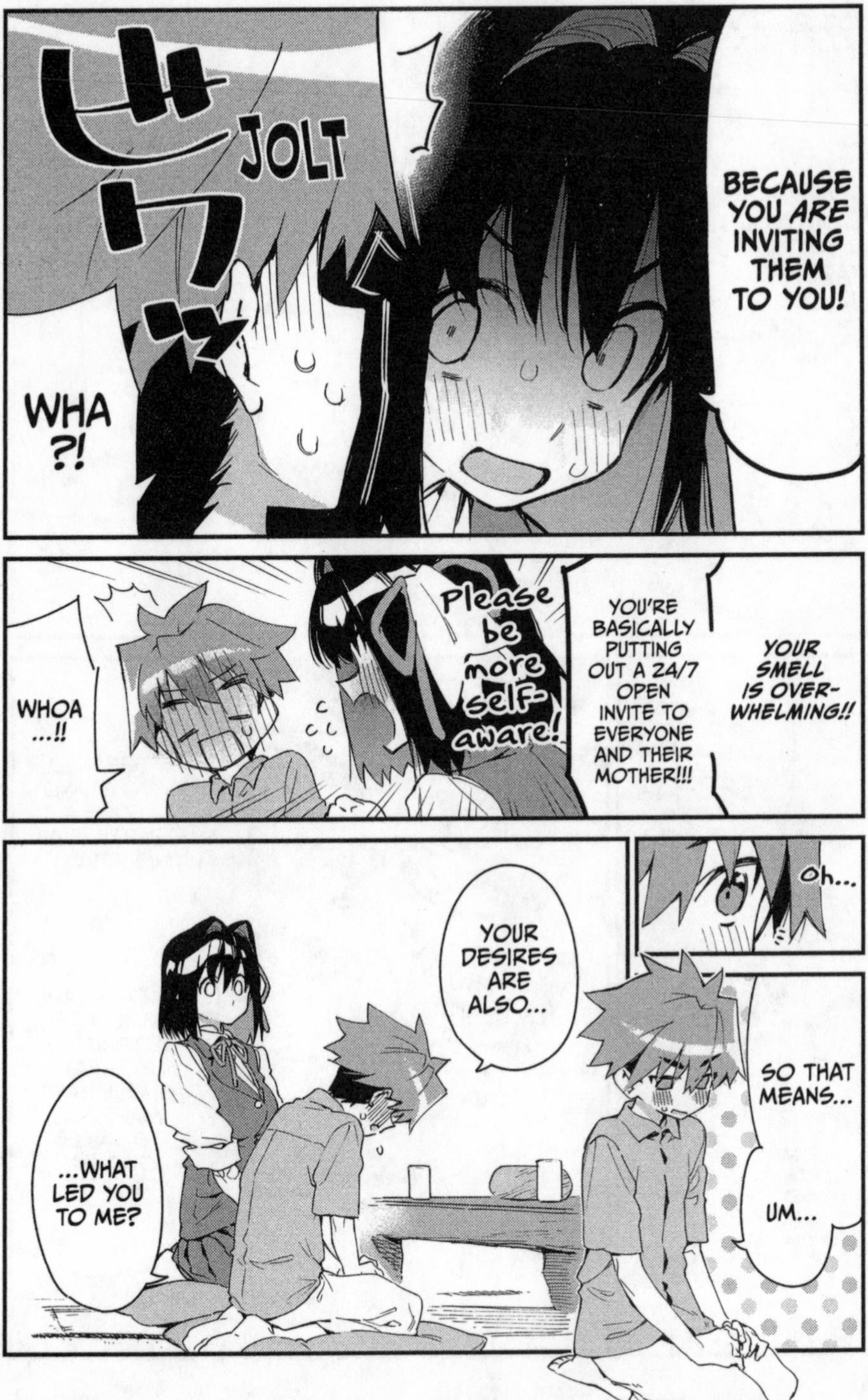
BECAUSE YOU ARE INVITING THEM TO YOU!
JOLT
WHA ?!
YOUR SMELL IS OVER-WHELMING!!
YOU'RE BASICALLY PUTTING OUT A 24/7 OPEN INVITE TO EVERYONE AND THEIR MOTHER!!!
Please be more self-aware!
WHOA ...!!
Oh...
SO THAT MEANS...
UM...
YOUR DESIRES ARE ALSO...
...WHAT LED YOU TO ME?

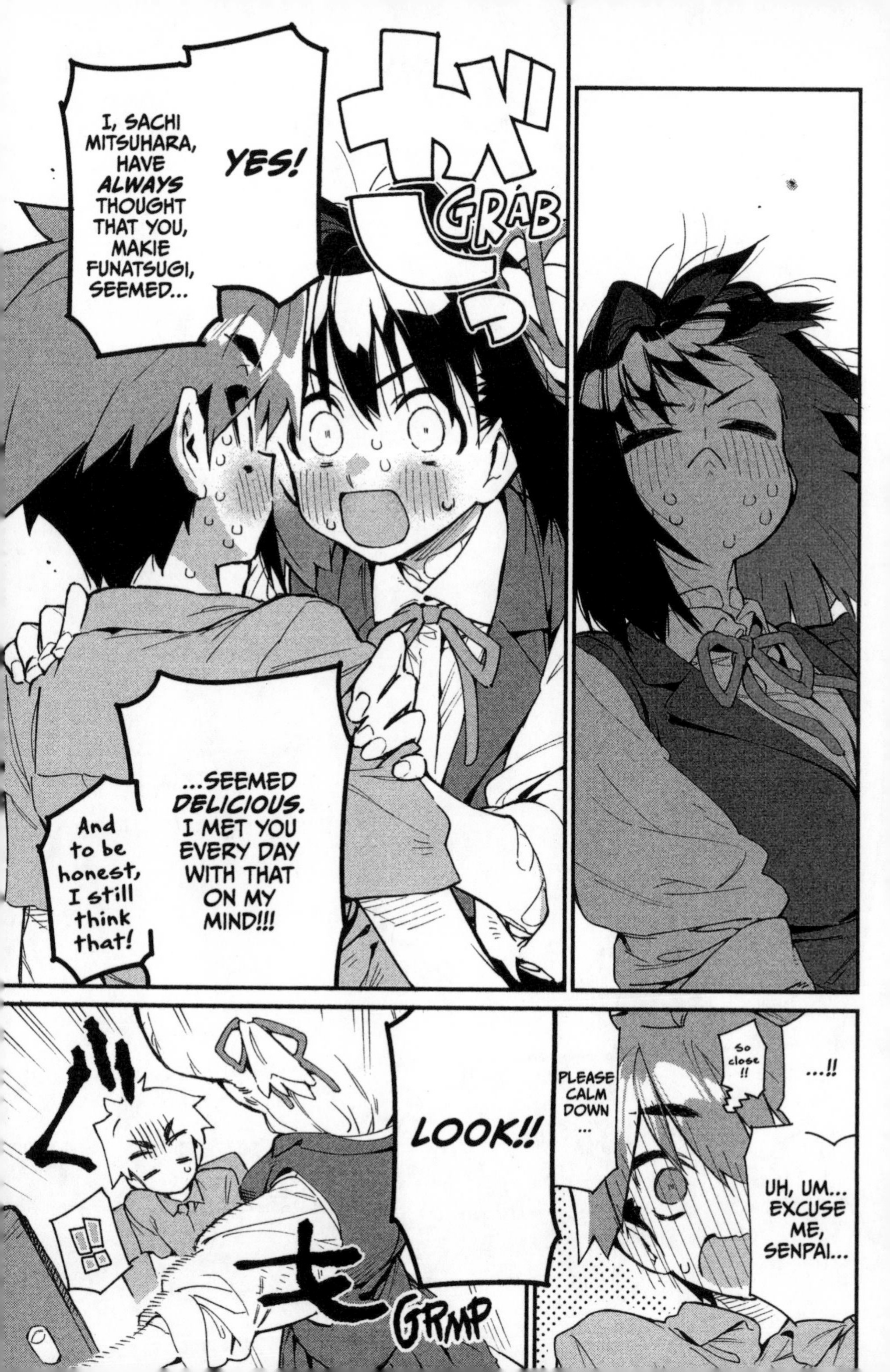

GRAB
YES!
I, SACHI MITSUHARA, HAVE ***ALWAYS*** THOUGHT THAT YOU, MAKIE FUNATSUGI, SEEMED...
...SEEMED ***DELICIOUS.*** I MET YOU EVERY DAY WITH THAT ON MY MIND!!!
And to be honest, I still think that!
...!!
So close!!
UH, UM... EXCUSE ME, SENPAI...
PLEASE CALM DOWN...
LOOK!!
GRMP

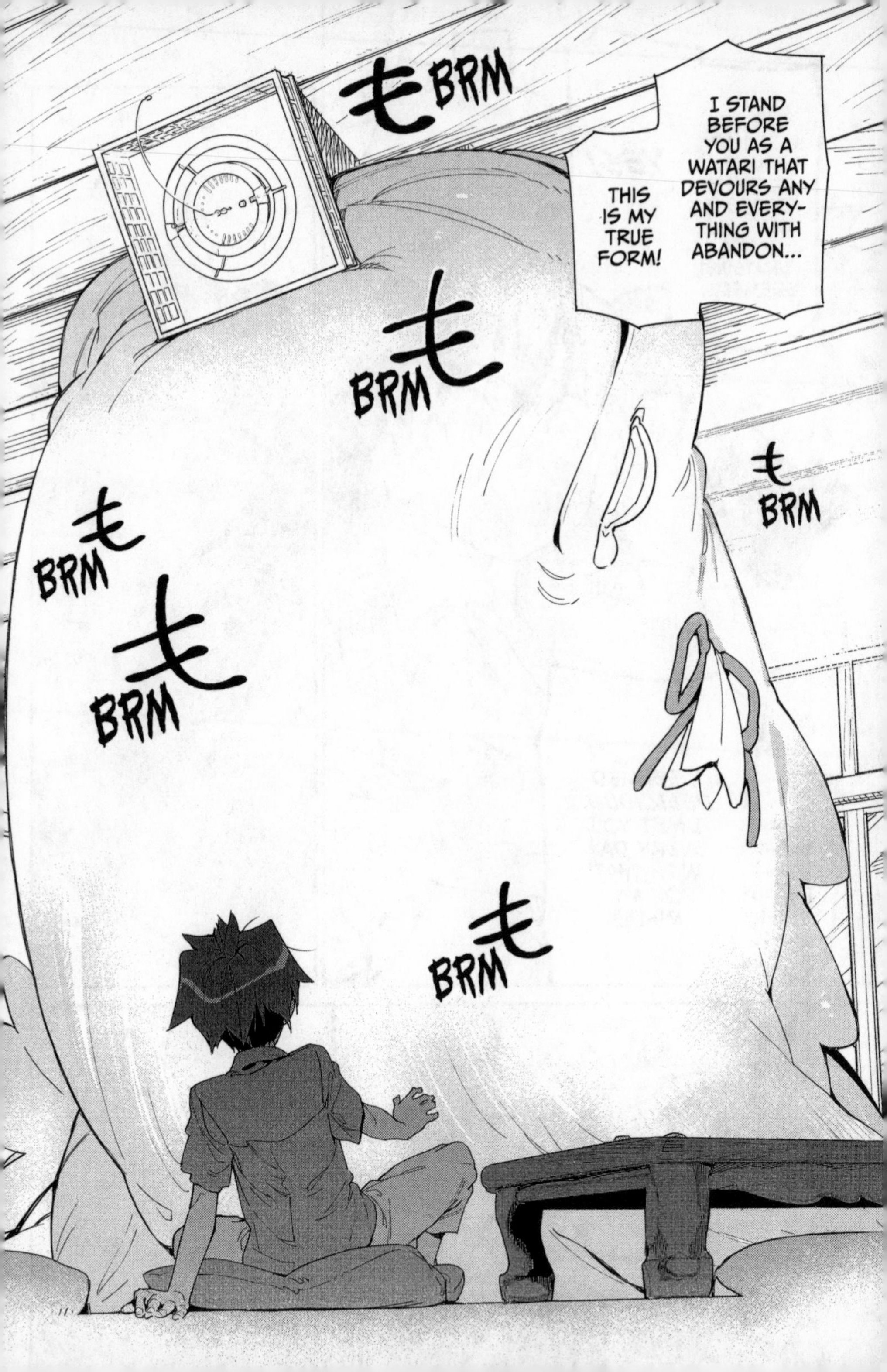
I STAND BEFORE YOU AS A WATARI THAT DEVOURS ANY AND EVERY-THING WITH ABANDON...
THIS IS MY TRUE FORM!
も BRM
も BRM
も BRM
も BRM
も BRM
も BRM

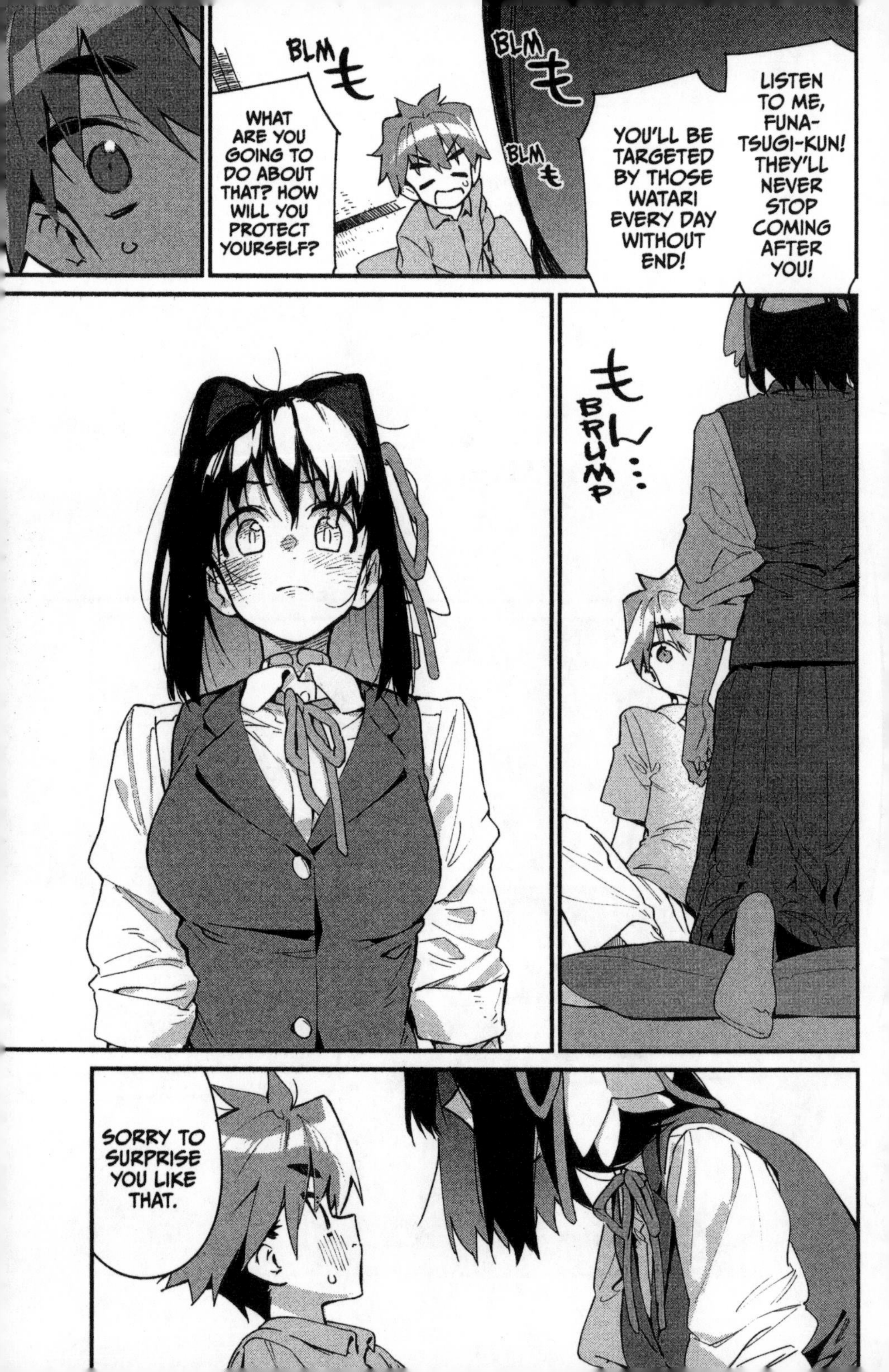
BLM も
BLM も
LISTEN TO ME, FUNA-TSUGI-KUN! THEY'LL NEVER STOP COMING AFTER YOU!
YOU'LL BE TARGETED BY THOSE WATARI EVERY DAY WITHOUT END!
BLM も
WHAT ARE YOU GOING TO DO ABOUT THAT? HOW WILL YOU PROTECT YOURSELF?
もん…
BRUMP
SORRY TO SURPRISE YOU LIKE THAT.

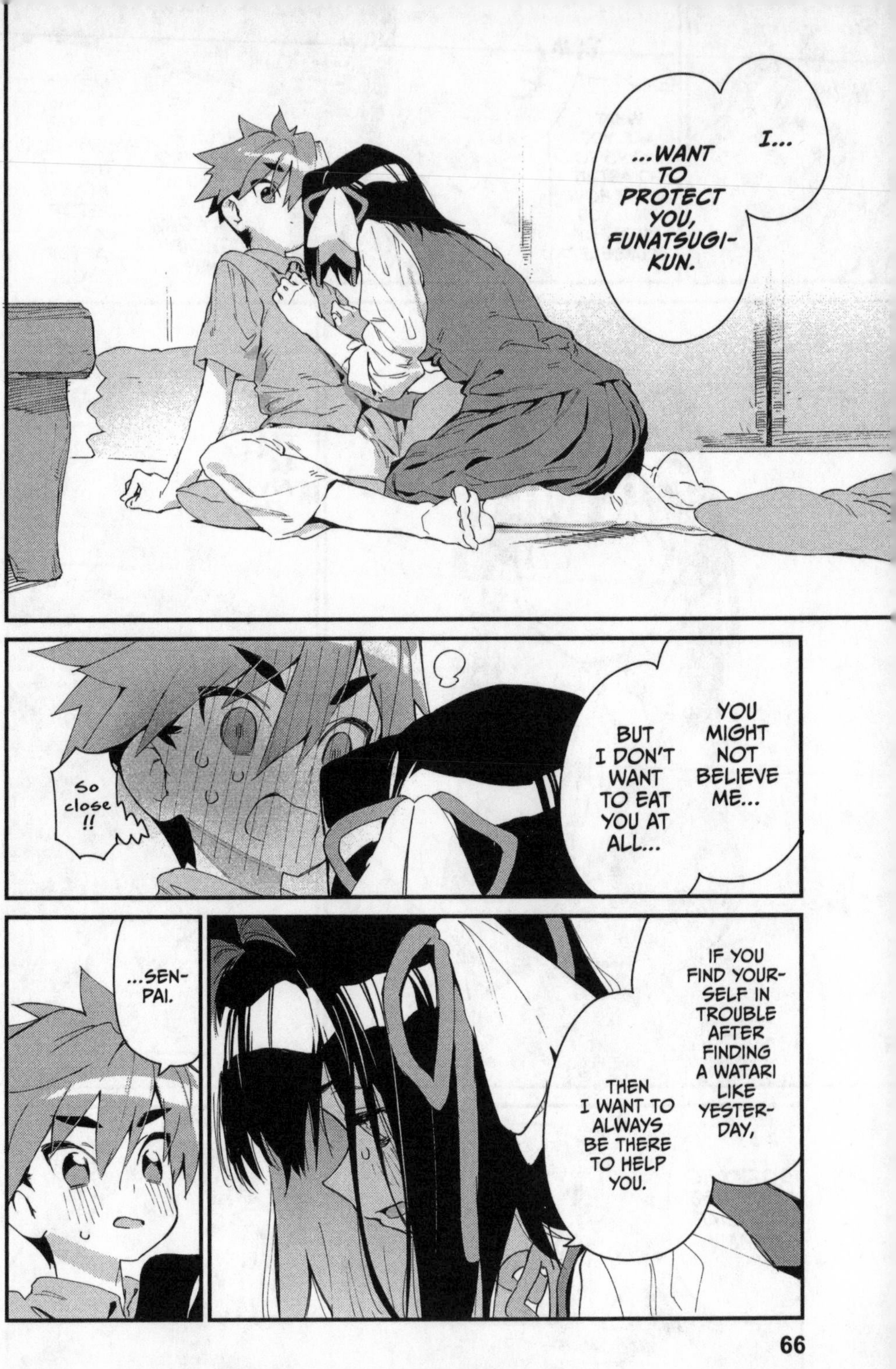
I...
...WANT TO PROTECT YOU, FUNATSUGI-KUN.
YOU MIGHT NOT BELIEVE ME...
BUT I DON'T WANT TO EAT YOU AT ALL...
So close!!
IF YOU FIND YOURSELF IN TROUBLE AFTER FINDING A WATARI LIKE YESTERDAY,
THEN I WANT TO ALWAYS BE THERE TO HELP YOU.
...SENPAI.

BUT YOU REALLY DO SMELL GOO-OOO-OOD!
You seem so, so tasty! I'm really sorry.
...
THANK YOU...
...FOR SAVING ME YESTERDAY.
BUT, UM...
I'VE BEEN WONDERING ABOUT ONE THING...

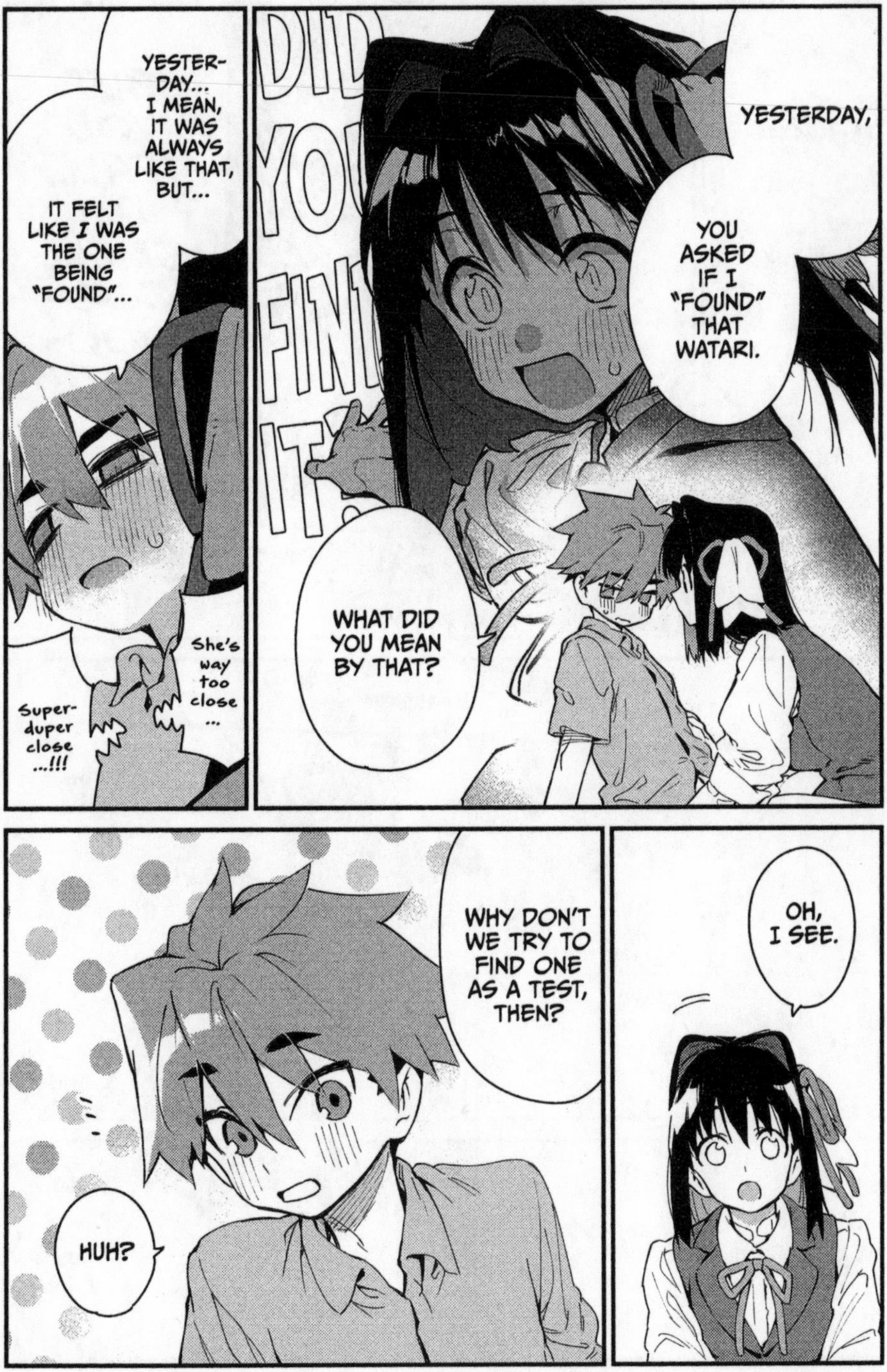
YESTERDAY,
YOU ASKED IF I "FOUND" THAT WATARI.
DID YOU FIN IT?
WHAT DID YOU MEAN BY THAT?
YESTER-DAY... I MEAN, IT WAS ALWAYS LIKE THAT, BUT...
IT FELT LIKE I WAS THE ONE BEING "FOUND"...
She's way too close...
Super-duper close...!!!
OH, I SEE.
WHY DON'T WE TRY TO FIND ONE AS A TEST, THEN?
HUH?

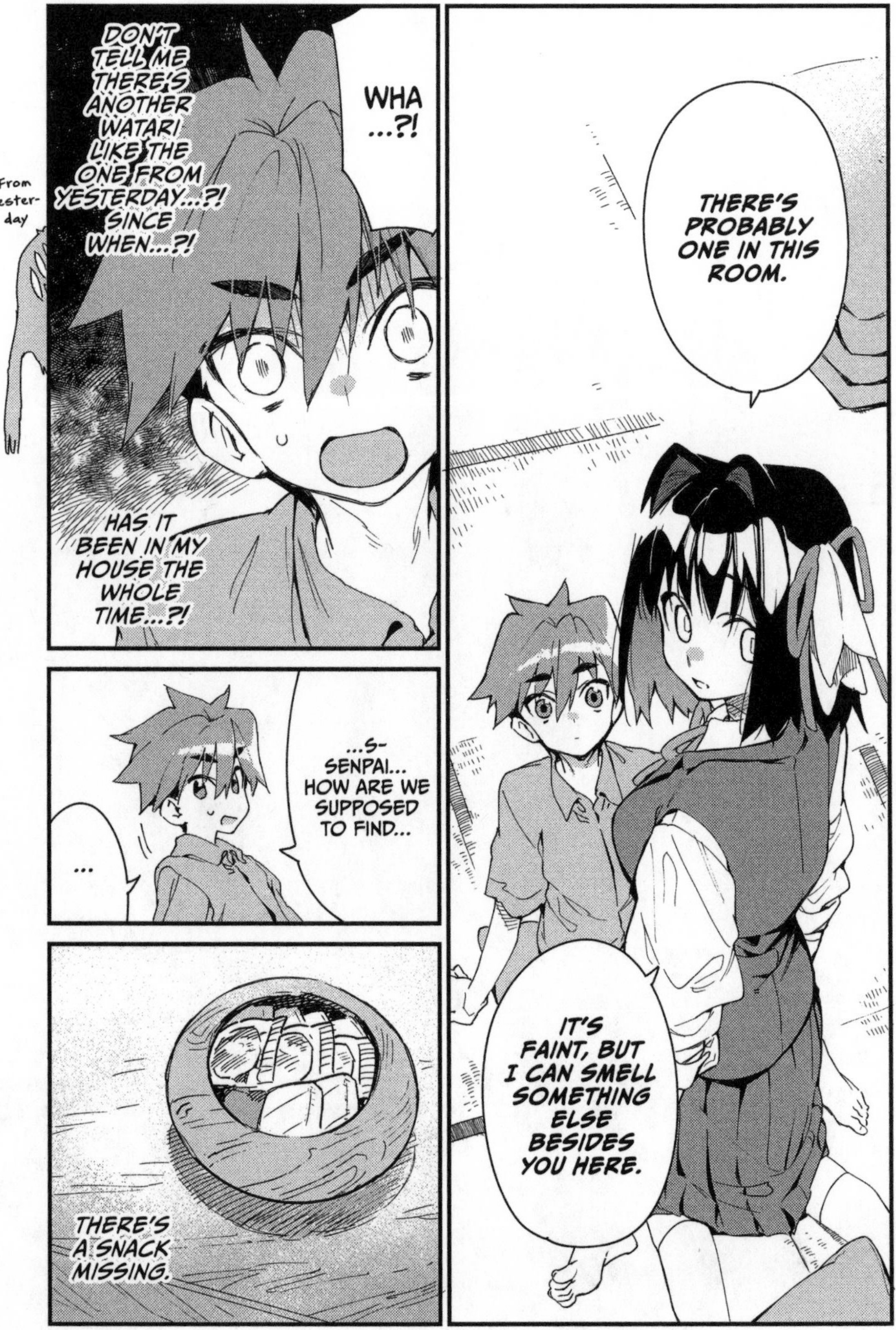
THERE'S PROBABLY ONE IN THIS ROOM.
IT'S FAINT, BUT I CAN SMELL SOMETHING ELSE BESIDES YOU HERE.
WHA ...?!
DON'T TELL ME THERE'S ANOTHER WATARI LIKE THE ONE FROM YESTERDAY...?! SINCE WHEN...?!
From yester-day
HAS IT BEEN IN MY HOUSE THE WHOLE TIME...?!
...S-SENPAI... HOW ARE WE SUPPOSED TO FIND...
...
THERE'S A SNACK MISSING.

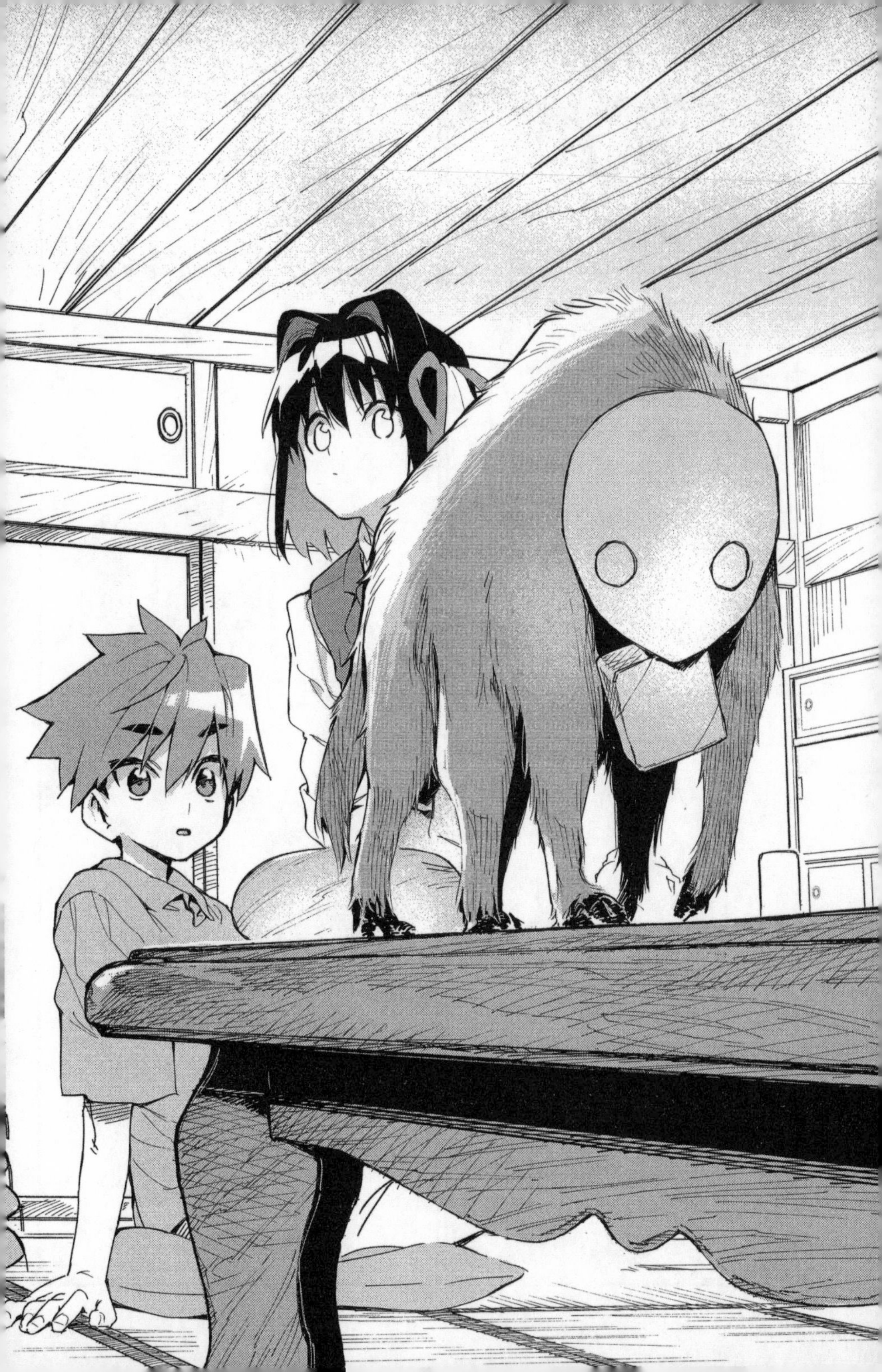

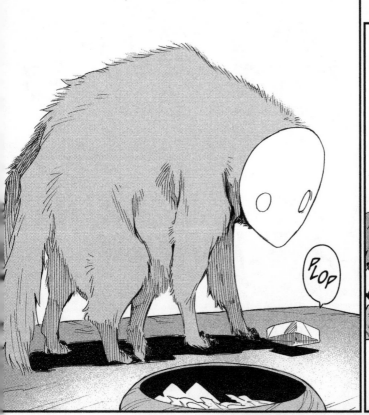

PLOP

IT APPEAR-ED!

YOU FOUND IT!

...

That's my...

...bento...

FROM BACK THEN...?

IT'S YOU...

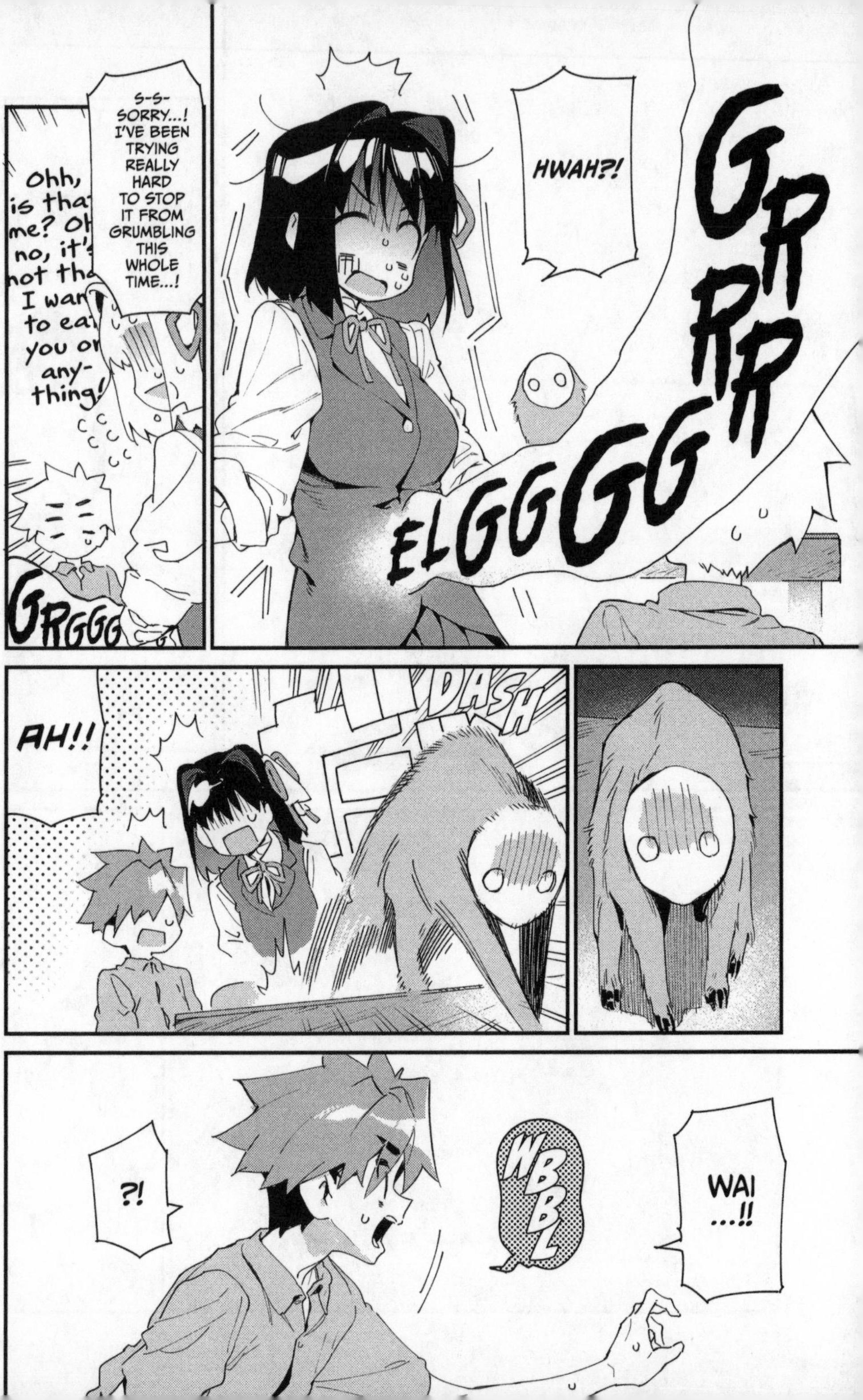
GRRR
ELGGGG
HWAH?!
S-S-SORRY...! I'VE BEEN TRYING REALLY HARD TO STOP IT FROM GRUMBLING THIS WHOLE TIME...!
Ohh, is tha me? Oh no, it's not tha I wan to ea you or any-thing!
GRGGG
DASH
AH!!
WAI ...!!
WBBL
?!

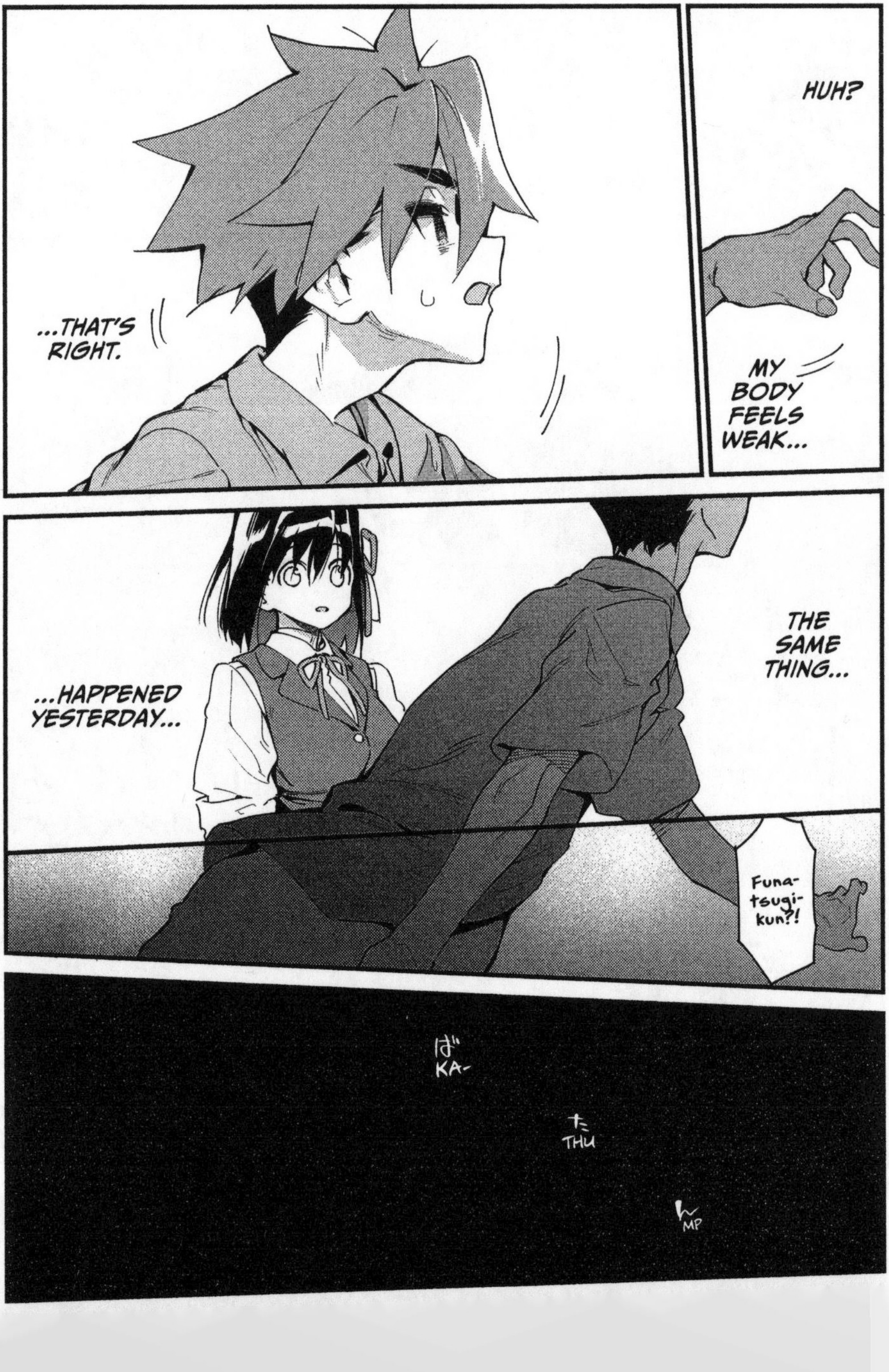
HUH?
MY BODY FEELS WEAK...
...THAT'S RIGHT.
THE SAME THING...
...HAPPENED YESTERDAY...
Funa-tsugi-kun?!
ばKA-
たTHU
んMP

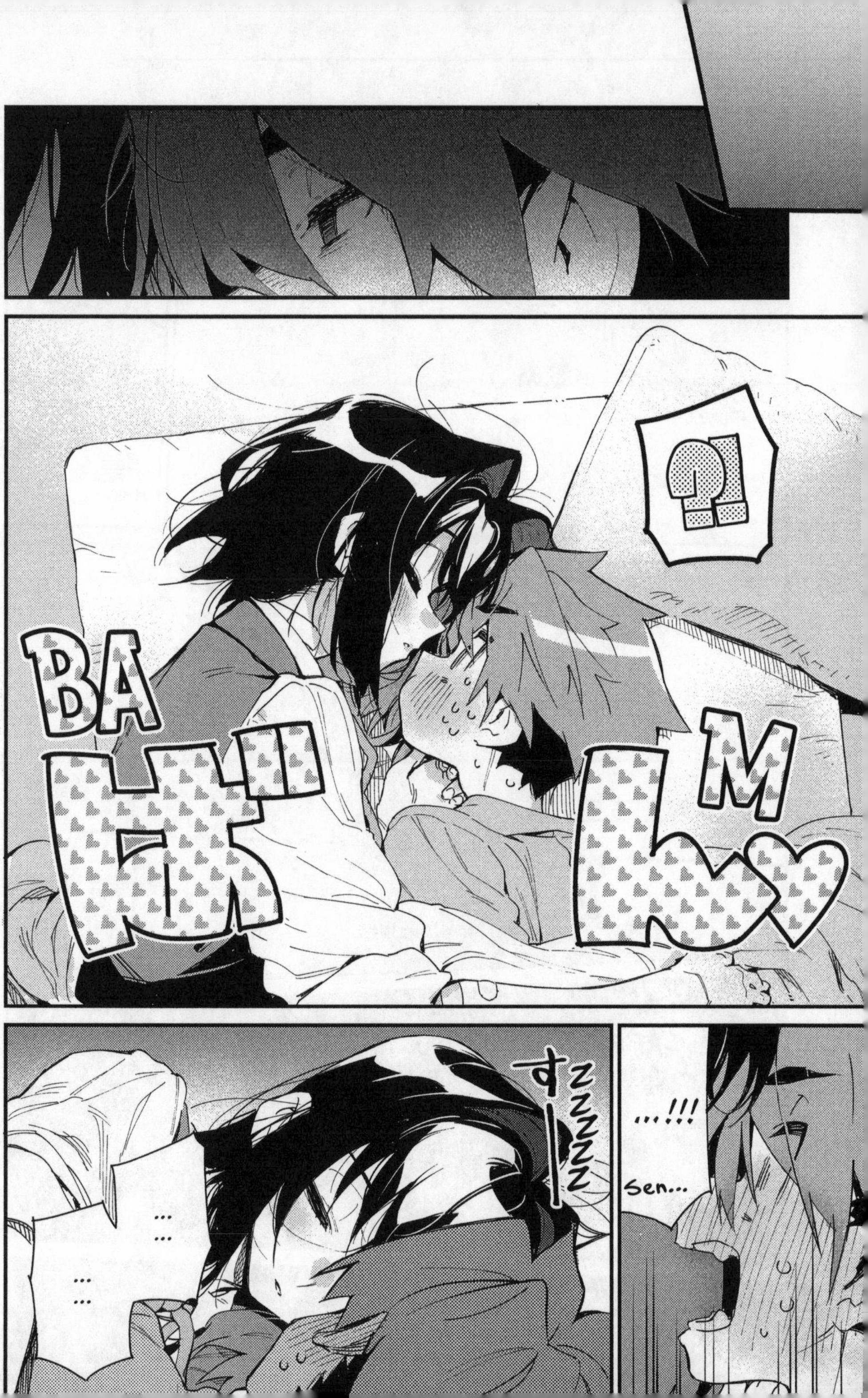
?!
BA
M
...!!!
Sen...
すZZZZZ
...
...
...
...
...

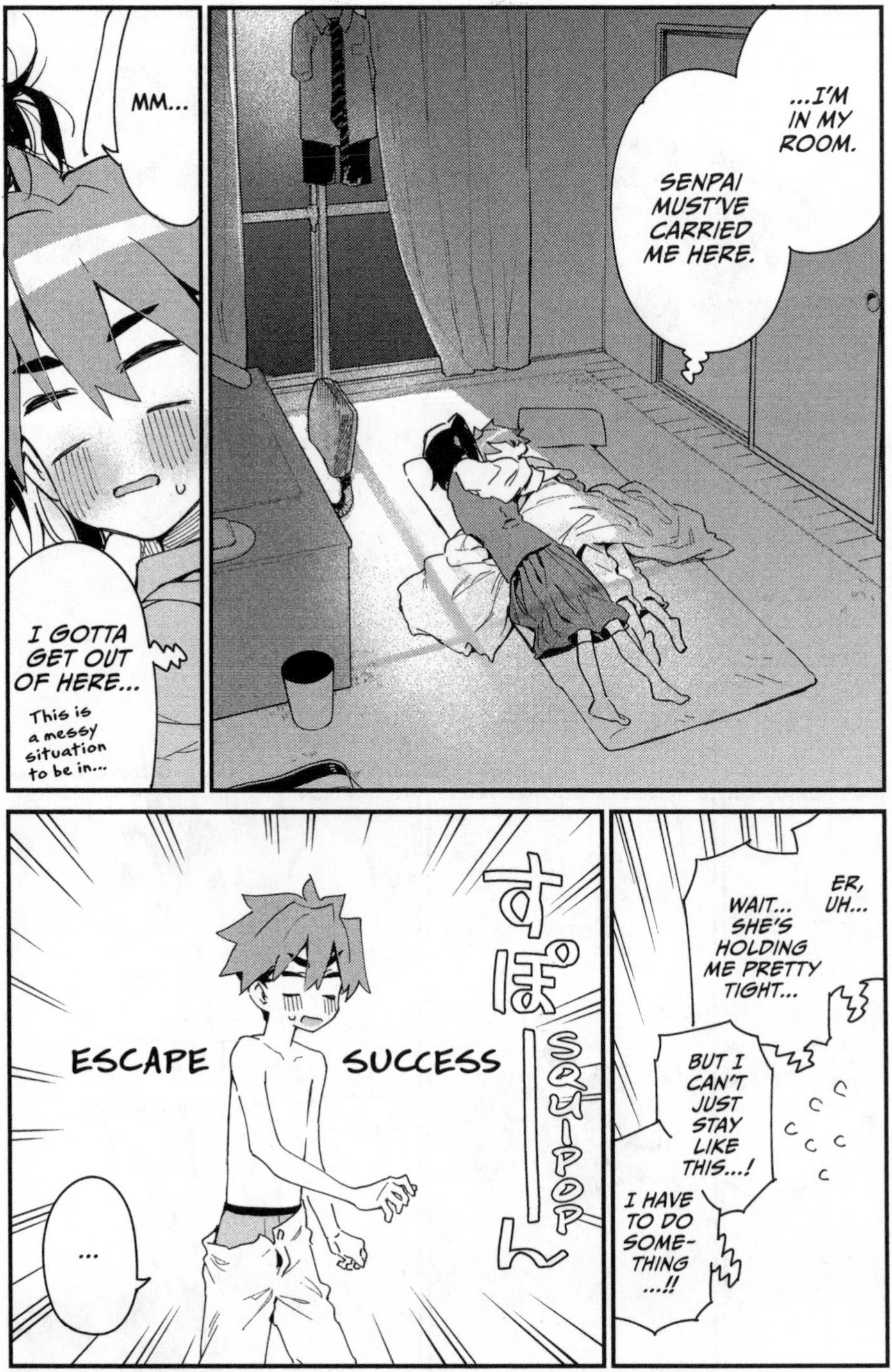
...I'M IN MY ROOM.
SENPAI MUST'VE CARRIED ME HERE.
MM...
I GOTTA GET OUT OF HERE...
This is a messy situation to be in...
ER, UH...
WAIT... SHE'S HOLDING ME PRETTY TIGHT...
BUT I CAN'T JUST STAY LIKE THIS...!
I HAVE TO DO SOME-THING ...!!
すぽーん
SQU-POP
ESCAPE SUCCESS
...

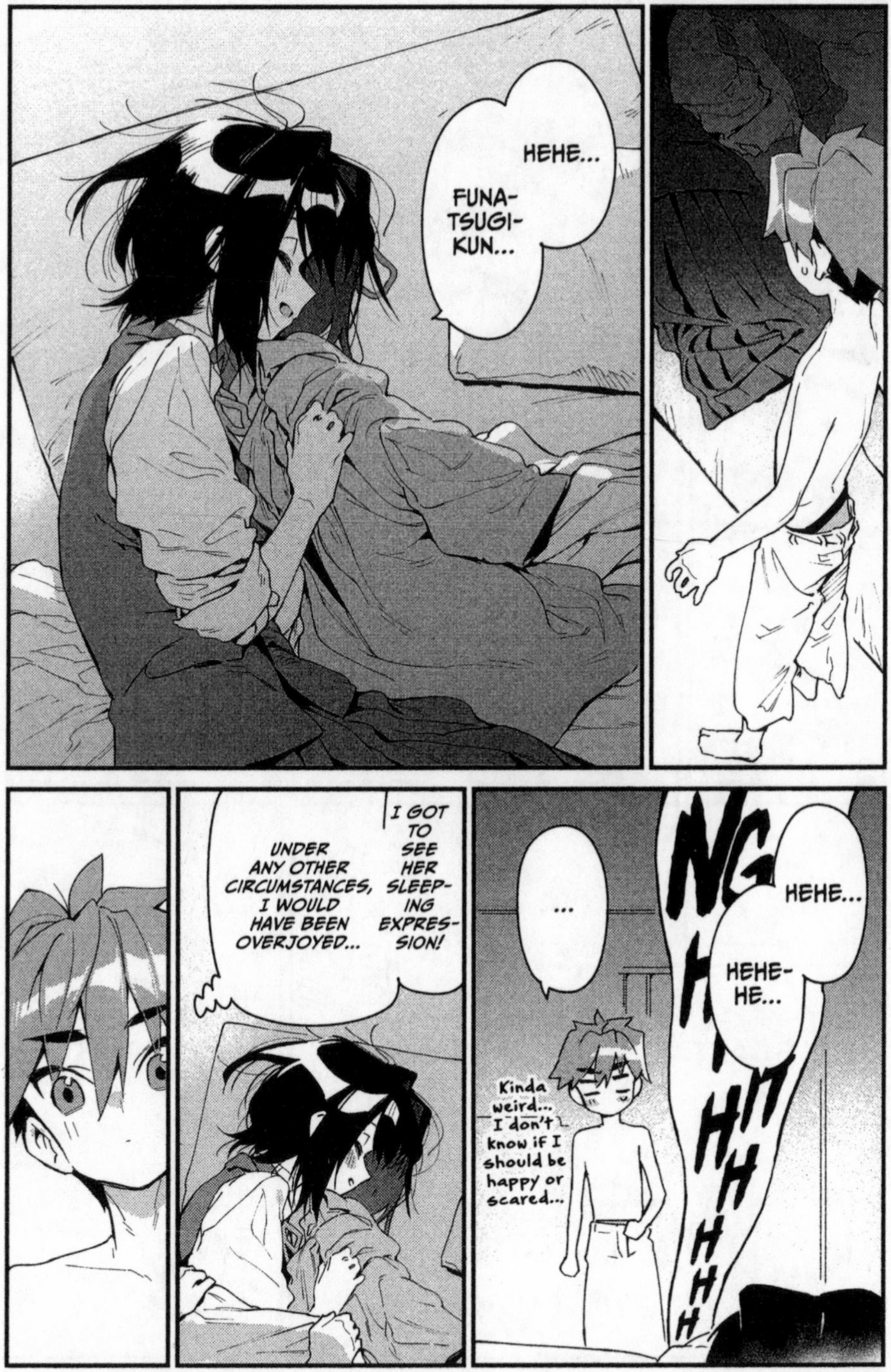

HEHE...
FUNA-TSUGI-KUN...
NGHHHHHHHHH
HEHE...
HEHE-HE...
...
Kinda weird... I don't know if I should be happy or scared...
I GOT TO SEE HER SLEEP-ING EXPRES-SION!
UNDER ANY OTHER CIRCUMSTANCES, I WOULD HAVE BEEN OVERJOYED...

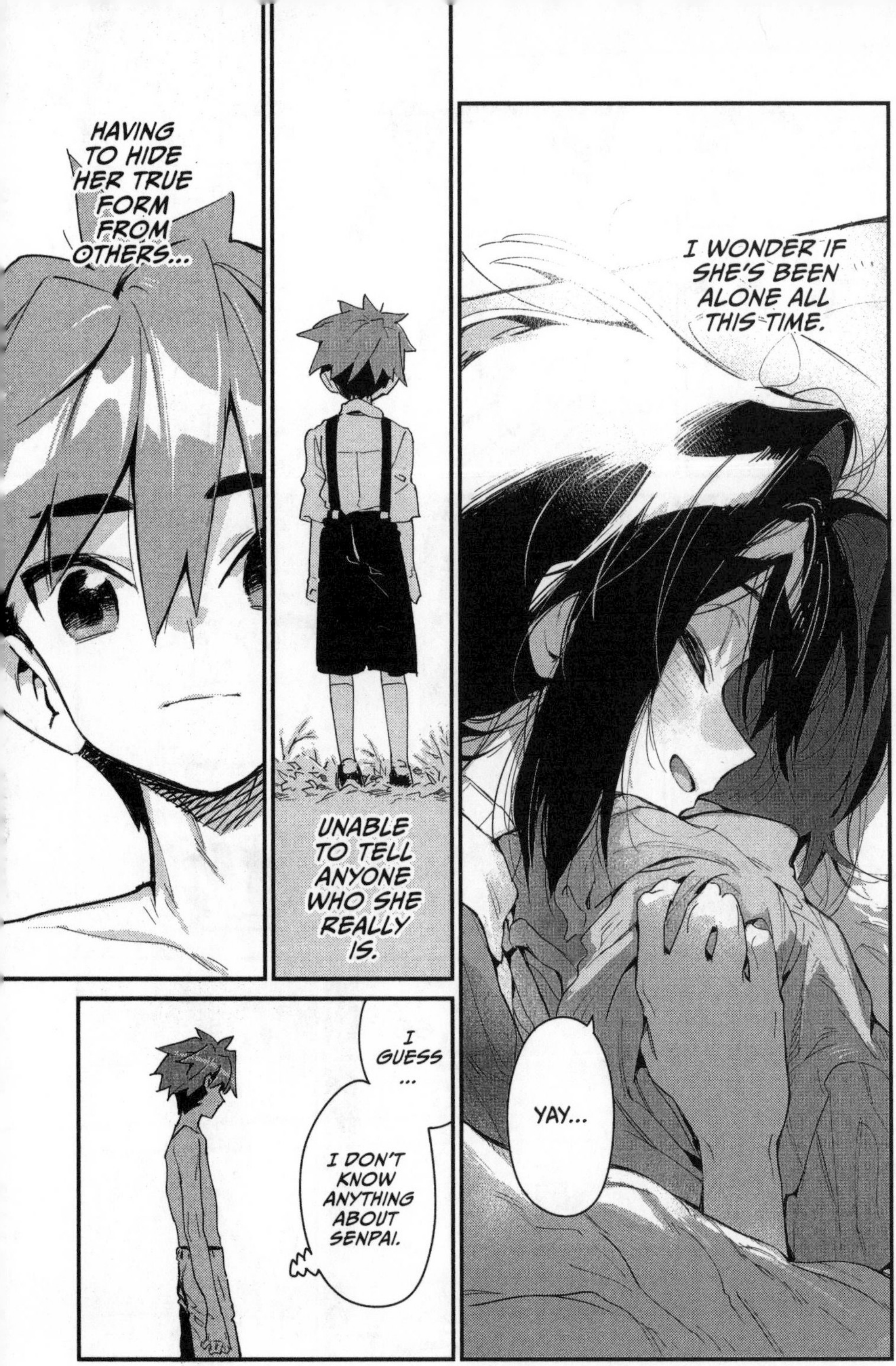
I WONDER IF SHE'S BEEN ALONE ALL THIS TIME.
YAY...
UNABLE TO TELL ANYONE WHO SHE REALLY IS.
HAVING TO HIDE HER TRUE FORM FROM OTHERS...
I GUESS ...
I DON'T KNOW ANYTHING ABOUT SENPAI.

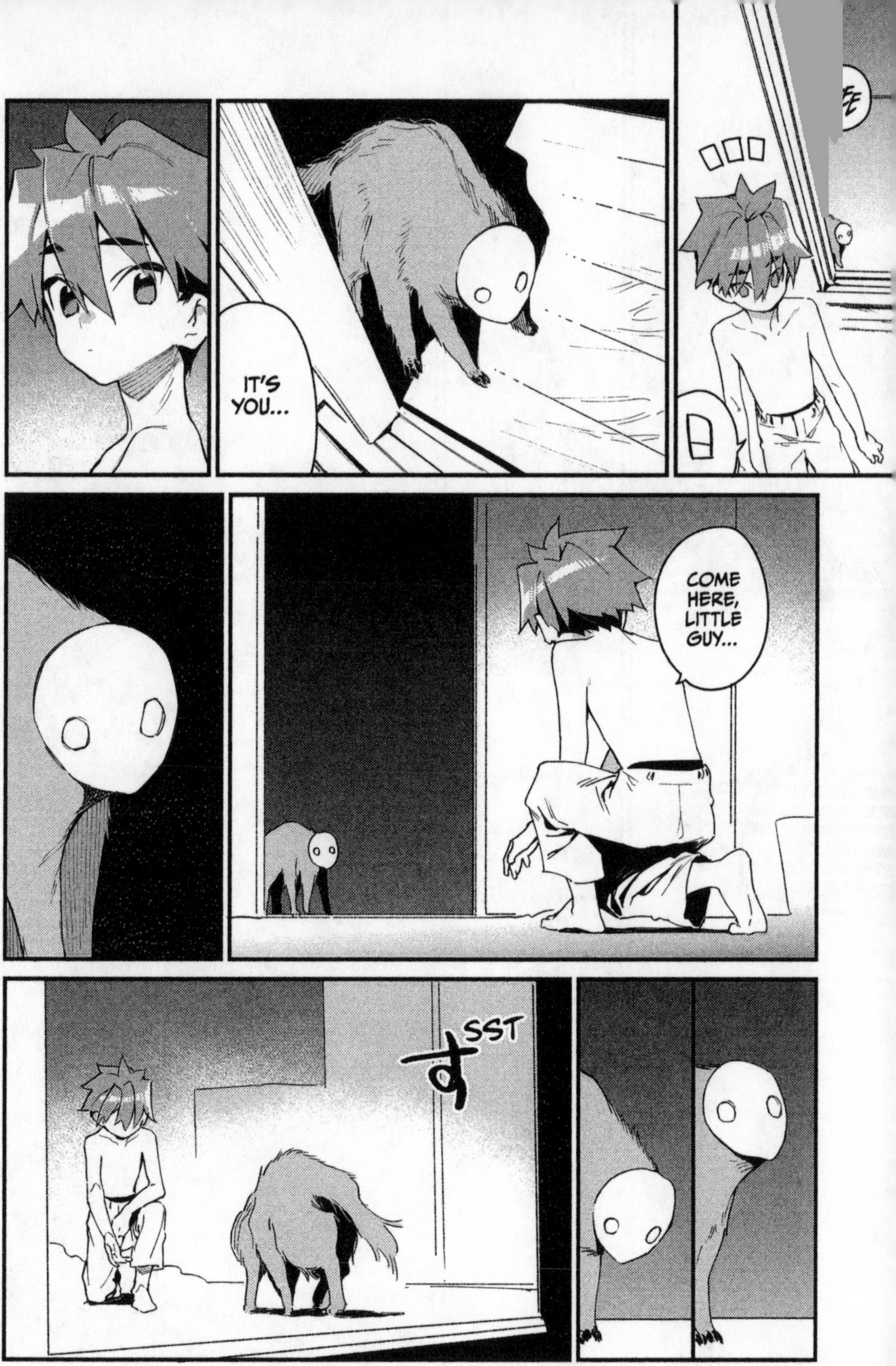
IT'S YOU...
COME HERE, LITTLE GUY...
SST
す

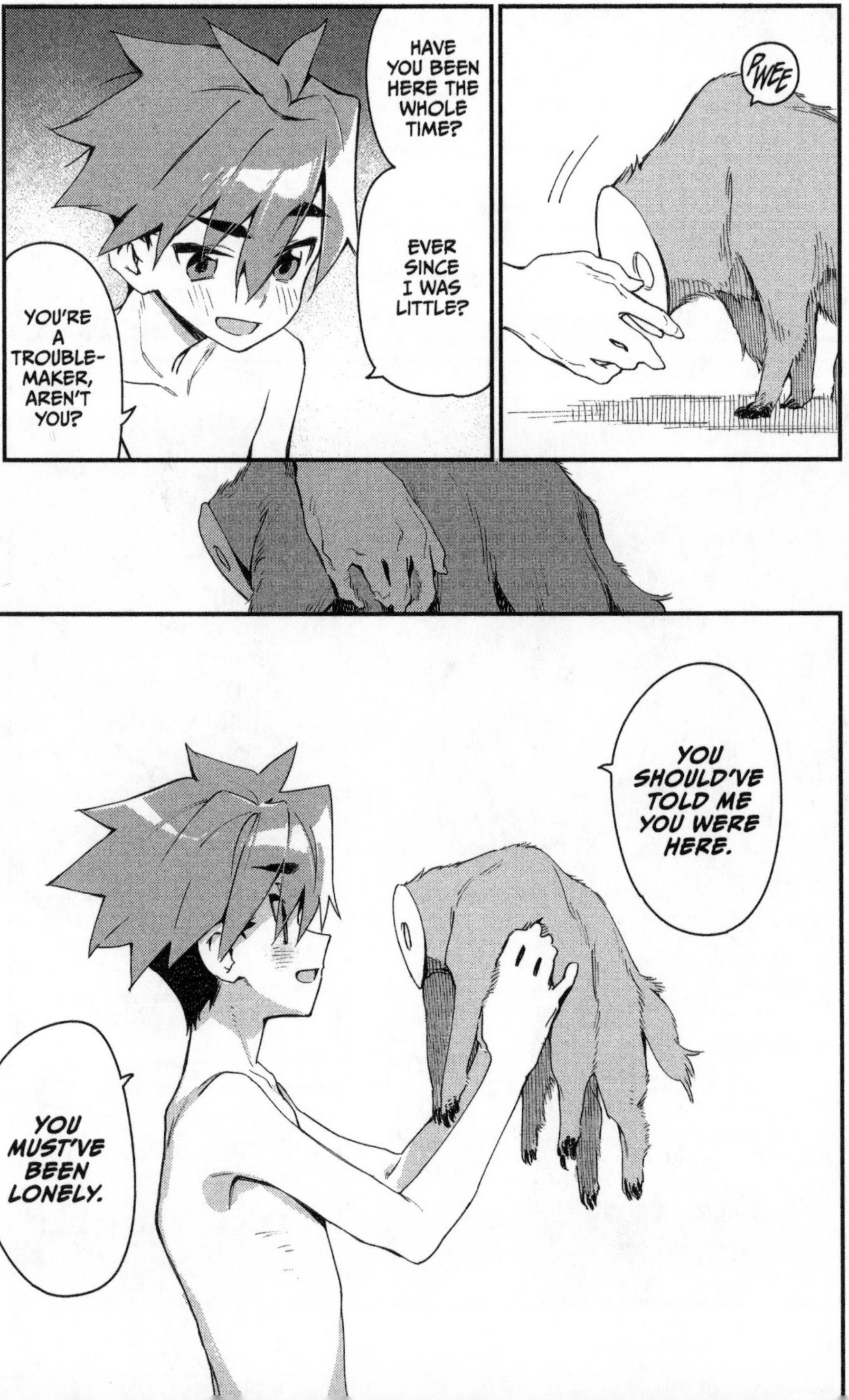
PWEE
HAVE YOU BEEN HERE THE WHOLE TIME?
EVER SINCE I WAS LITTLE?
YOU'RE A TROUBLE-MAKER, AREN'T YOU?
YOU SHOULD'VE TOLD ME YOU WERE HERE.
YOU MUST'VE BEEN LONELY.

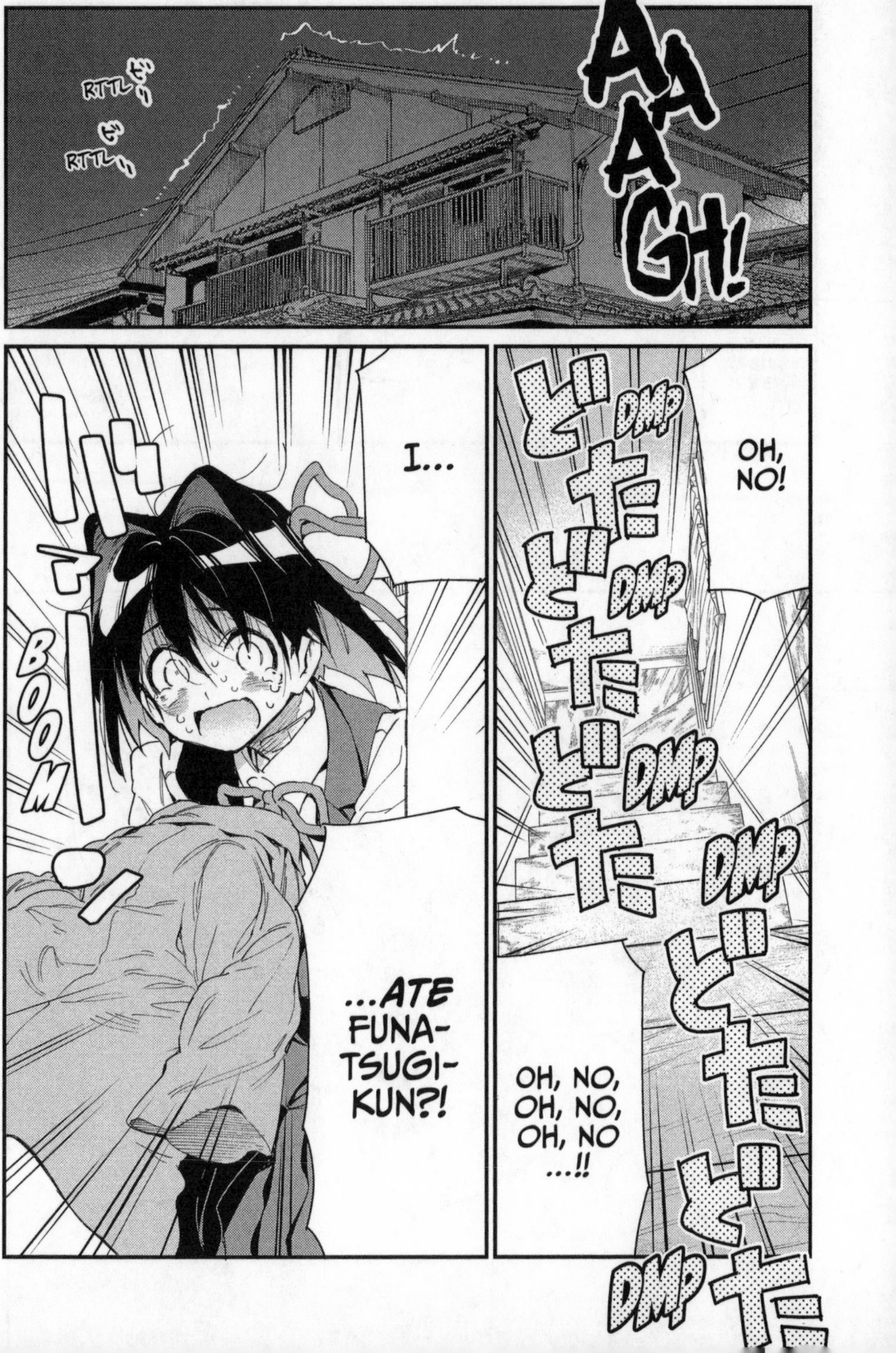
RTTL
RTTL
AAAGH!
DMP
DMP
DMP
DMP
DMP
OH, NO!
OH, NO, OH, NO, OH, NO ...!!
I...
BOOM
...ATE FUNA-TSUGI-KUN?!

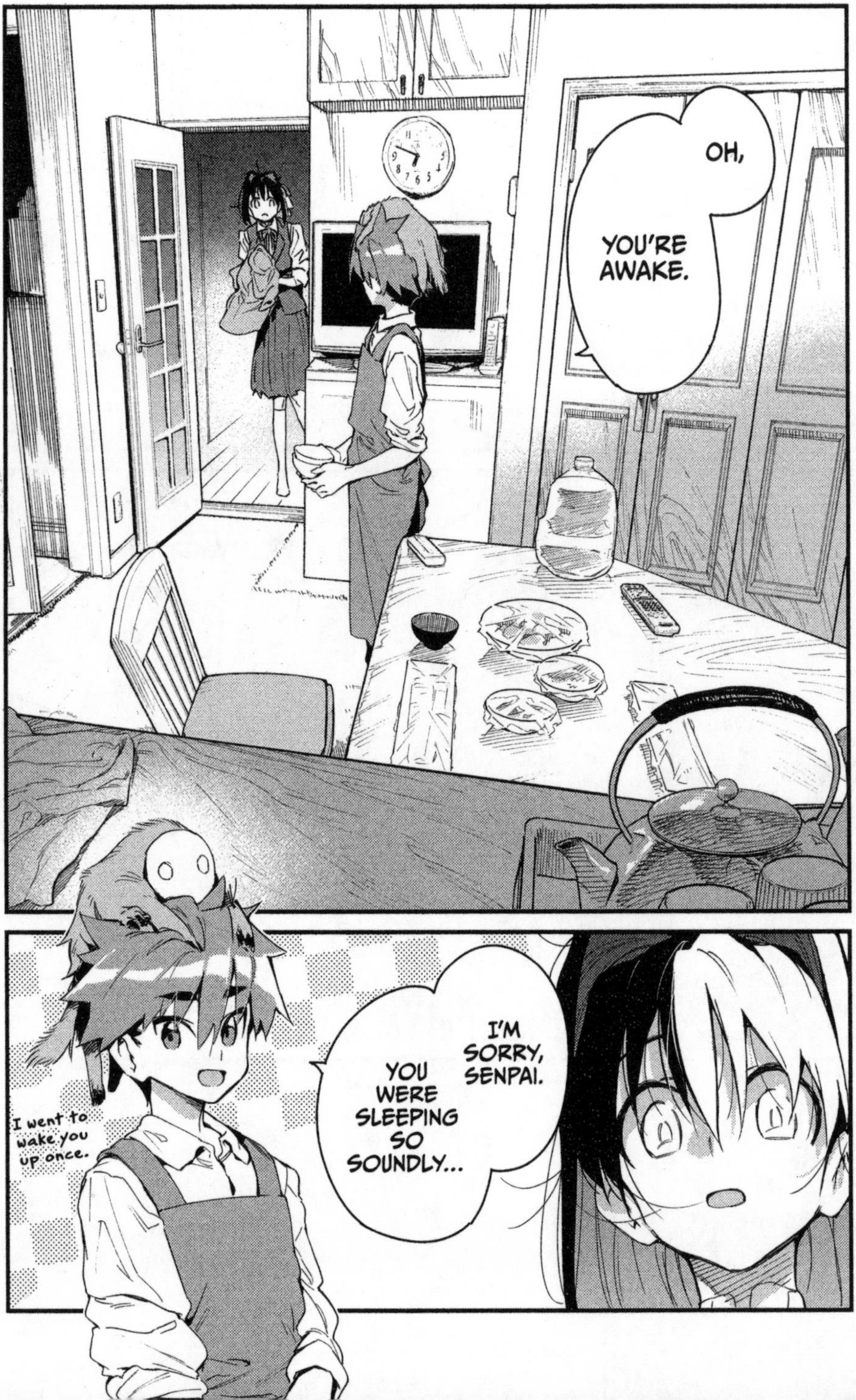
OH,
YOU'RE AWAKE.
I'M SORRY, SENPAI.
YOU WERE SLEEPING SO SOUNDLY...
I went to wake you up once.

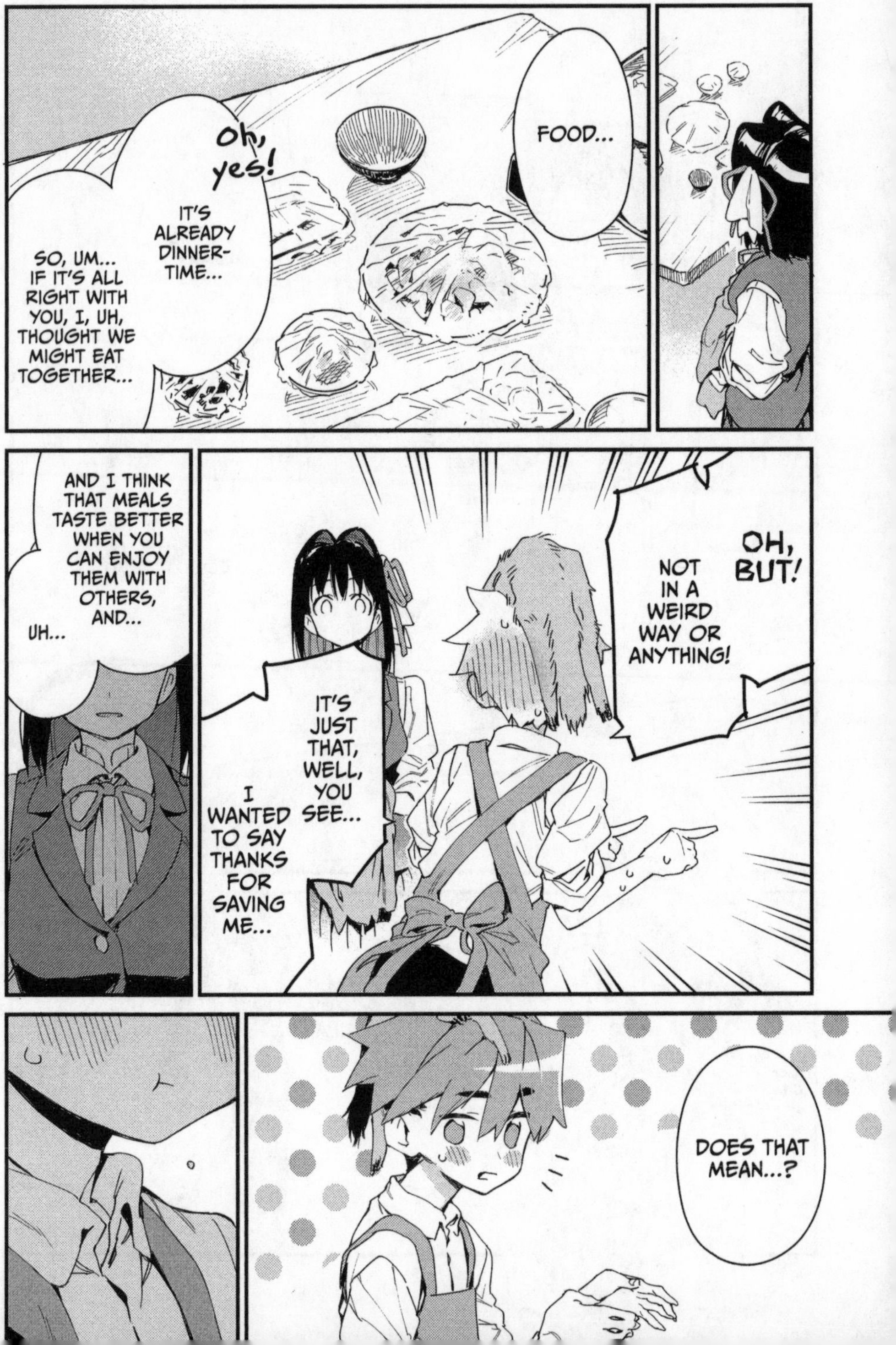
FOOD...
Oh, yes!
IT'S ALREADY DINNER-TIME...
SO, UM... IF IT'S ALL RIGHT WITH YOU, I, UH, THOUGHT WE MIGHT EAT TOGETHER...
OH, BUT!
NOT IN A WEIRD WAY OR ANYTHING!
IT'S JUST THAT, WELL, YOU SEE...
I WANTED TO SAY THANKS FOR SAVING ME...
AND I THINK THAT MEALS TASTE BETTER WHEN YOU CAN ENJOY THEM WITH OTHERS, AND...
UH...
DOES THAT MEAN...?

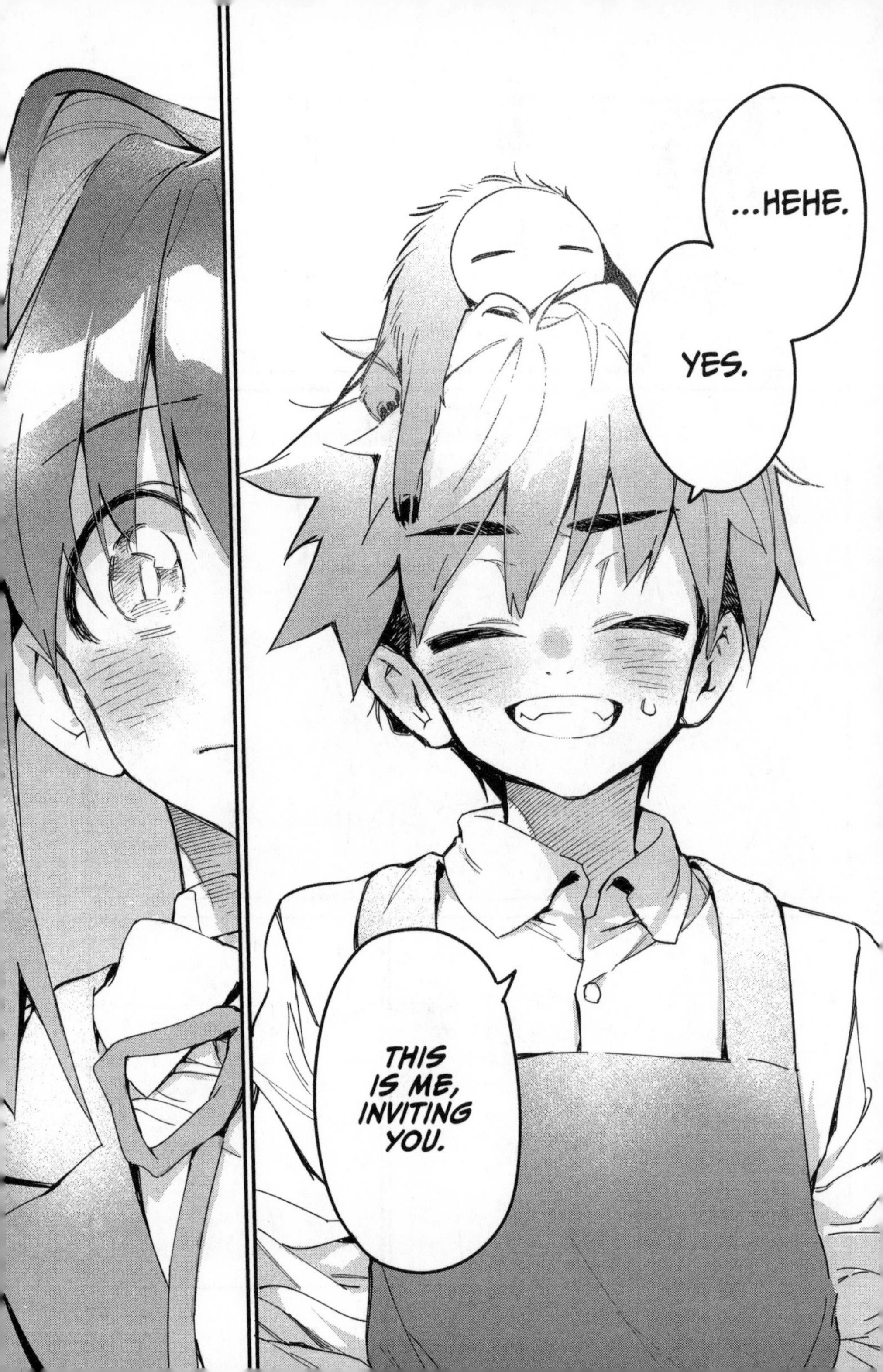
...HEHE.
YES.
THIS IS ME, INVITING YOU.

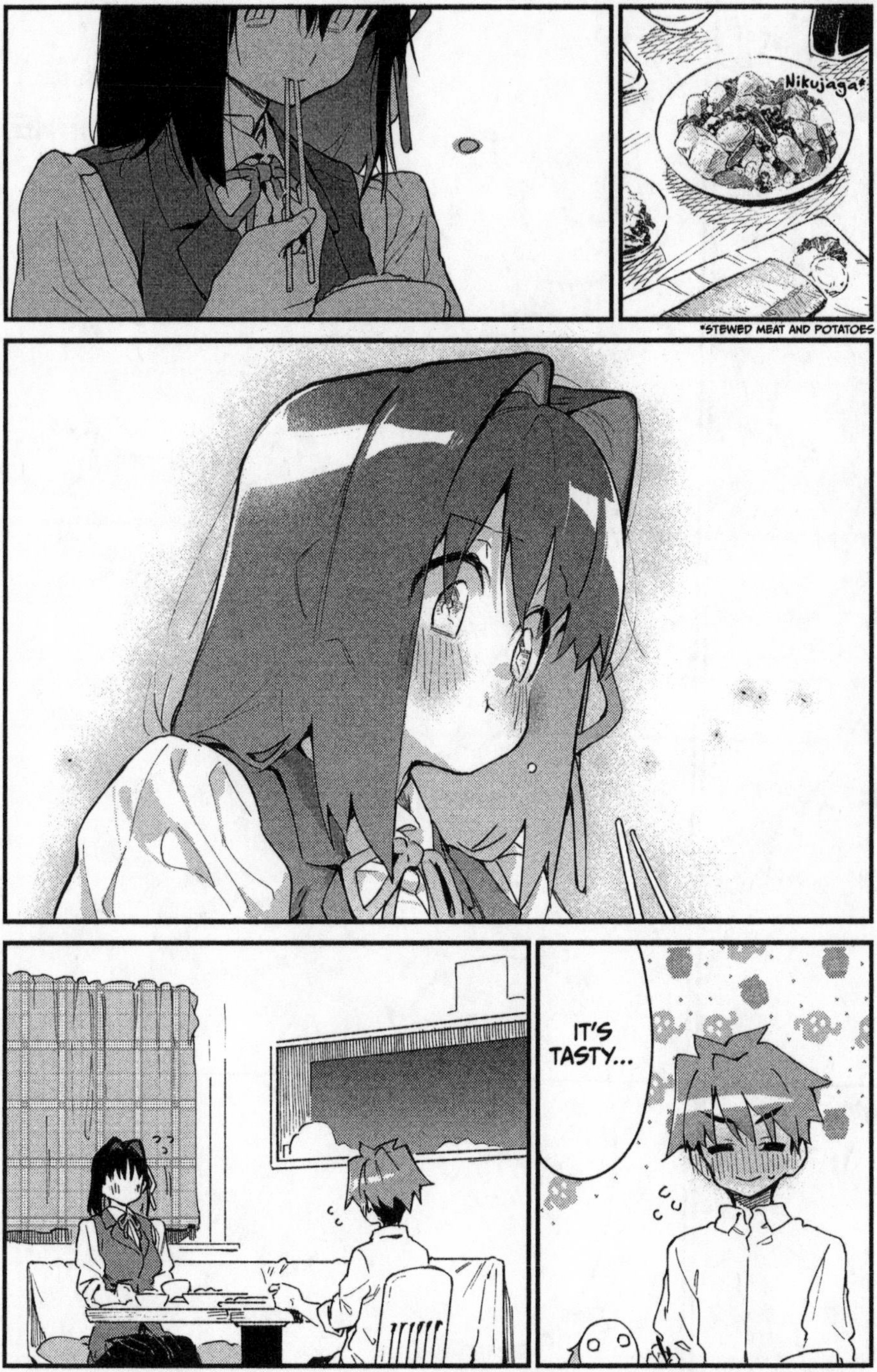
Nikujaga*
IT'S TASTY...
*STEWED MEAT AND POTATOES

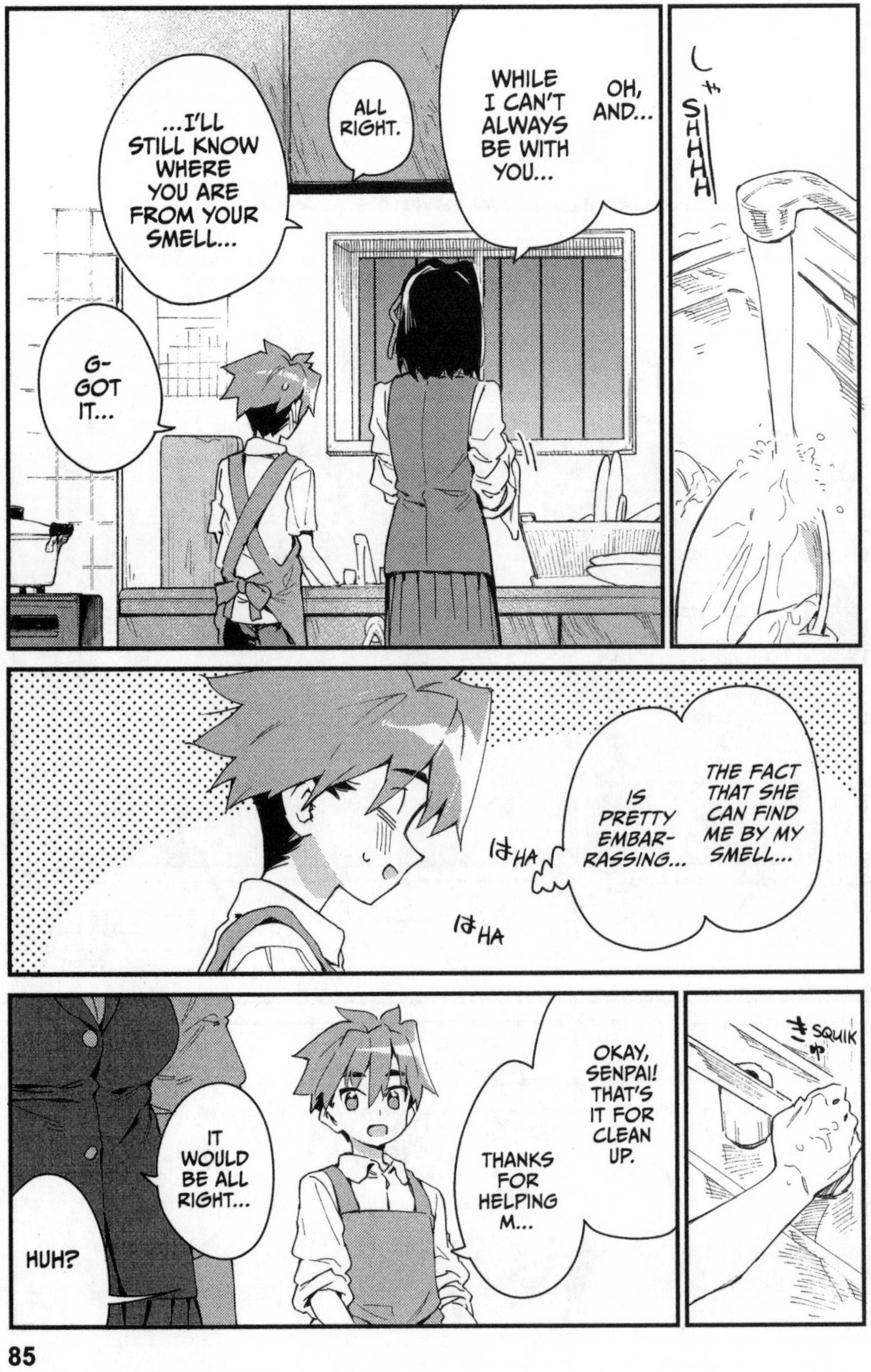
しゃ SHHHH
OH, AND...
WHILE I CAN'T ALWAYS BE WITH YOU...
ALL RIGHT.
...I'LL STILL KNOW WHERE YOU ARE FROM YOUR SMELL...
G-GOT IT...
THE FACT THAT SHE CAN FIND ME BY MY SMELL...
IS PRETTY EMBARRASSING...
は HA
は HA
きゅ SQUIK
OKAY, SENPAI! THAT'S IT FOR CLEAN UP.
THANKS FOR HELPING M...
IT WOULD BE ALL RIGHT...
HUH?

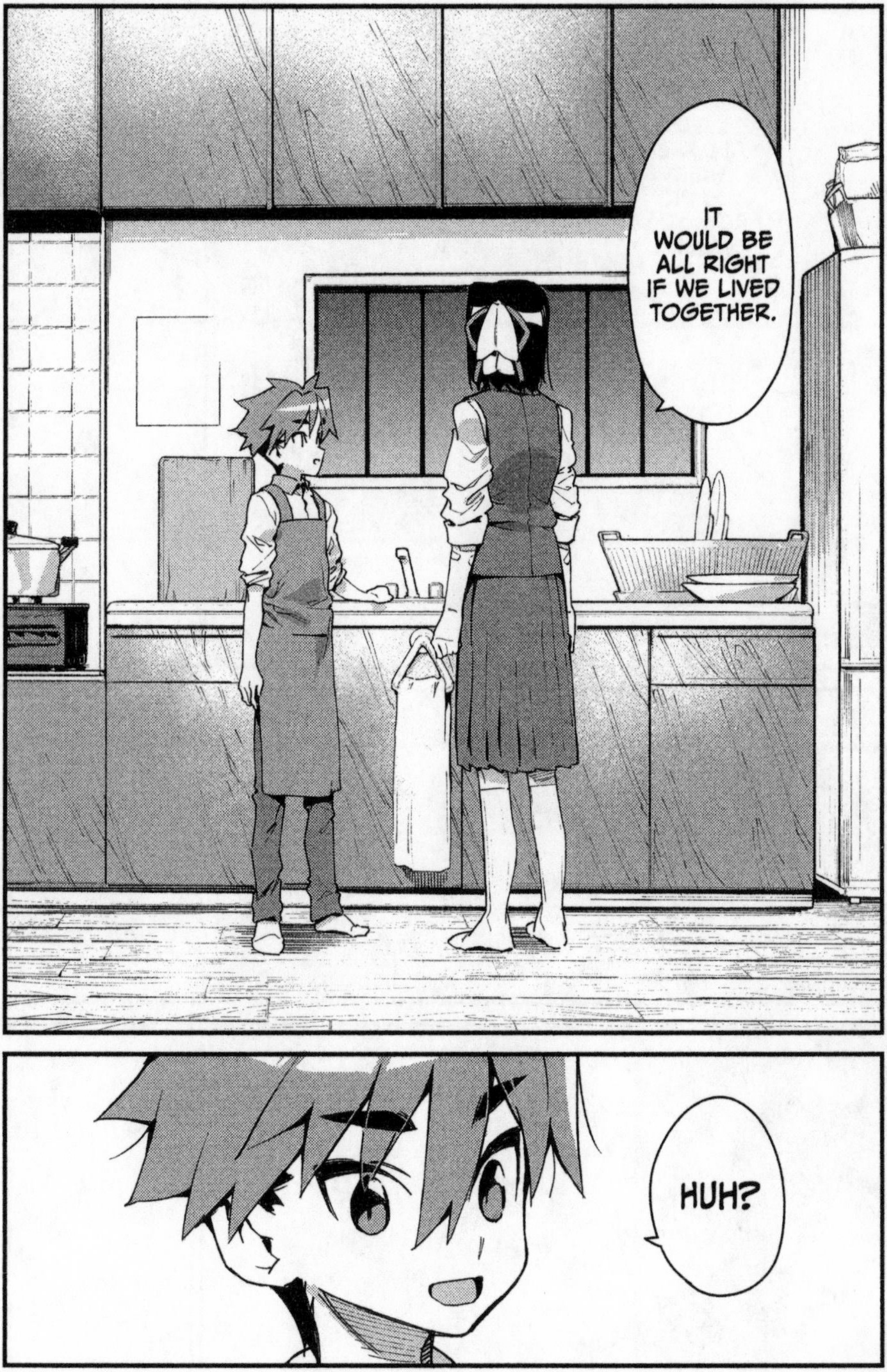
IT WOULD BE ALL RIGHT IF WE LIVED TOGETHER.
HUH?

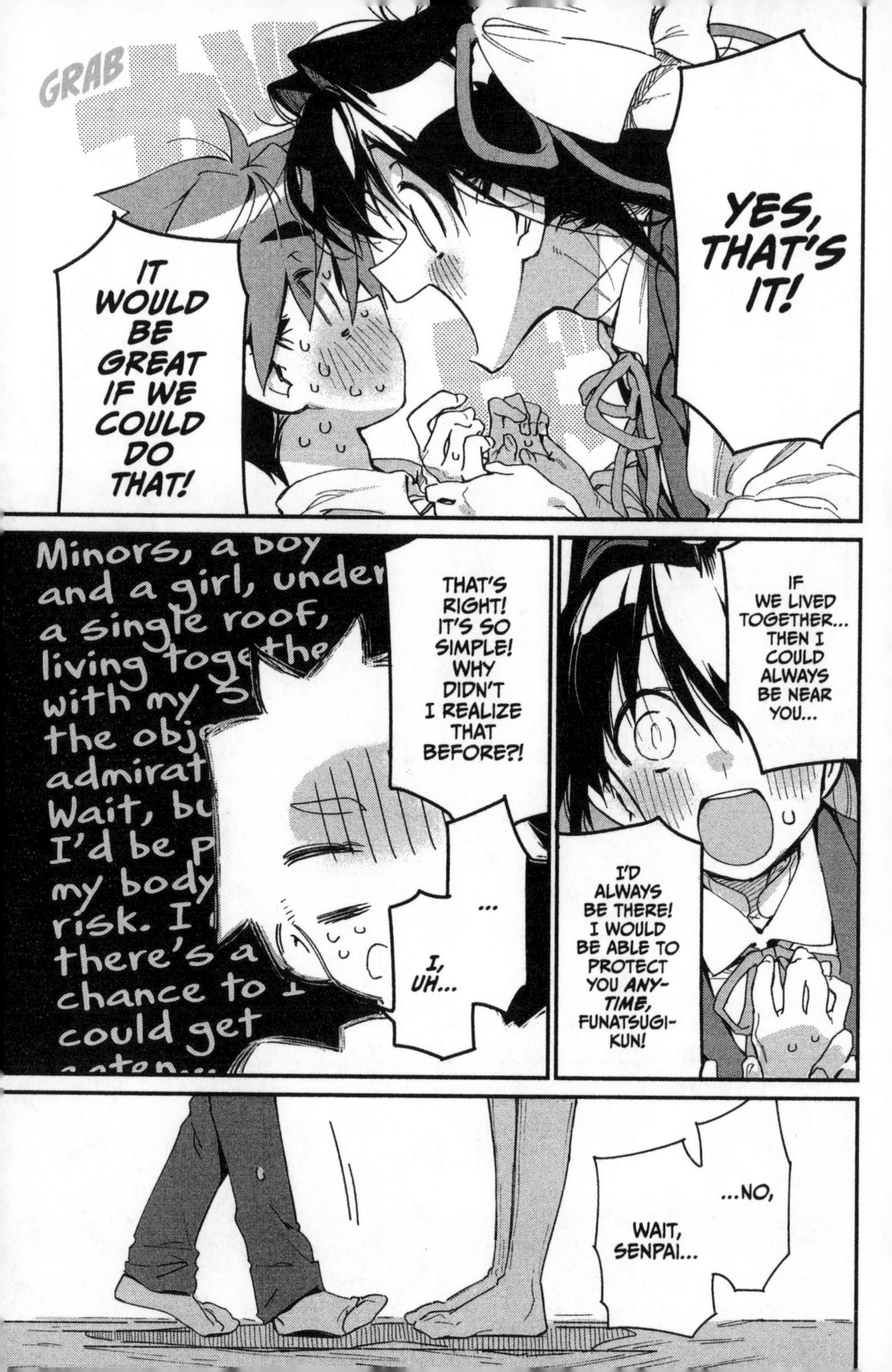
YES, THAT'S IT!
GRAB
IT WOULD BE GREAT IF WE COULD DO THAT!
IF WE LIVED TOGETHER... THEN I COULD ALWAYS BE NEAR YOU...
I'D ALWAYS BE THERE! I WOULD BE ABLE TO PROTECT YOU ANY-TIME, FUNATSUGI-KUN!
THAT'S RIGHT! IT'S SO SIMPLE! WHY DIDN'T I REALIZE THAT BEFORE?!
...
I, UH...
Minors, a boy and a girl, under a single roof, living togethe with my the obj admirat Wait, bu I'd be my body risk. I there's a chance to could get
...NO,
WAIT, SENPAI...

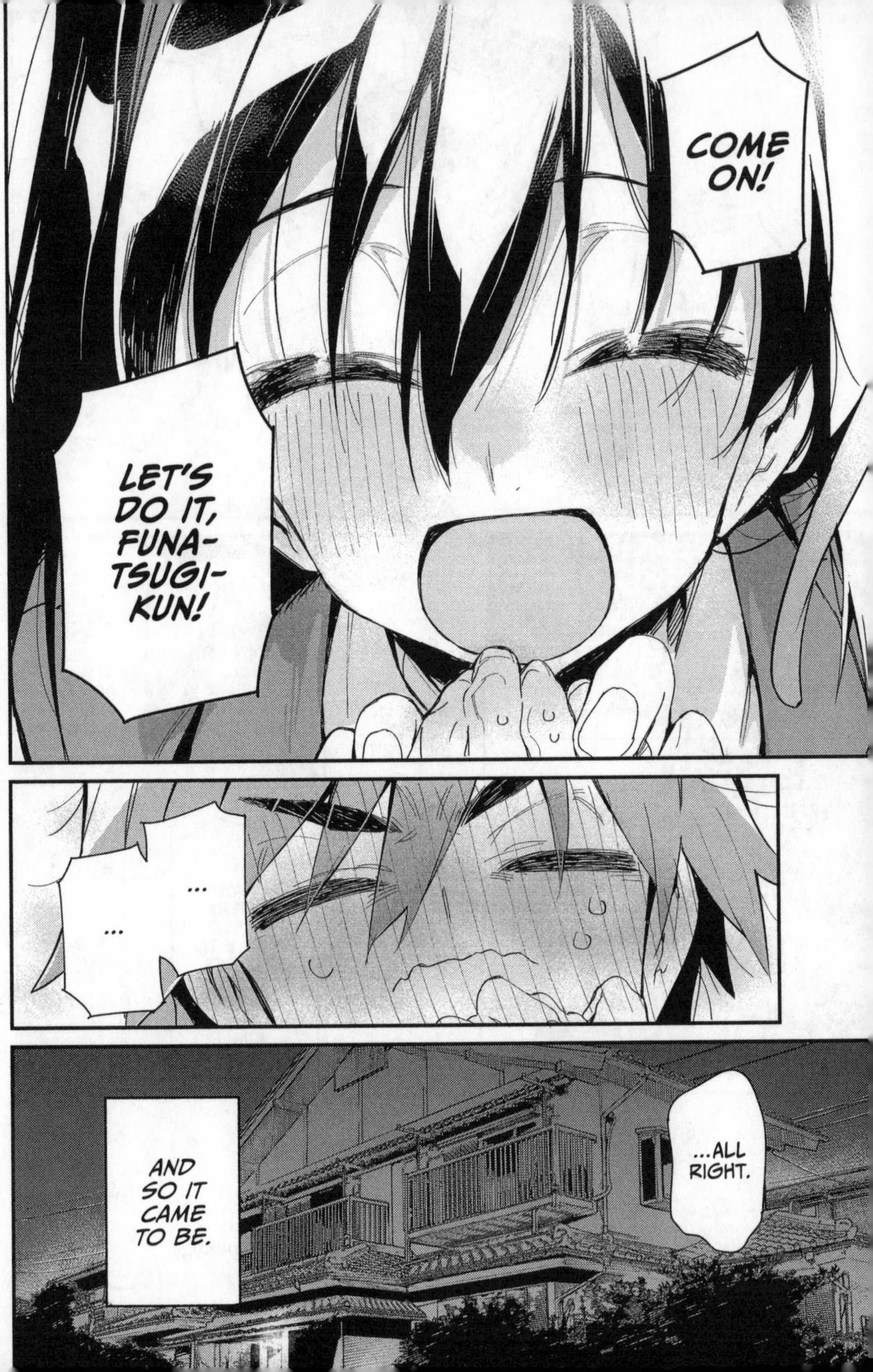
COME ON!
LET'S DO IT, FUNA-TSUGI-KUN!
...
...
...ALL RIGHT.
AND SO IT CAME TO BE.

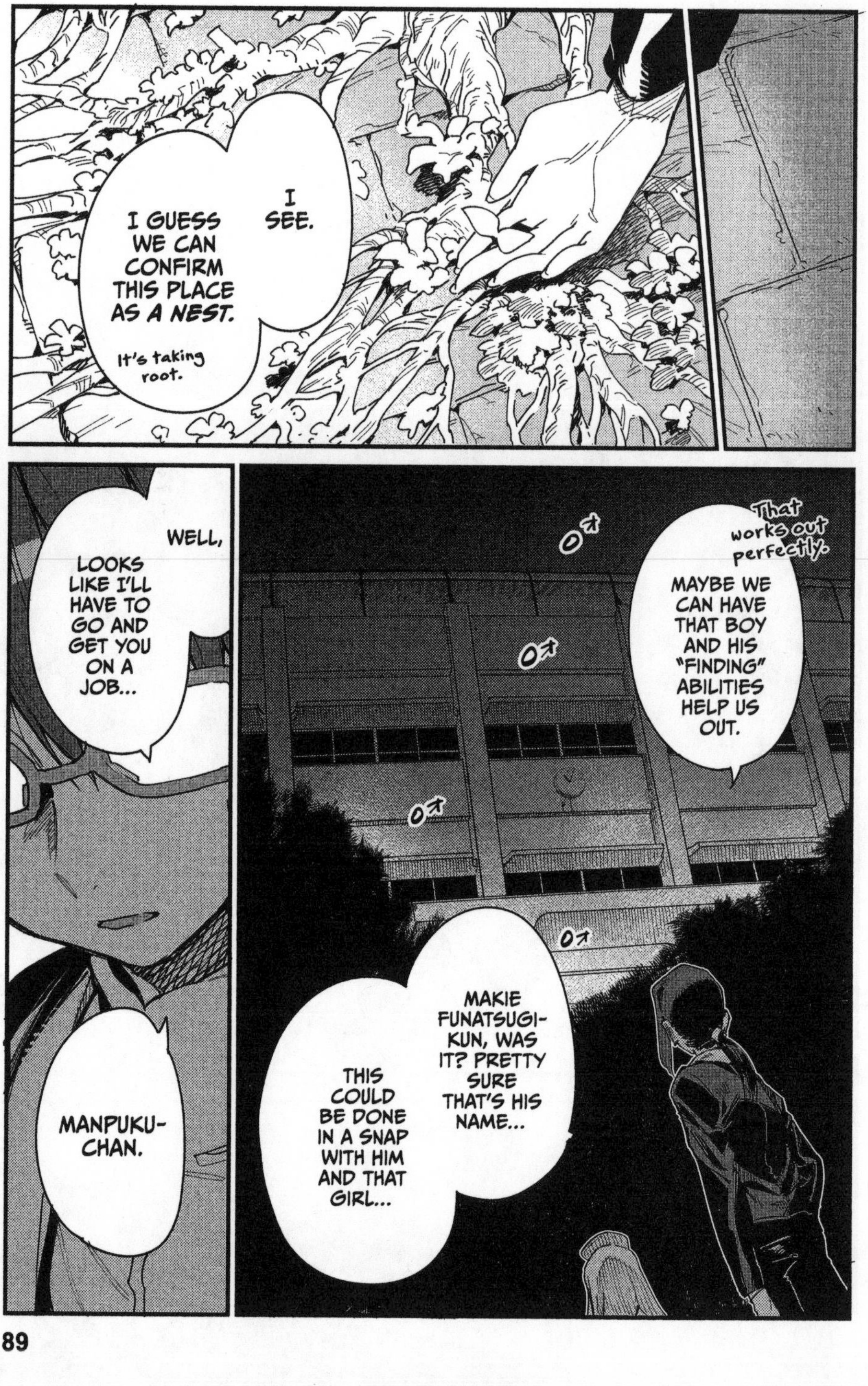

I SEE.
I GUESS WE CAN CONFIRM THIS PLACE AS A *NEST.*
It's taking root.
That works out perfectly.
MAYBE WE CAN HAVE THAT BOY AND HIS "FINDING" ABILITIES HELP US OUT.
MAKIE FUNATSUGI-KUN, WAS IT? PRETTY SURE THAT'S HIS NAME...
THIS COULD BE DONE IN A SNAP WITH HIM AND THAT GIRL...
WELL,
LOOKS LIKE I'LL HAVE TO GO AND GET YOU ON A JOB...
MANPUKU-CHAN.

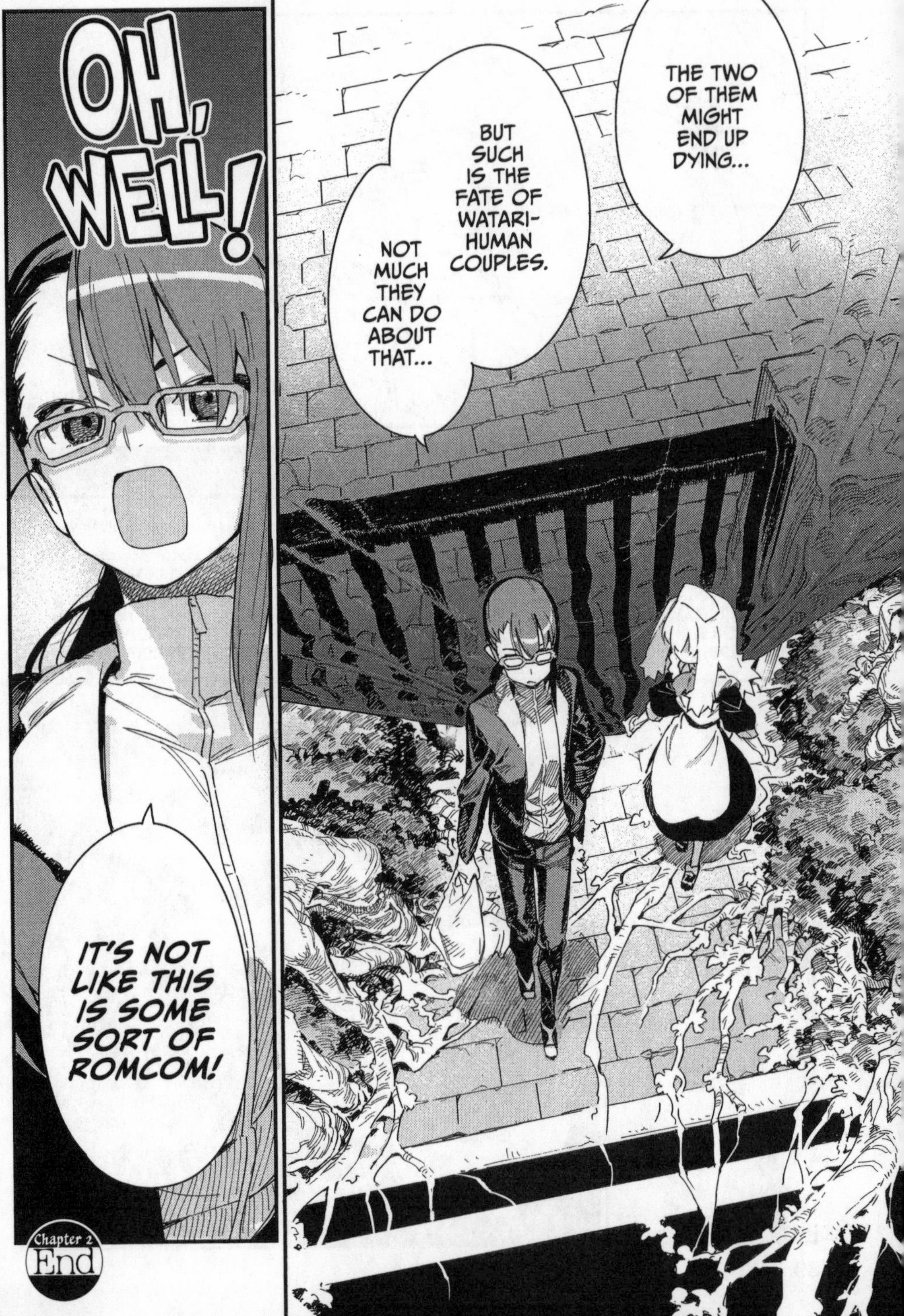
THE TWO OF THEM MIGHT END UP DYING...
BUT SUCH IS THE FATE OF WATARI-HUMAN COUPLES.
NOT MUCH THEY CAN DO ABOUT THAT...
OH, WELL!
IT'S NOT LIKE THIS IS SOME SORT OF ROMCOM!
Chapter 2 End

Chapter 3: You Wanna Look Cool for Her, Don't You?

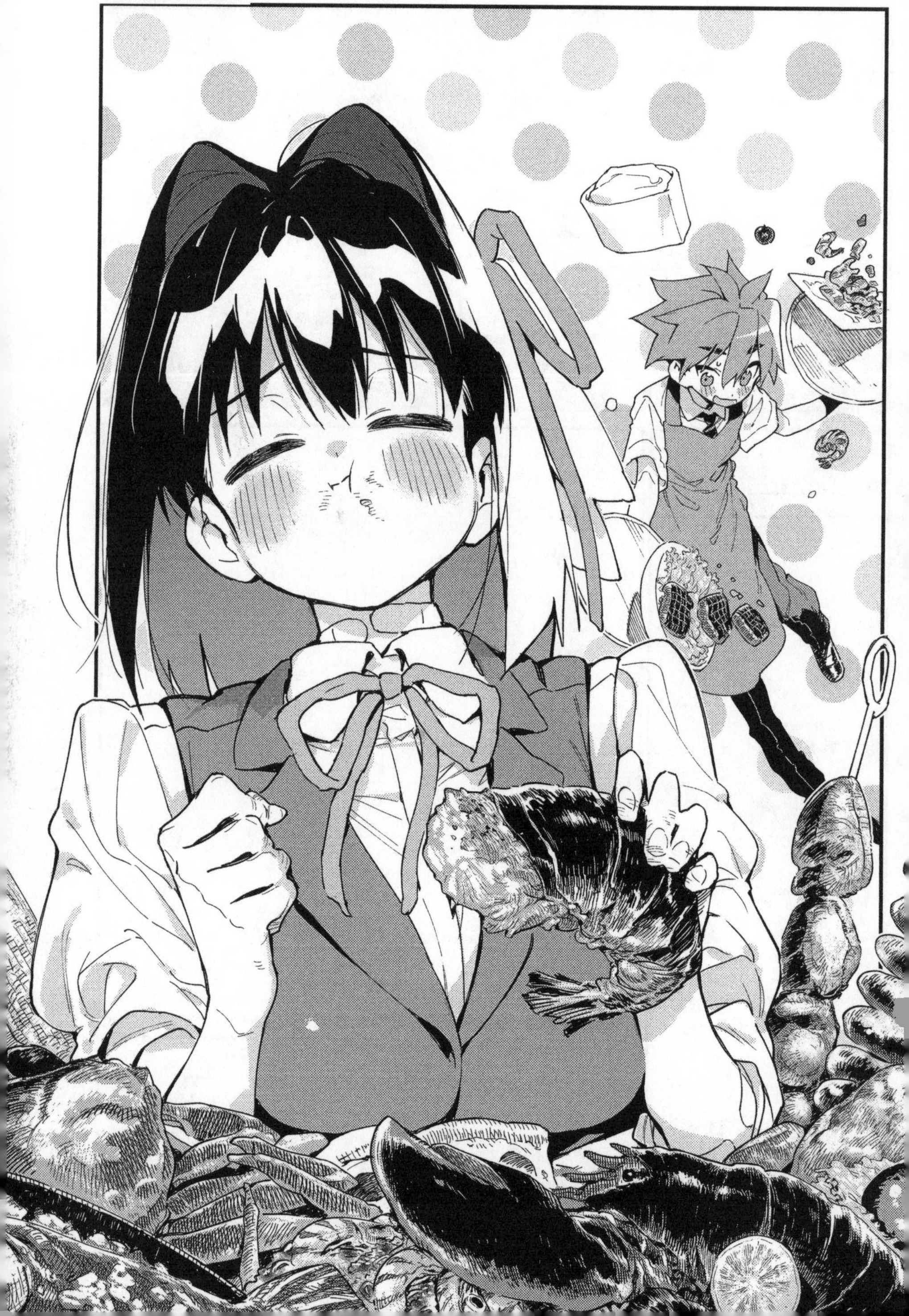

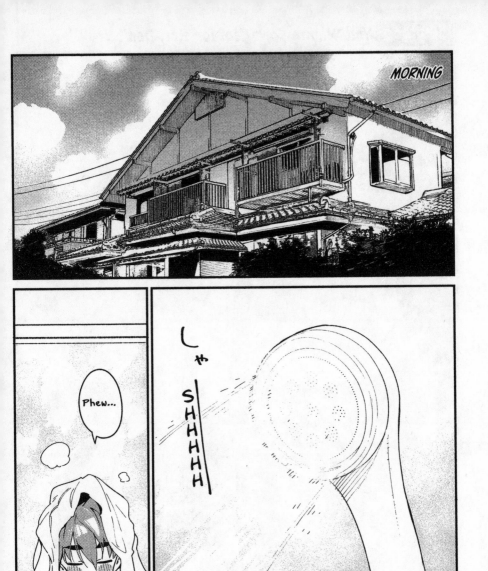

MORNING

Phew...

SHHHH
しゃ

SQUIK
き ゅ

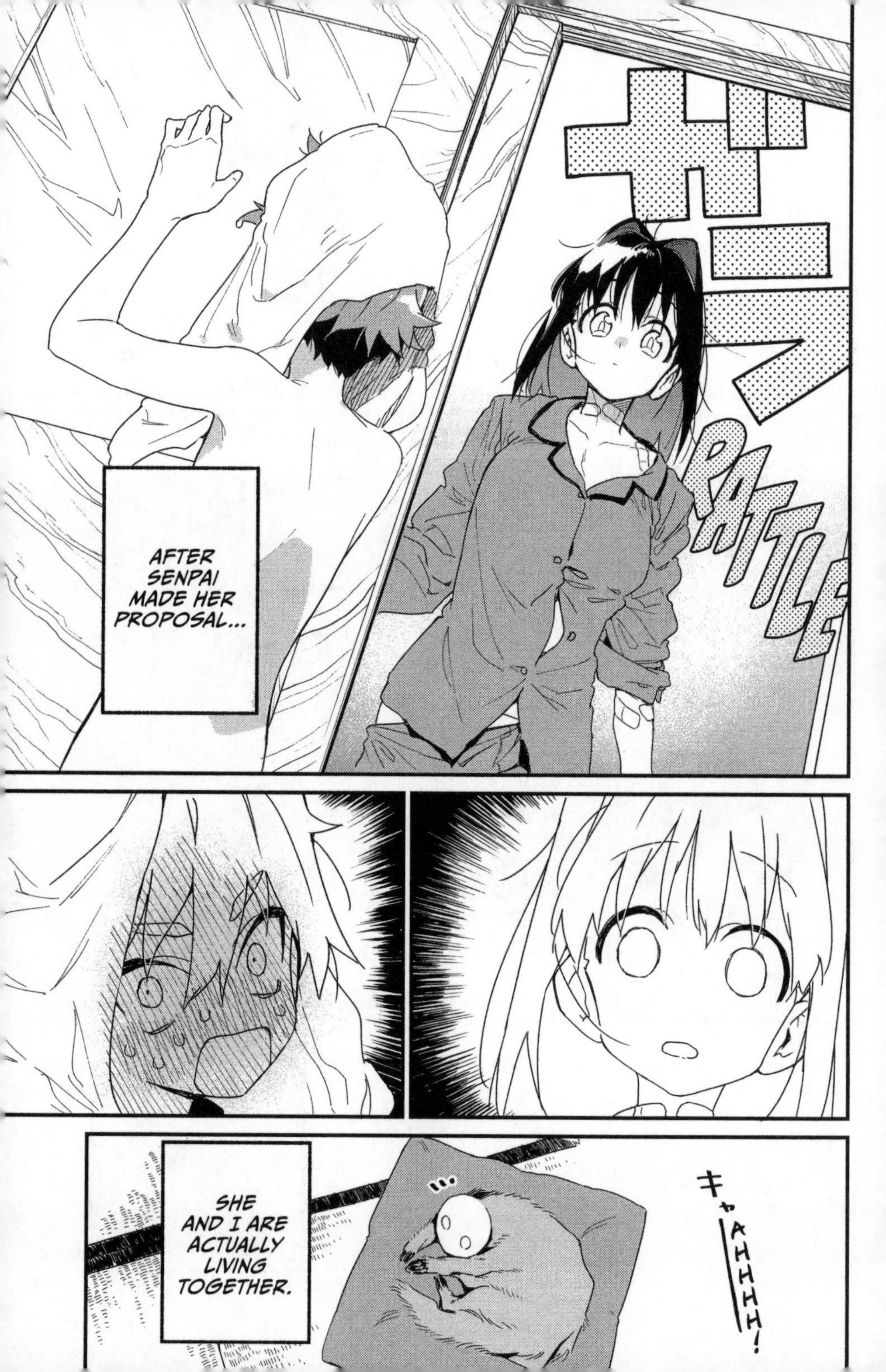
ガラッ
RATTLE
AFTER SENPAI MADE HER PROPOSAL...
キャAHHHH!
SHE AND I ARE ACTUALLY LIVING TOGETHER.

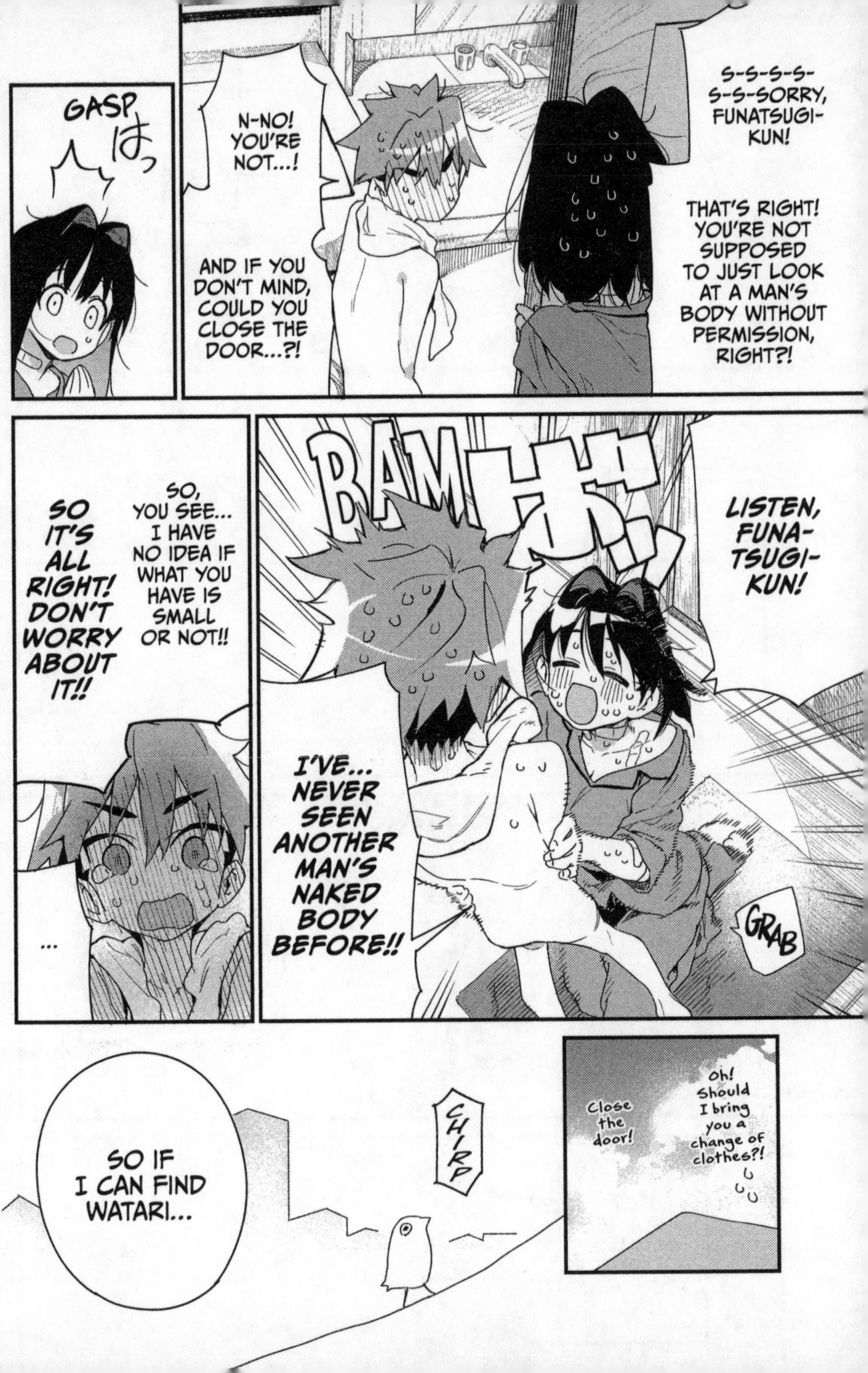
S-S-S-S-S-S-SORRY, FUNATSUGI-KUN!
N-NO! YOU'RE NOT...!
THAT'S RIGHT! YOU'RE NOT SUPPOSED TO JUST LOOK AT A MAN'S BODY WITHOUT PERMISSION, RIGHT?!
AND IF YOU DON'T MIND, COULD YOU CLOSE THE DOOR...?!
GASP はっ
BAM
LISTEN, FUNATSUGI-KUN!
I'VE... NEVER SEEN ANOTHER MAN'S NAKED BODY BEFORE!!
GRAB
SO, YOU SEE... I HAVE NO IDEA IF WHAT YOU HAVE IS SMALL OR NOT!!
SO IT'S ALL RIGHT! DON'T WORRY ABOUT IT!!
...
Oh! Should I bring you a change of clothes?!
Close the door!
CHIRP
SO IF I CAN FIND WATARI...

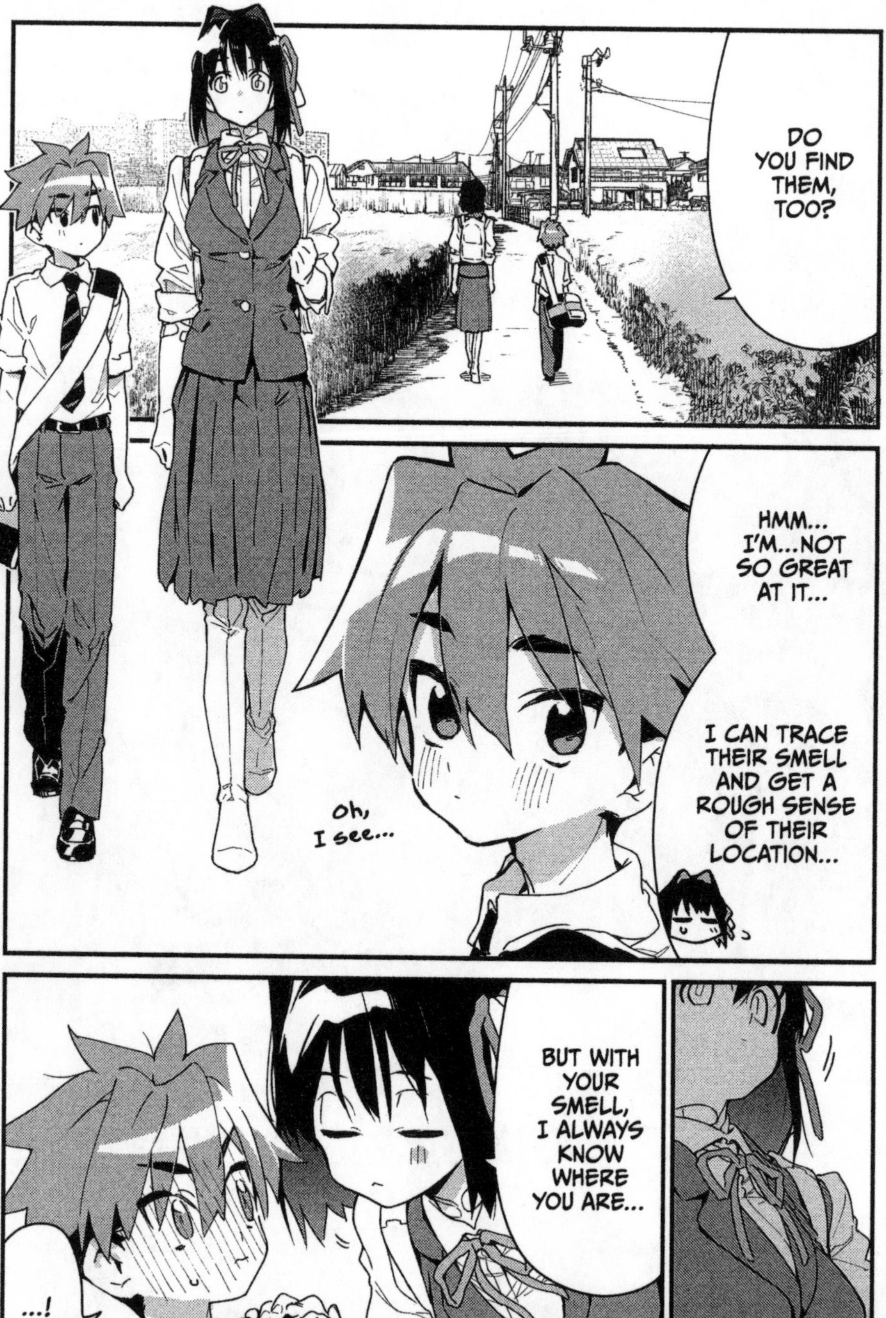
DO YOU FIND THEM, TOO?
HMM... I'M...NOT SO GREAT AT IT...
I CAN TRACE THEIR SMELL AND GET A ROUGH SENSE OF THEIR LOCATION...
Oh, I see...
BUT WITH YOUR SMELL, I ALWAYS KNOW WHERE YOU ARE...
...!

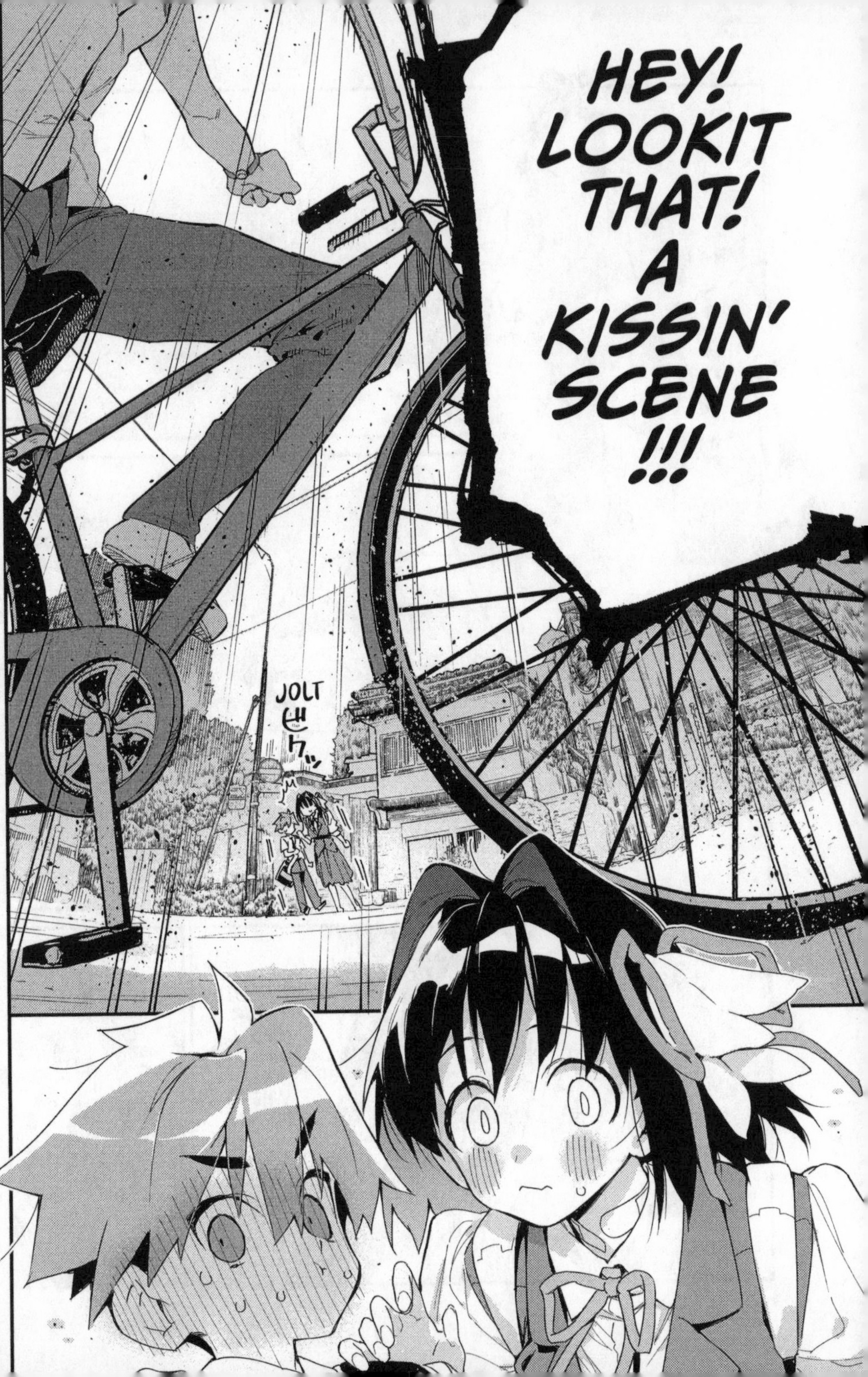
HEY! LOOKIT THAT! A KISSIN' SCENE !!!
JOLT
ビクッ

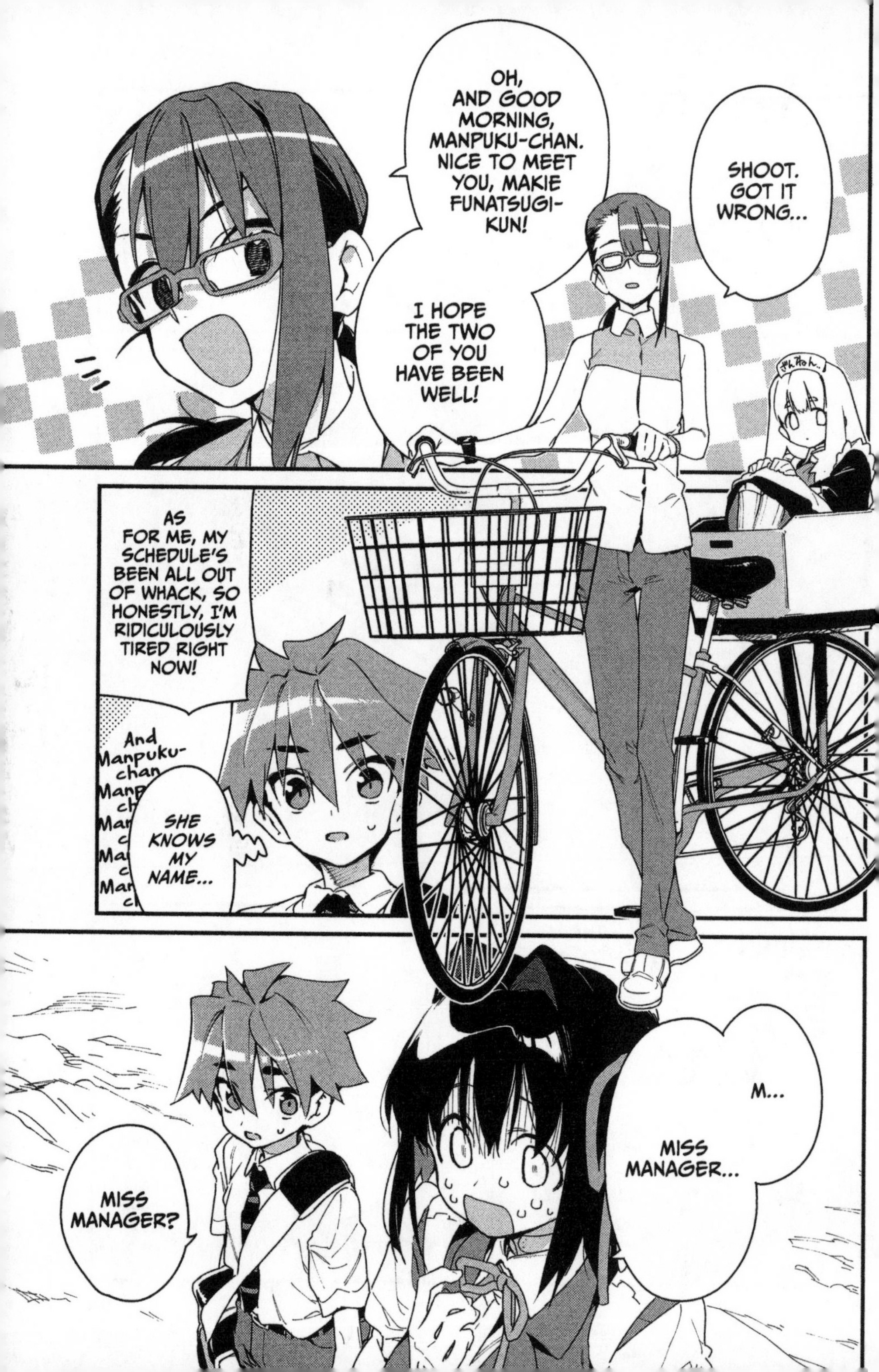
SHOOT. GOT IT WRONG...
ざんねん..
OH, AND GOOD MORNING, MANPUKU-CHAN. NICE TO MEET YOU, MAKIE FUNATSUGI-KUN!
I HOPE THE TWO OF YOU HAVE BEEN WELL!
AS FOR ME, MY SCHEDULE'S BEEN ALL OUT OF WHACK, SO HONESTLY, I'M RIDICULOUSLY TIRED RIGHT NOW!
SHE KNOWS MY NAME...
And Manpuku-chan
M...
MISS MANAGER...
MISS MANAGER?

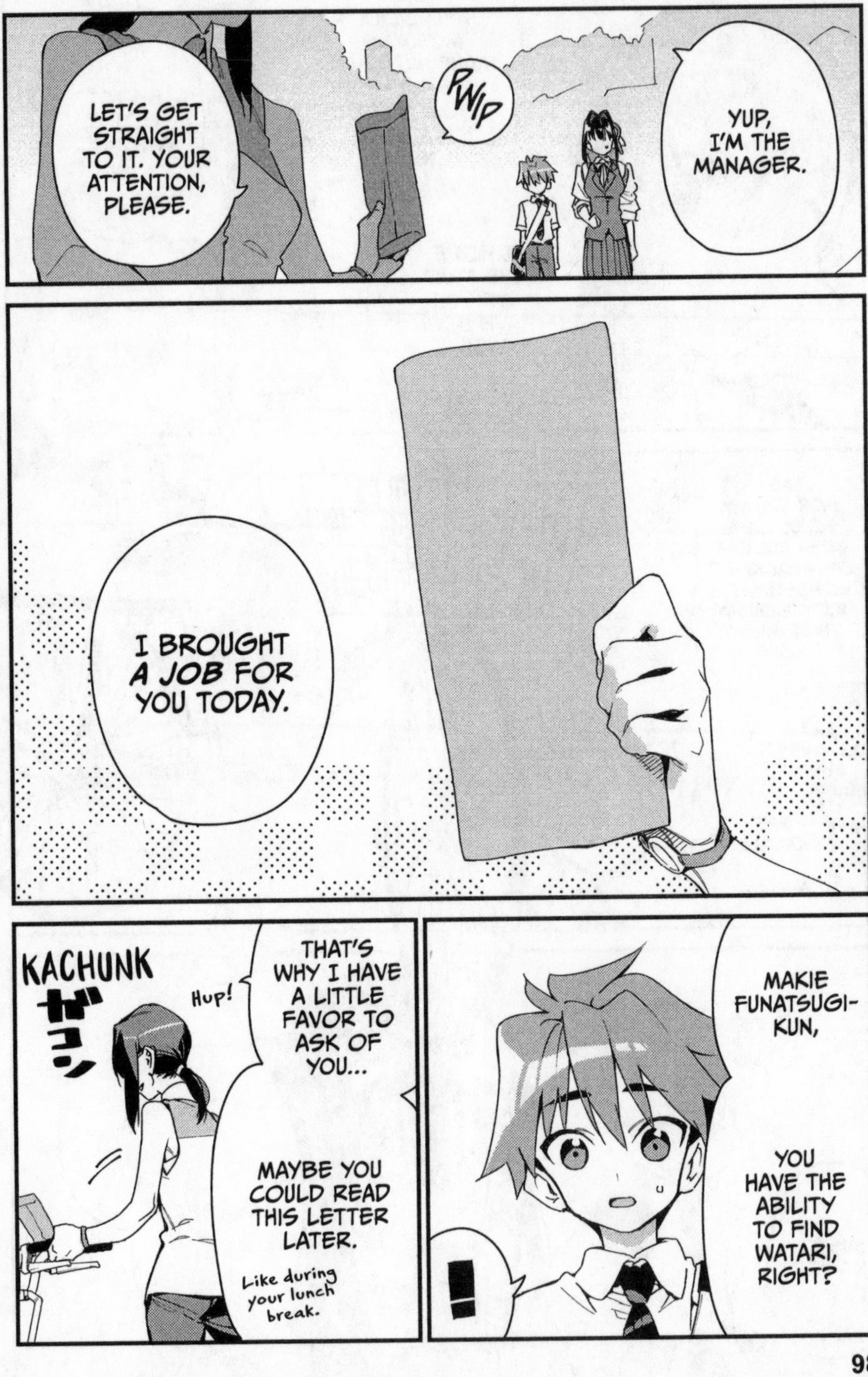
YUP, I'M THE MANAGER.
PWIP
LET'S GET STRAIGHT TO IT. YOUR ATTENTION, PLEASE.
I BROUGHT *A JOB* FOR YOU TODAY.
MAKIE FUNATSUGI-KUN,
YOU HAVE THE ABILITY TO FIND WATARI, RIGHT?
!
THAT'S WHY I HAVE A LITTLE FAVOR TO ASK OF YOU...
Hup!
KACHUNK
ガコン
MAYBE YOU COULD READ THIS LETTER LATER.
Like during your lunch break.

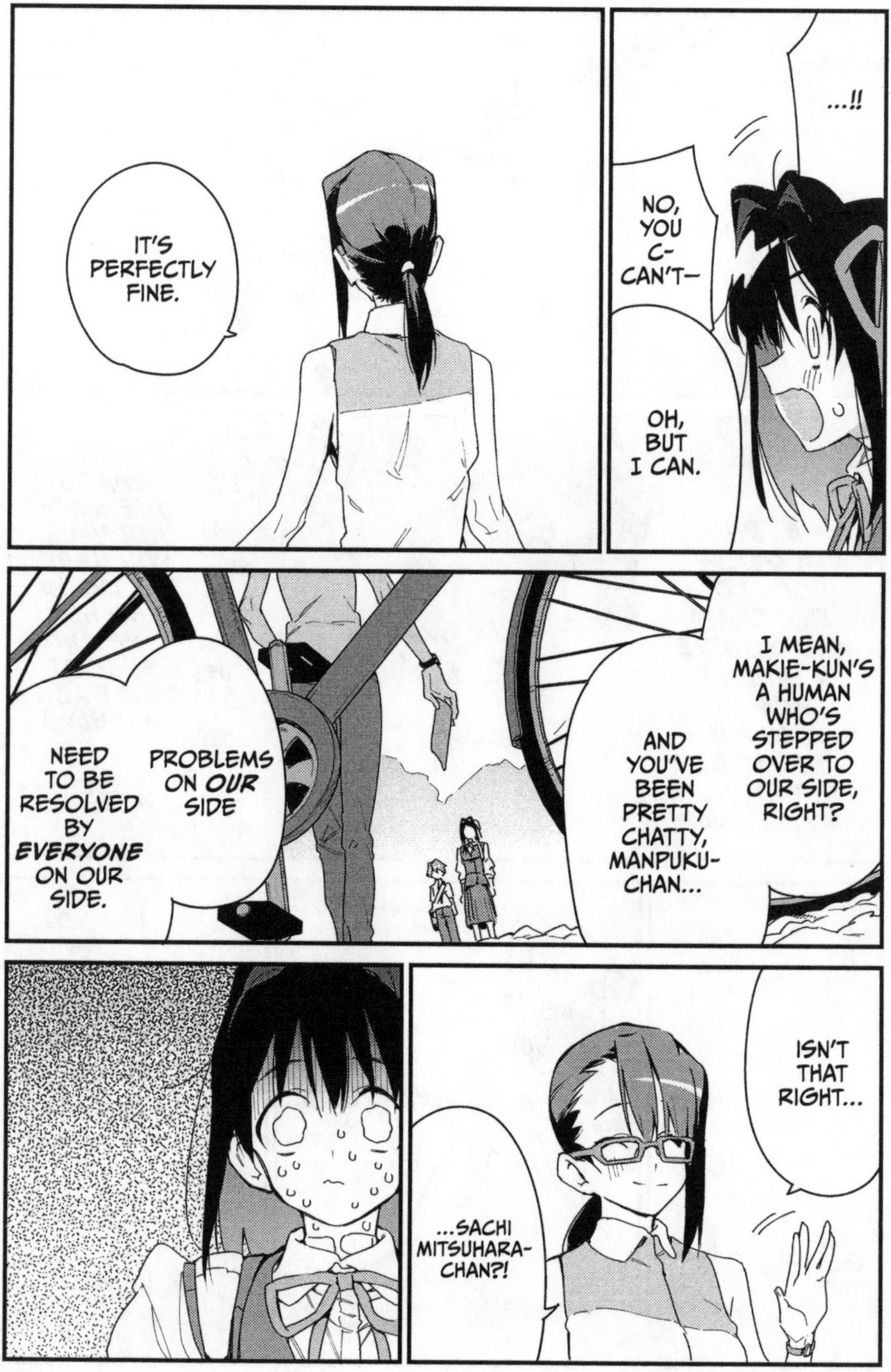
...!!
NO, YOU C-CAN'T—
OH, BUT I CAN.
IT'S PERFECTLY FINE.
I MEAN, MAKIE-KUN'S A HUMAN WHO'S STEPPED OVER TO OUR SIDE, RIGHT?
AND YOU'VE BEEN PRETTY CHATTY, MANPUKU-CHAN...
PROBLEMS ON OUR SIDE
NEED TO BE RESOLVED BY EVERYONE ON OUR SIDE.
ISN'T THAT RIGHT...
...SACHI MITSUHARA-CHAN?!

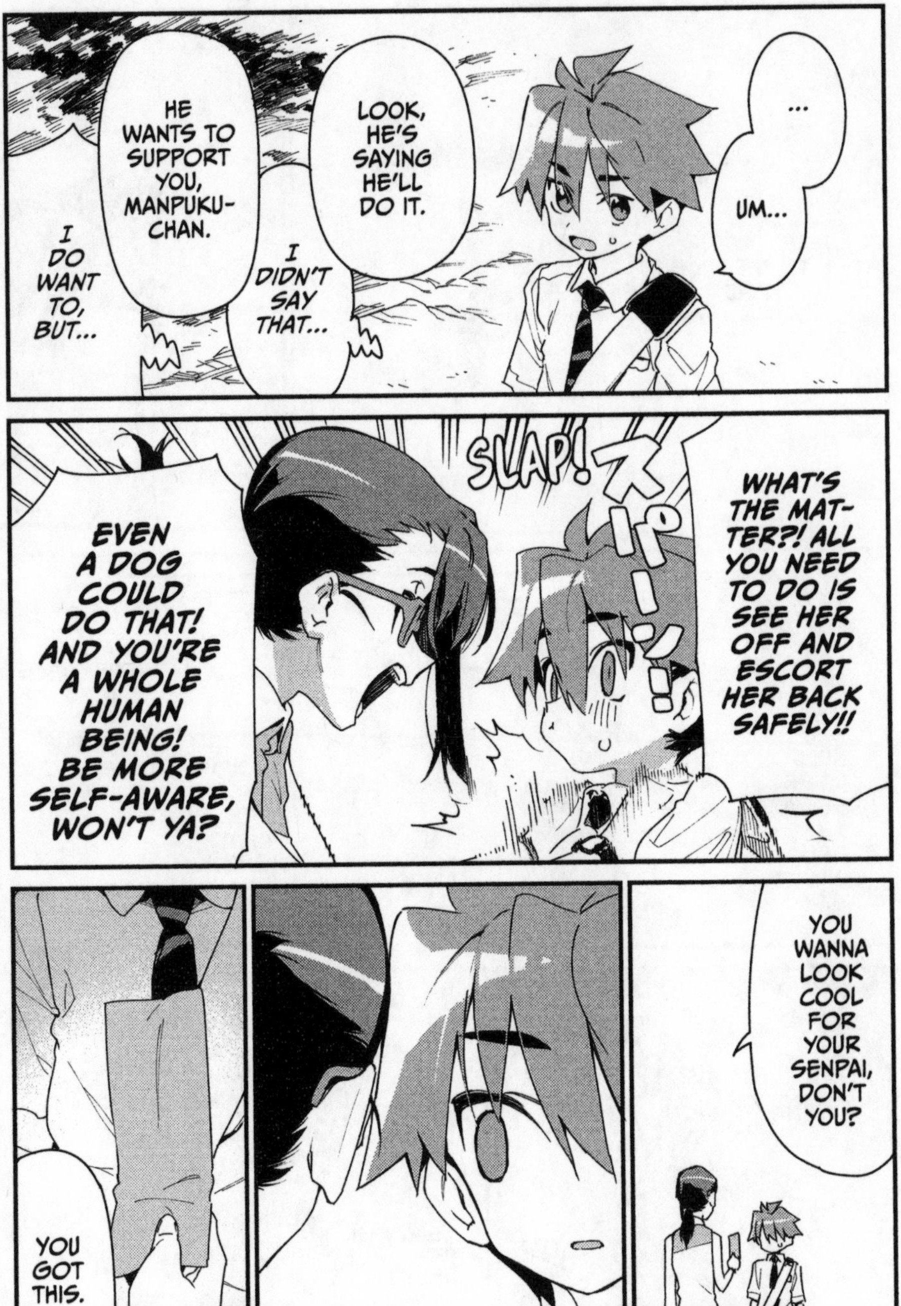
...
UM...
LOOK, HE'S SAYING HE'LL DO IT.
I DIDN'T SAY THAT...
HE WANTS TO SUPPORT YOU, MANPUKU-CHAN.
I DO WANT TO, BUT...
WHAT'S THE MATTER?! ALL YOU NEED TO DO IS SEE HER OFF AND ESCORT HER BACK SAFELY!!
SLAP!
スパーン!
EVEN A DOG COULD DO THAT! AND YOU'RE A WHOLE HUMAN BEING! BE MORE SELF-AWARE, WON'T YA?
YOU WANNA LOOK COOL FOR YOUR SENPAI, DON'T YOU?
YOU GOT THIS.

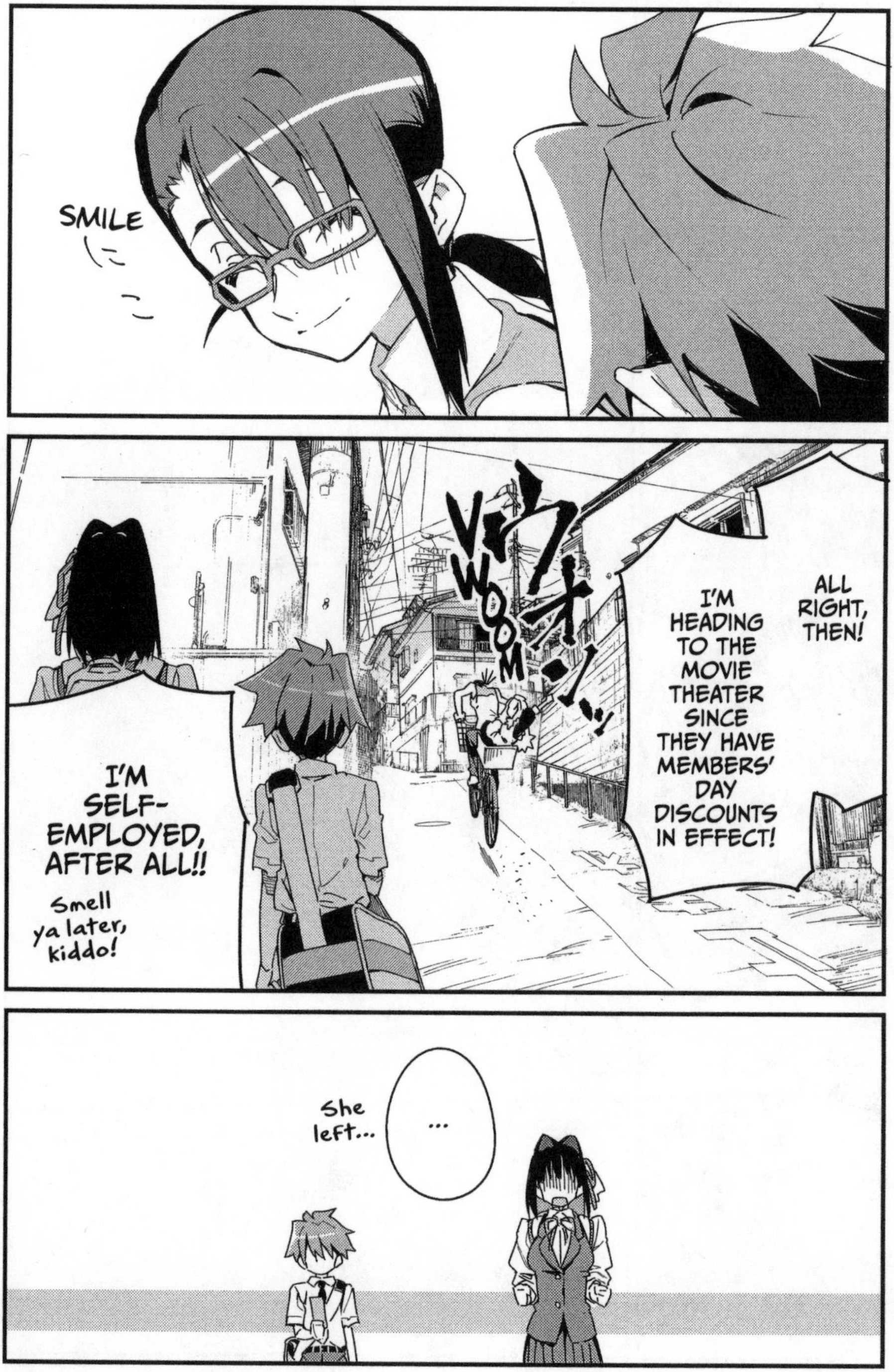
SMILE
ALL RIGHT, THEN!
I'M HEADING TO THE MOVIE THEATER SINCE THEY HAVE MEMBERS' DAY DISCOUNTS IN EFFECT!
VWOOM
I'M SELF-EMPLOYED, AFTER ALL!!
Smell ya later, kiddo!
...
She left...

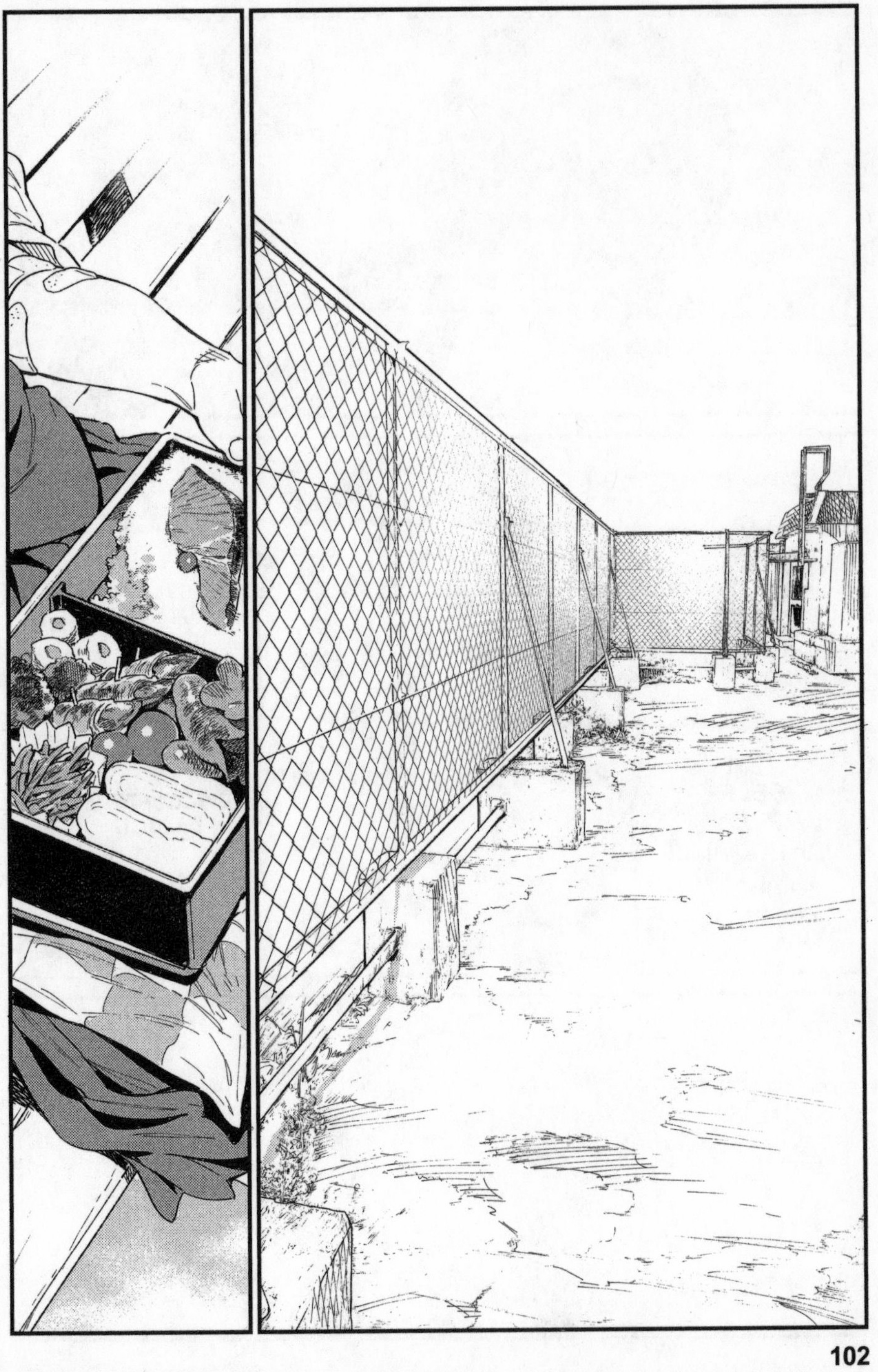

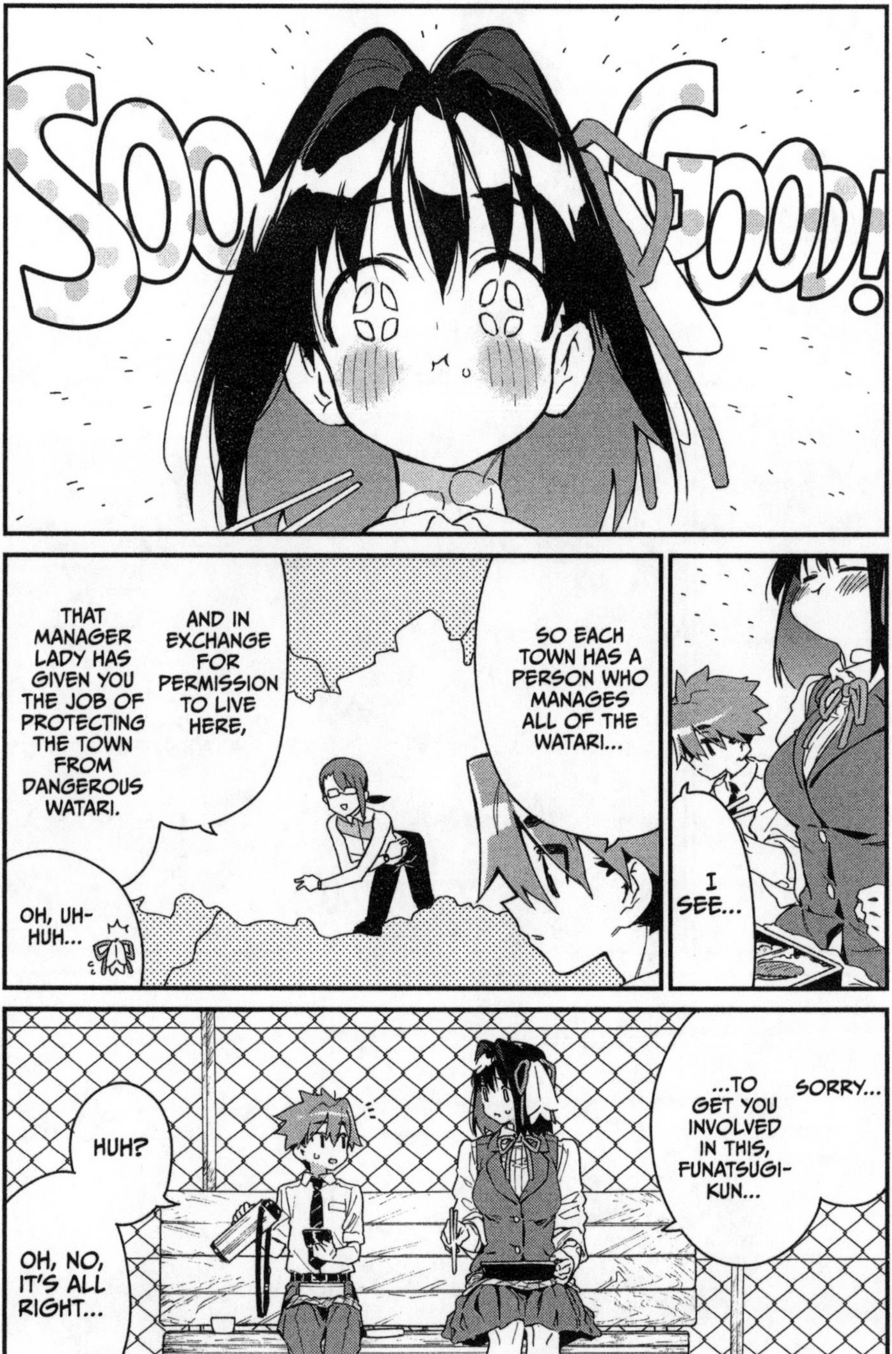
SOOO GOOD!
I SEE...
SO EACH TOWN HAS A PERSON WHO MANAGES ALL OF THE WATARI...
AND IN EXCHANGE FOR PERMISSION TO LIVE HERE,
THAT MANAGER LADY HAS GIVEN YOU THE JOB OF PROTECTING THE TOWN FROM DANGEROUS WATARI.
OH, UH-HUH...
SORRY...
...TO GET YOU INVOLVED IN THIS, FUNATSUGI-KUN...
HUH?
OH, NO, IT'S ALL RIGHT...

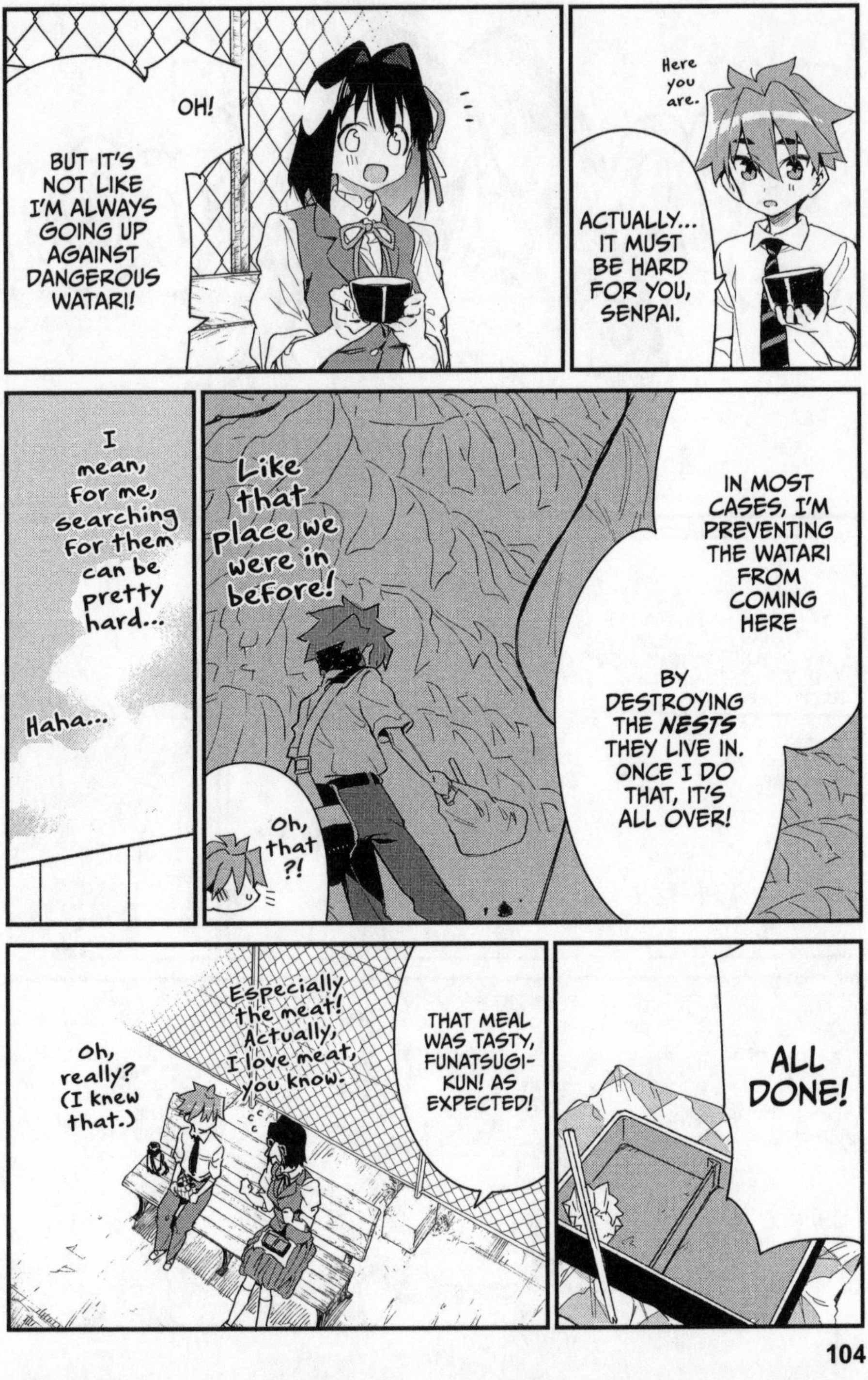
Here you are.
ACTUALLY... IT MUST BE HARD FOR YOU, SENPAI.
OH!
BUT IT'S NOT LIKE I'M ALWAYS GOING UP AGAINST DANGEROUS WATARI!
IN MOST CASES, I'M PREVENTING THE WATARI FROM COMING HERE
BY DESTROYING THE *NESTS* THEY LIVE IN. ONCE I DO THAT, IT'S ALL OVER!
Like that place we were in before!
Oh, that?!
I mean, for me, searching for them can be pretty hard...
Haha...
ALL DONE!
THAT MEAL WAS TASTY, FUNATSUGI-KUN! AS EXPECTED!
Especially the meat! Actually, I love meat, you know.
Oh, really? (I knew that.)

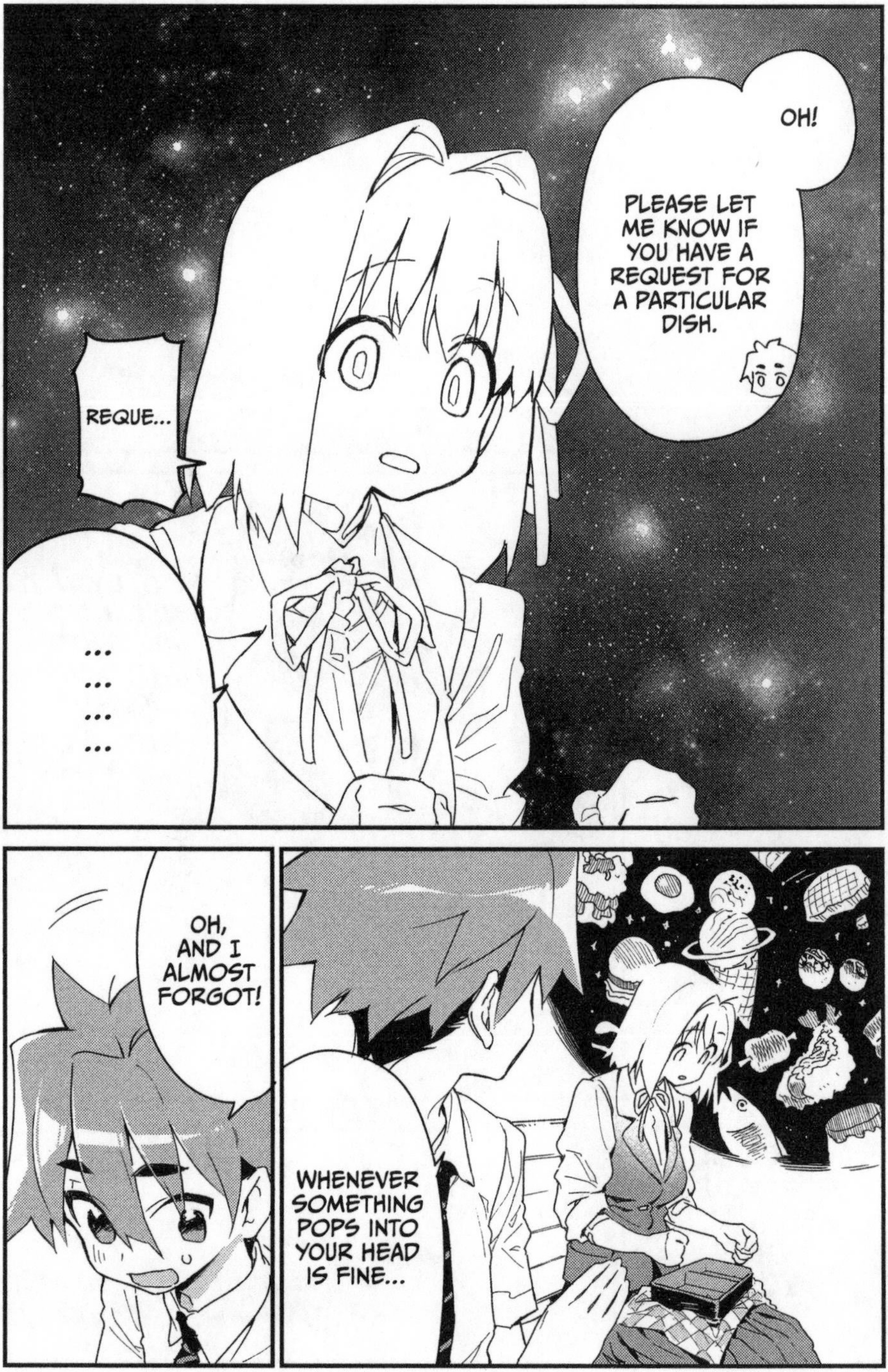
OH!
PLEASE LET ME KNOW IF YOU HAVE A REQUEST FOR A PARTICULAR DISH.
REQUE...
...
...
...
...
WHENEVER SOMETHING POPS INTO YOUR HEAD IS FINE...
OH, AND I ALMOST FORGOT!

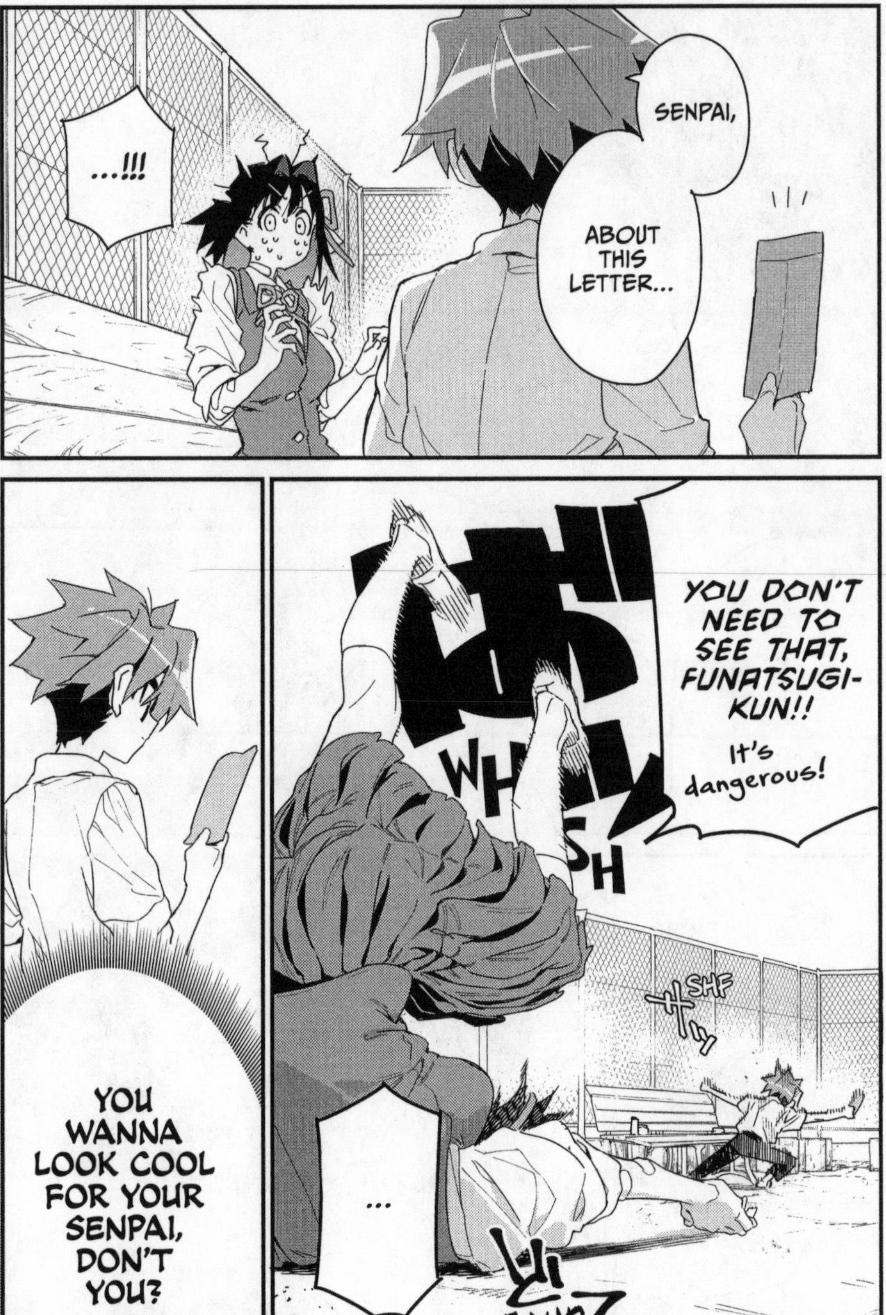
SENPAI,
ABOUT THIS LETTER...
...!!!
YOU DON'T NEED TO SEE THAT, FUNATSUGI-KUN!!
It's dangerous!
WHSH
SHF
...
THUD
YOU WANNA LOOK COOL FOR YOUR SENPAI, DON'T YOU?

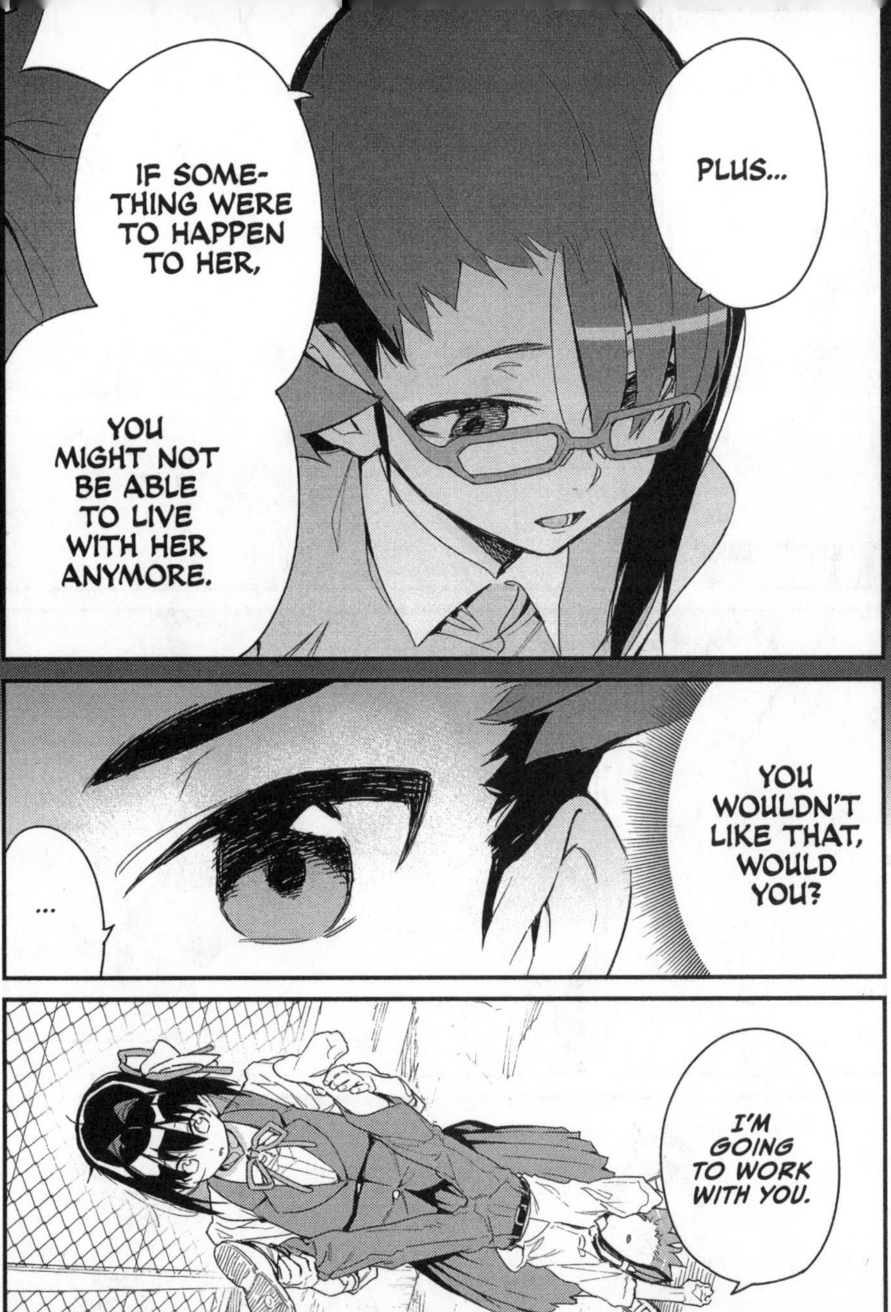
PLUS...
IF SOME-THING WERE TO HAPPEN TO HER,
YOU MIGHT NOT BE ABLE TO LIVE WITH HER ANYMORE.
YOU WOULDN'T LIKE THAT, WOULD YOU?
...
I'M GOING TO WORK WITH YOU.

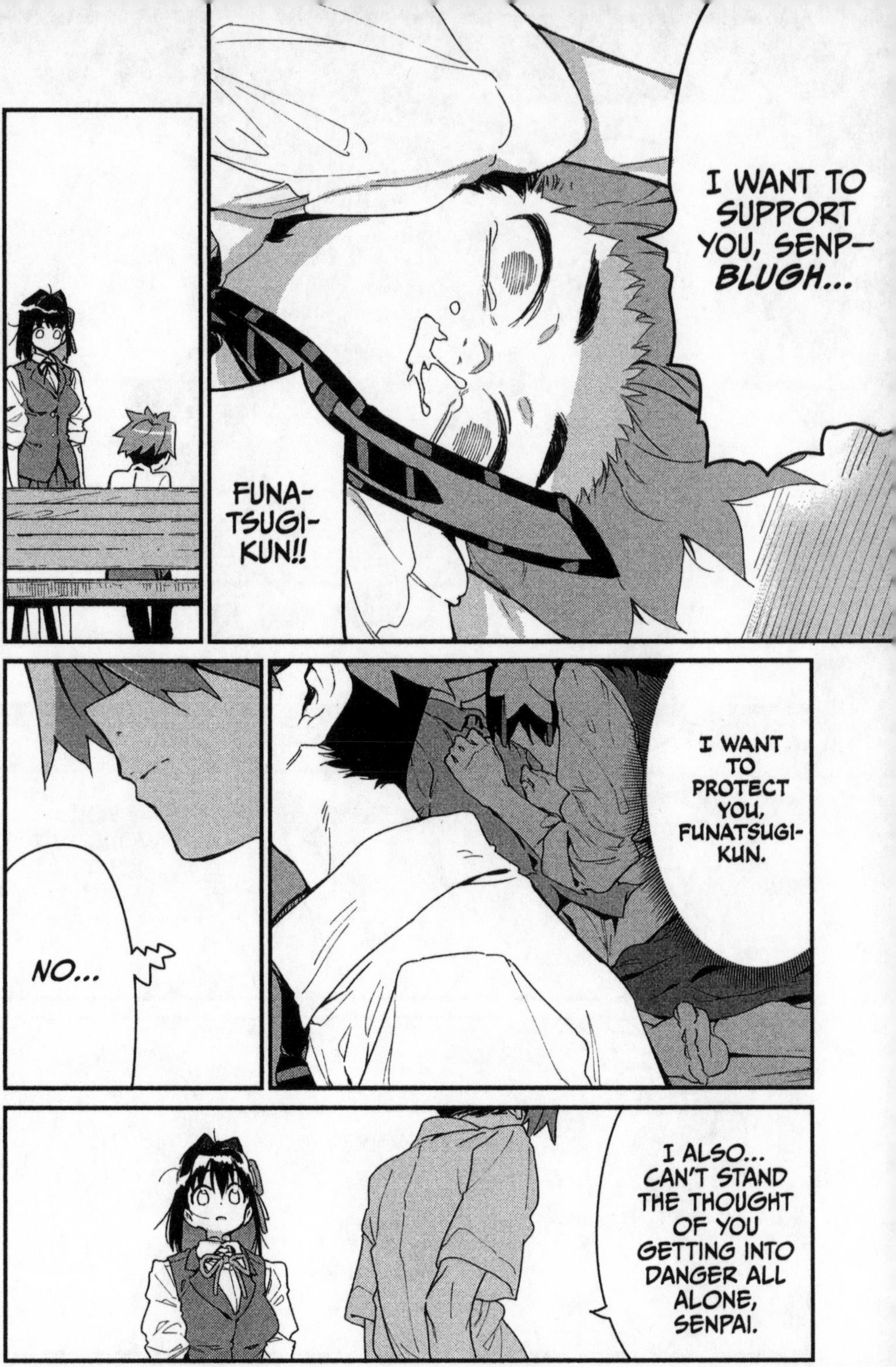
I WANT TO SUPPORT YOU, SENP— BLUGH...
FUNA-TSUGI-KUN!!
I WANT TO PROTECT YOU, FUNATSUGI-KUN.
NO...
I ALSO... CAN'T STAND THE THOUGHT OF YOU GETTING INTO DANGER ALL ALONE, SENPAI.

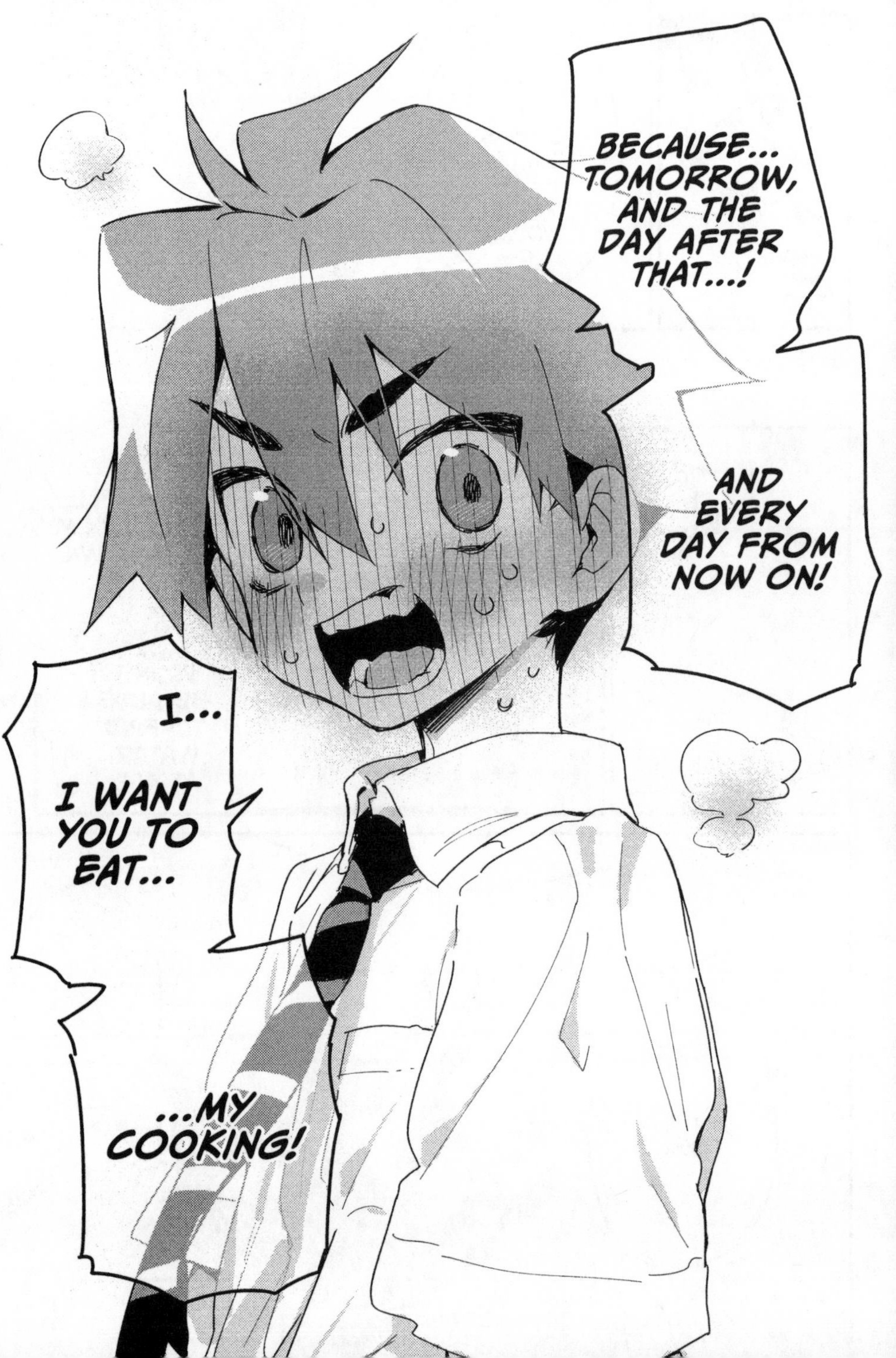
BECAUSE... TOMORROW, AND THE DAY AFTER THAT...!
AND EVERY DAY FROM NOW ON!
I...
I WANT YOU TO EAT...
...MY COOKING!

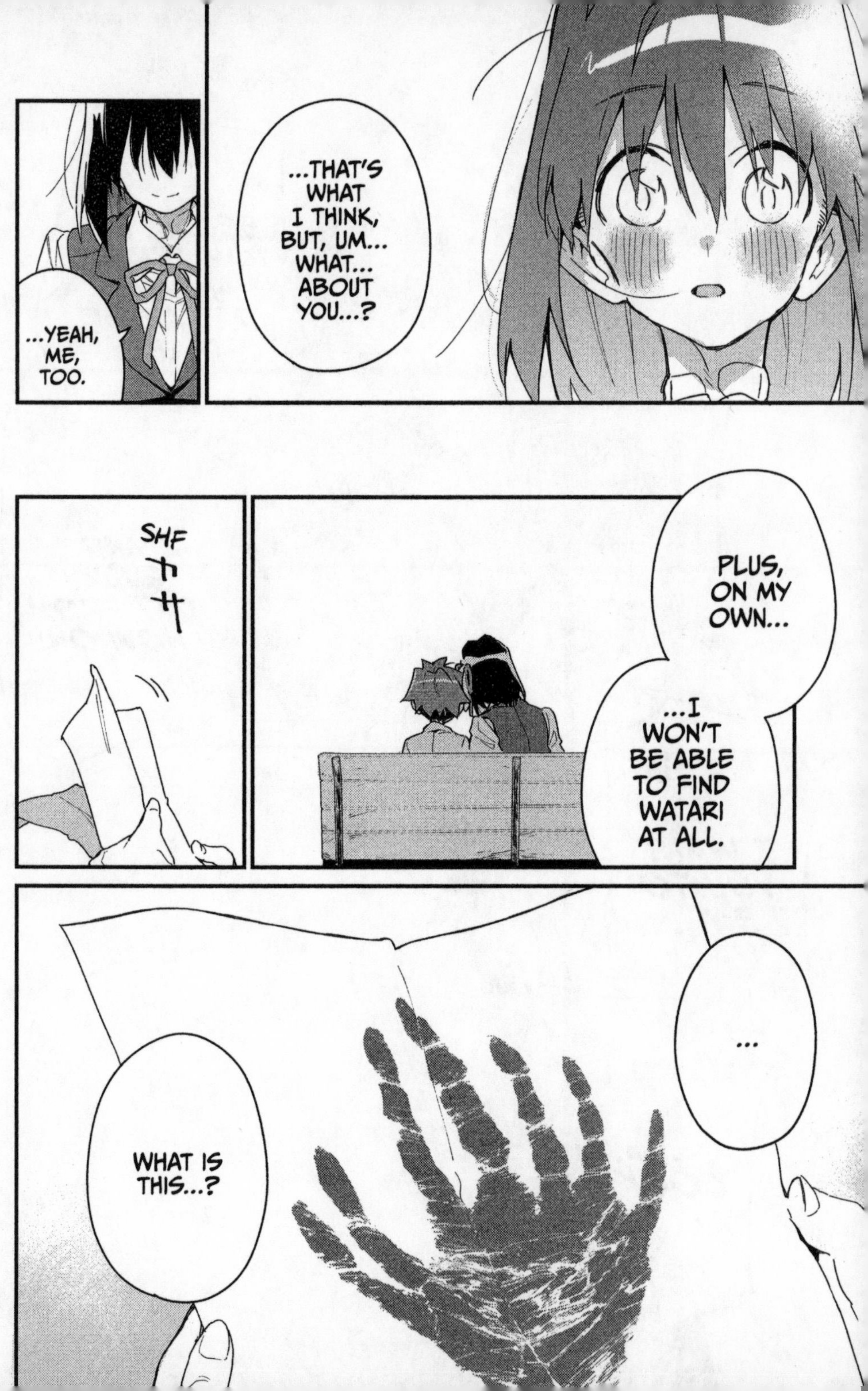
...THAT'S WHAT I THINK, BUT, UM... WHAT... ABOUT YOU...?
...YEAH, ME, TOO.
PLUS, ON MY OWN...
...I WON'T BE ABLE TO FIND WATARI AT ALL.
SHF
...
WHAT IS THIS...?

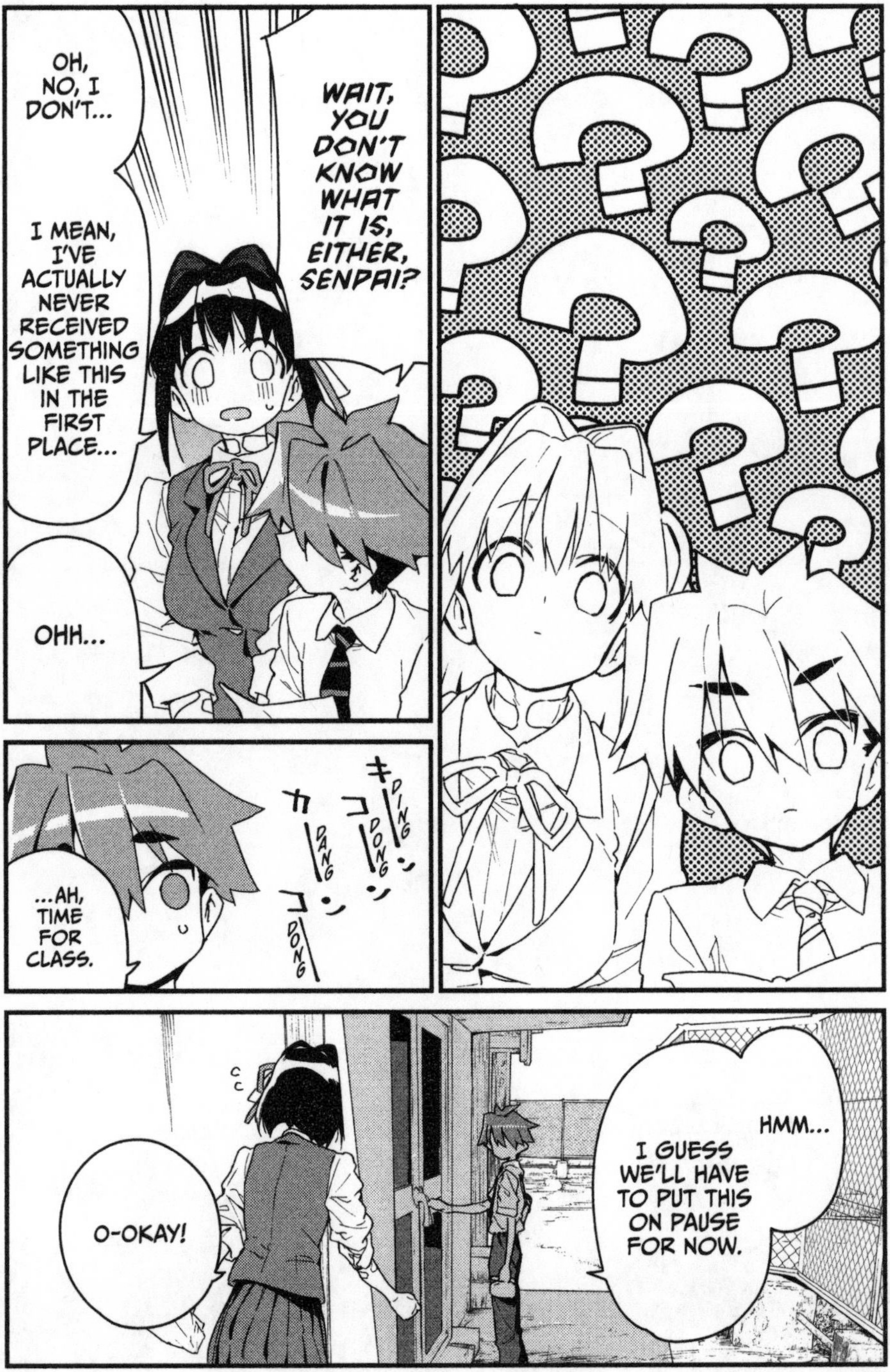
WAIT, YOU DON'T KNOW WHAT IT IS, EITHER, SENPAI?
OH, NO, I DON'T...
I MEAN, I'VE ACTUALLY NEVER RECEIVED SOMETHING LIKE THIS IN THE FIRST PLACE...
OHH...
キーン DING コーン DONG カーン DANG コーン DONG
...AH, TIME FOR CLASS.
HMM...
I GUESS WE'LL HAVE TO PUT THIS ON PAUSE FOR NOW.
O-OKAY!

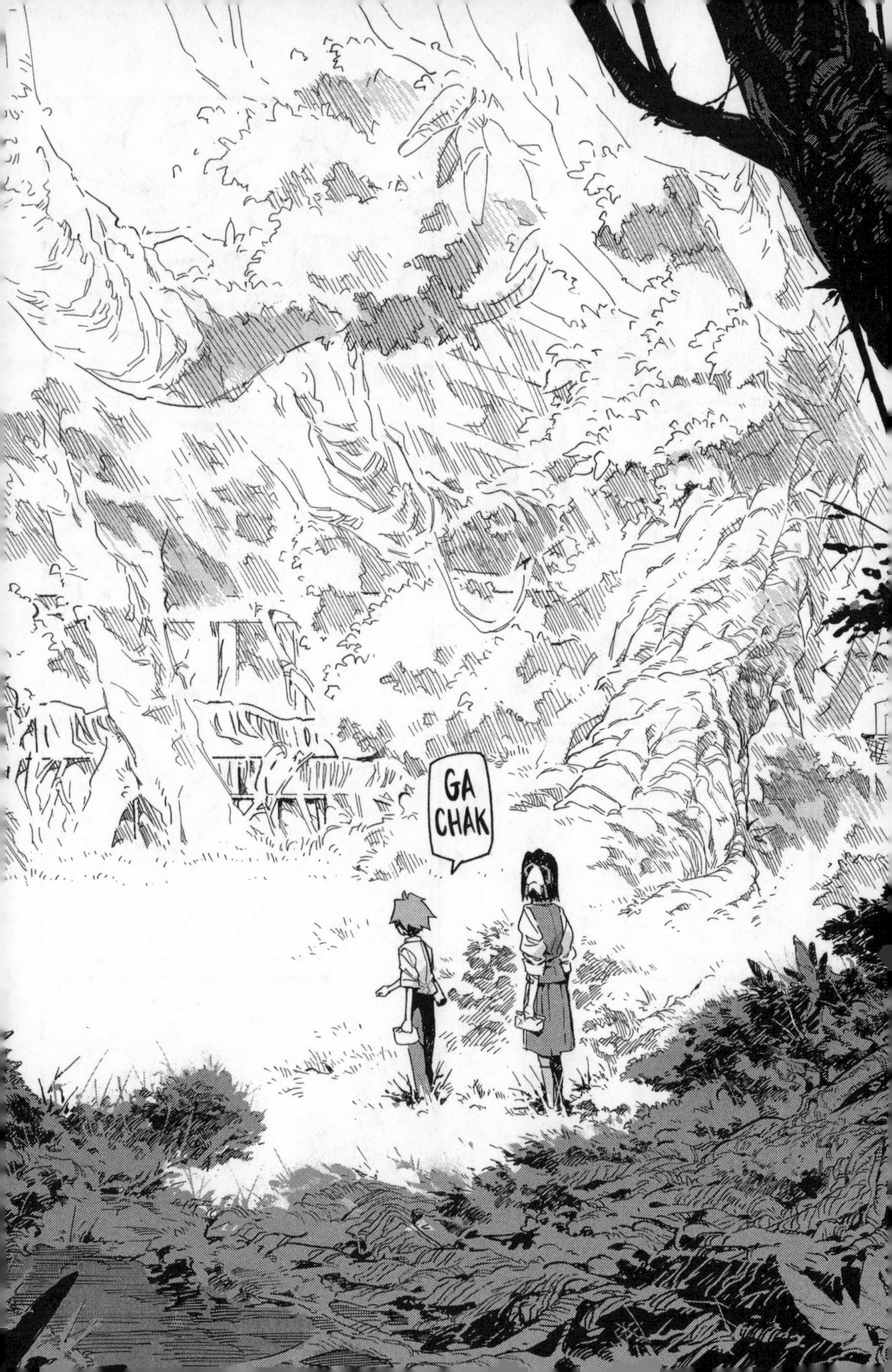
GA CHAK

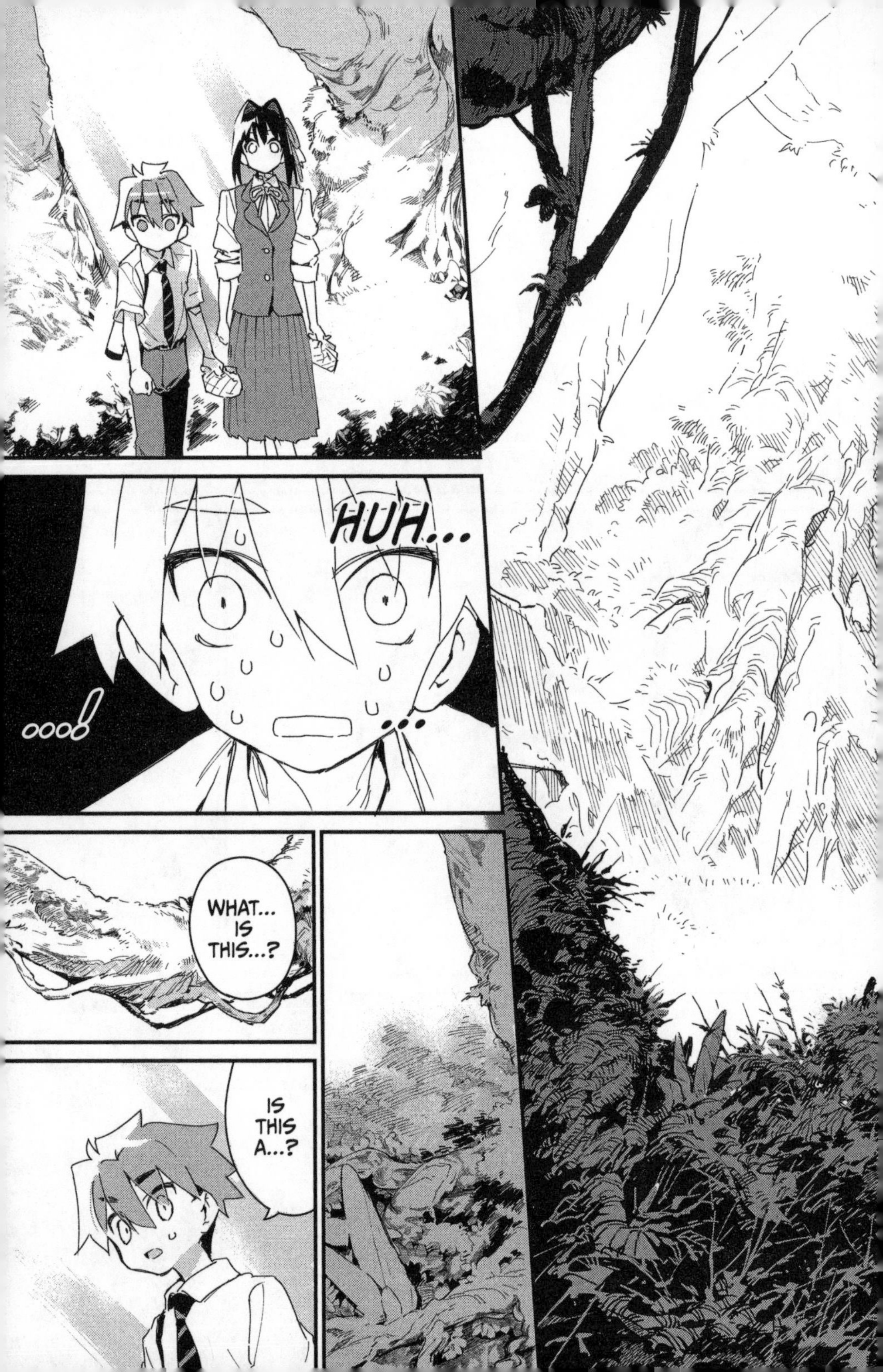
HUH...
ooo!
WHAT... IS THIS...?
IS THIS A...?

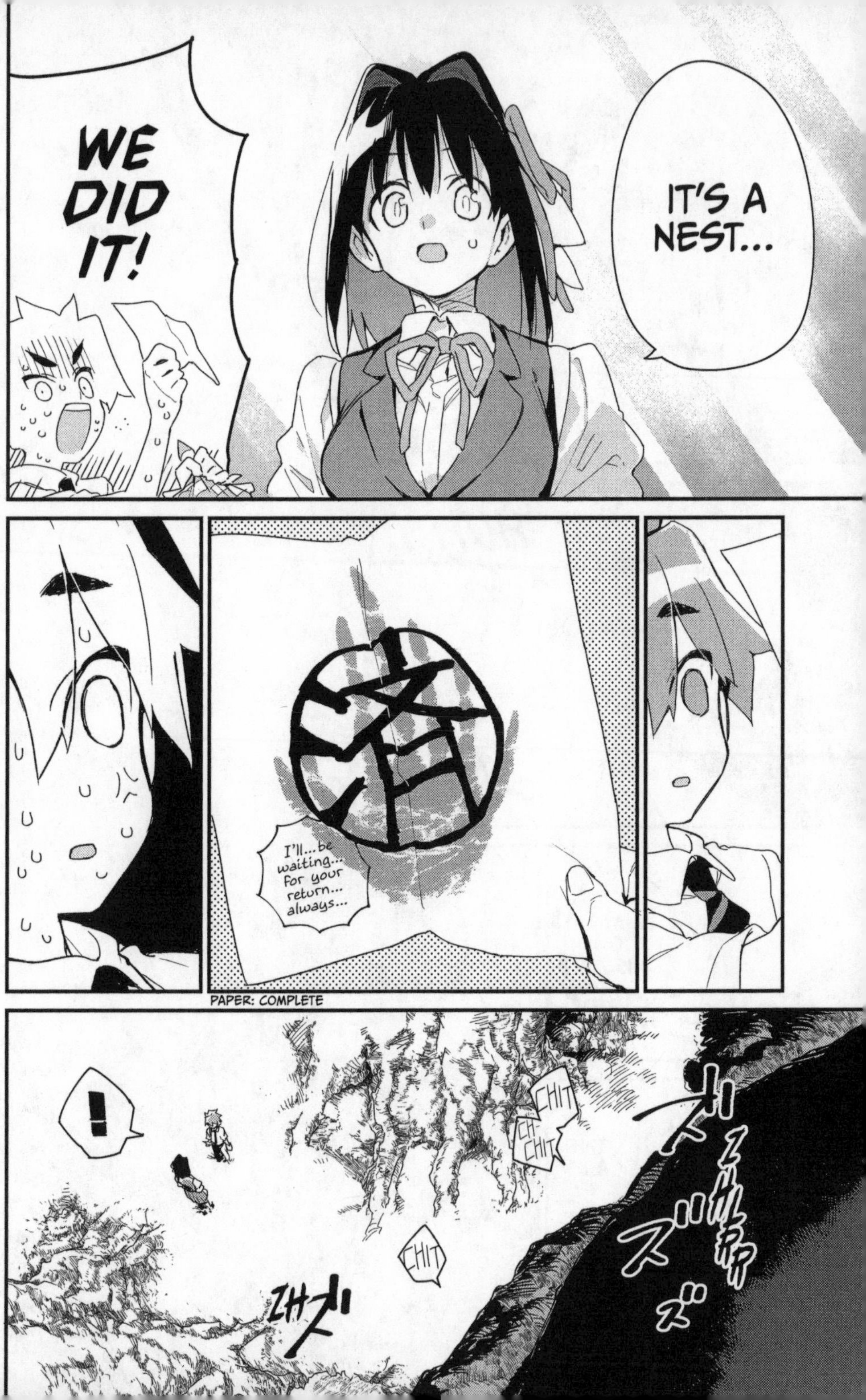
IT'S A NEST...
WE DID IT!
I'll... be waiting... for your return... always...
PAPER: COMPLETE
ZHHRRR
CHIT
CH-CHIT
CHIT
ZH
!

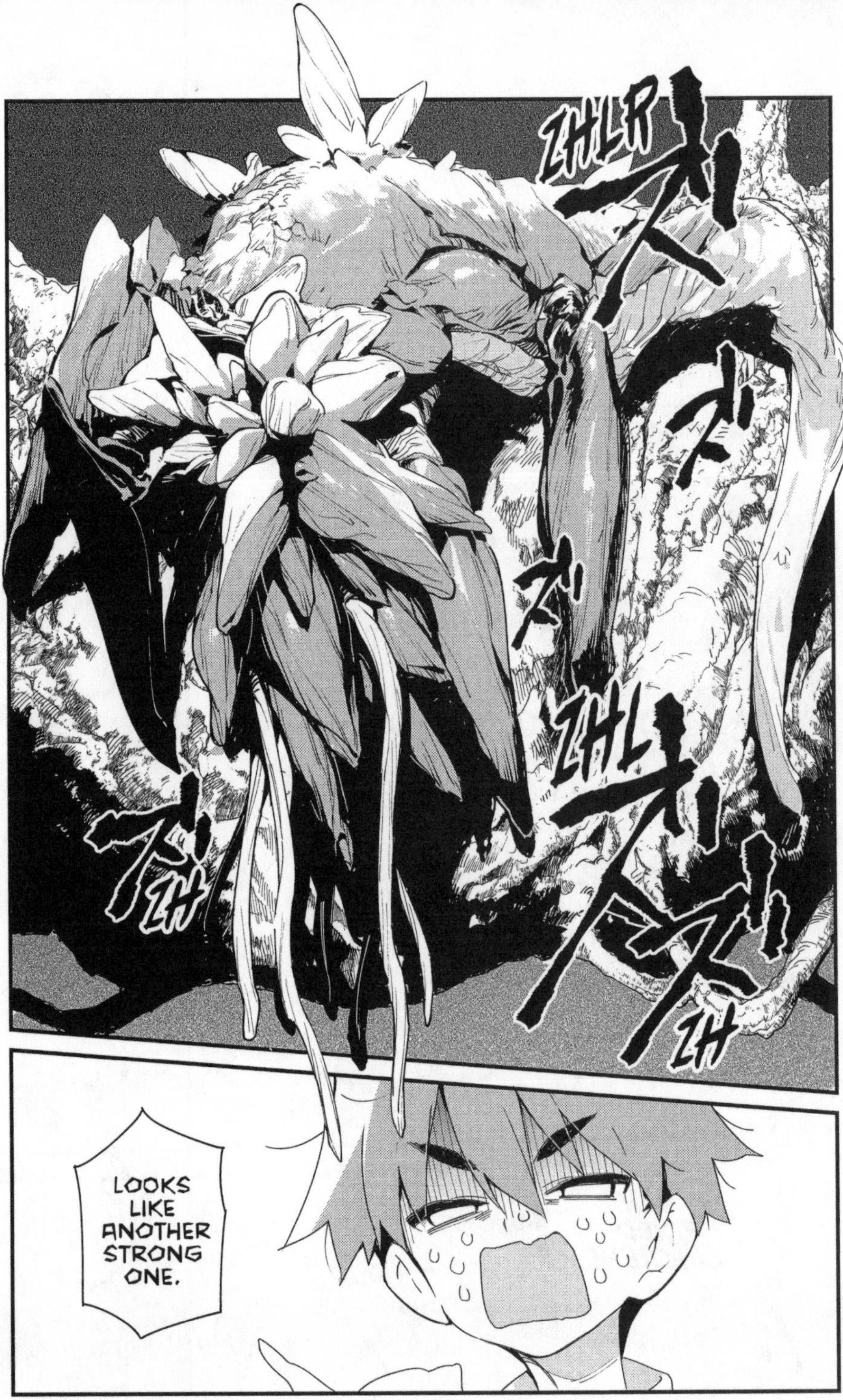
ZHLR
ZHL
ZH
ZH
LOOKS LIKE ANOTHER STRONG ONE.

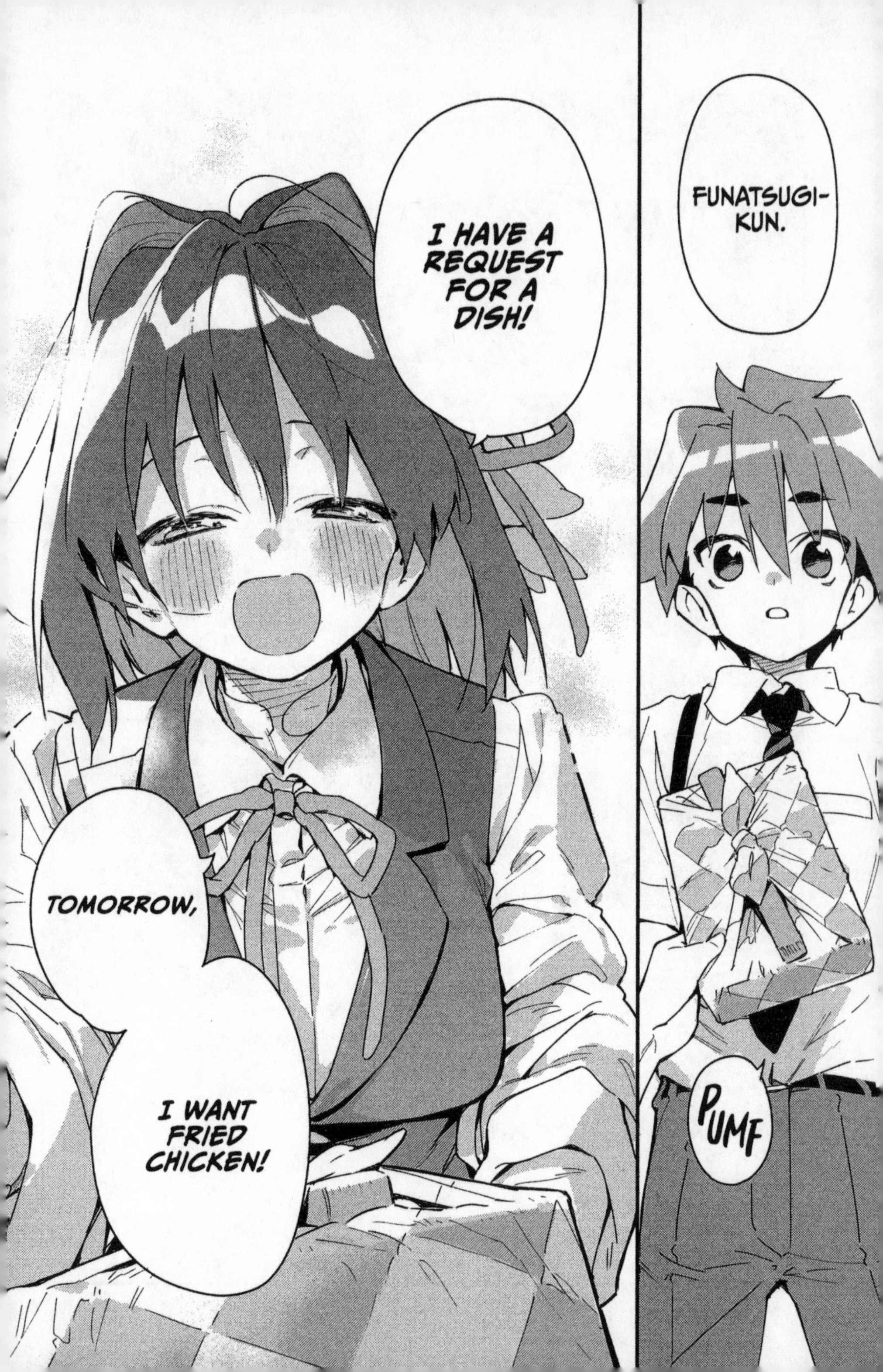
FUNATSUGI-KUN.
PUMF
I HAVE A REQUEST FOR A DISH!
TOMORROW,
I WANT FRIED CHICKEN!

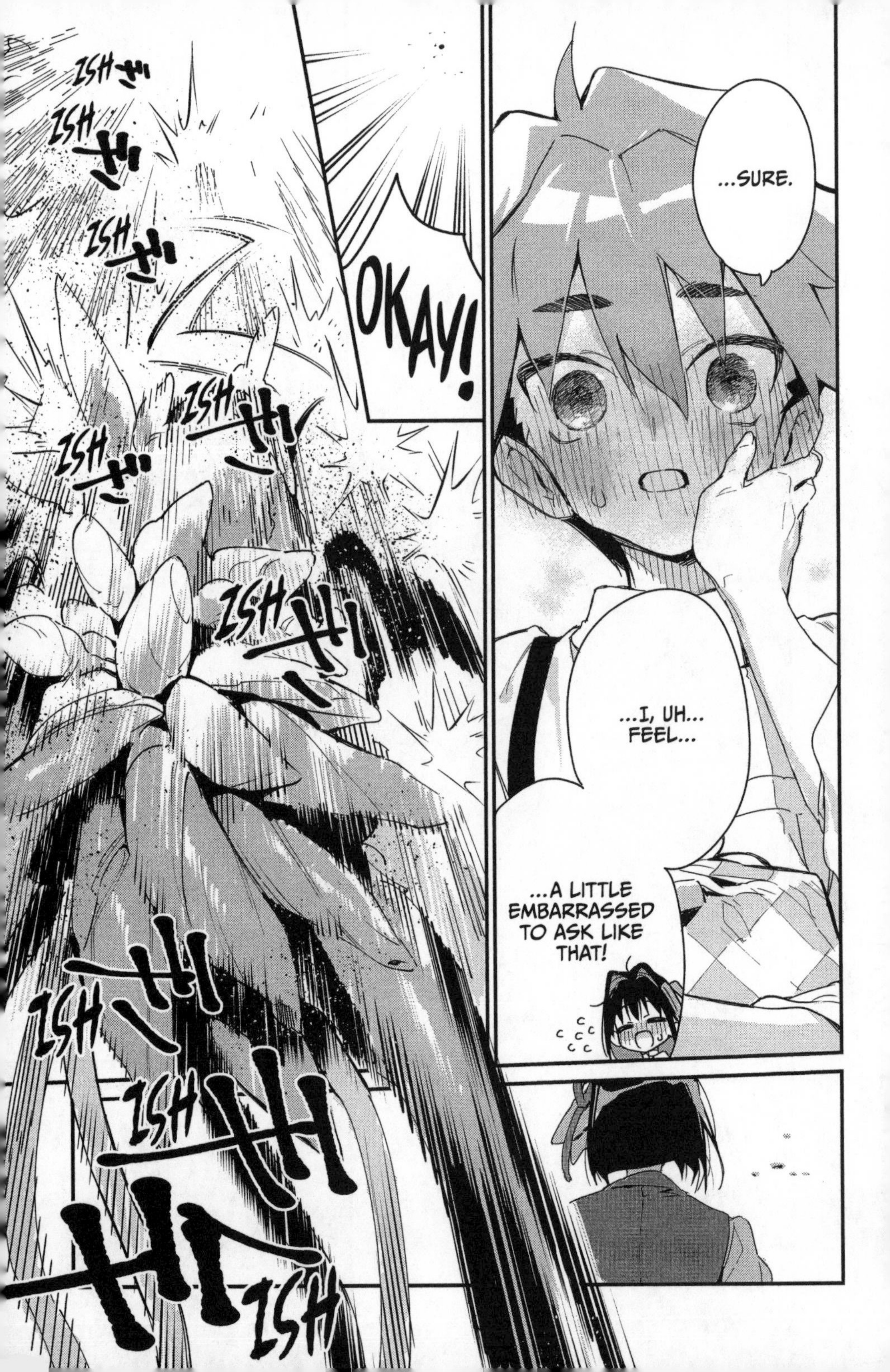
...SURE.
...I, UH... FEEL...
...A LITTLE EMBARRASSED TO ASK LIKE THAT!
OKAY!
ISH
ISH
ISH
ISH
ISH
ISH
ISH
ISH
ISH

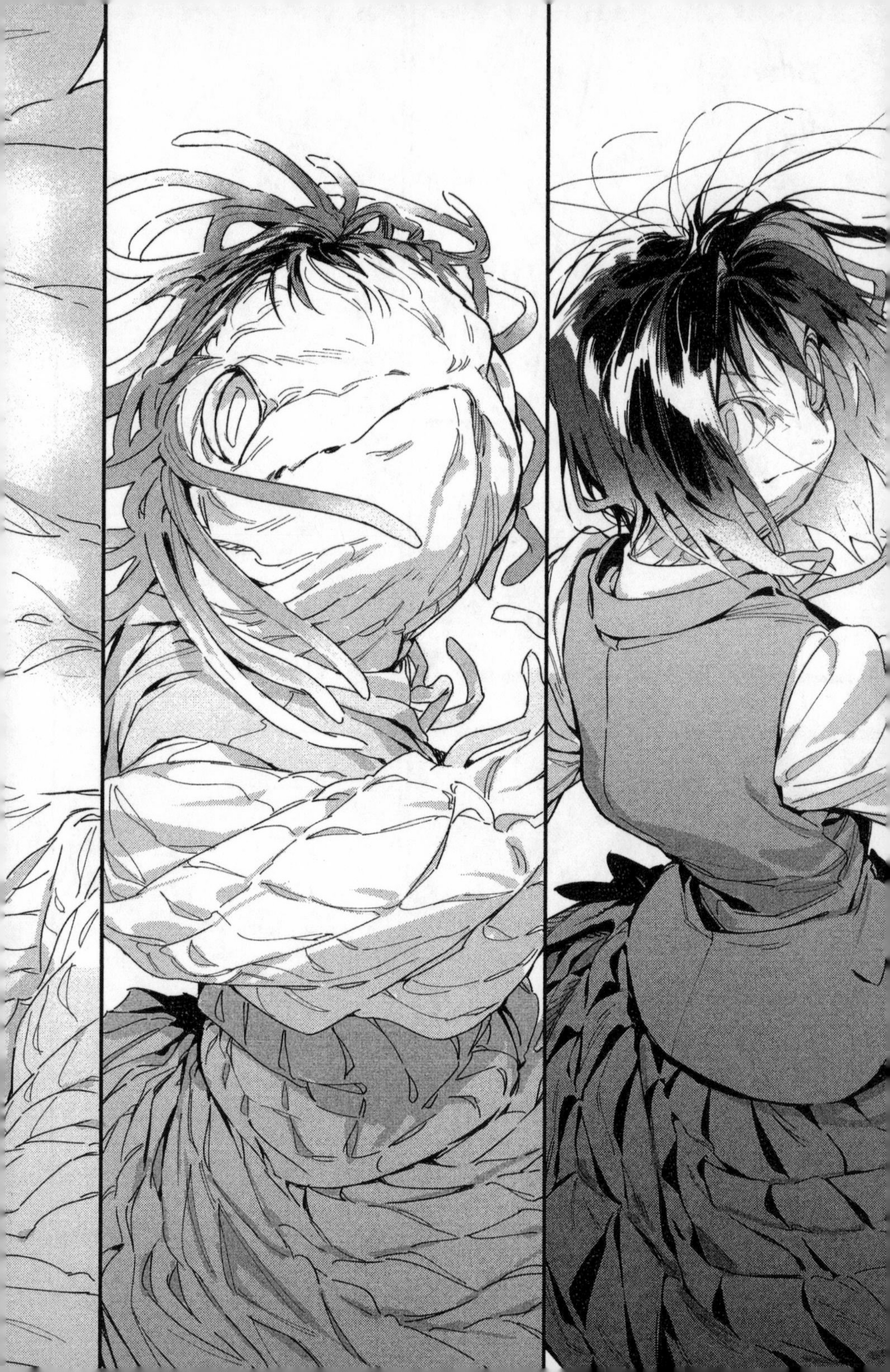

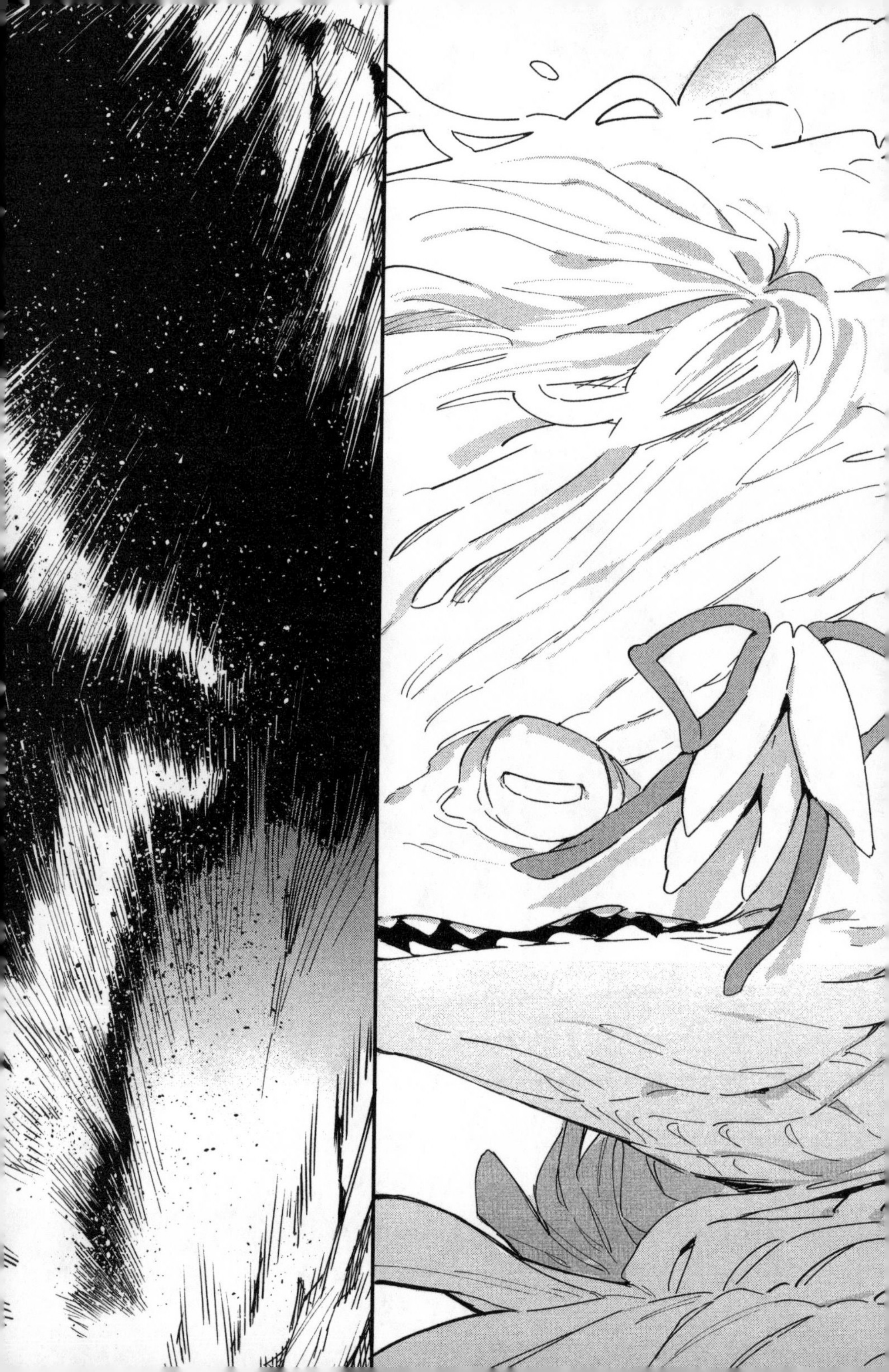

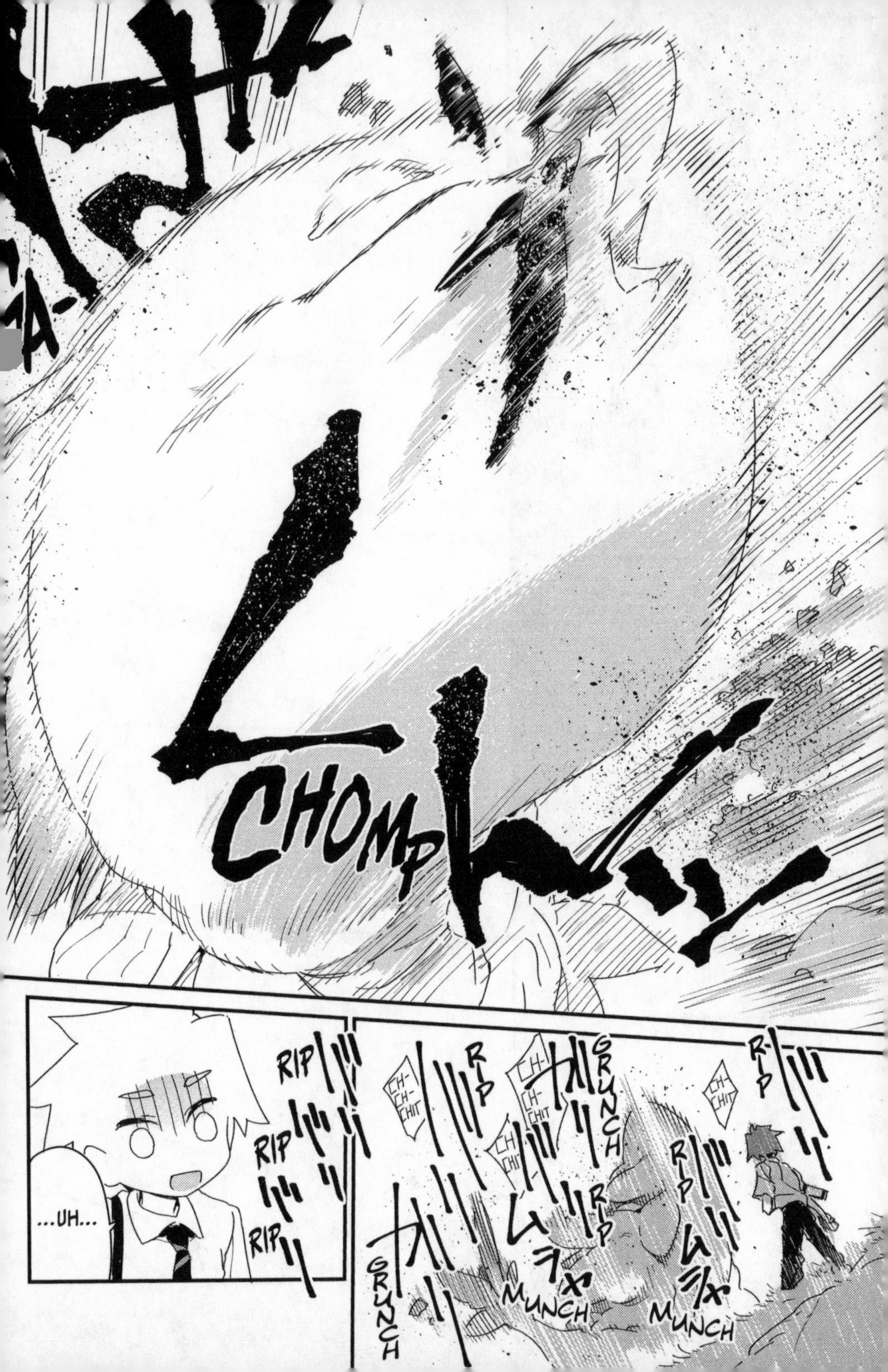
A-
CHOMP
R-IP
CH-CHIT
RIP
MUNCH
GRUNCH
CH-CH-CHIT
RIP
RIP
CH-CHIT
CH-CHIT
MUNCH
GRUNCH
RIP
RIP
RIP
...UH...

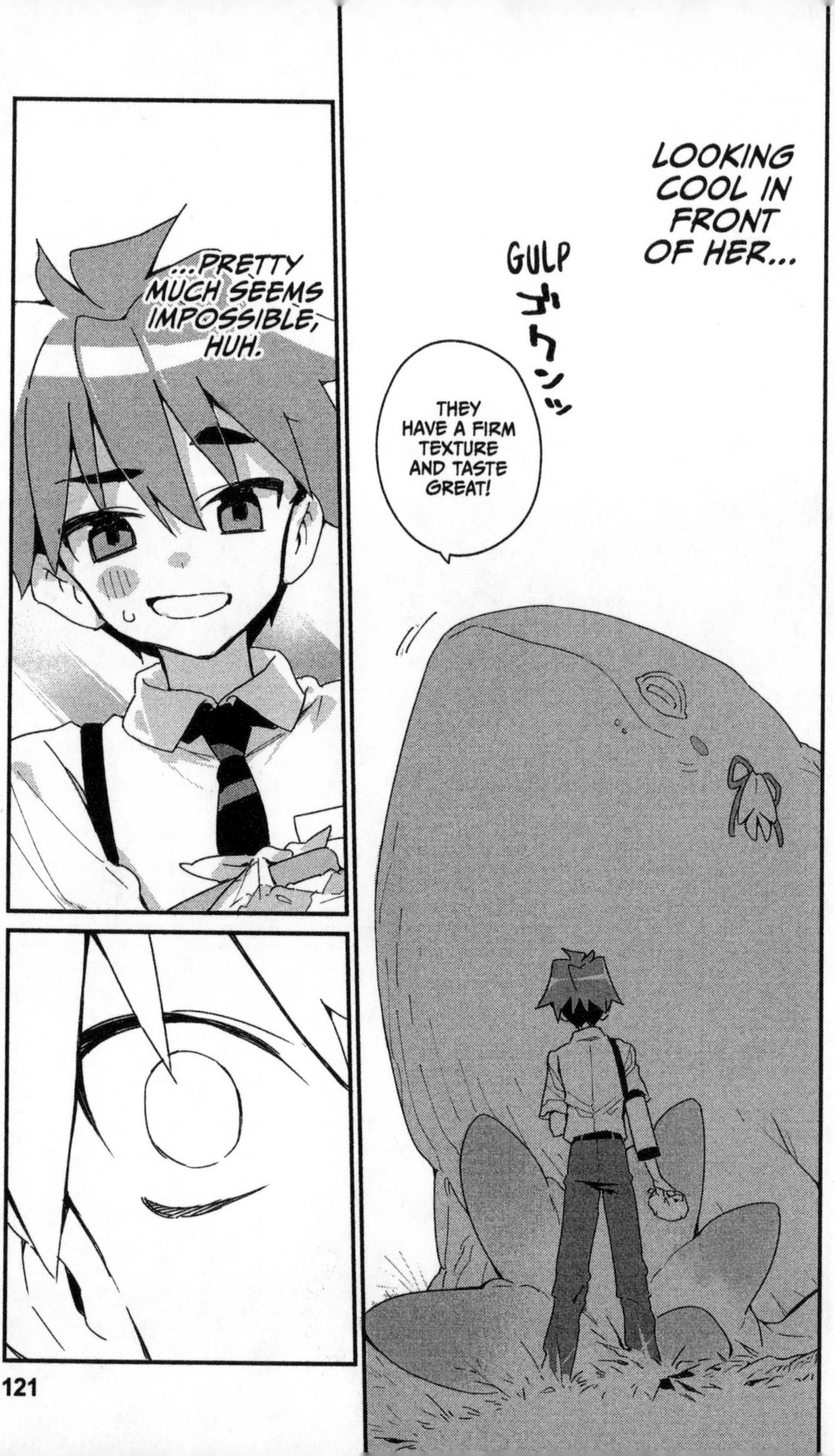
LOOKING COOL IN FRONT OF HER...
GULP
ゴクンッ
THEY HAVE A FIRM TEXTURE AND TASTE GREAT!
...PRETTY MUCH SEEMS IMPOSSIBLE, HUH.

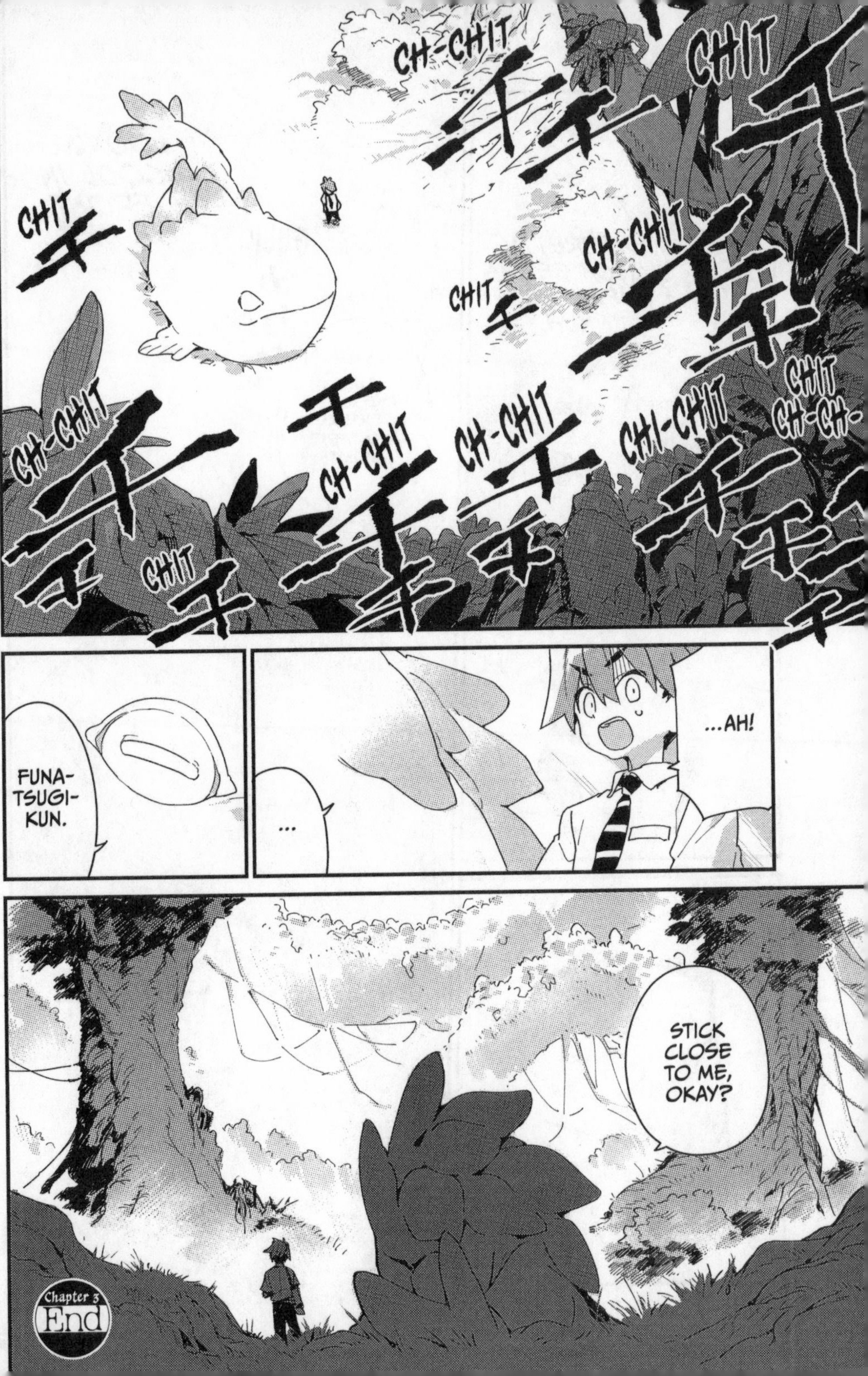
CHIT
CH-CHIT
CH-CHIT
CHIT
CHIT
CHIT
CH-CH-
CHI-CHIT
CH-CHIT
CH-CHIT
CH-CHIT
CHIT
...AH!
...
FUNA-TSUGI-KUN.
STICK CLOSE TO ME, OKAY?
Chapter 3
End

Chapter 4: Now That's Just Ridiculous...

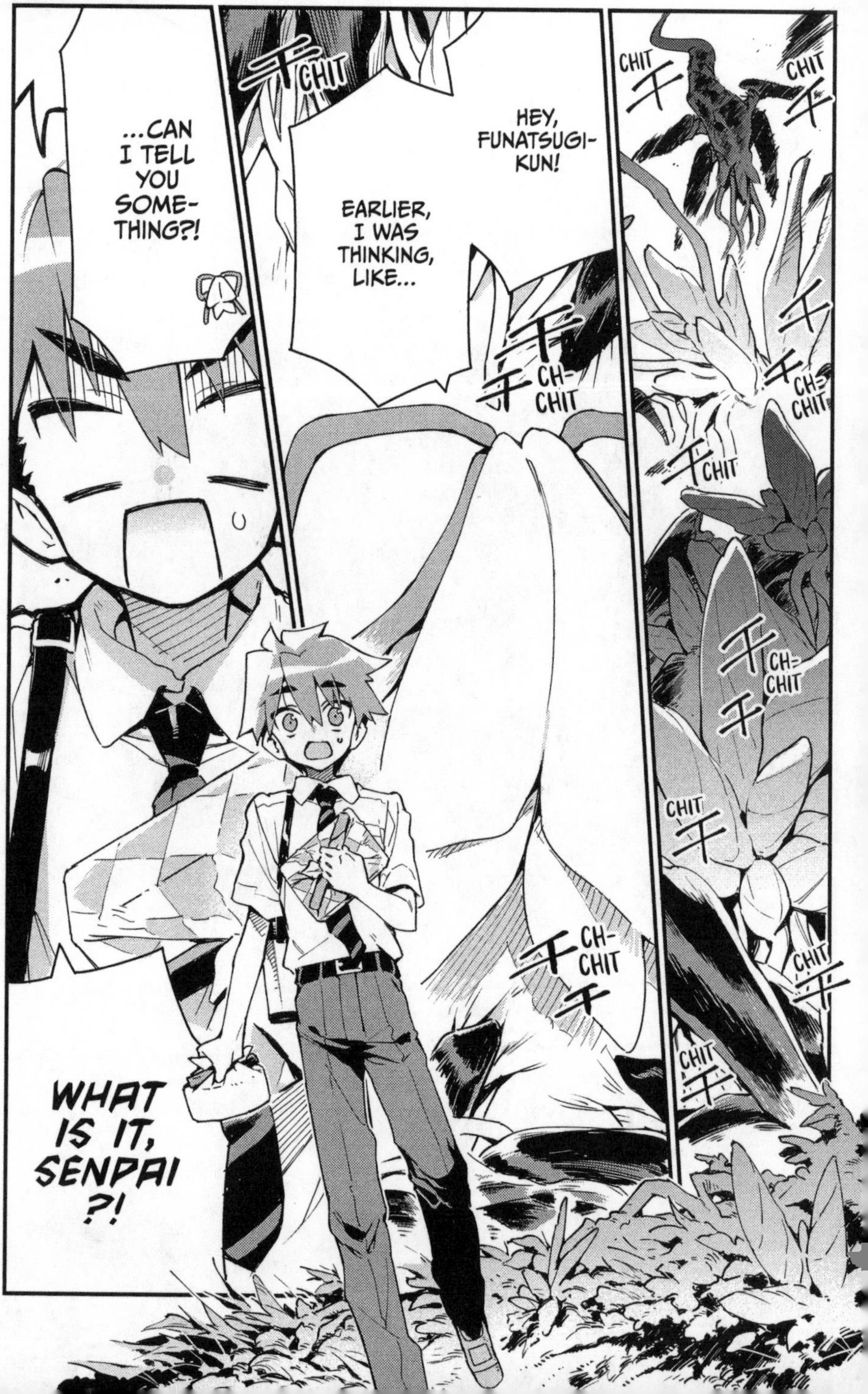
CHIT
CHIT
CH-CHIT
CHIT
CH-CHIT
CHIT
CHIT
CHIT
CHIT
HEY, FUNATSUGI-KUN!
EARLIER, I WAS THINKING, LIKE...
CH-CHIT
CH-CHIT
...CAN I TELL YOU SOME-THING?!
WHAT IS IT, SENPAI?!

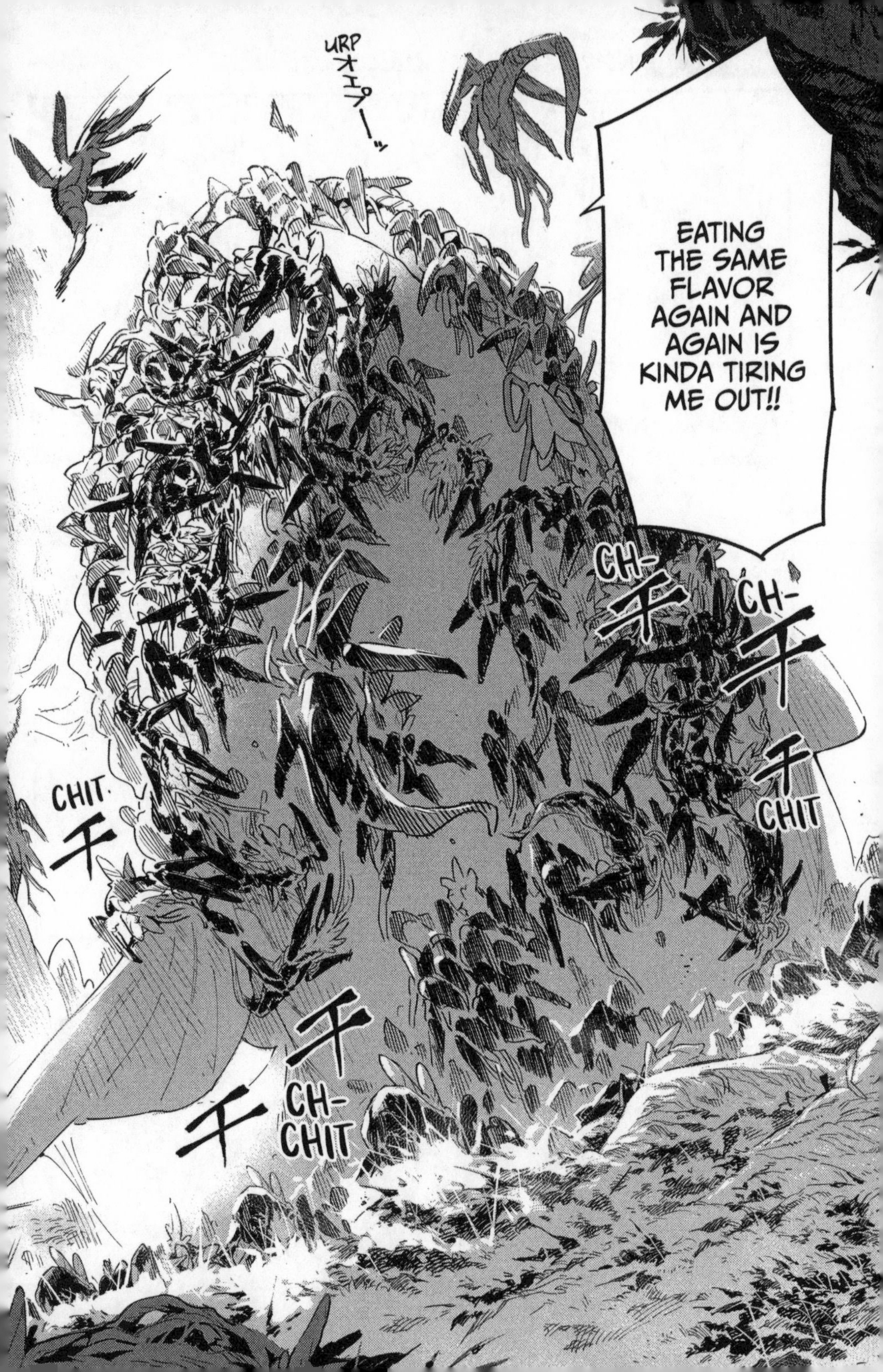
EATING THE SAME FLAVOR AGAIN AND AGAIN IS KINDA TIRING ME OUT!!
URP
オエプーーッ
CH- チ
CH- チ
チ CHIT
CHIT チ
チ チ CH-CHIT

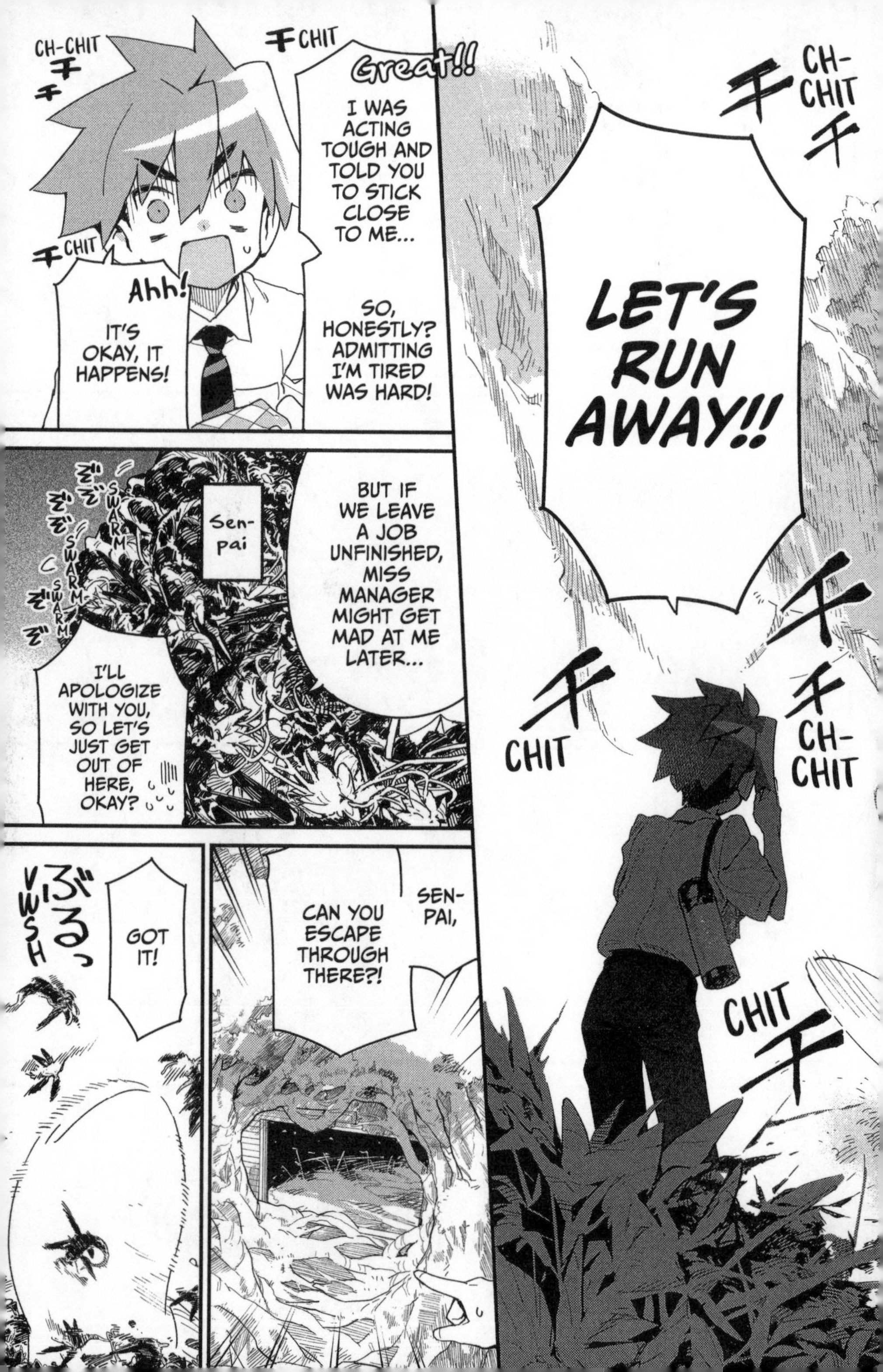
CH-CHIT
LET'S RUN AWAY!!
CHIT
CH-CHIT
CHIT
CHIT
Great!!
I WAS ACTING TOUGH AND TOLD YOU TO STICK CLOSE TO ME...
SO, HONESTLY? ADMITTING I'M TIRED WAS HARD!
CH-CHIT
CHIT
Ahh!
IT'S OKAY, IT HAPPENS!
BUT IF WE LEAVE A JOB UNFINISHED, MISS MANAGER MIGHT GET MAD AT ME LATER...
Sen-pai
ぞぞ SWARM
ぞぞ SWARM
ぞぞ SWARM
I'LL APOLOGIZE WITH YOU, SO LET'S JUST GET OUT OF HERE, OKAY?
SEN-PAI,
CAN YOU ESCAPE THROUGH THERE?!
ぶるっ VWSH
GOT IT!

FUNA-TSUGI-KUN, JUMP OUT OF THE WAY!

HYAH!

BAM

FUNATSUGI-KUN!!

SMALL BRANCH

KA-KLONK!

WHA—

ACK?!

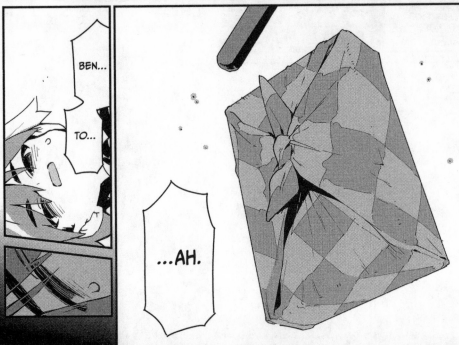

BEN...

TO...

...AH.

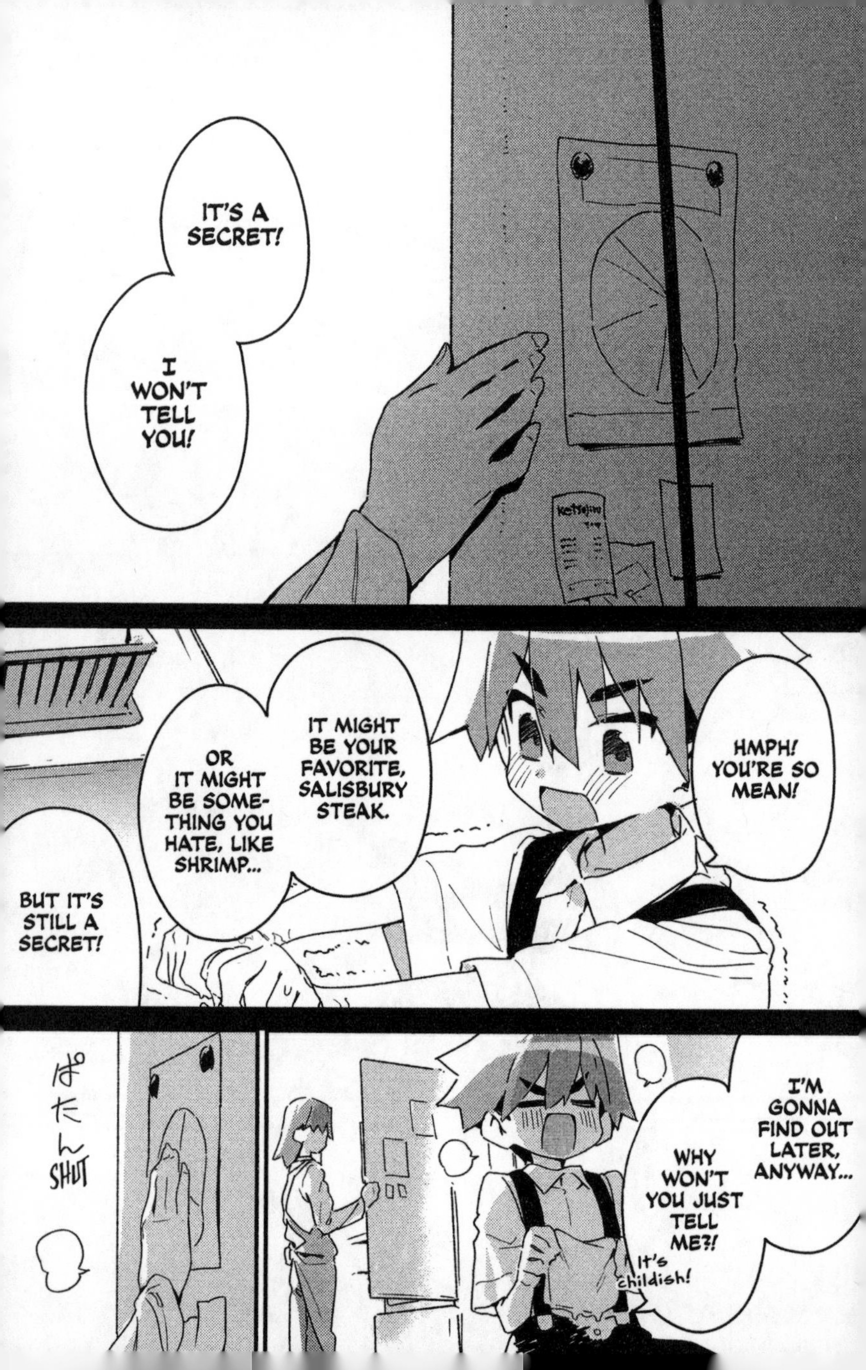
IT'S A SECRET!
I WON'T TELL YOU!
HMPH! YOU'RE SO MEAN!
IT MIGHT BE YOUR FAVORITE, SALISBURY STEAK.
OR IT MIGHT BE SOME-THING YOU HATE, LIKE SHRIMP...
BUT IT'S STILL A SECRET!
I'M GONNA FIND OUT LATER, ANYWAY...
WHY WON'T YOU JUST TELL ME?!
It's childish!
ぱたん
SHUT

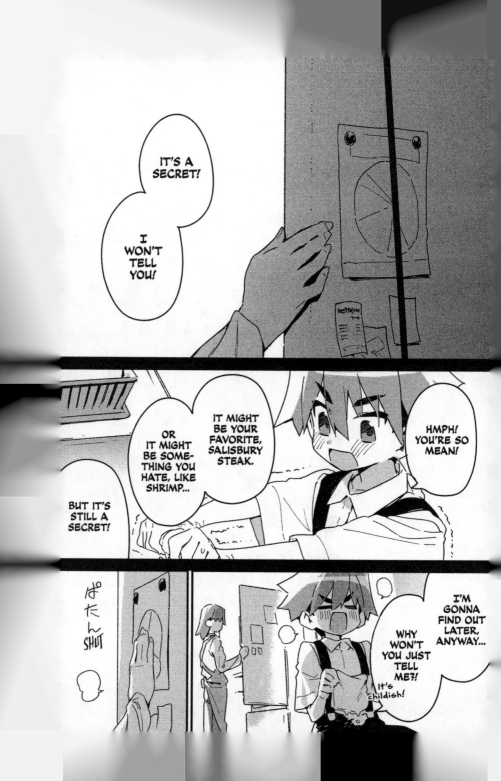

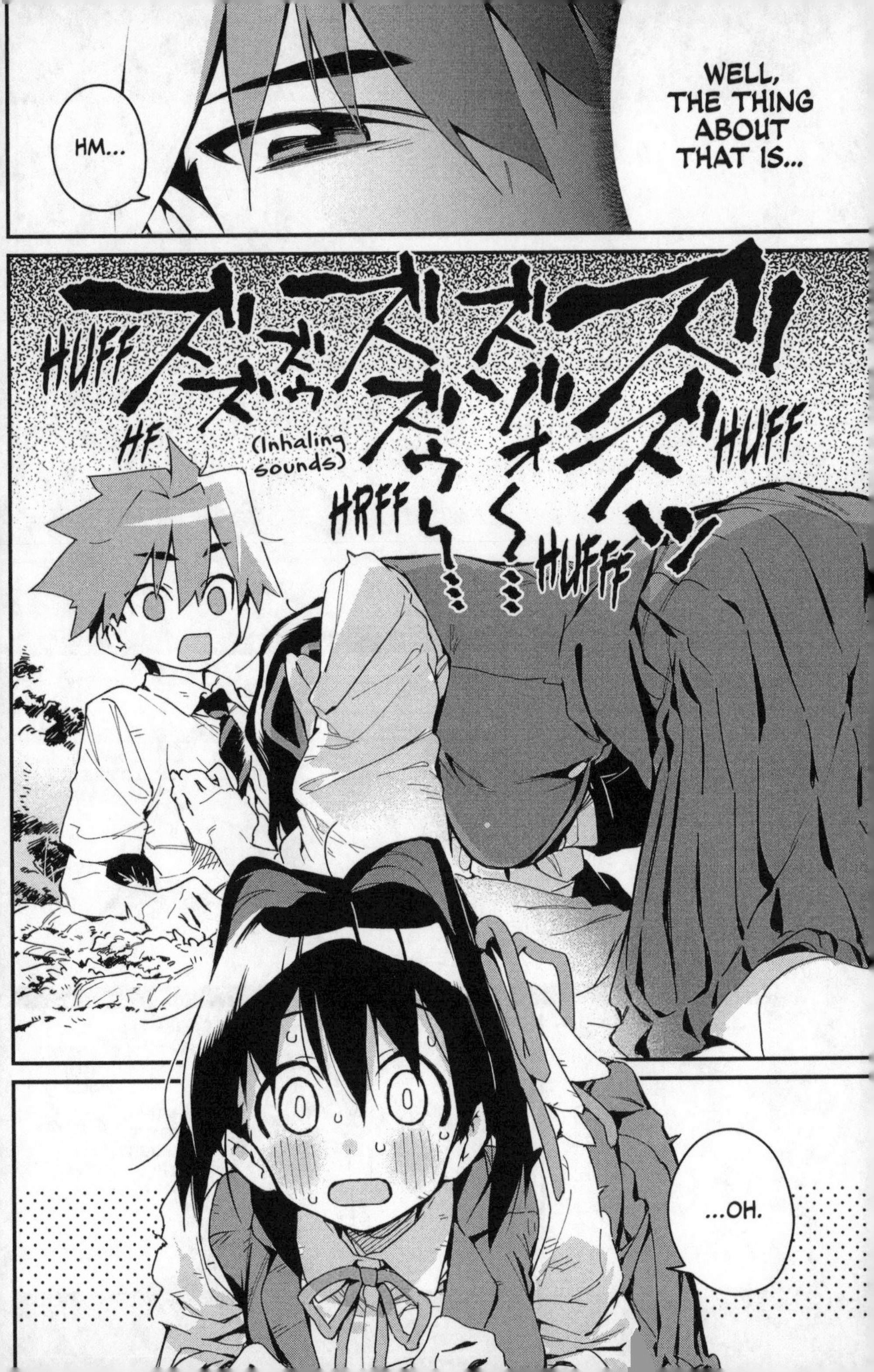
WELL, THE THING ABOUT THAT IS...
HM...
HUFF
HUFFF
HRFF
(Inhaling sounds)
HUFF
HF
...OH.

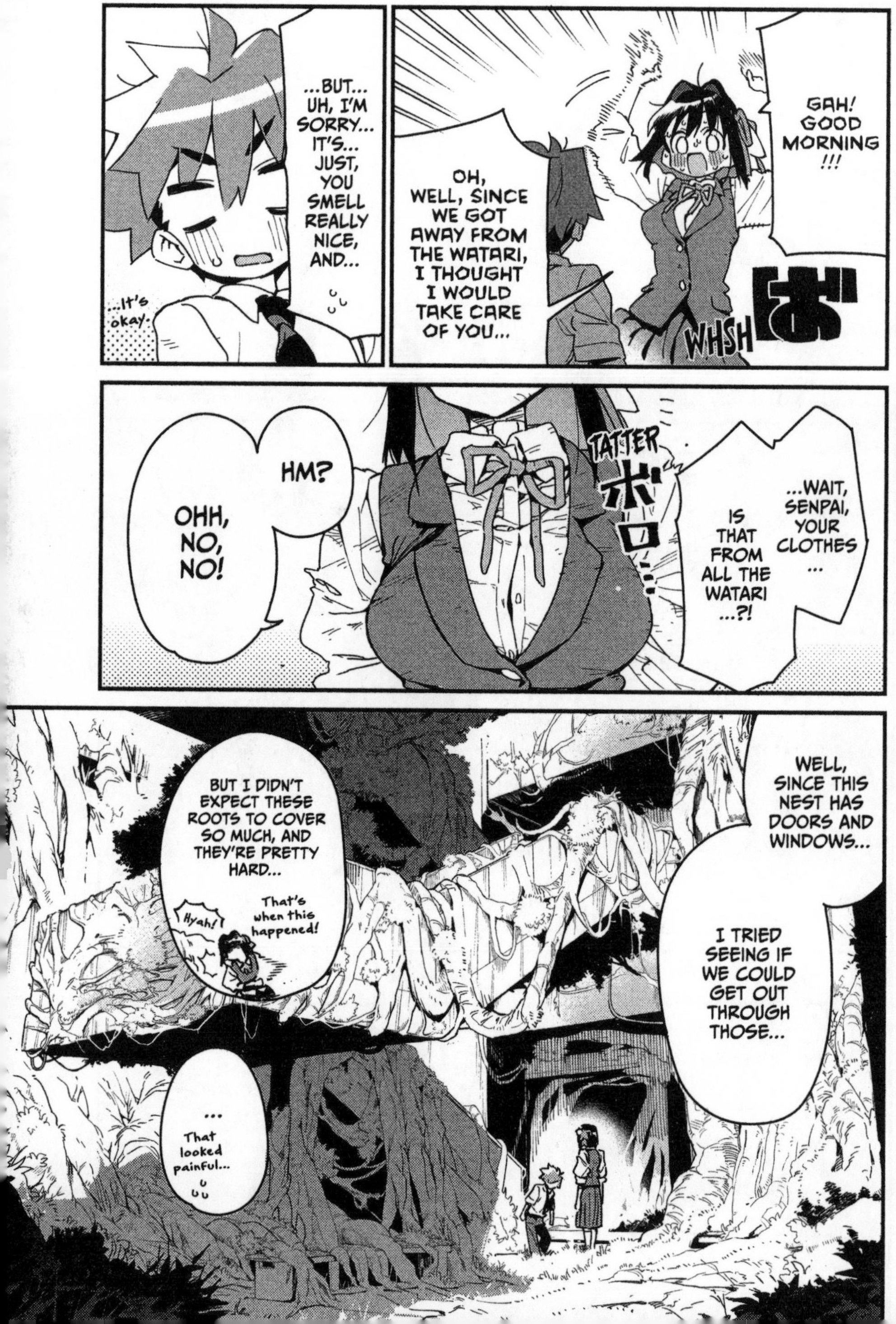
GAH! GOOD MORNING !!!
OH, WELL, SINCE WE GOT AWAY FROM THE WATARI, I THOUGHT I WOULD TAKE CARE OF YOU...
WHSH
ば
...BUT... UH, I'M SORRY... IT'S... JUST, YOU SMELL REALLY NICE, AND...
...It's okay.
...WAIT, SENPAI, YOUR CLOTHES ...
IS THAT FROM ALL THE WATARI ...?!
TATTER
ボロ
HM?
OHH, NO, NO!
WELL, SINCE THIS NEST HAS DOORS AND WINDOWS...
I TRIED SEEING IF WE COULD GET OUT THROUGH THOSE...
BUT I DIDN'T EXPECT THESE ROOTS TO COVER SO MUCH, AND THEY'RE PRETTY HARD...
That's when this happened!
Hyah!
... That looked painful...

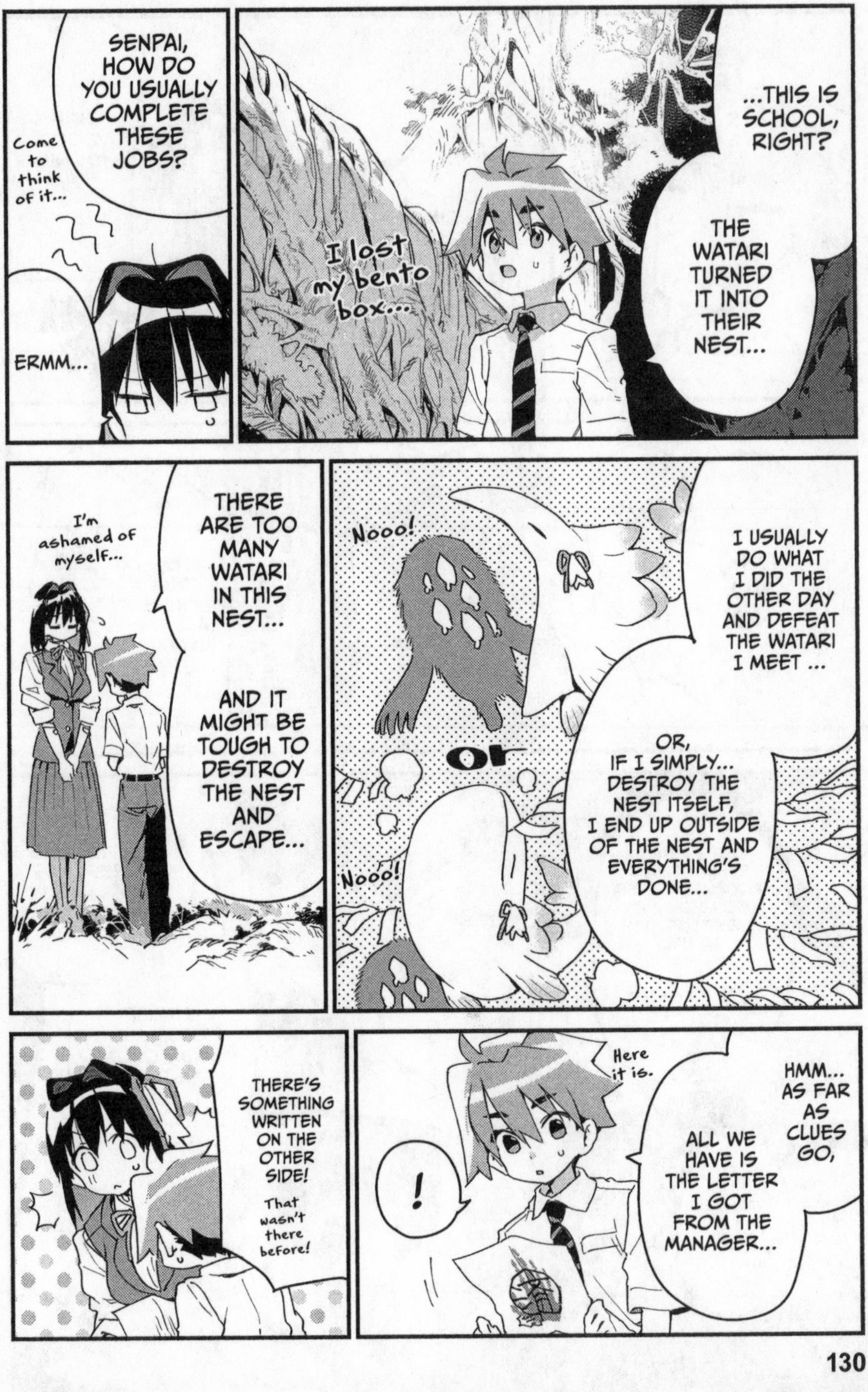
...THIS IS SCHOOL, RIGHT?
THE WATARI TURNED IT INTO THEIR NEST...
I lost my bento box...
SENPAI, HOW DO YOU USUALLY COMPLETE THESE JOBS?
Come to think of it...
ERMM...
I USUALLY DO WHAT I DID THE OTHER DAY AND DEFEAT THE WATARI I MEET ...
Nooo!
or
OR, IF I SIMPLY... DESTROY THE NEST ITSELF, I END UP OUTSIDE OF THE NEST AND EVERYTHING'S DONE...
Nooo!
THERE ARE TOO MANY WATARI IN THIS NEST...
AND IT MIGHT BE TOUGH TO DESTROY THE NEST AND ESCAPE...
I'm ashamed of myself...
HMM... AS FAR AS CLUES GO,
ALL WE HAVE IS THE LETTER I GOT FROM THE MANAGER...
Here it is.
!
THERE'S SOMETHING WRITTEN ON THE OTHER SIDE!
That wasn't there before!

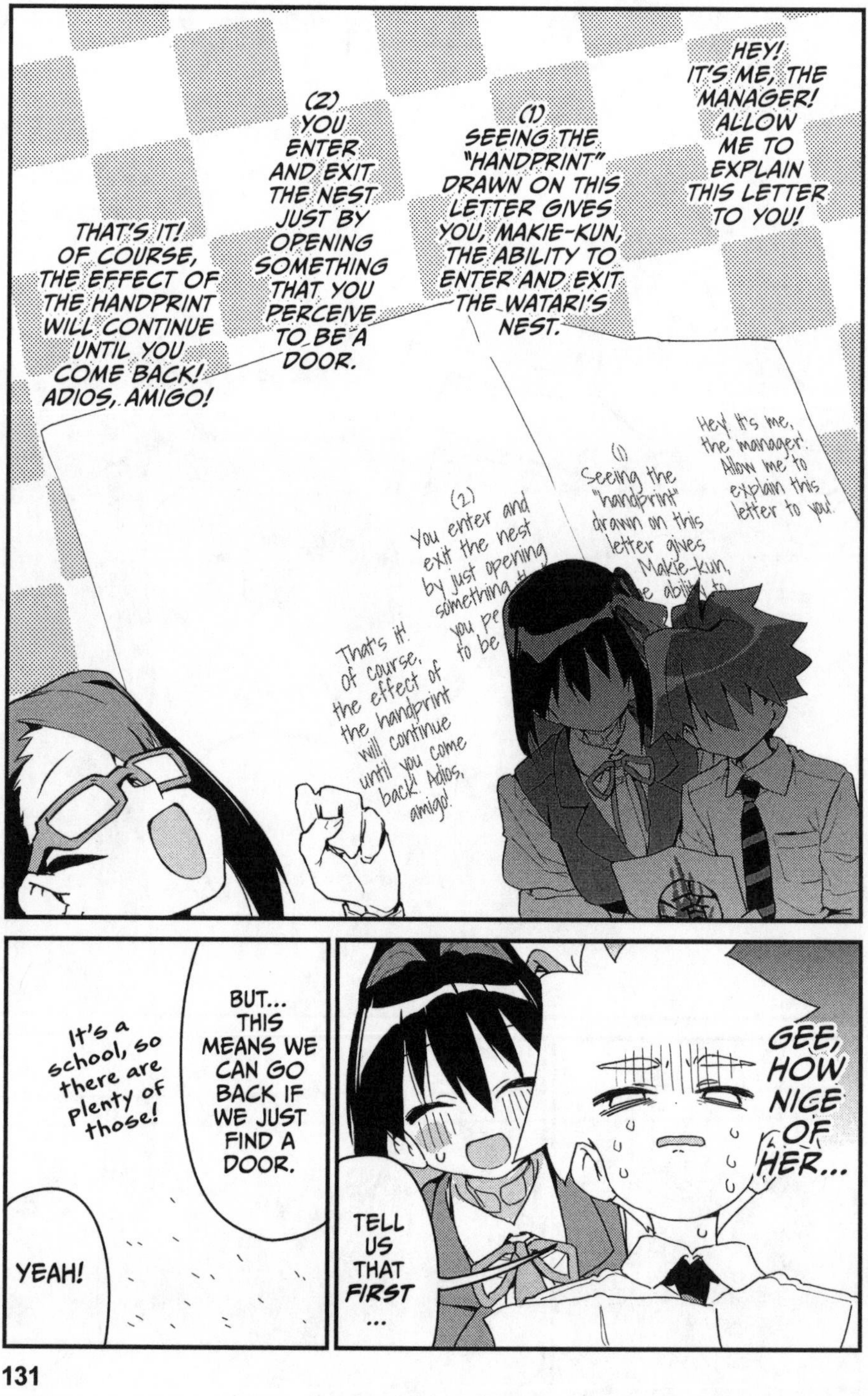
HEY! IT'S ME, THE MANAGER! ALLOW ME TO EXPLAIN THIS LETTER TO YOU!
(1) SEEING THE "HANDPRINT" DRAWN ON THIS LETTER GIVES YOU, MAKIE-KUN, THE ABILITY TO ENTER AND EXIT THE WATARI'S NEST.
(2) YOU ENTER AND EXIT THE NEST JUST BY OPENING SOMETHING THAT YOU PERCEIVE TO BE A DOOR.
THAT'S IT! OF COURSE, THE EFFECT OF THE HANDPRINT WILL CONTINUE UNTIL YOU COME BACK! ADIOS, AMIGO!
Hey! It's me, the manager! Allow me to explain this letter to you!
That's it! Of course, the effect of the handprint will continue until you come back! Adios, amigo!
GEE, HOW NICE OF HER...
TELL US THAT FIRST ...
BUT... THIS MEANS WE CAN GO BACK IF WE JUST FIND A DOOR.
It's a school, so there are plenty of those!
YEAH!

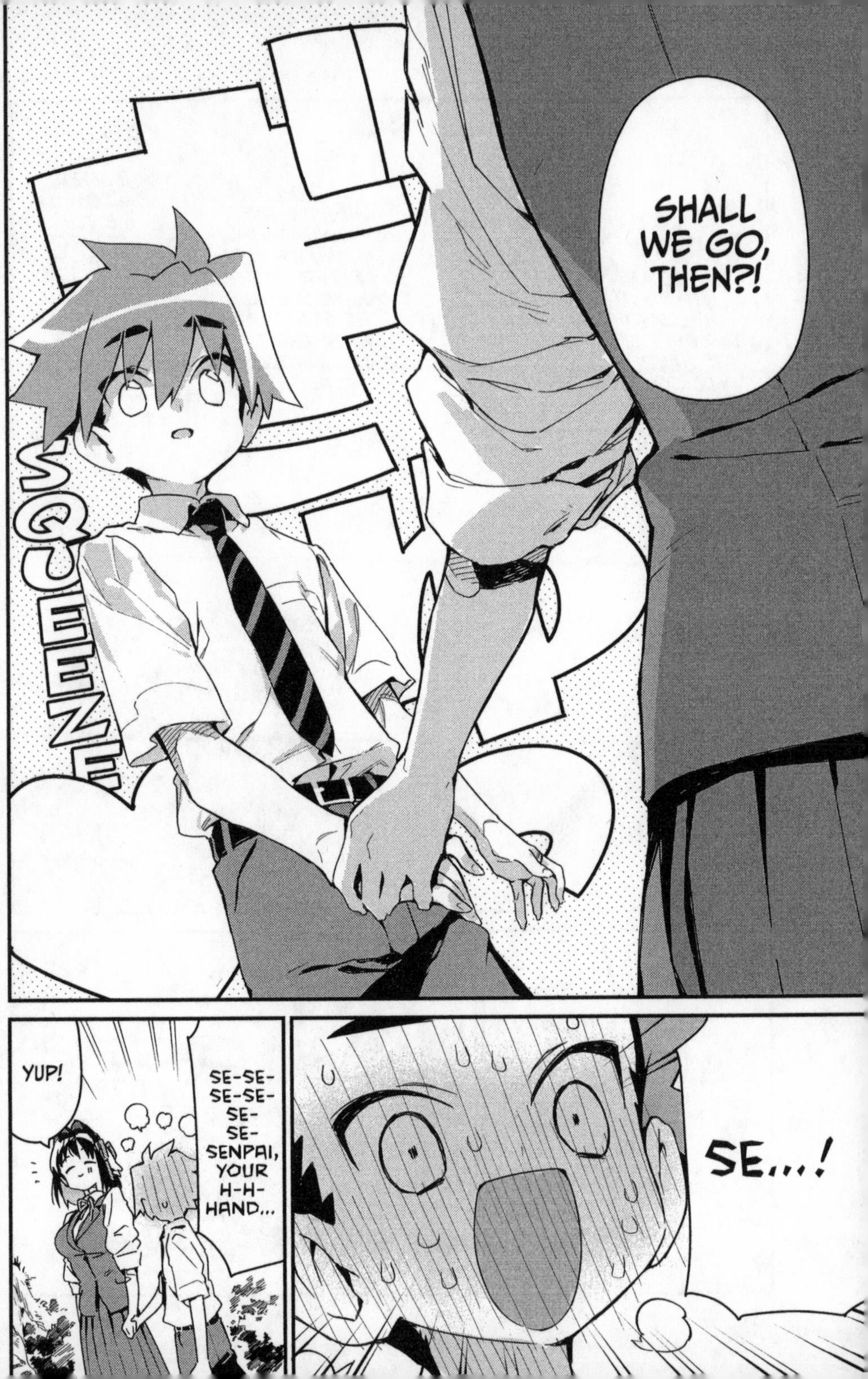
SHALL WE GO, THEN?!
SQUEEZE
SE...!
SE-SE-SE-SE-SE-SE-SENPAI, YOUR H-H-HAND...
YUP!

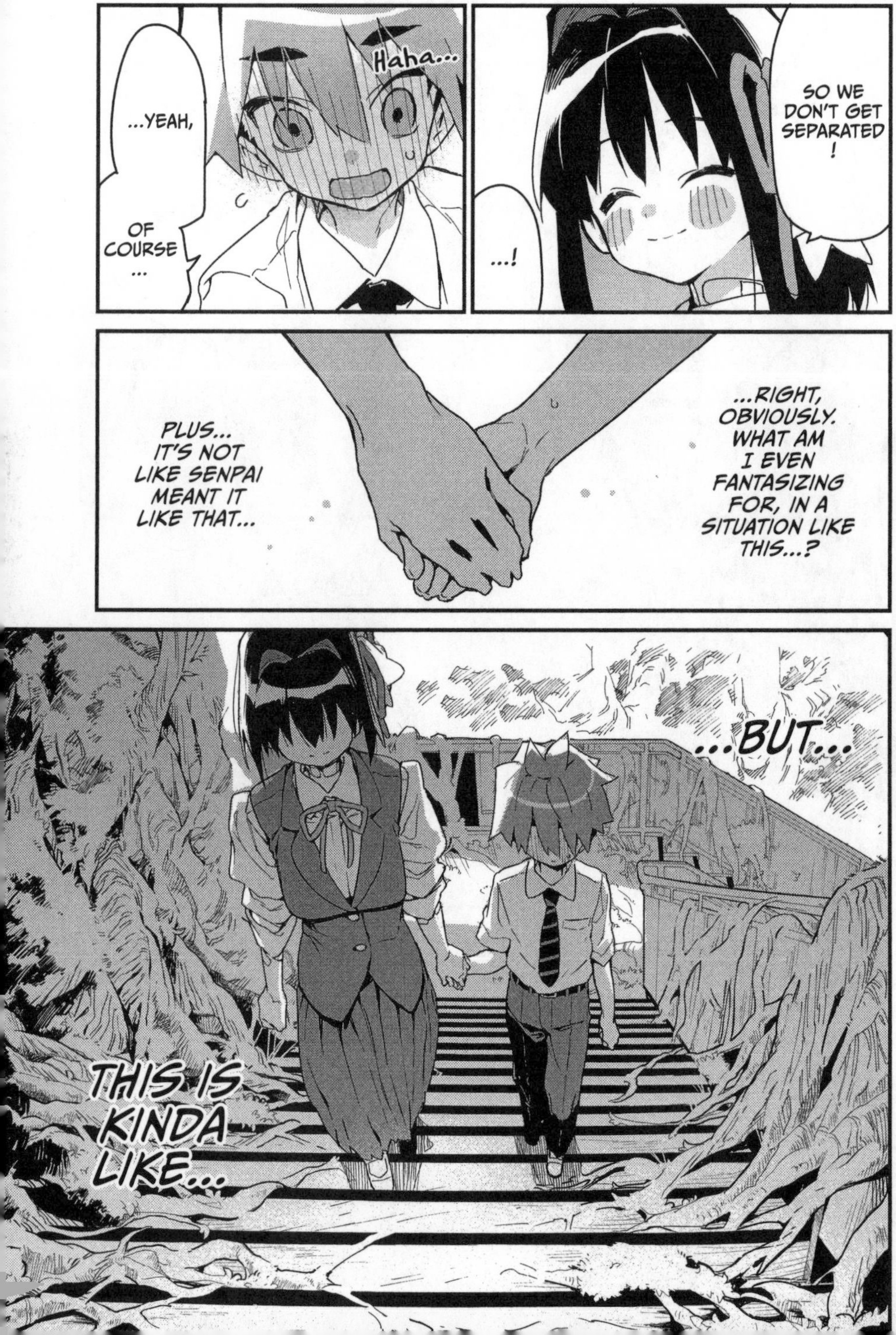
SO WE DON'T GET SEPARATED!
...!
Haha...
...YEAH,
OF COURSE...
...RIGHT, OBVIOUSLY. WHAT AM I EVEN FANTASIZING FOR, IN A SITUATION LIKE THIS...?
PLUS... IT'S NOT LIKE SENPAI MEANT IT LIKE THAT...
...BUT...
THIS IS KINDA LIKE...

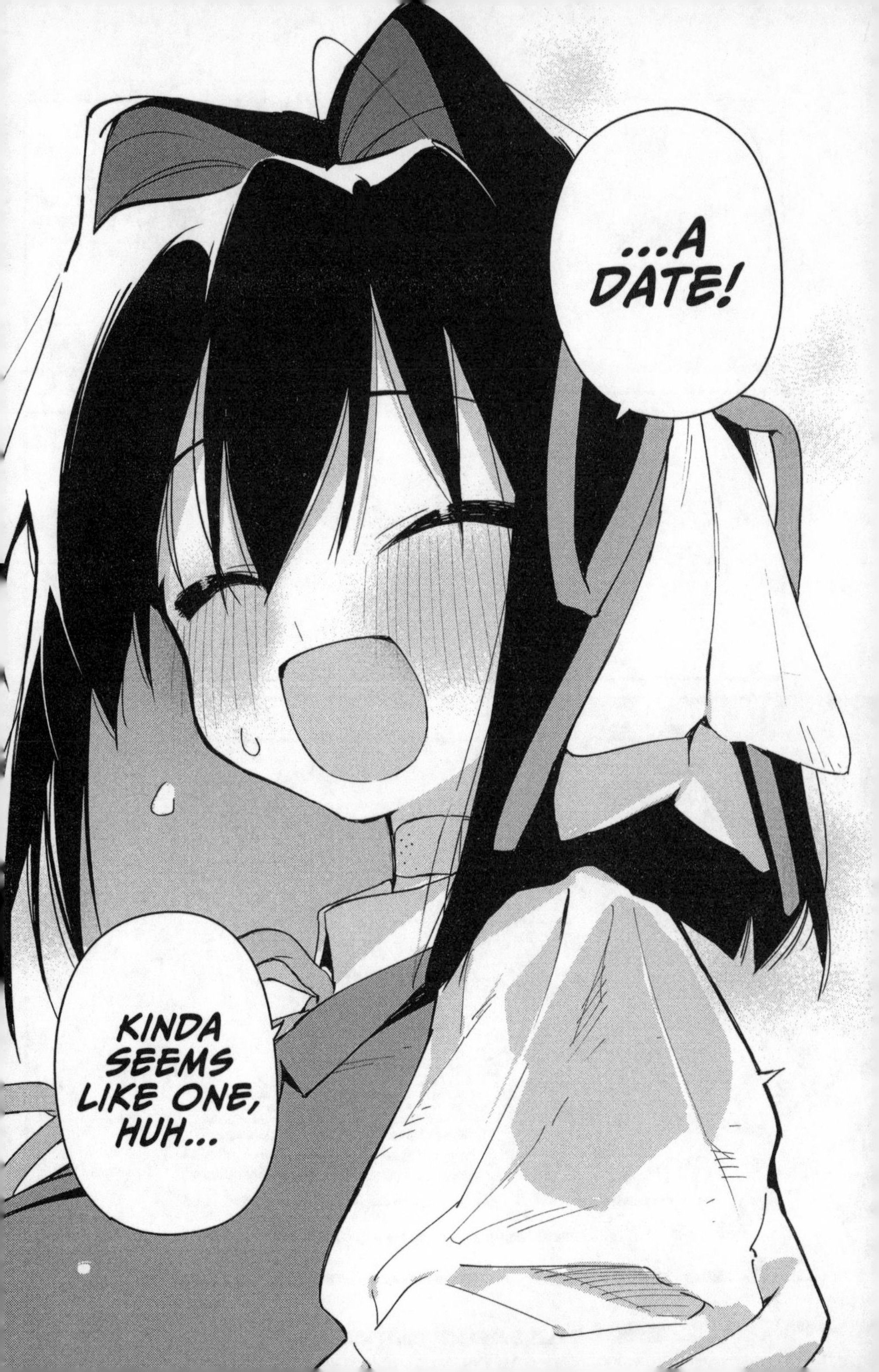
...A DATE!
KINDA SEEMS LIKE ONE, HUH...

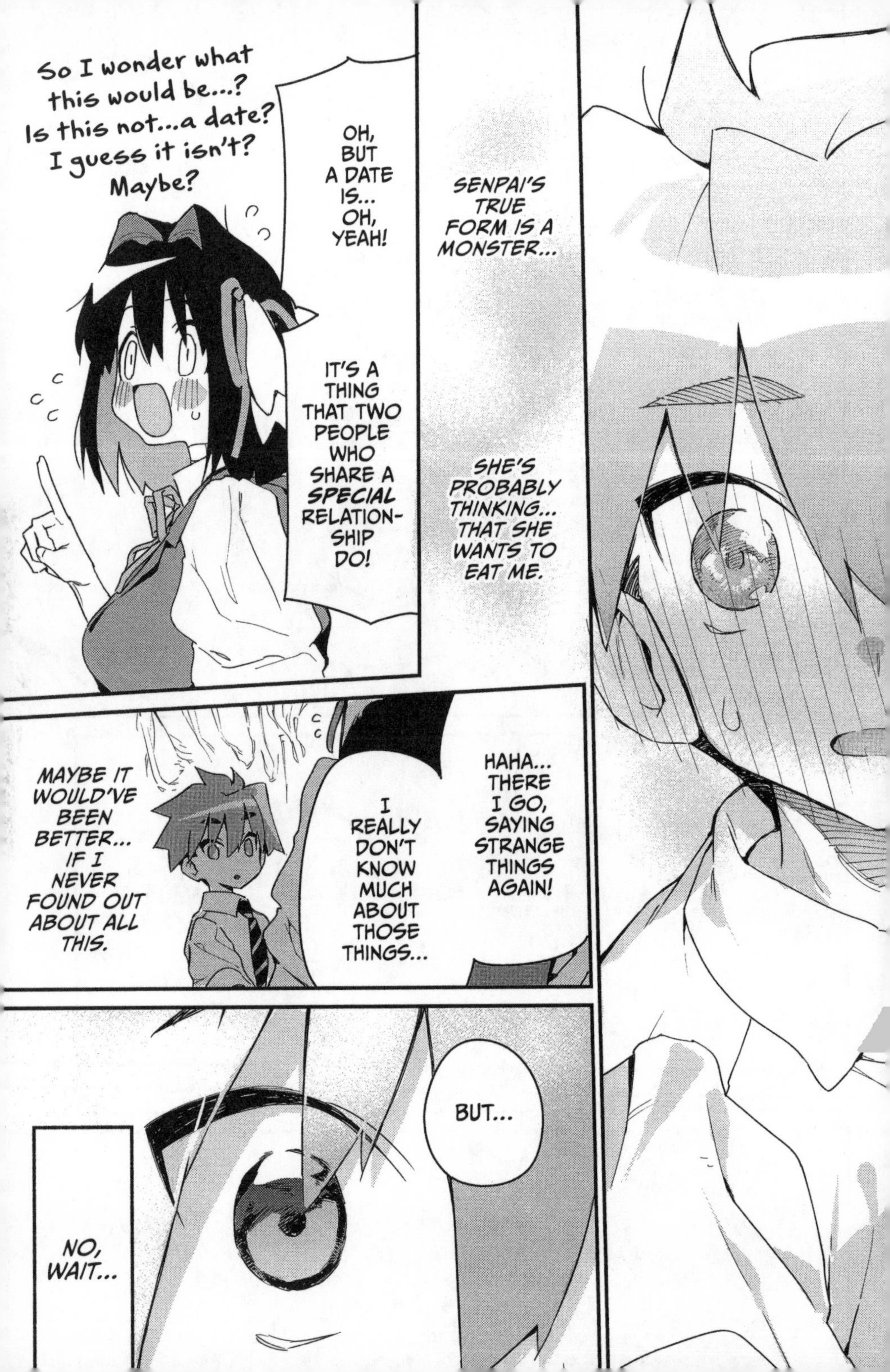
SENPAI'S TRUE FORM IS A MONSTER...
SHE'S PROBABLY THINKING... THAT SHE WANTS TO EAT ME.
So I wonder what this would be...? Is this not...a date? I guess it isn't? Maybe?
OH, BUT A DATE IS... OH, YEAH!
IT'S A THING THAT TWO PEOPLE WHO SHARE A SPECIAL RELATION-SHIP DO!
HAHA... THERE I GO, SAYING STRANGE THINGS AGAIN!
I REALLY DON'T KNOW MUCH ABOUT THOSE THINGS...
MAYBE IT WOULD'VE BEEN BETTER... IF I NEVER FOUND OUT ABOUT ALL THIS.
BUT...
NO, WAIT...

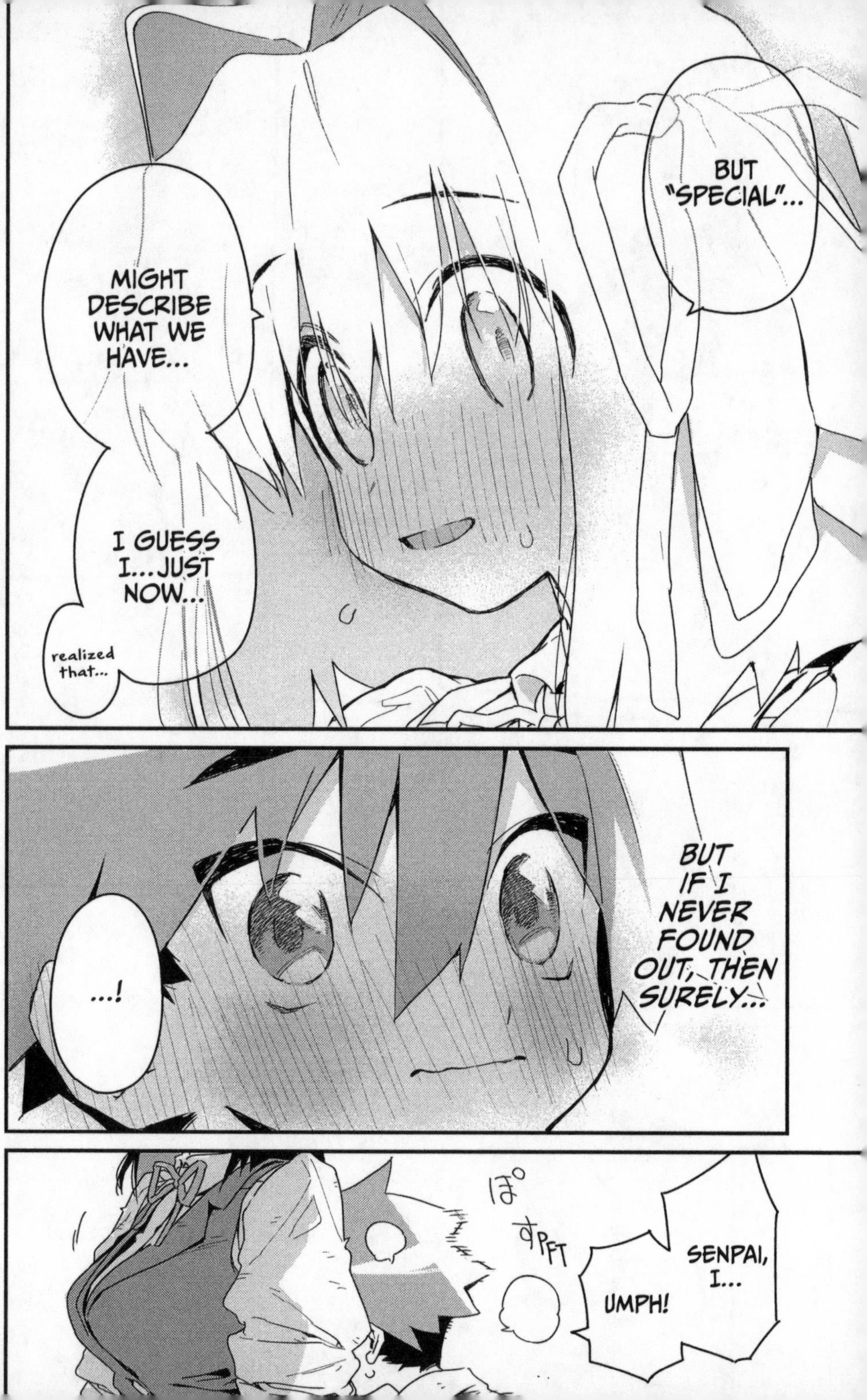
BUT "SPECIAL"...
MIGHT DESCRIBE WHAT WE HAVE...
I GUESS I...JUST NOW...
realized that...
BUT IF I NEVER FOUND OUT, THEN SURELY...
...!
SENPAI, I...
UMPH!
ぽす PFFT

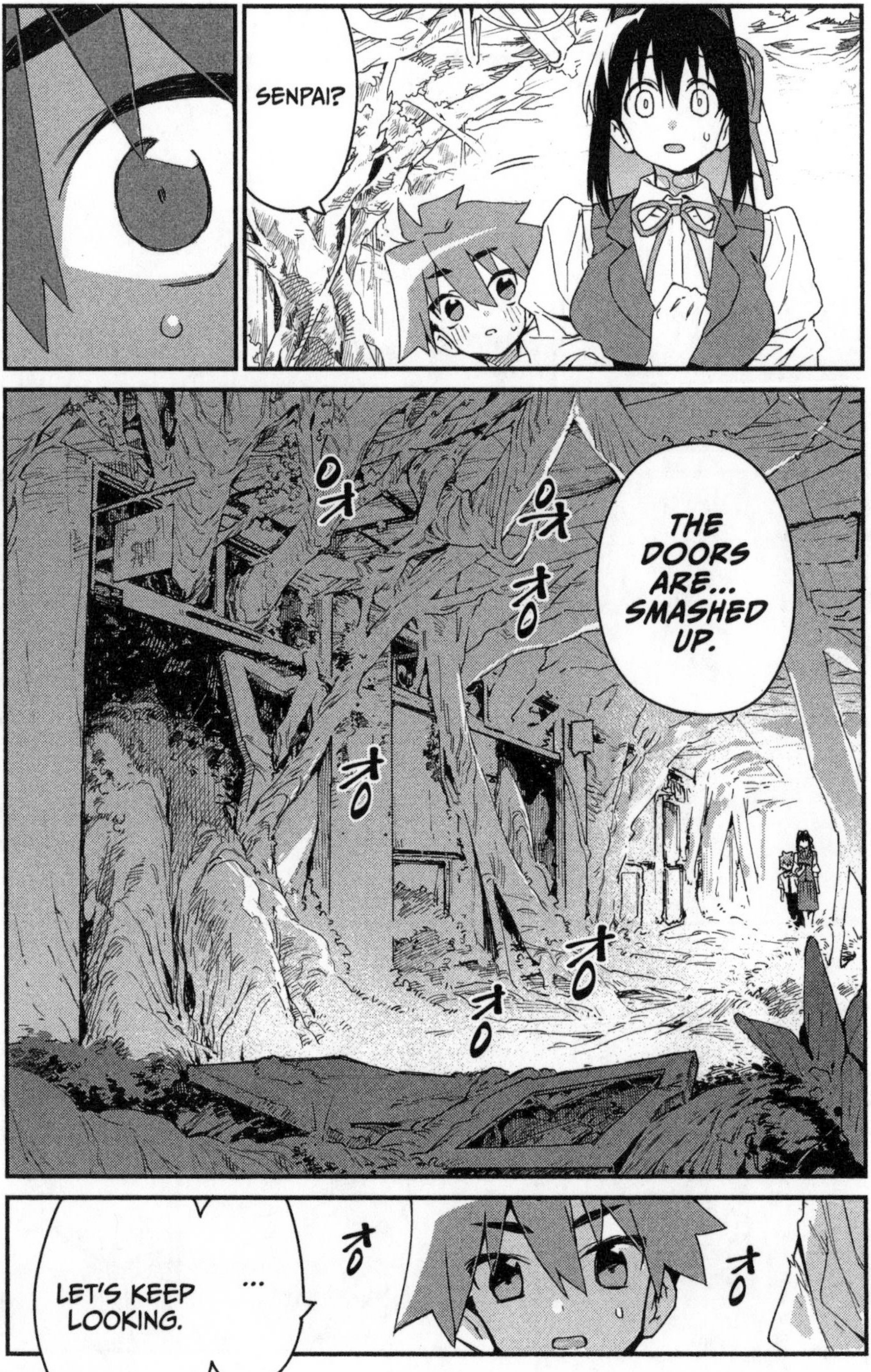
SENPAI?
THE DOORS ARE... SMASHED UP.
...
LET'S KEEP LOOKING.

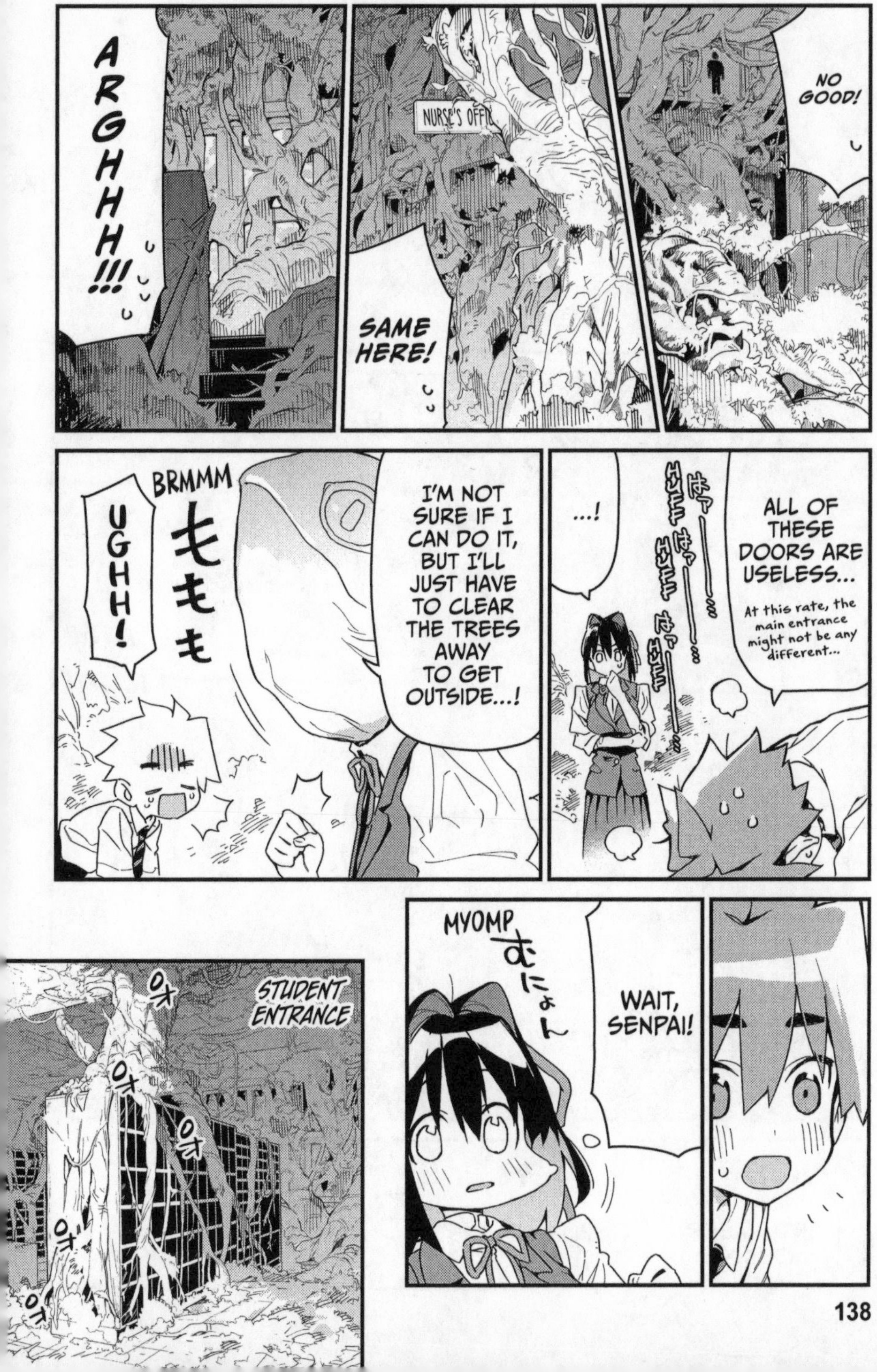
NO GOOD!
NURSE'S OFFIC
SAME HERE!
ARGHHHH!!!
ALL OF THESE DOORS ARE USELESS...
At this rate, the main entrance might not be any different...
HUFF HUFF HUFF
はァ――… はァ――… はァ――…
...!
I'M NOT SURE IF I CAN DO IT, BUT I'LL JUST HAVE TO CLEAR THE TREES AWAY TO GET OUTSIDE...!
BRMMM
もももも
UGHH!
WAIT, SENPAI!
MYOMP
むにょん
STUDENT ENTRANCE
オオオオオ

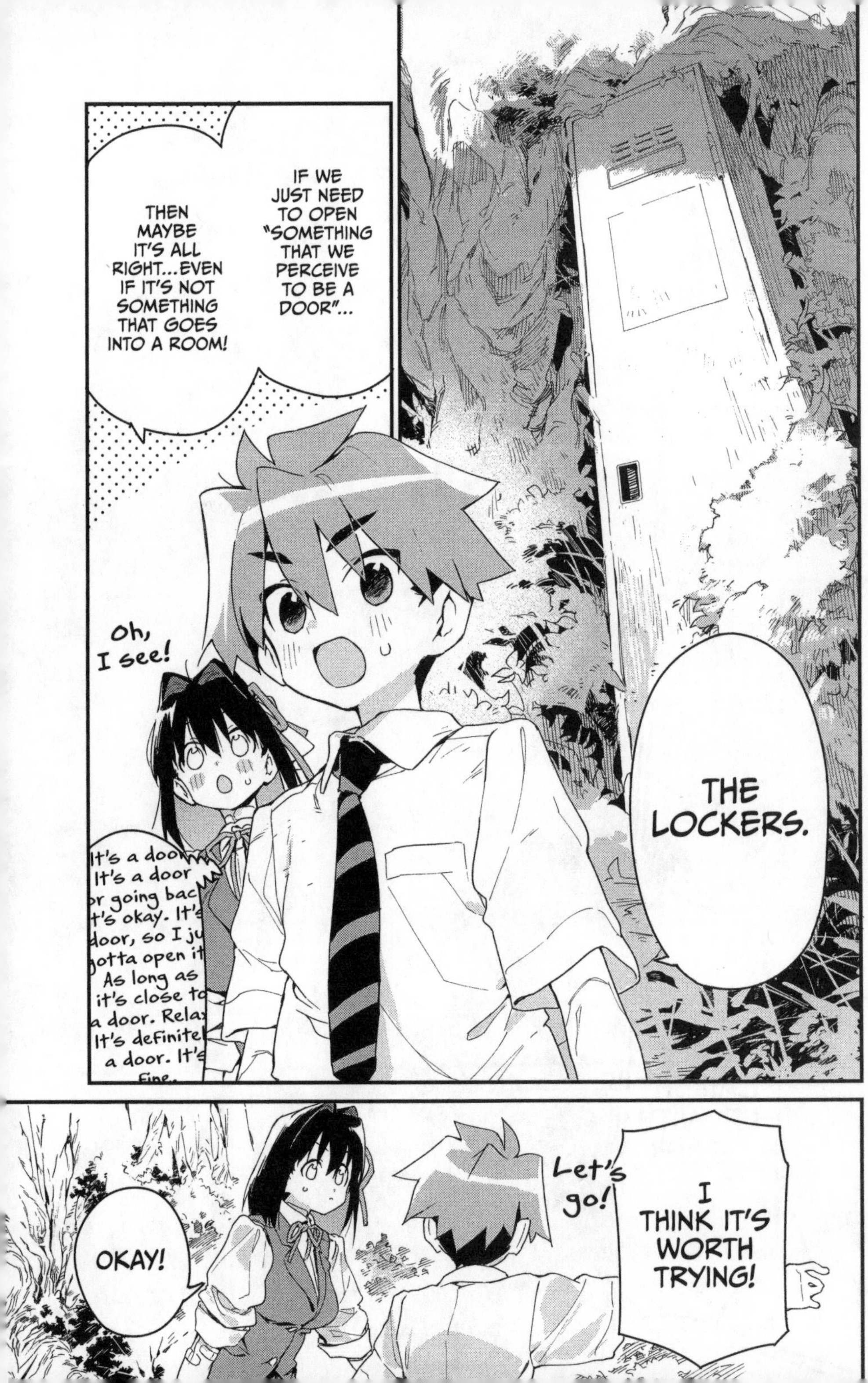
IF WE JUST NEED TO OPEN "SOMETHING THAT WE PERCEIVE TO BE A DOOR"...
THEN MAYBE IT'S ALL RIGHT...EVEN IF IT'S NOT SOMETHING THAT GOES INTO A ROOM!
THE LOCKERS.
Oh, I see!
It's a doo It's a door or going bac it's okay. It's door, so I ju gotta open it As long as it's close to a door. Rela It's definite a door. It's
I THINK IT'S WORTH TRYING!
Let's go!
OKAY!

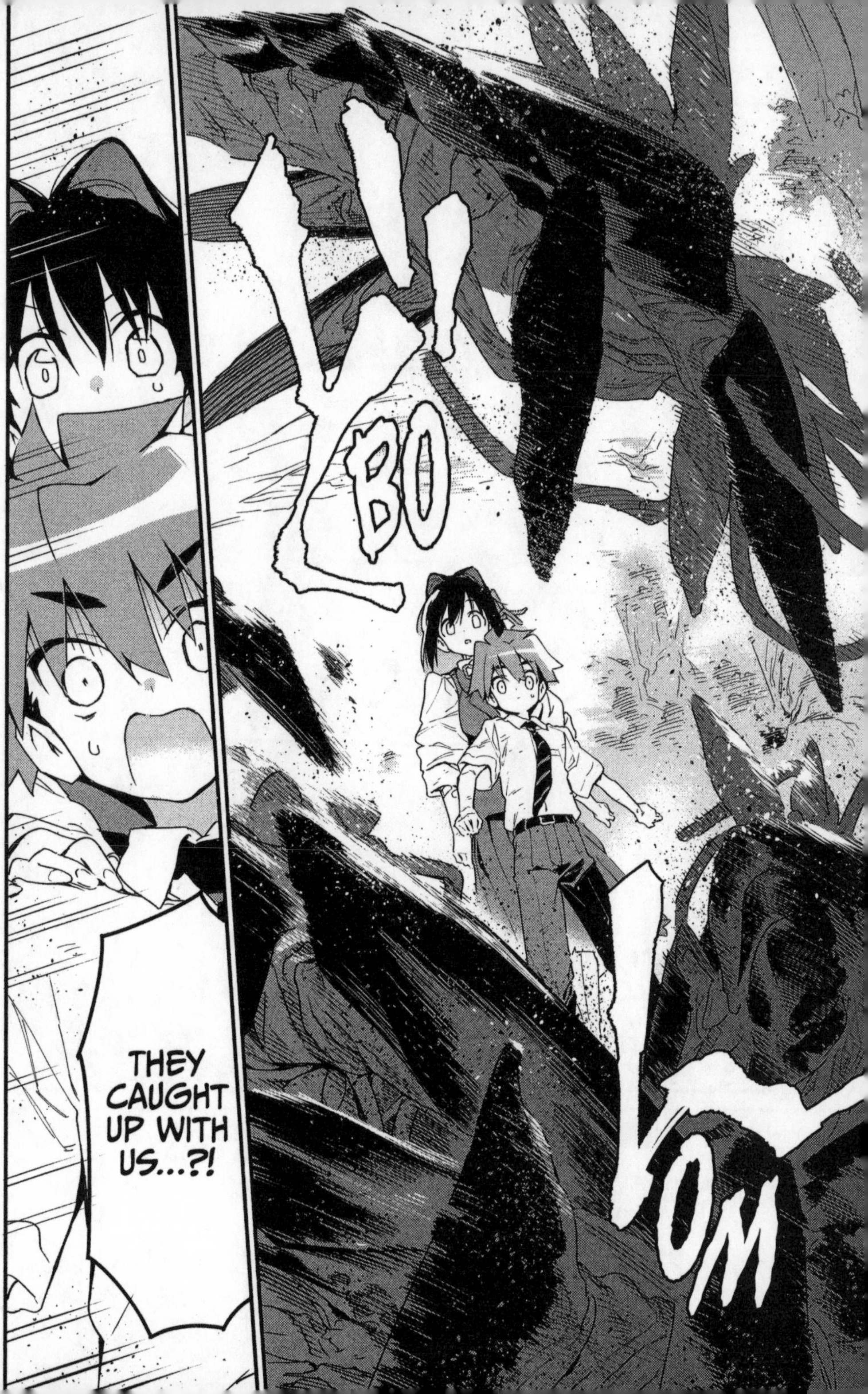
BO
OM
THEY CAUGHT UP WITH US...?!

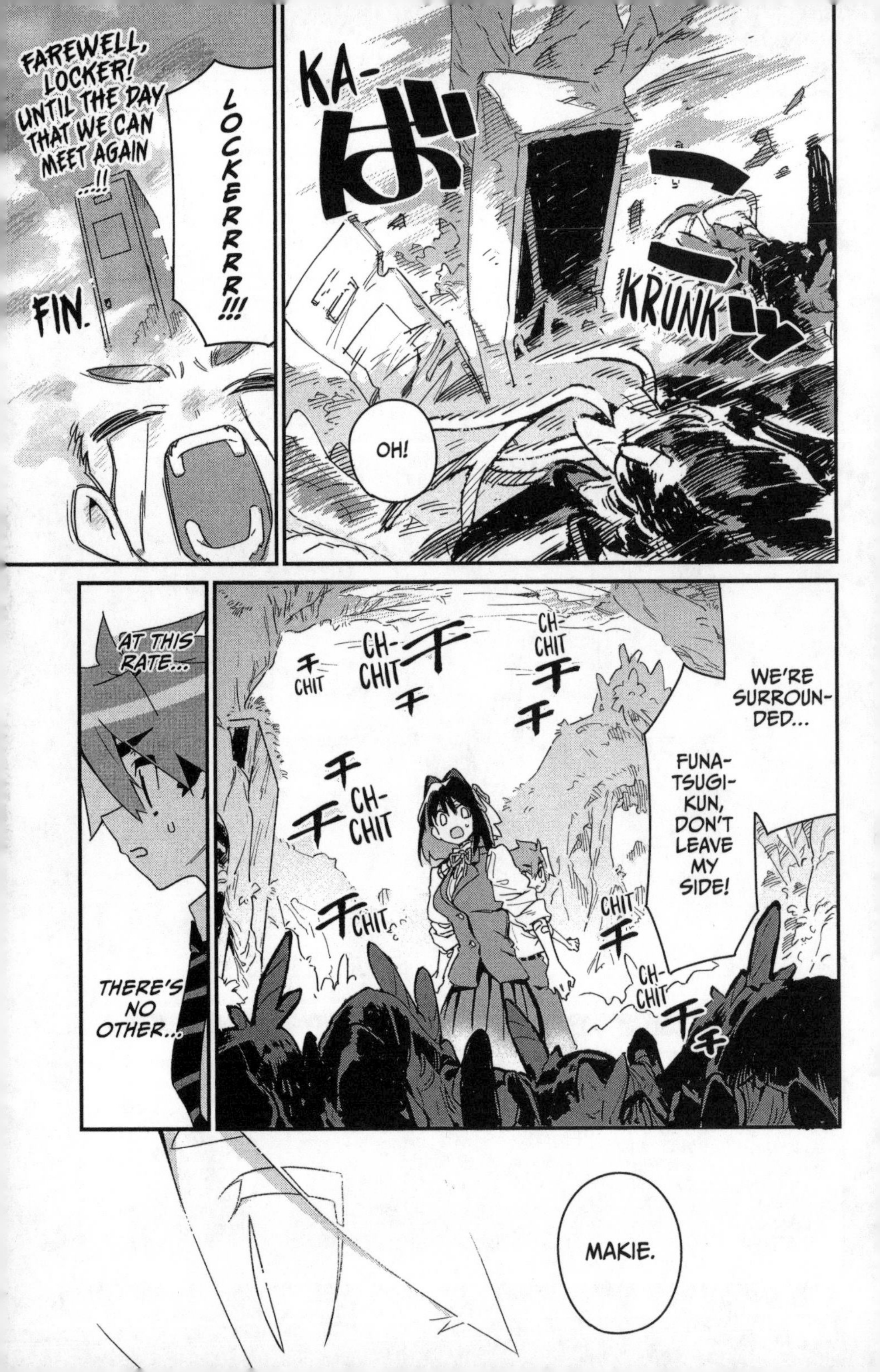
KA-
KRUNK
OH!
LOCKERRRR!!!
FAREWELL, LOCKER! UNTIL THE DAY THAT WE CAN MEET AGAIN ...!!
FIN.
WE'RE SURROUNDED...
FUNATSUGI-KUN, DON'T LEAVE MY SIDE!
CH-CHIT
CH-CHIT
CHIT
CH-CHIT
CHIT
CHIT
CH-CHIT
AT THIS RATE...
THERE'S NO OTHER...
MAKIE.

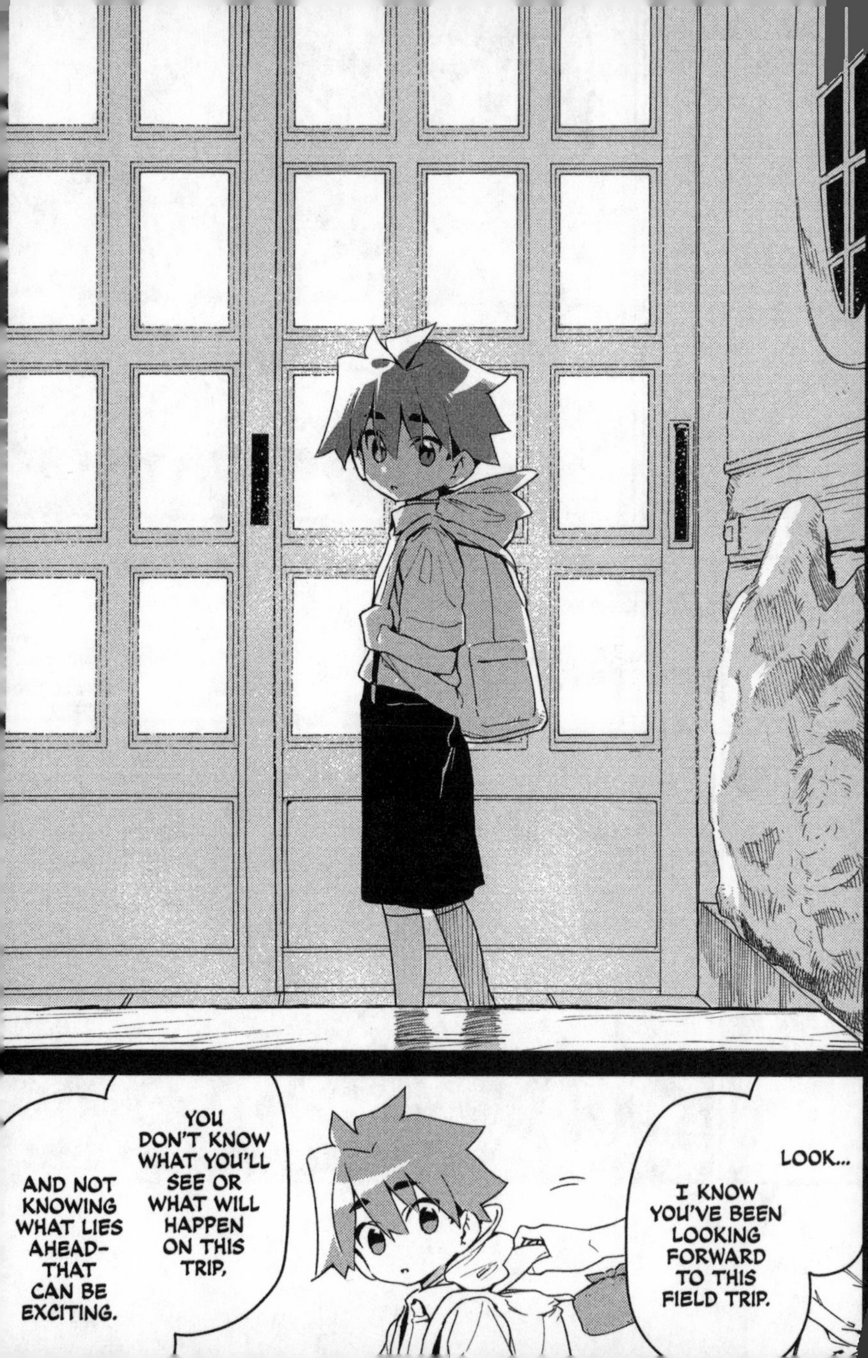
LOOK...
I KNOW YOU'VE BEEN LOOKING FORWARD TO THIS FIELD TRIP.
YOU DON'T KNOW WHAT YOU'LL SEE OR WHAT WILL HAPPEN ON THIS TRIP,
AND NOT KNOWING WHAT LIES AHEAD—THAT CAN BE EXCITING.

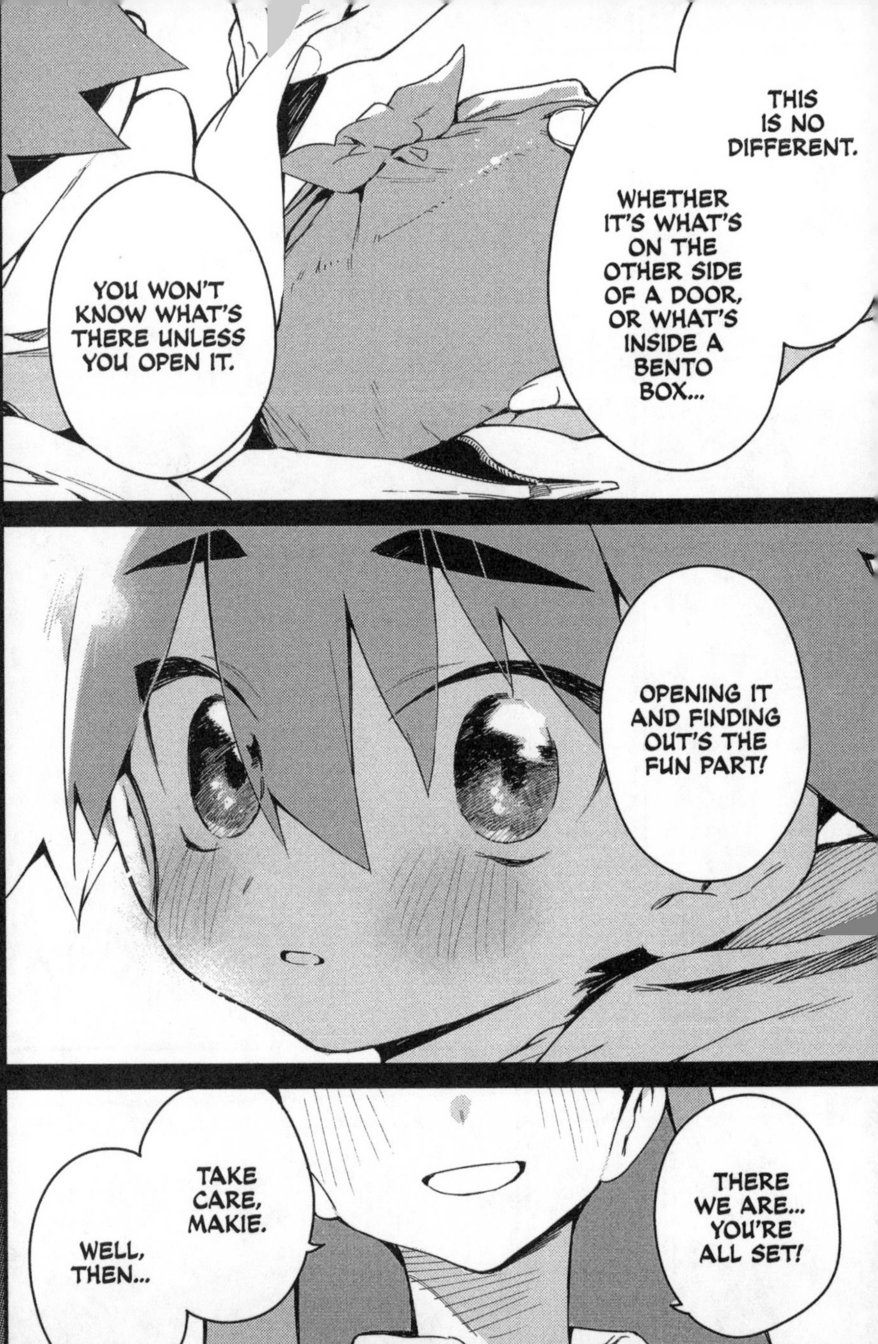
THIS IS NO DIFFERENT.
WHETHER IT'S WHAT'S ON THE OTHER SIDE OF A DOOR, OR WHAT'S INSIDE A BENTO BOX...
YOU WON'T KNOW WHAT'S THERE UNLESS YOU OPEN IT.
OPENING IT AND FINDING OUT'S THE FUN PART!
THERE WE ARE... YOU'RE ALL SET!
TAKE CARE, MAKIE.
WELL, THEN...

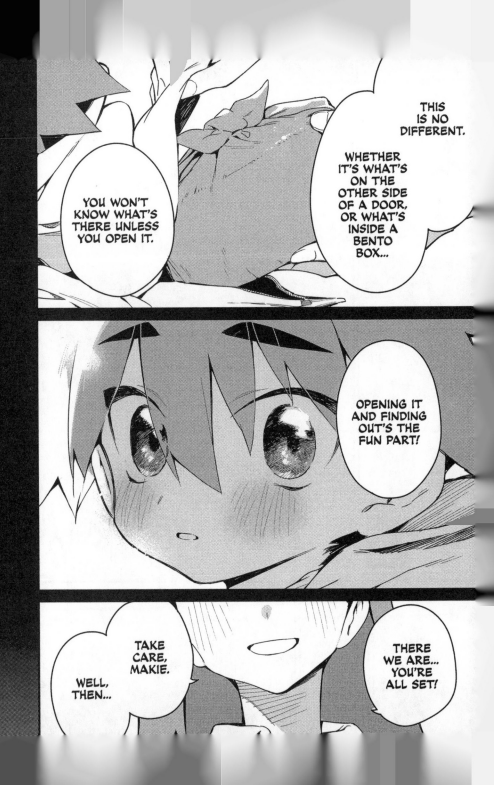

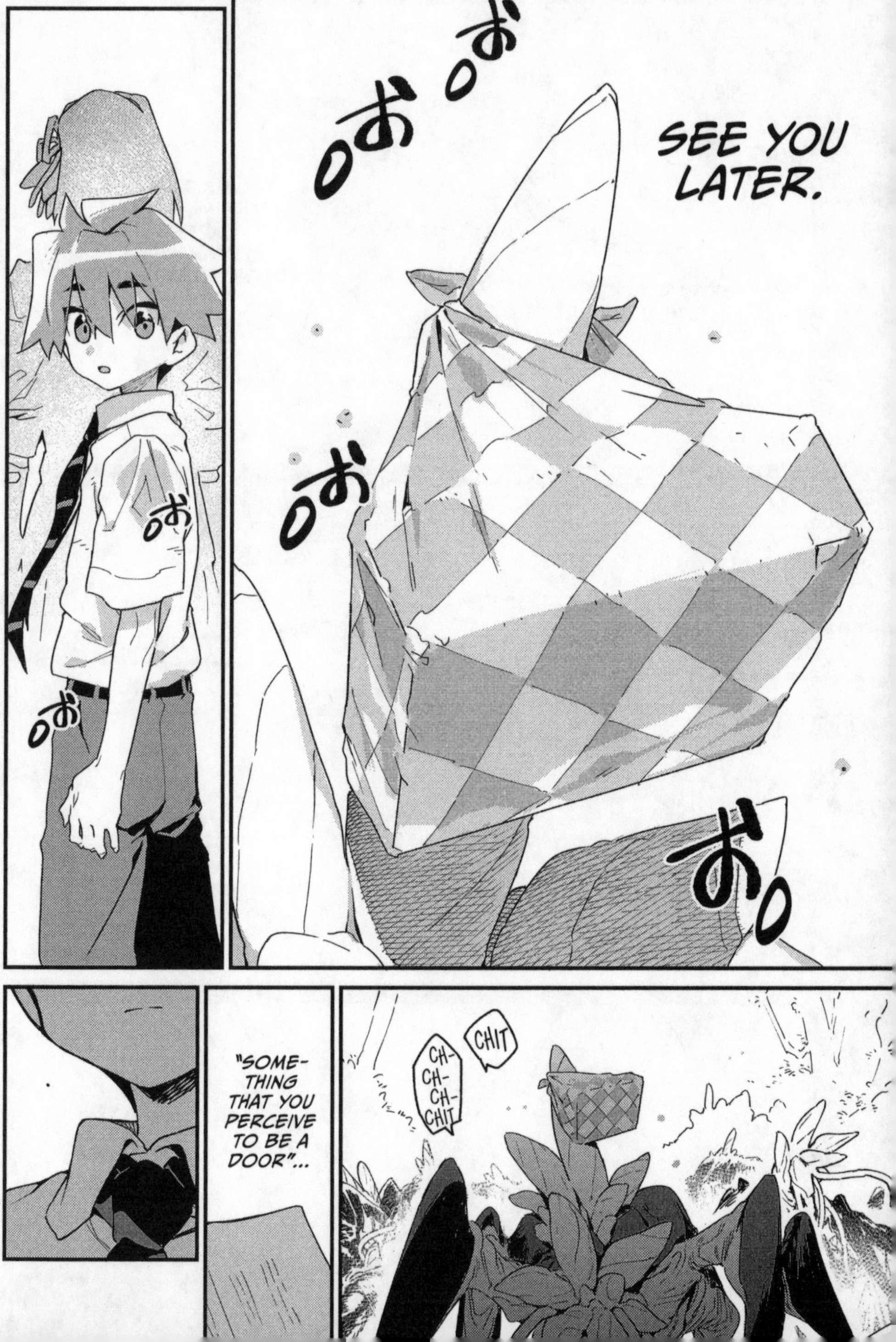
SEE YOU LATER.
CHIT
CH-CH-CH-CHIT
"SOMETHING THAT YOU PERCEIVE TO BE A DOOR"...

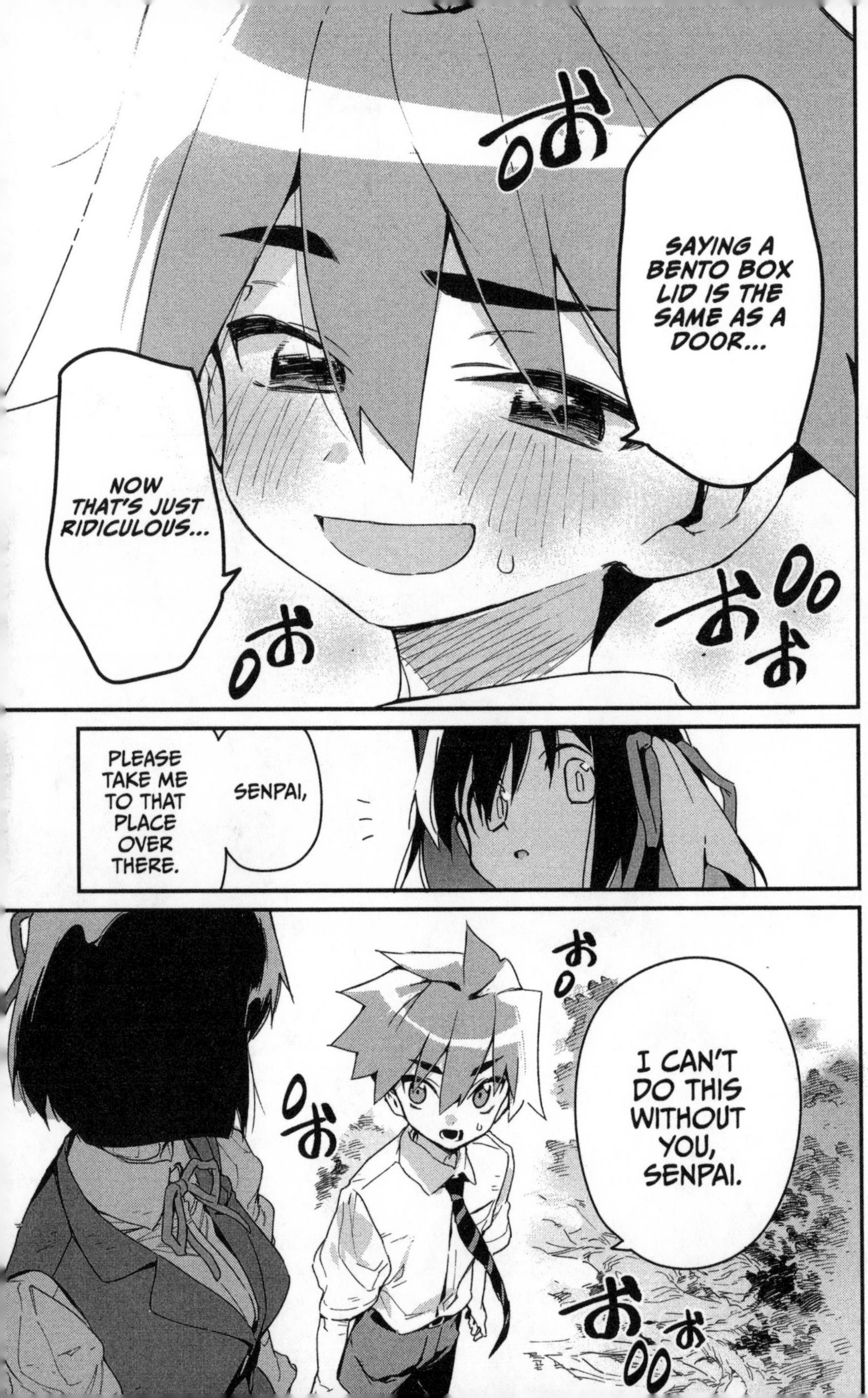
SAYING A BENTO BOX LID IS THE SAME AS A DOOR...
NOW THAT'S JUST RIDICULOUS...
SENPAI,
PLEASE TAKE ME TO THAT PLACE OVER THERE.
I CAN'T DO THIS WITHOUT YOU, SENPAI.

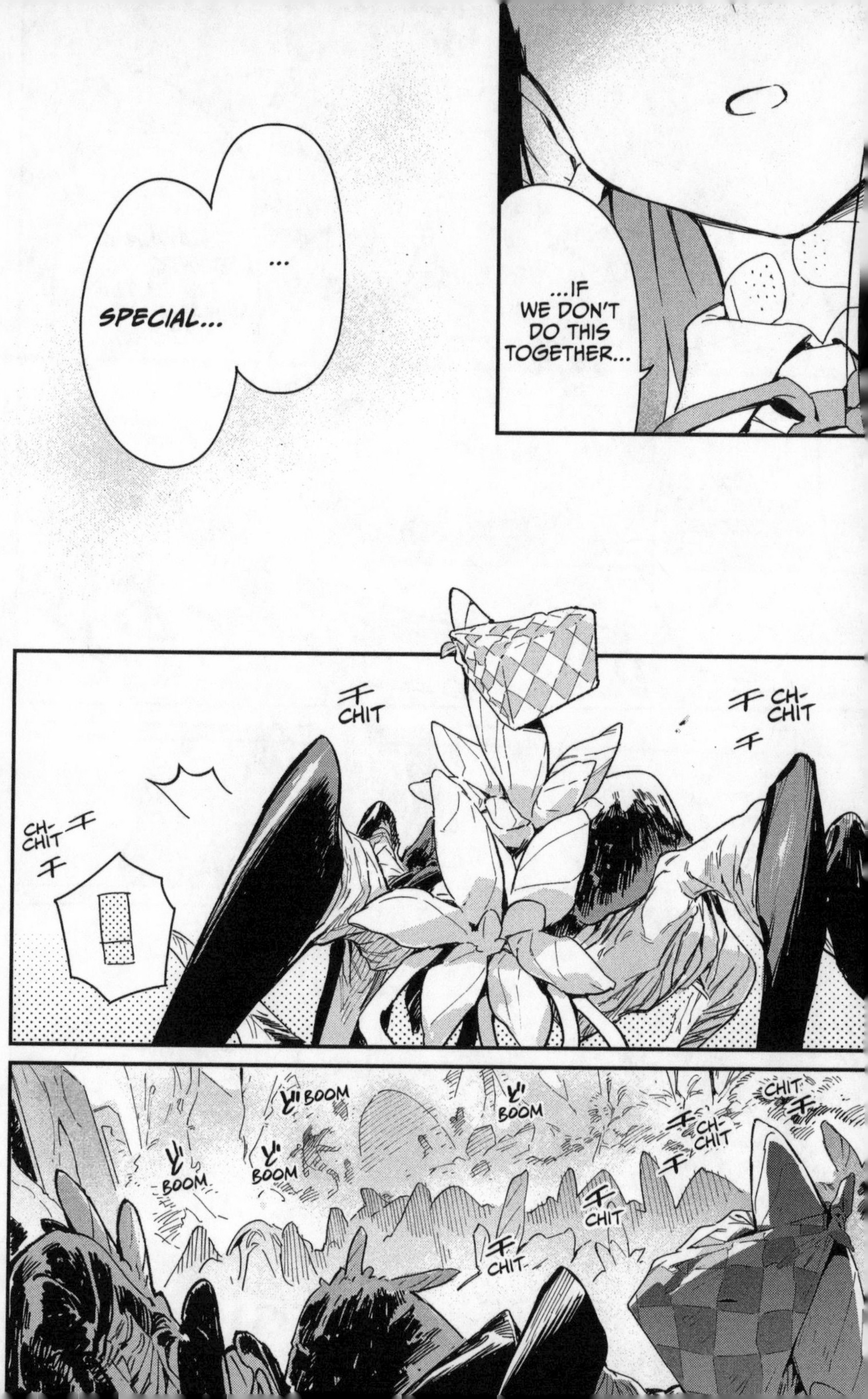
...IF WE DON'T DO THIS TOGETHER...
...
SPECIAL...
チ CH-CHIT
チ
チ CHIT
CH-CHIT チ
チ
CHIT チ
チ CH-CHIT
チ
チ CHIT
チ CHIT
ど BOOM
ど BOOM
ど BOOM
ど BOOM

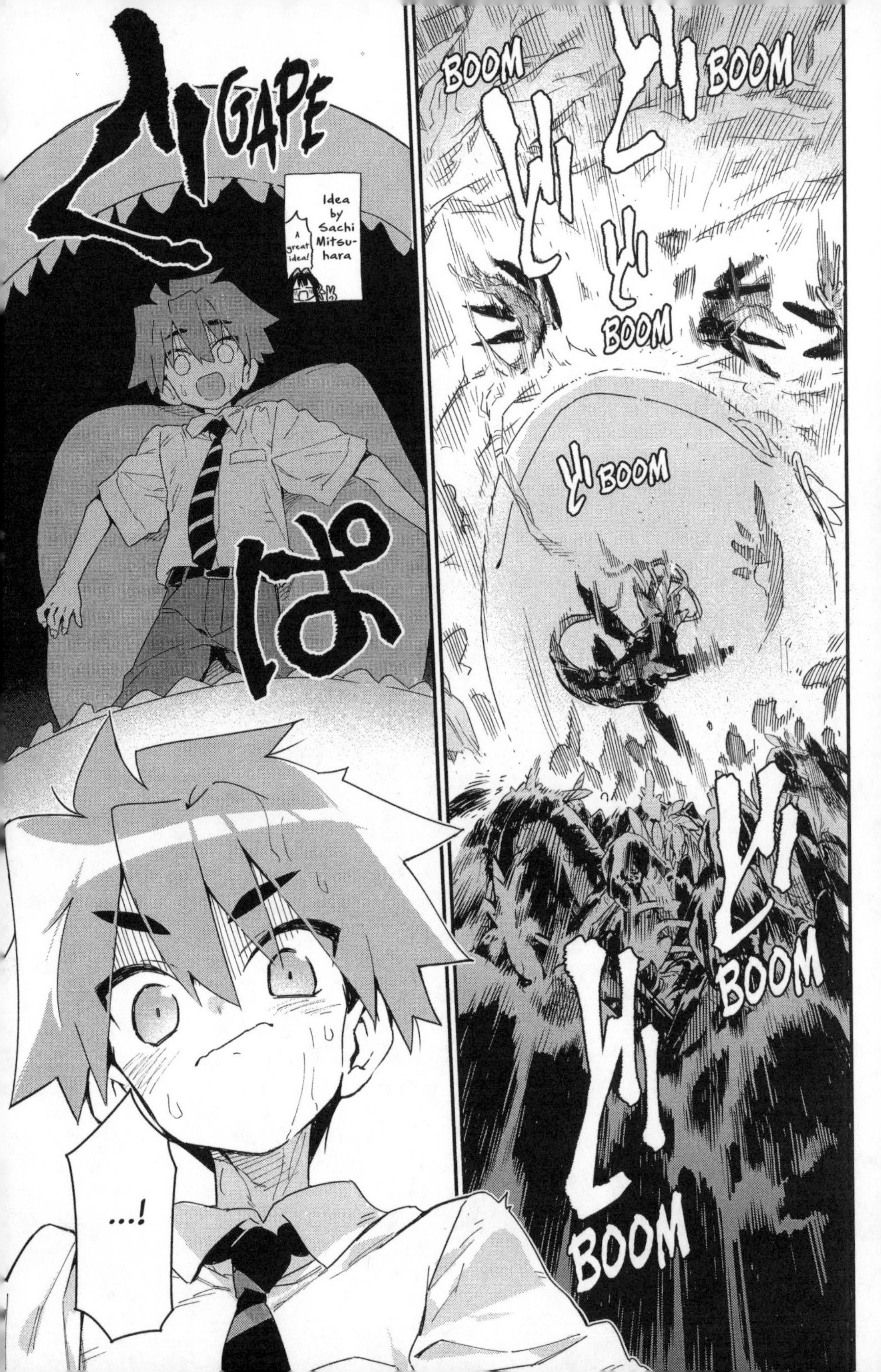
BOOM
BOOM
BOOM
BOOM
BOOM
BOOM
GAPE
Idea by Sachi Mitsu-hara
A great idea!
ぱ
...!

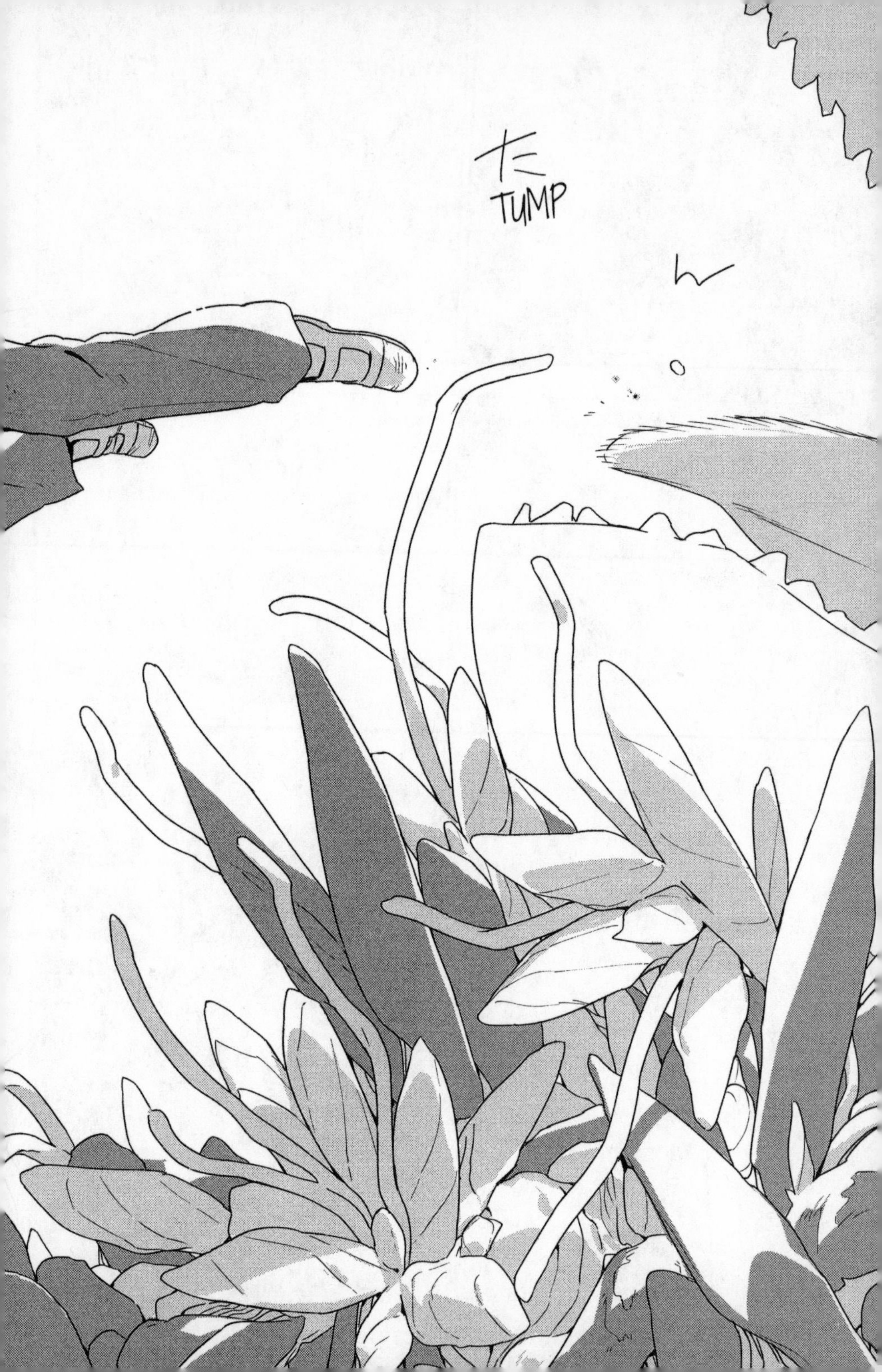
TUMP

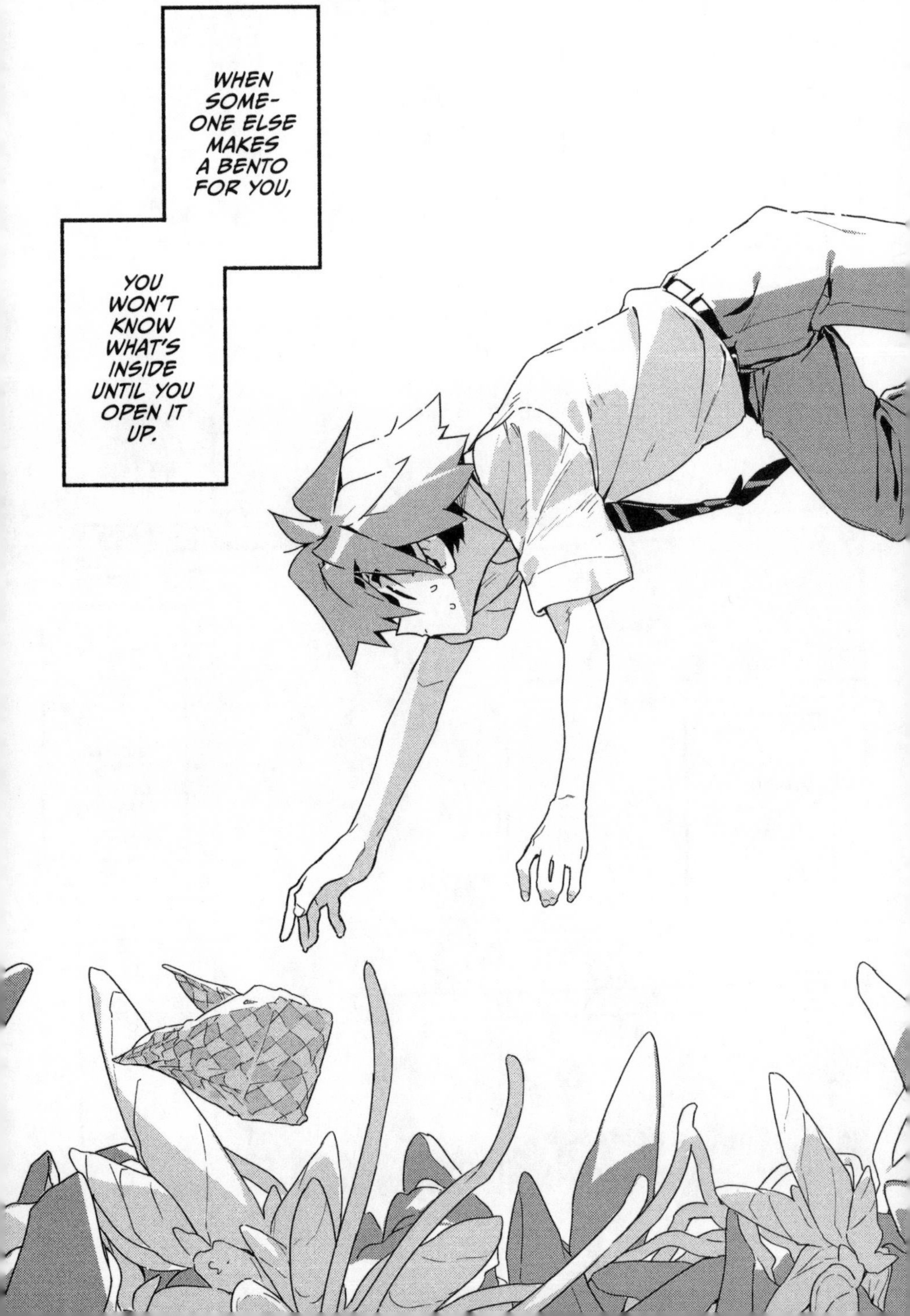
WHEN SOME-ONE ELSE MAKES A BENTO FOR YOU,
YOU WON'T KNOW WHAT'S INSIDE UNTIL YOU OPEN IT UP.

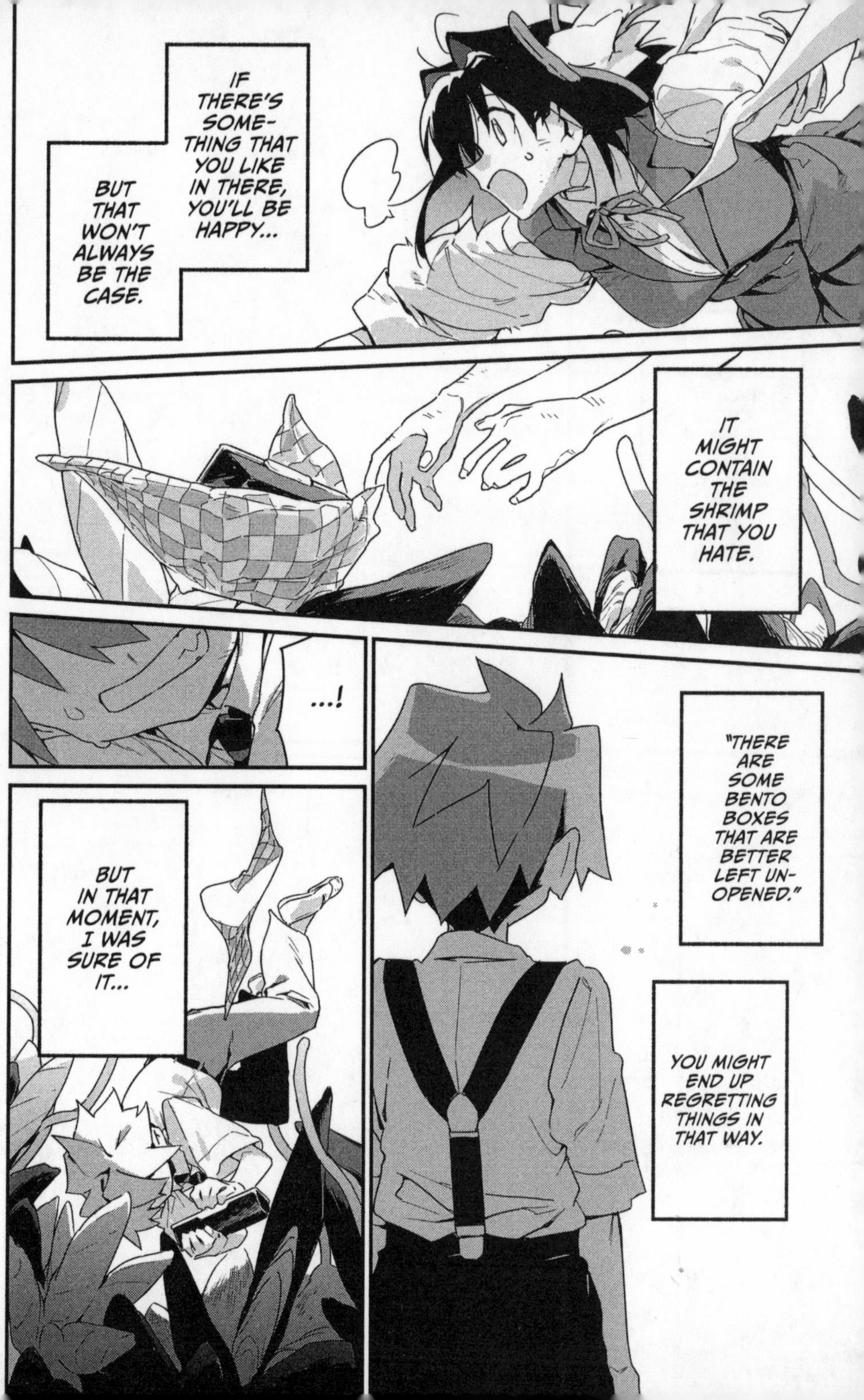
IF THERE'S SOME-THING THAT YOU LIKE IN THERE, YOU'LL BE HAPPY...
BUT THAT WON'T ALWAYS BE THE CASE.
IT MIGHT CONTAIN THE SHRIMP THAT YOU HATE.
"THERE ARE SOME BENTO BOXES THAT ARE BETTER LEFT UN-OPENED."
YOU MIGHT END UP REGRETTING THINGS IN THAT WAY.
...!
BUT IN THAT MOMENT, I WAS SURE OF IT...

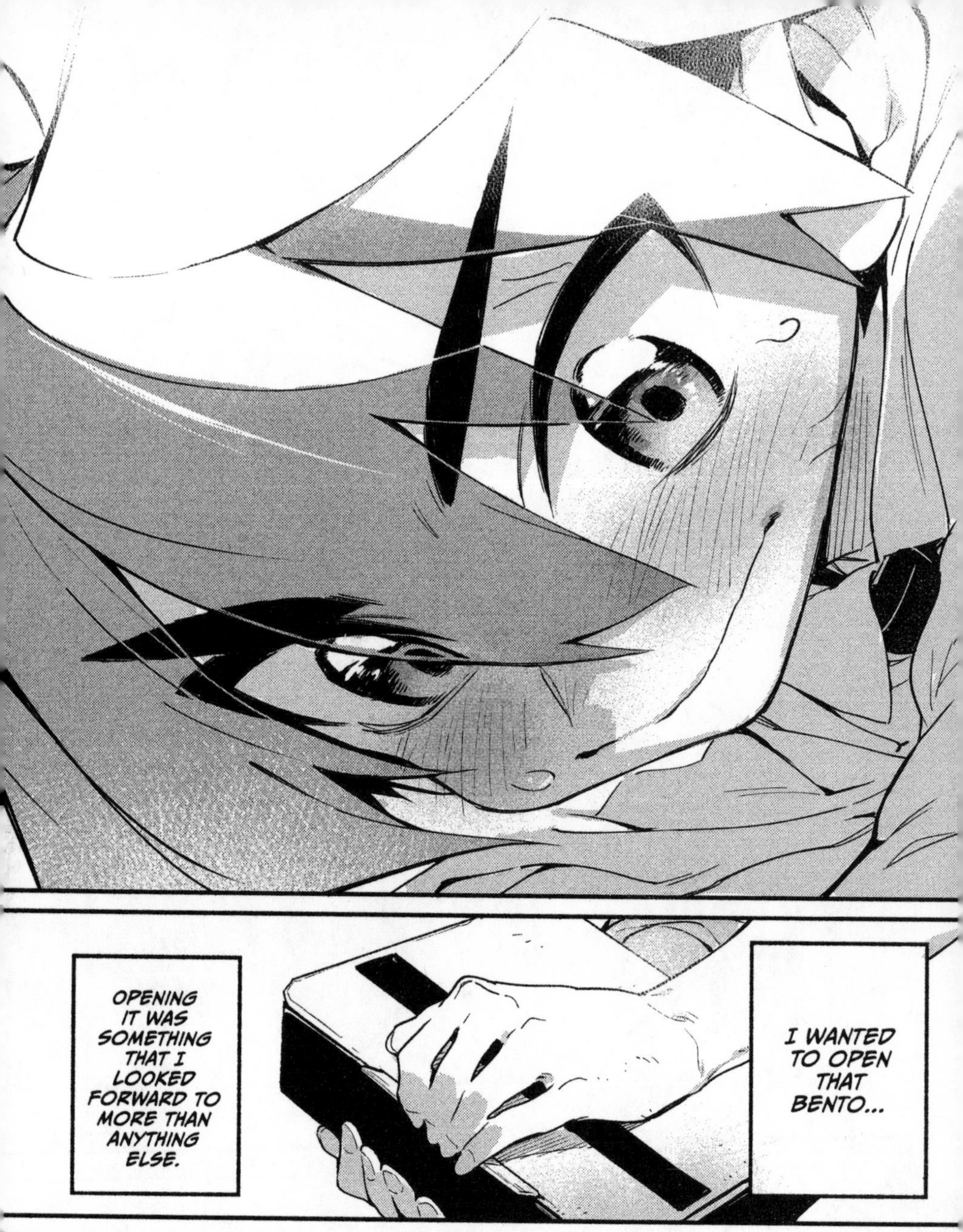
I WANTED TO OPEN THAT BENTO...
OPENING IT WAS SOMETHING THAT I LOOKED FORWARD TO MORE THAN ANYTHING ELSE.
KA-POP

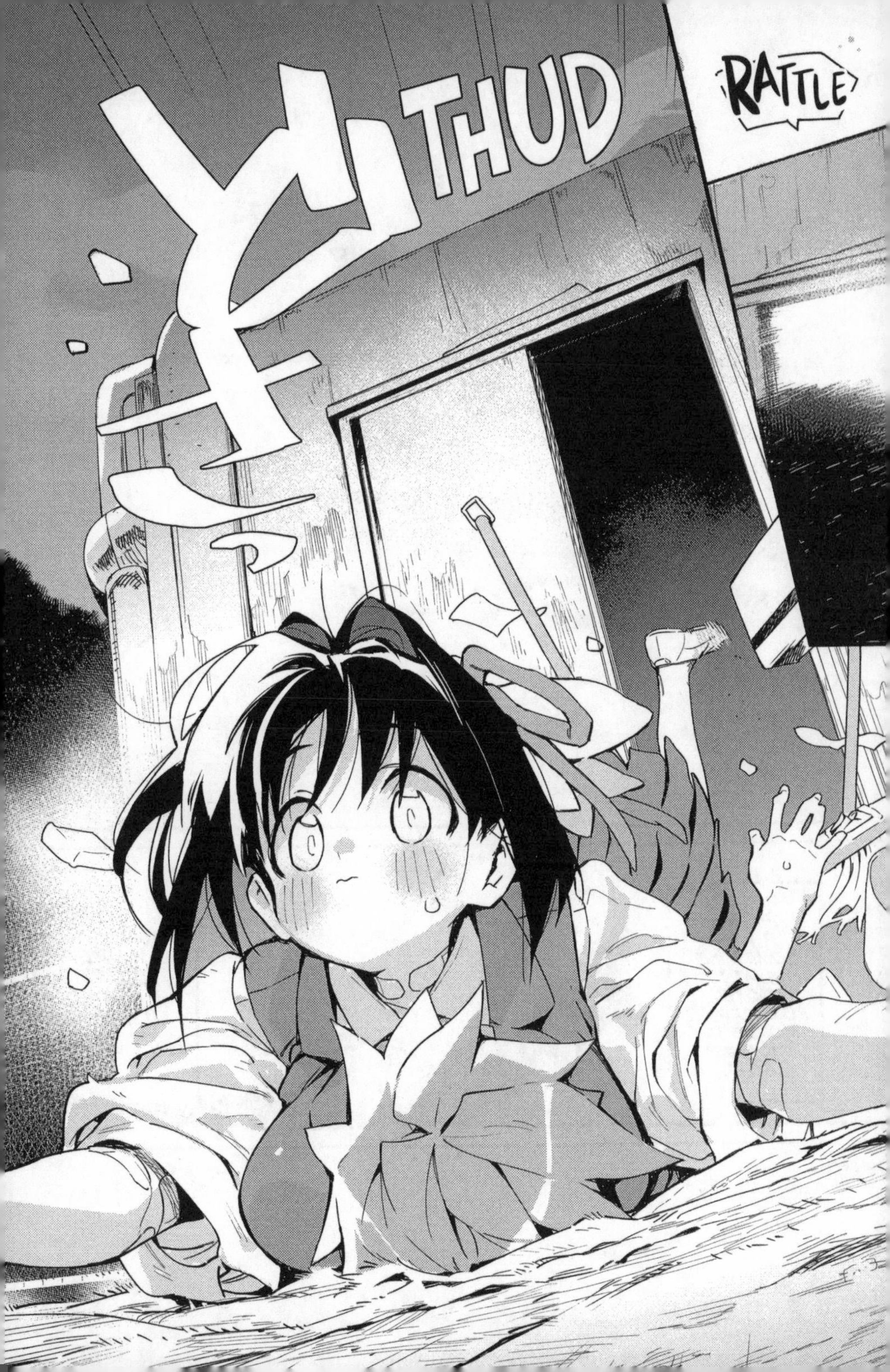
RATTLE
THUD

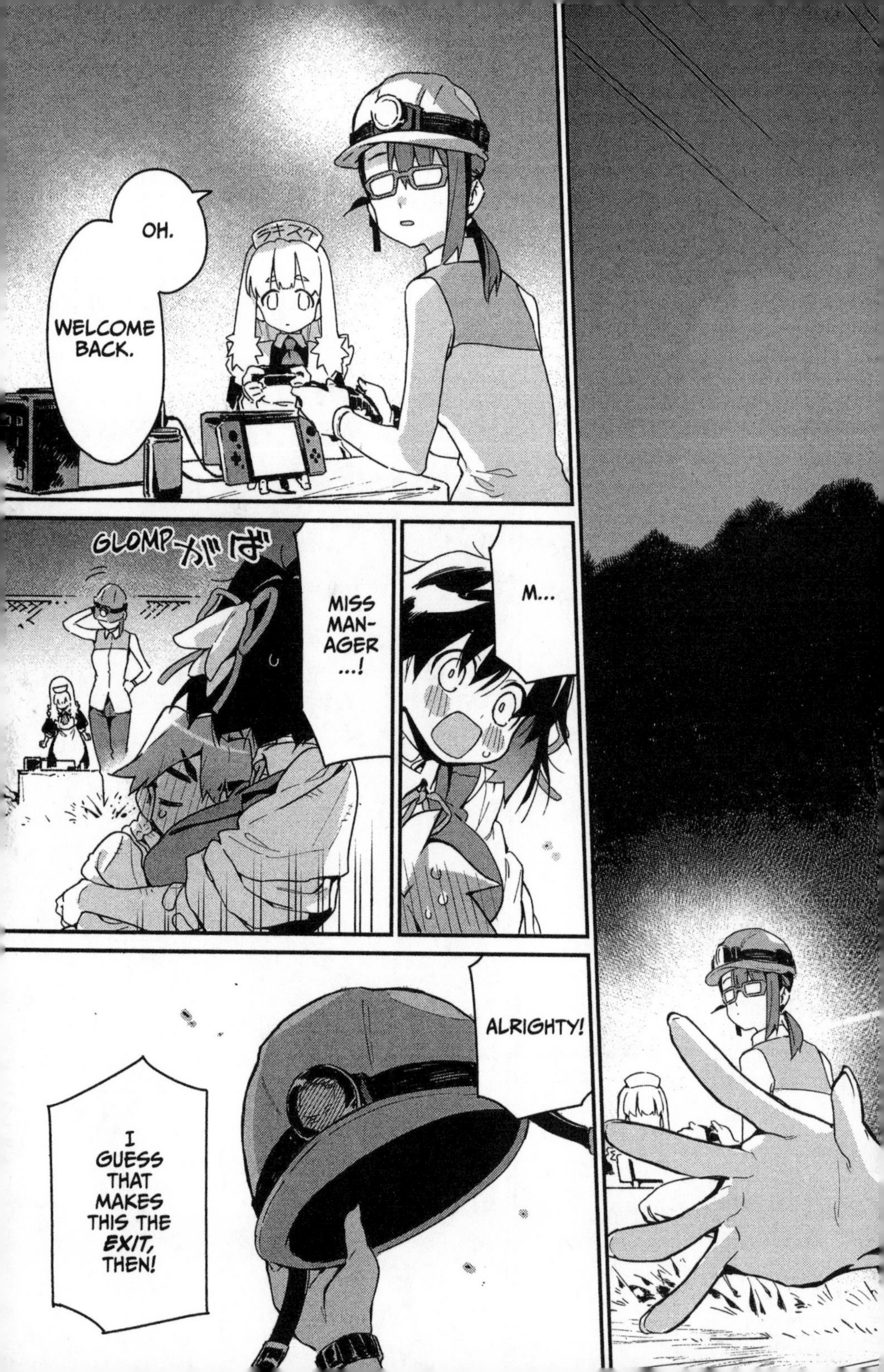
OH.
WELCOME BACK.
ラキスケ
M...
MISS MAN-AGER ...!
GLOMP がば
ALRIGHTY!
I GUESS THAT MAKES THIS THE *EXIT,* THEN!

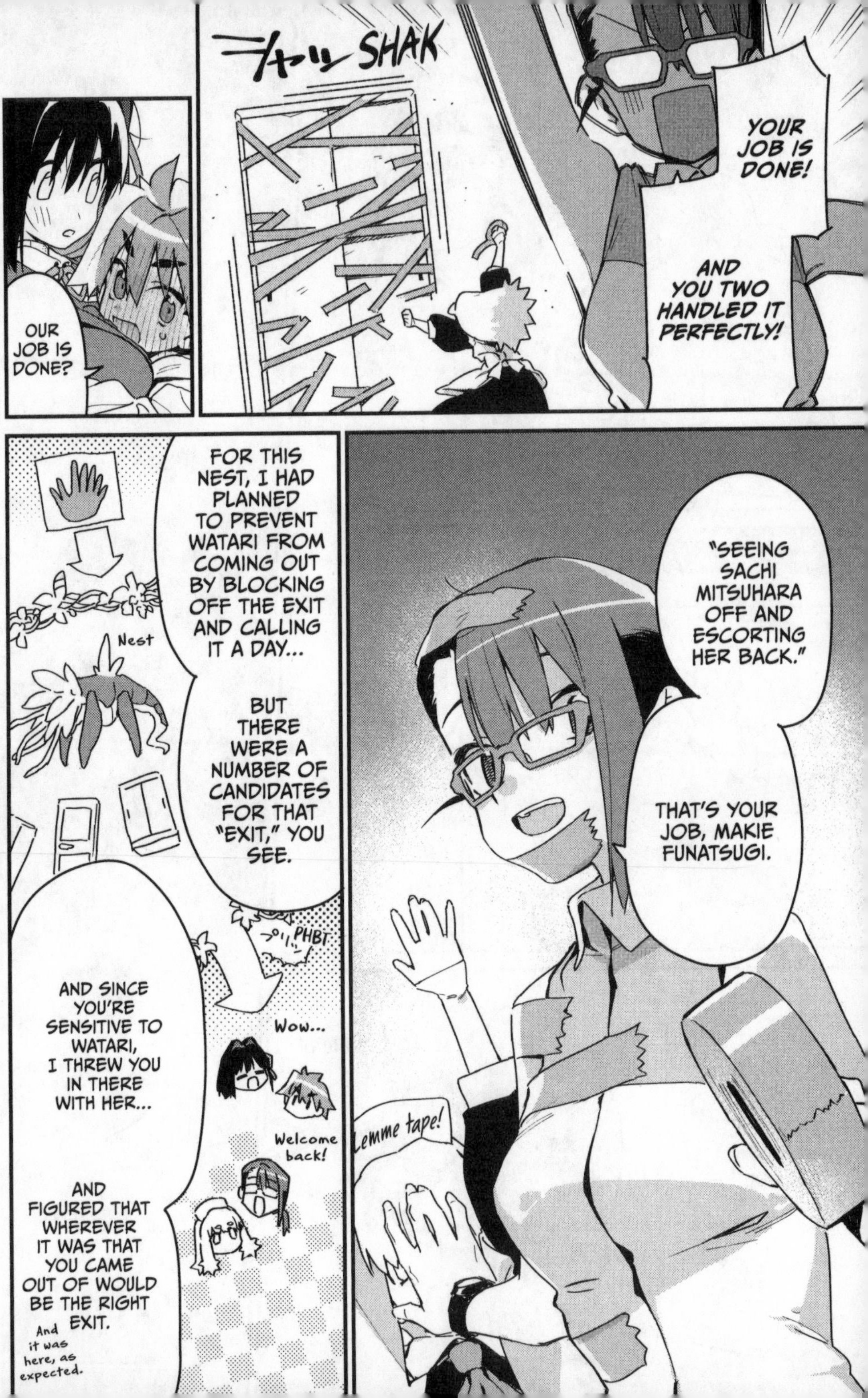
YOUR JOB IS DONE!
AND YOU TWO HANDLED IT PERFECTLY!
SHAK
OUR JOB IS DONE?
"SEEING SACHI MITSUHARA OFF AND ESCORTING HER BACK."
THAT'S YOUR JOB, MAKIE FUNATSUGI.
Lemme tape!
FOR THIS NEST, I HAD PLANNED TO PREVENT WATARI FROM COMING OUT BY BLOCKING OFF THE EXIT AND CALLING IT A DAY...
Nest
BUT THERE WERE A NUMBER OF CANDIDATES FOR THAT "EXIT," YOU SEE.
PHBT
AND SINCE YOU'RE SENSITIVE TO WATARI, I THREW YOU IN THERE WITH HER...
Wow...
Welcome back!
AND FIGURED THAT WHEREVER IT WAS THAT YOU CAME OUT OF WOULD BE THE RIGHT EXIT.
And it was here, as expected.

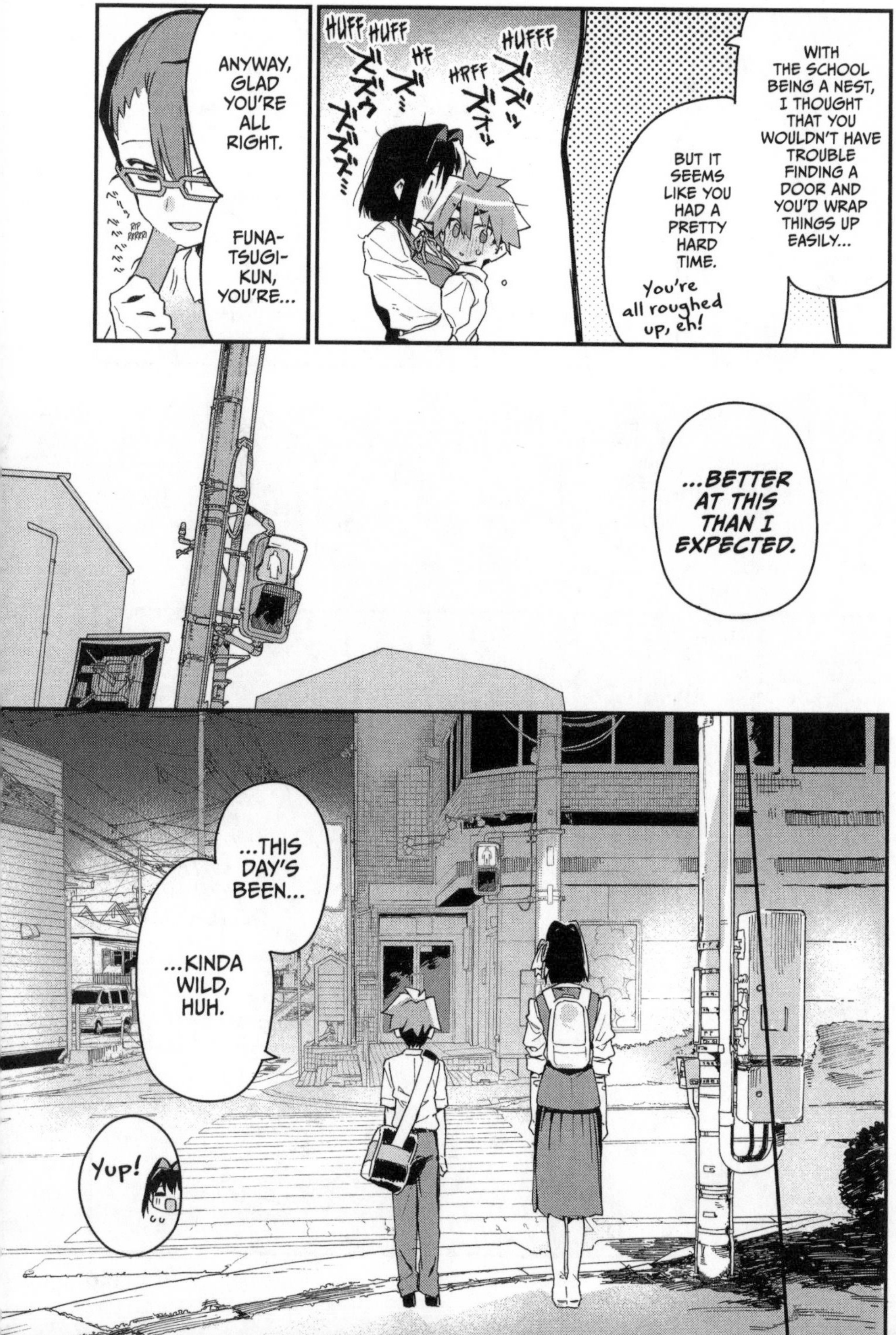
WITH THE SCHOOL BEING A NEST, I THOUGHT THAT YOU WOULDN'T HAVE TROUBLE FINDING A DOOR AND YOU'D WRAP THINGS UP EASILY...
BUT IT SEEMS LIKE YOU HAD A PRETTY HARD TIME.
You're all roughed up, eh!
HUFFF
HRFF
HF
HUFF HUFF
ANYWAY, GLAD YOU'RE ALL RIGHT.
FUNA-TSUGI-KUN, YOU'RE...
RIP RRRRR
...BETTER AT THIS THAN I EXPECTED.
...THIS DAY'S BEEN...
...KINDA WILD, HUH.
Yup!

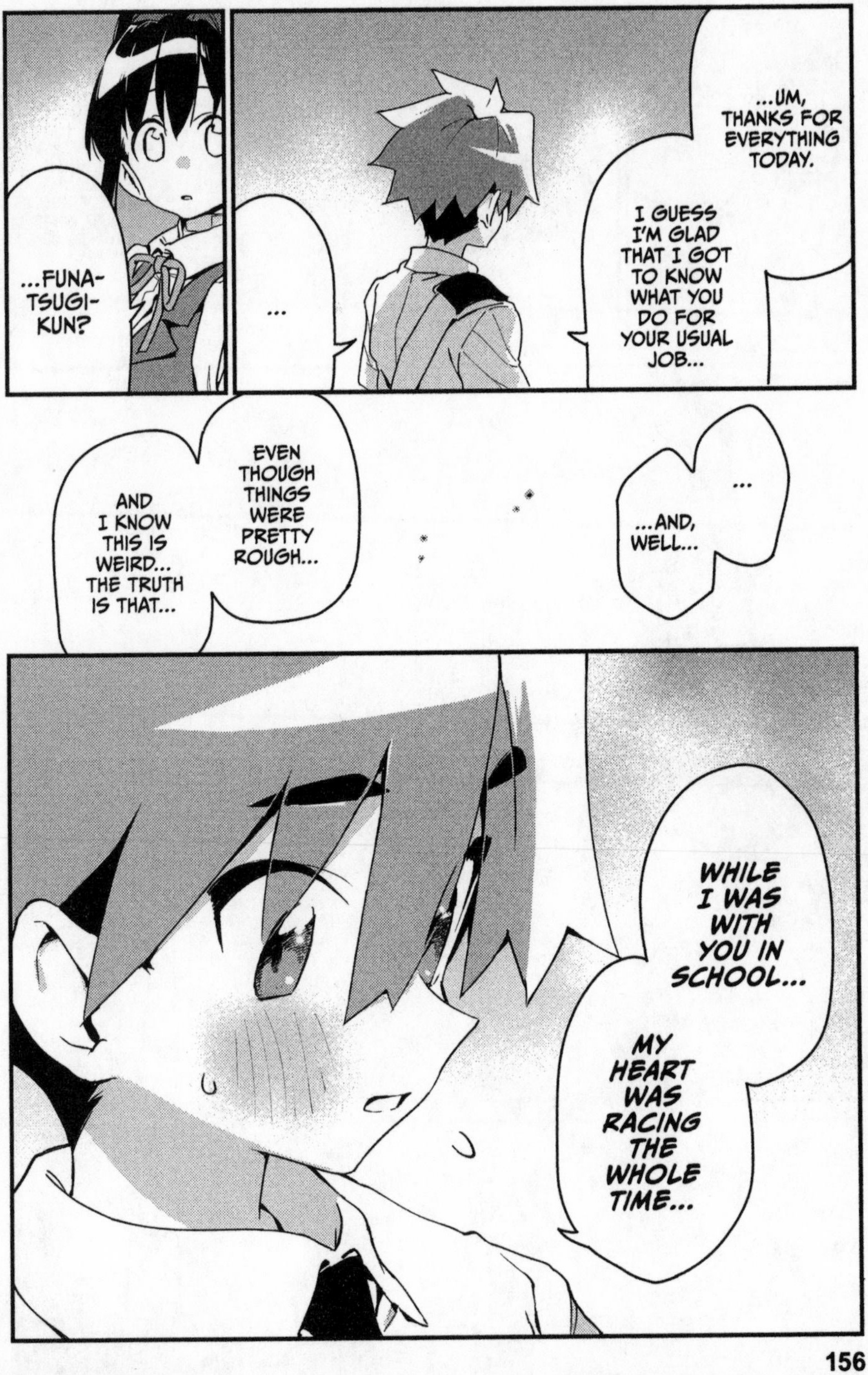
...UM, THANKS FOR EVERYTHING TODAY.
I GUESS I'M GLAD THAT I GOT TO KNOW WHAT YOU DO FOR YOUR USUAL JOB...
...
...FUNA-TSUGI-KUN?
...
...AND, WELL...
EVEN THOUGH THINGS WERE PRETTY ROUGH...
AND I KNOW THIS IS WEIRD... THE TRUTH IS THAT...
WHILE I WAS WITH YOU IN SCHOOL...
MY HEART WAS RACING THE WHOLE TIME...

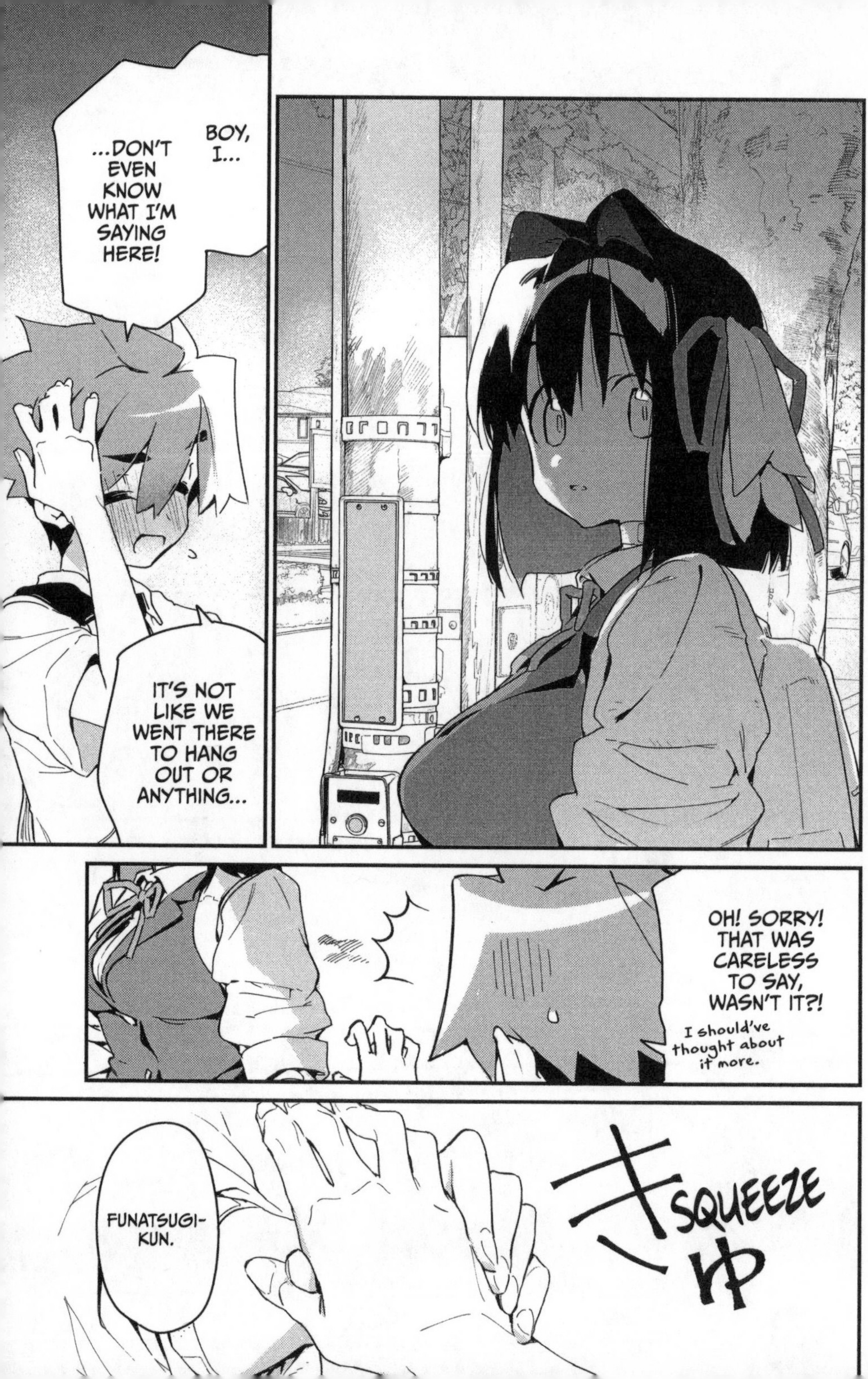
BOY, I...
...DON'T EVEN KNOW WHAT I'M SAYING HERE!
IT'S NOT LIKE WE WENT THERE TO HANG OUT OR ANYTHING...
OH! SORRY! THAT WAS CARELESS TO SAY, WASN'T IT?!
I should've thought about it more.
きゅ SQUEEZE
FUNATSUGI-KUN.

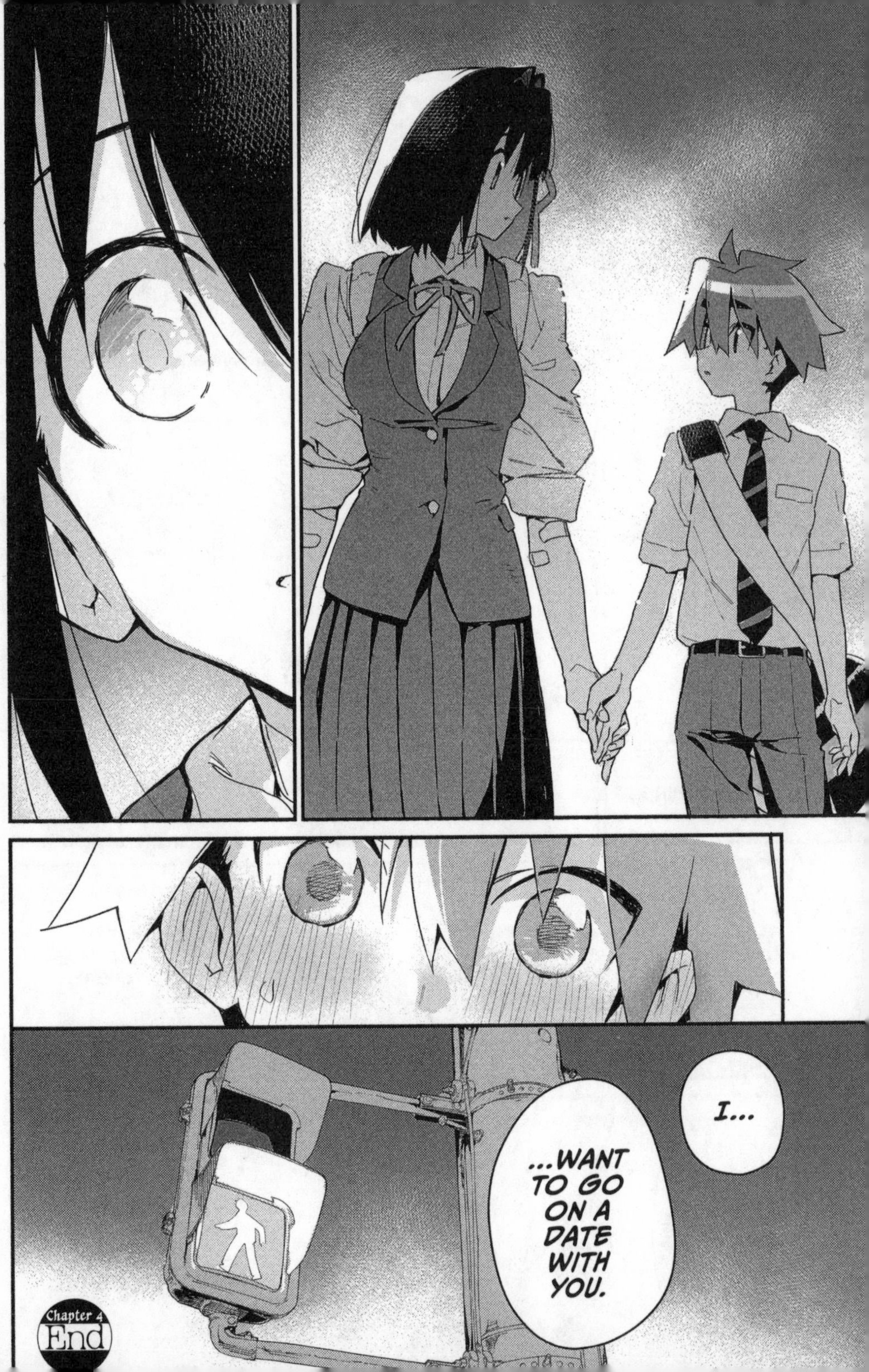
I...
...WANT TO GO ON A DATE WITH YOU.
Chapter 4 End

Chapter 5: Sachi's Monstrous Appetite

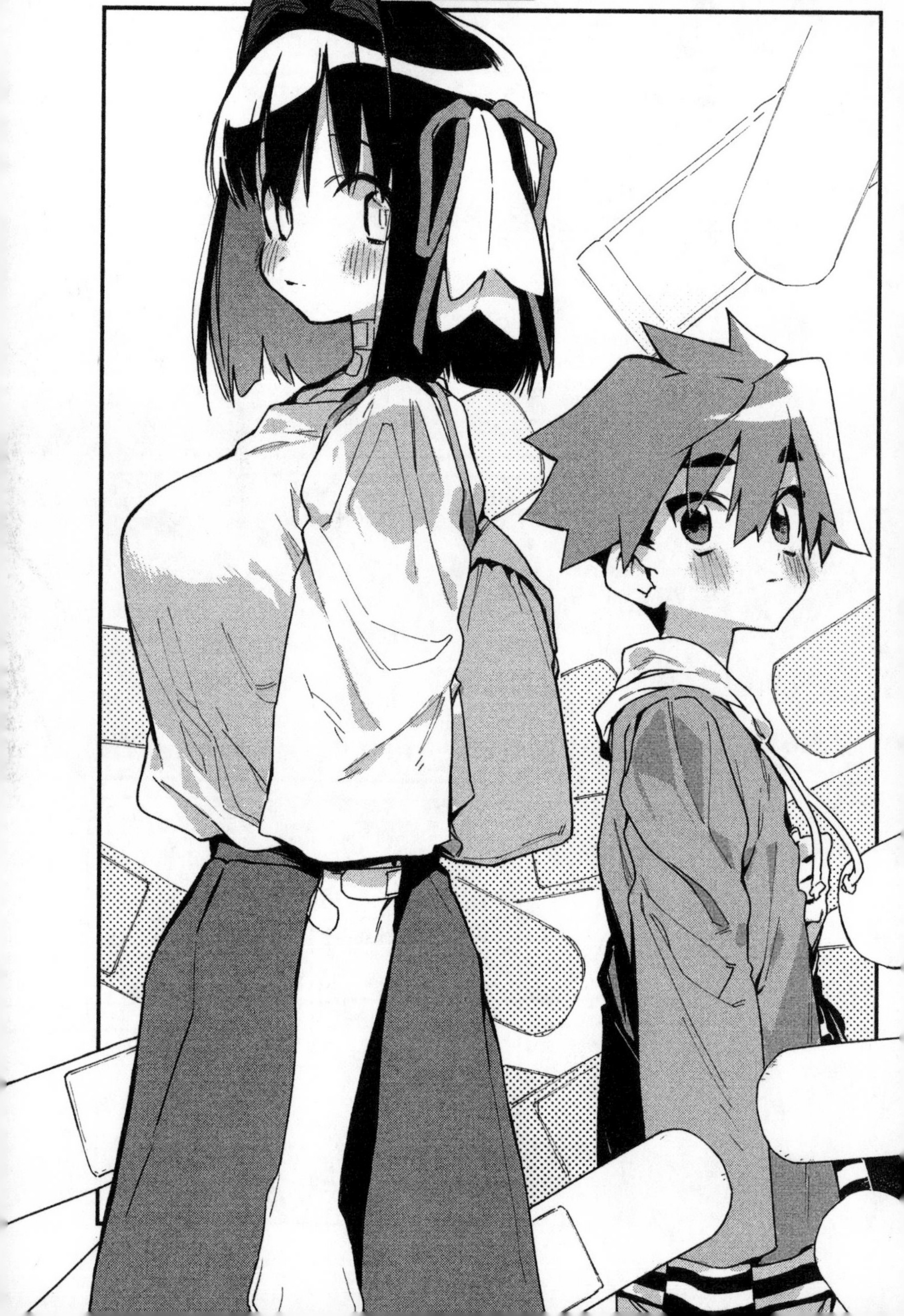

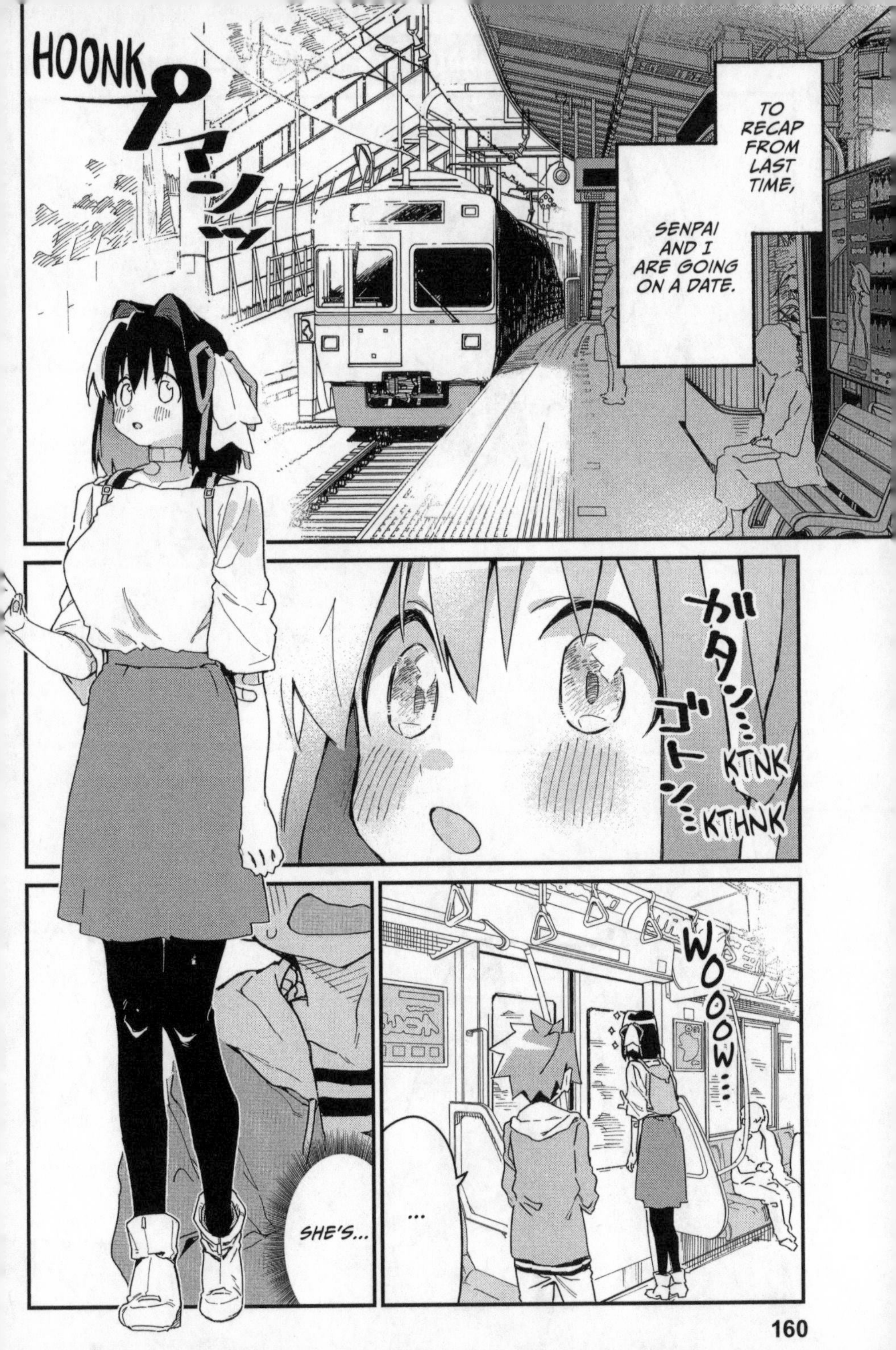
HOONK
TO RECAP FROM LAST TIME,
SENPAI AND I ARE GOING ON A DATE.
ガタン…
KTNK
ゴトン…
KTHNK
WOOOOW…
…
SHE'S…

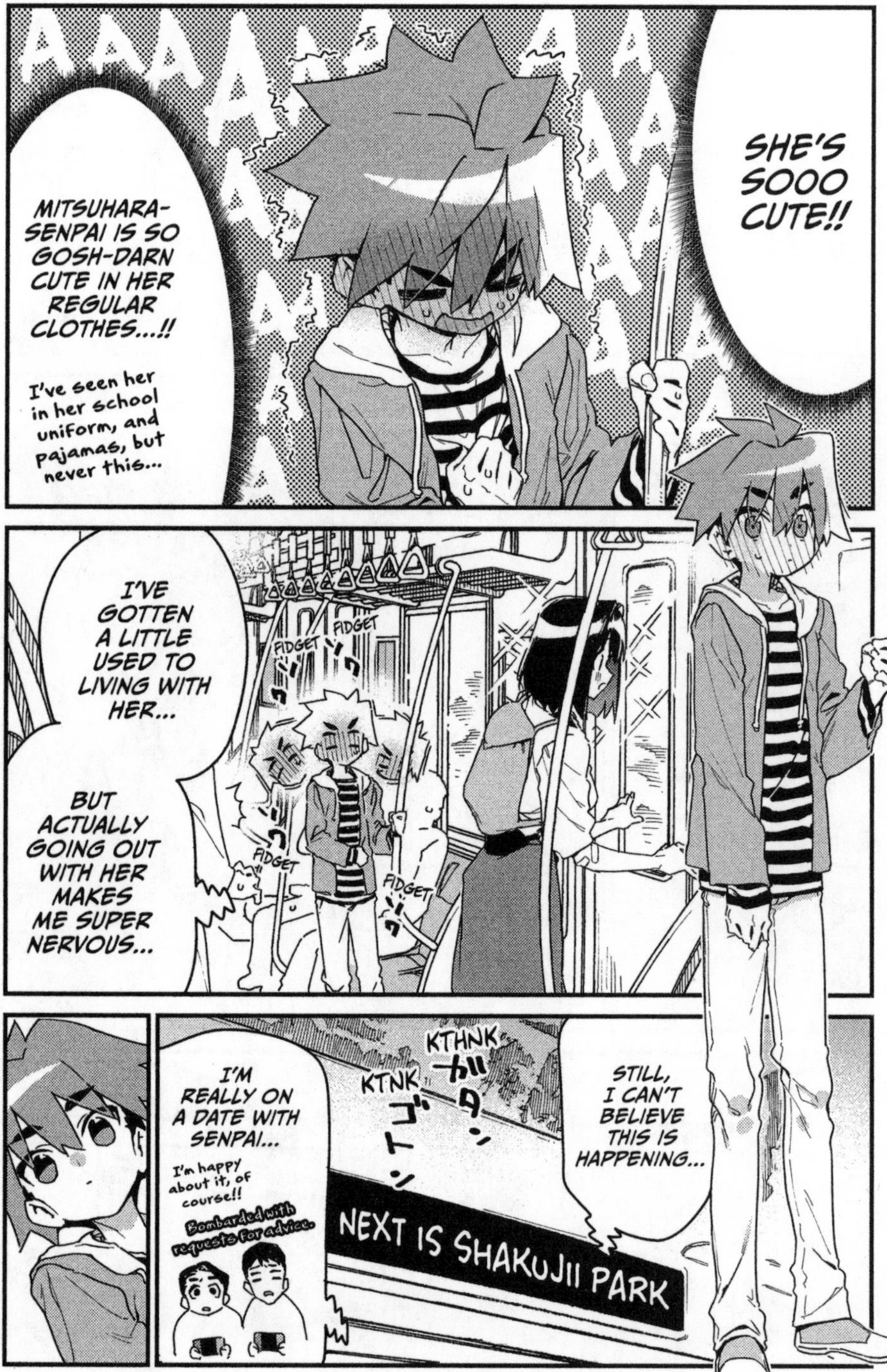
SHE'S SOOO CUTE!!
MITSUHARA-SENPAI IS SO GOSH-DARN CUTE IN HER REGULAR CLOTHES...!!
I've seen her in her school uniform, and pajamas, but never this...
I'VE GOTTEN A LITTLE USED TO LIVING WITH HER...
BUT ACTUALLY GOING OUT WITH HER MAKES ME SUPER NERVOUS...
FIDGET
FIDGET
FIDGET
FIDGET
STILL, I CAN'T BELIEVE THIS IS HAPPENING...
KTHNK
KTNK
NEXT IS SHAKUJII PARK
I'M REALLY ON A DATE WITH SENPAI...
I'm happy about it, of course!!
Bombarded with requests for advice.

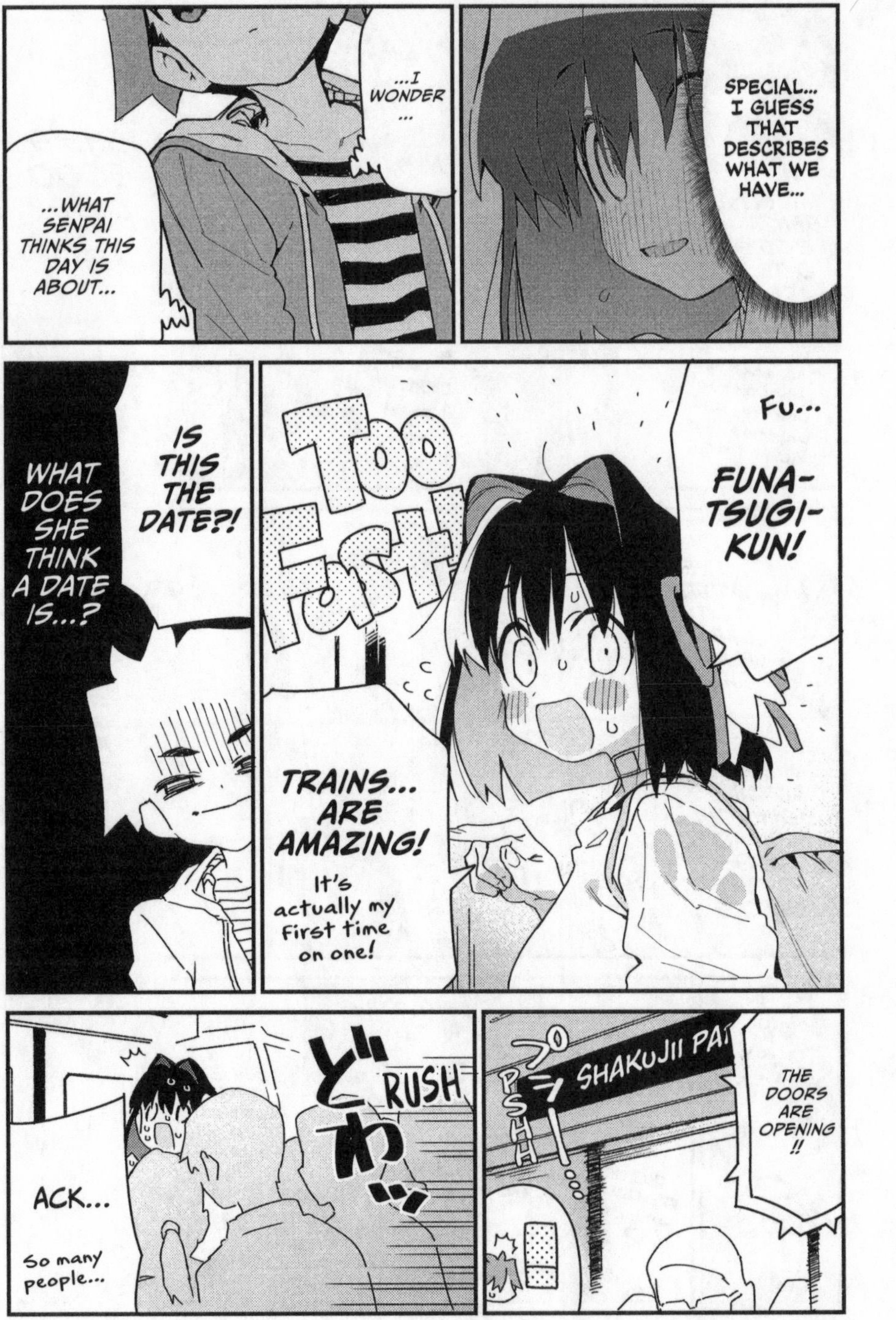
SPECIAL... I GUESS THAT DESCRIBES WHAT WE HAVE...
...I WONDER...
...WHAT SENPAI THINKS THIS DAY IS ABOUT...
FU...
FUNA-TSUGI-KUN!
TOO FAST!
TRAINS... ARE AMAZING!
It's actually my first time on one!
IS THIS THE DATE?!
WHAT DOES SHE THINK A DATE IS...?
THE DOORS ARE OPENING!!
SHAKUJII PA
PSHH
RUSH
ACK...
So many people...

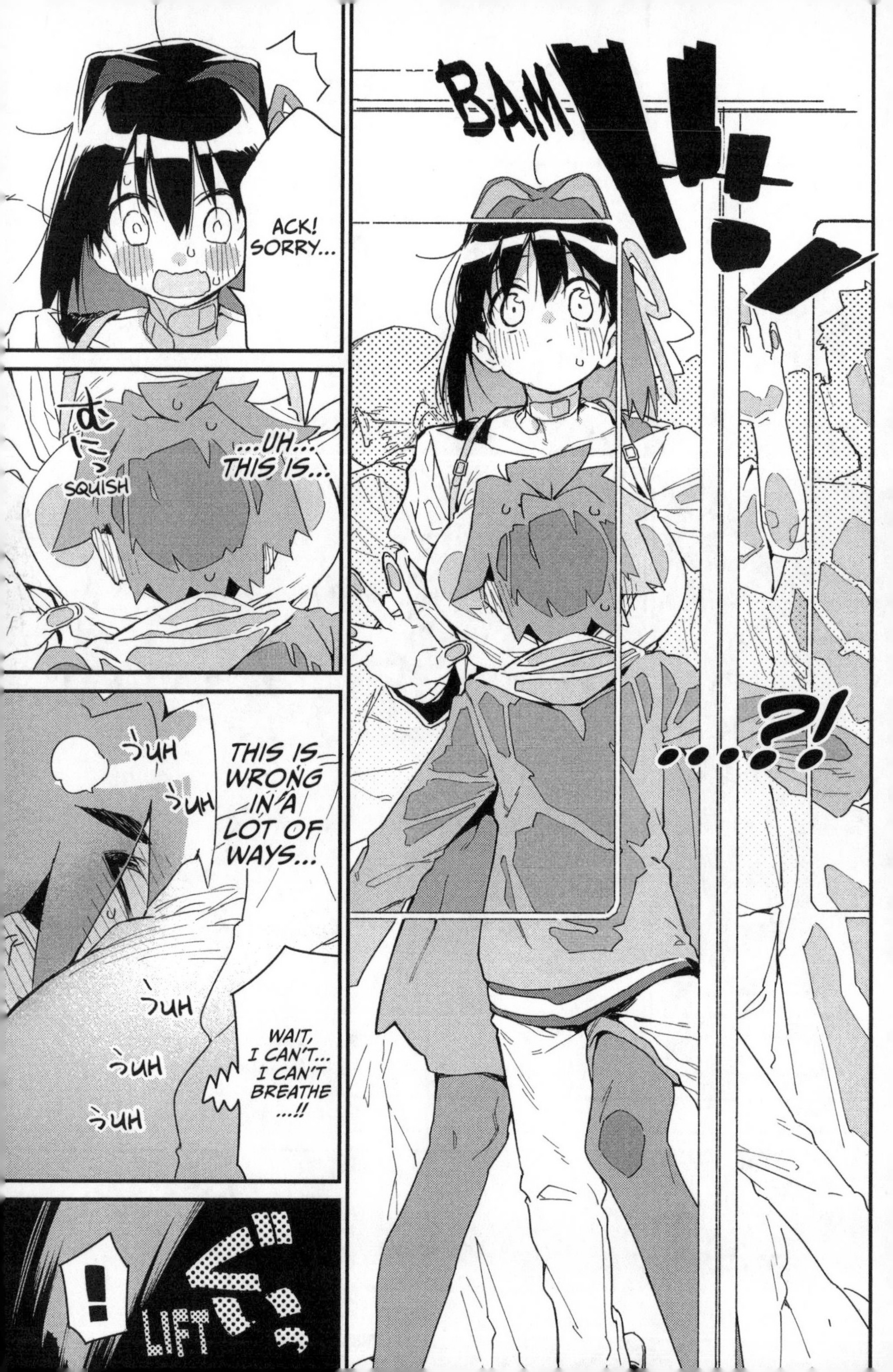
BAM!!
...?!
ACK! SORRY...
むにっ
SQUISH
...UH... THIS IS...
うUH
うUH
THIS IS WRONG IN A LOT OF WAYS...
うUH
うUH
うUH
WAIT, I CAN'T... I CAN'T BREATHE ...!!
!
LIFT

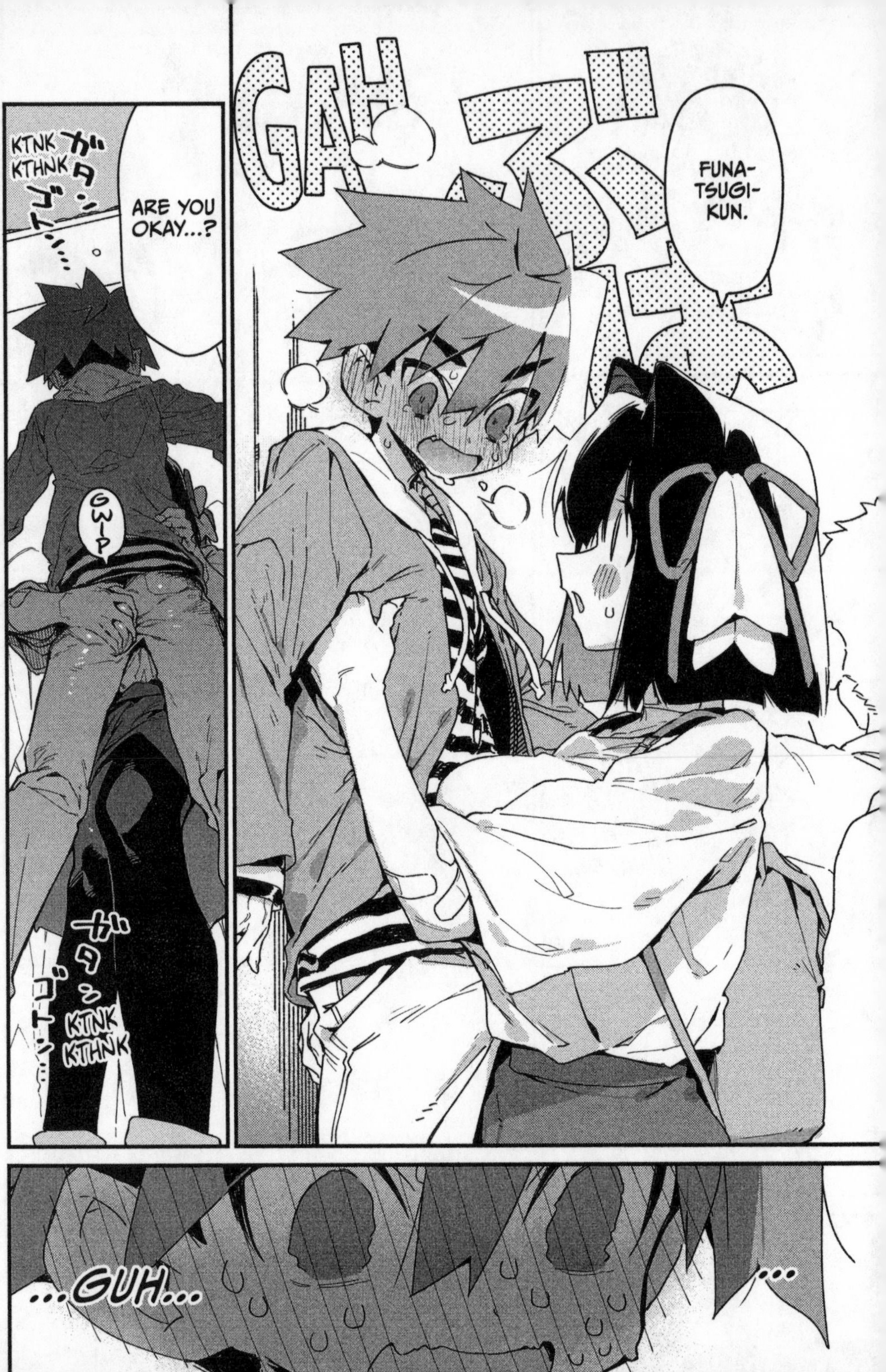
GAH
FUNA-TSUGI-KUN.
KTNK KTHNK
ARE YOU OKAY...?
GWIP
KTNK KTHNK
...GUH...
...

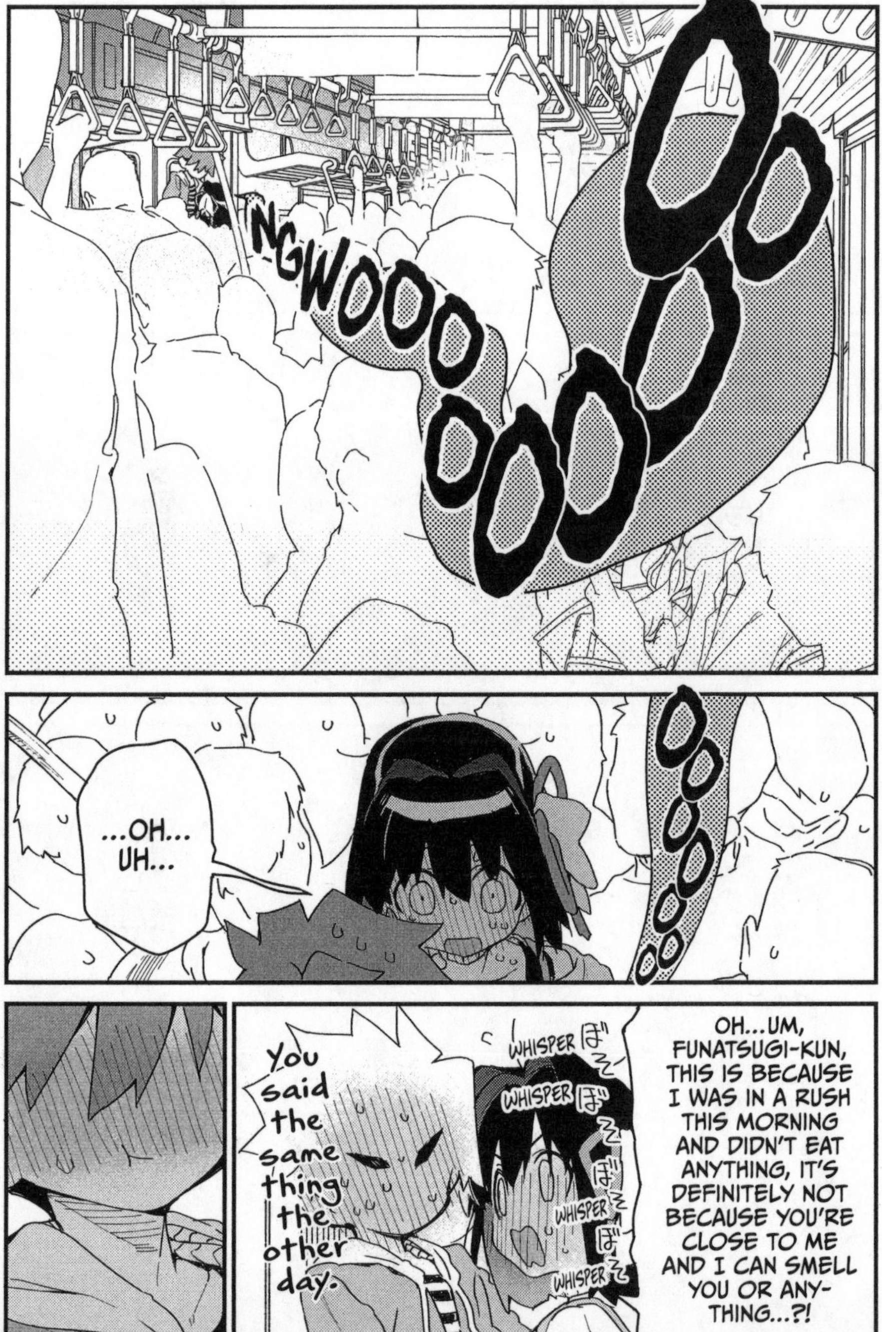
NGWOOOOOOOOOOO
...OH... UH...
OOOOOOOO
OH...UM, FUNATSUGI-KUN, THIS IS BECAUSE I WAS IN A RUSH THIS MORNING AND DIDN'T EAT ANYTHING, IT'S DEFINITELY NOT BECAUSE YOU'RE CLOSE TO ME AND I CAN SMELL YOU OR ANY-THING...?!
Whispered
WHISPER ぼそ
WHISPER ぼそ
ぼそ
WHISPER ぼそ
WHISPER ぼそ
You said the same thing the other day.

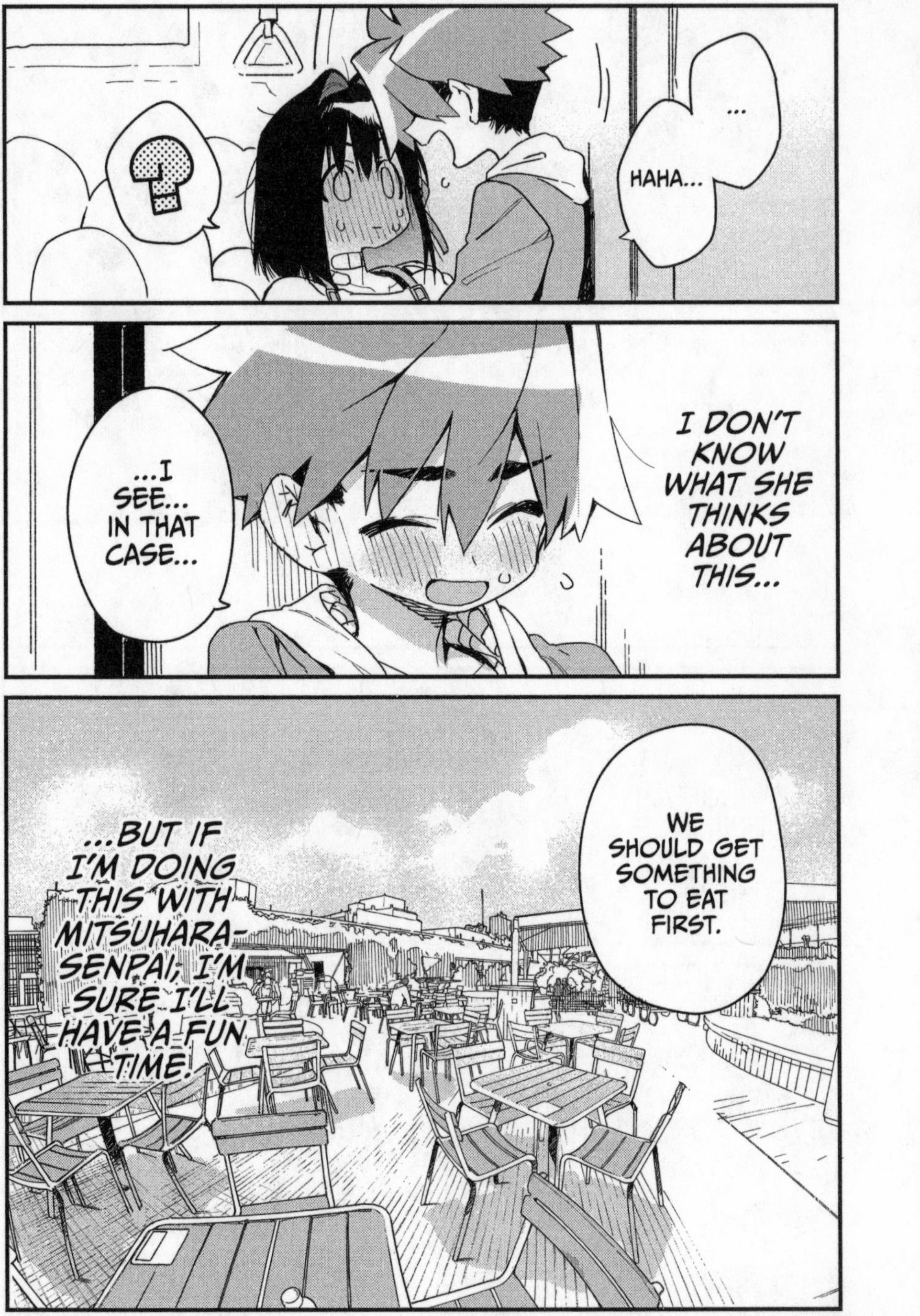
... HAHA...
?
I DON'T KNOW WHAT SHE THINKS ABOUT THIS...
...I SEE... IN THAT CASE...
WE SHOULD GET SOMETHING TO EAT FIRST.
...BUT IF I'M DOING THIS WITH MITSUHARA-SENPAI, I'M SURE I'LL HAVE A FUN TIME.

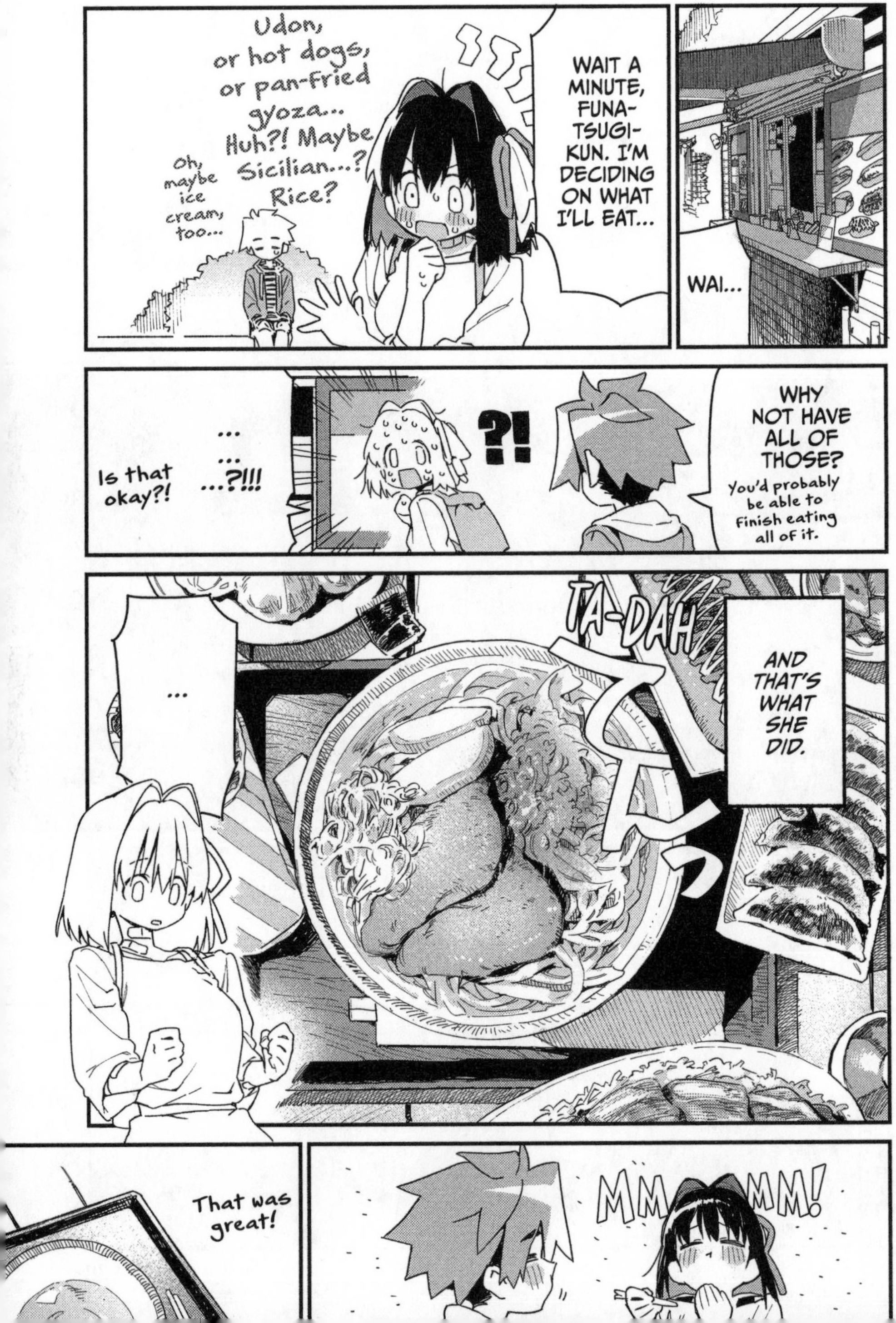
WAI...
WAIT A MINUTE, FUNA-TSUGI-KUN. I'M DECIDING ON WHAT I'LL EAT...
Udon, or hot dogs, or pan-fried gyoza.. Huh?! Maybe Sicilian...? Rice?
Oh, maybe ice cream, too...
WHY NOT HAVE ALL OF THOSE?
You'd probably be able to finish eating all of it.
?!
...
...
...?!!!
Is that okay?!
AND THAT'S WHAT SHE DID.
TA-DAH
...
MMMMMM!
That was great!

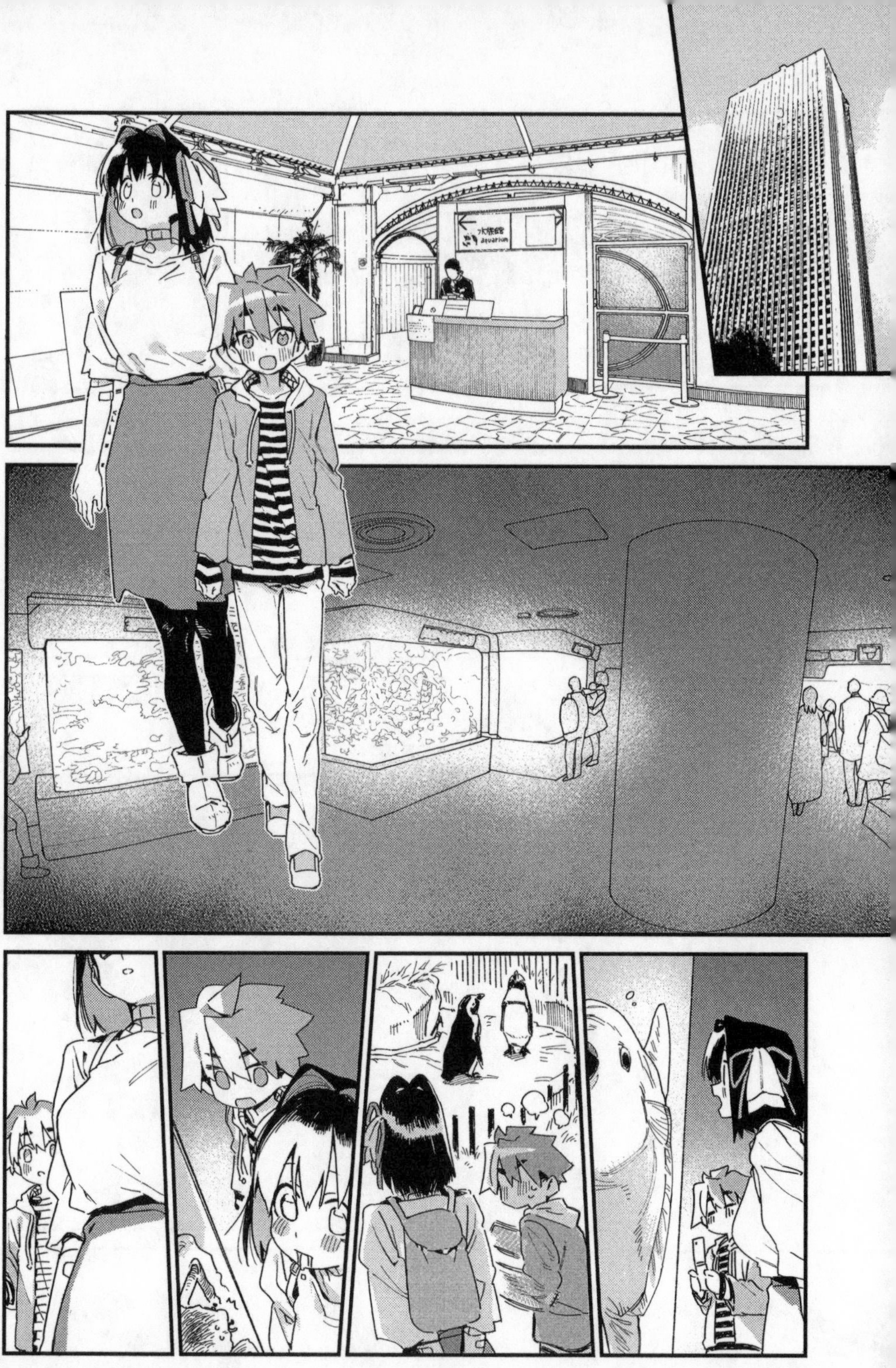
水族館
aquarium

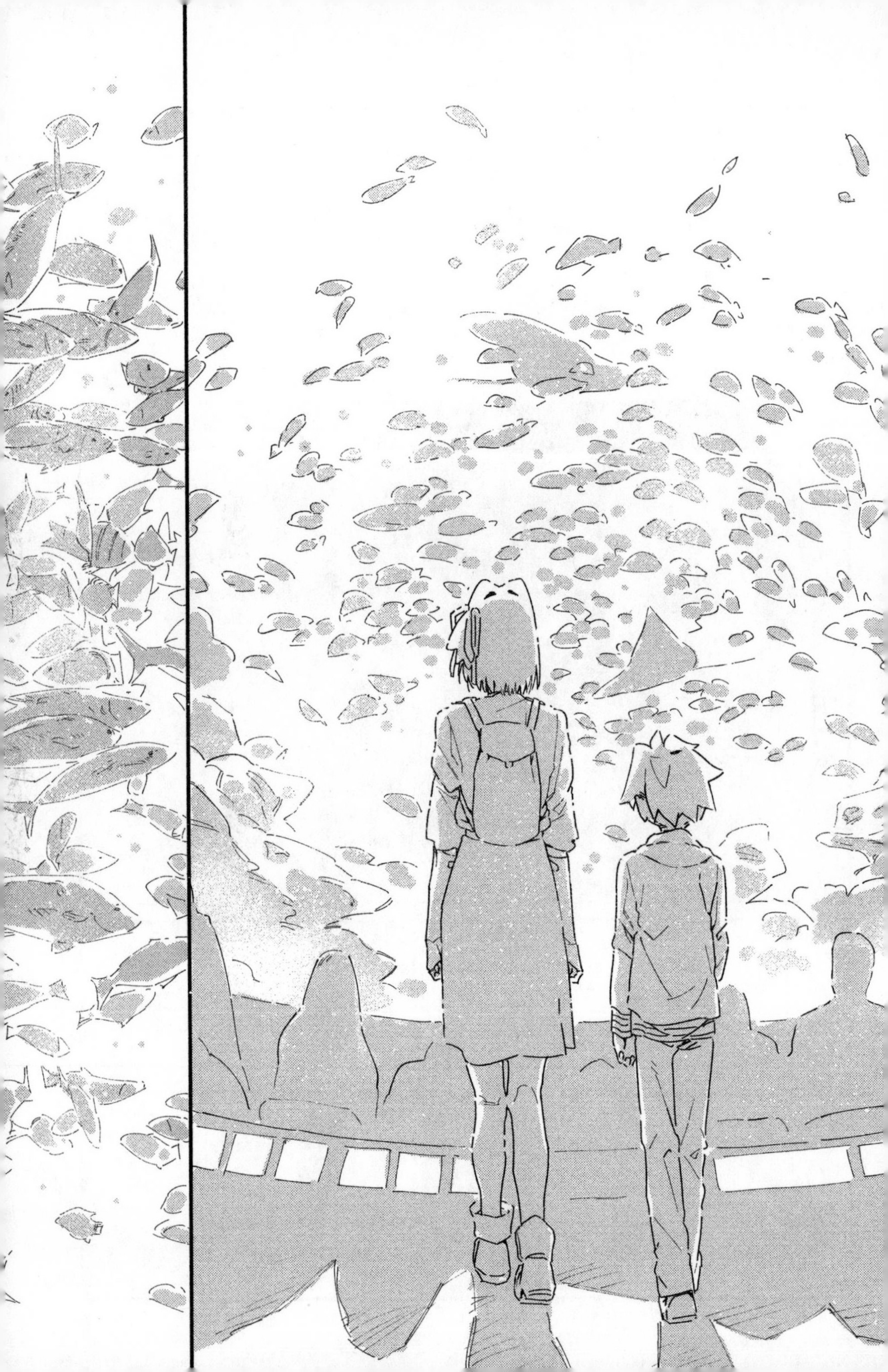

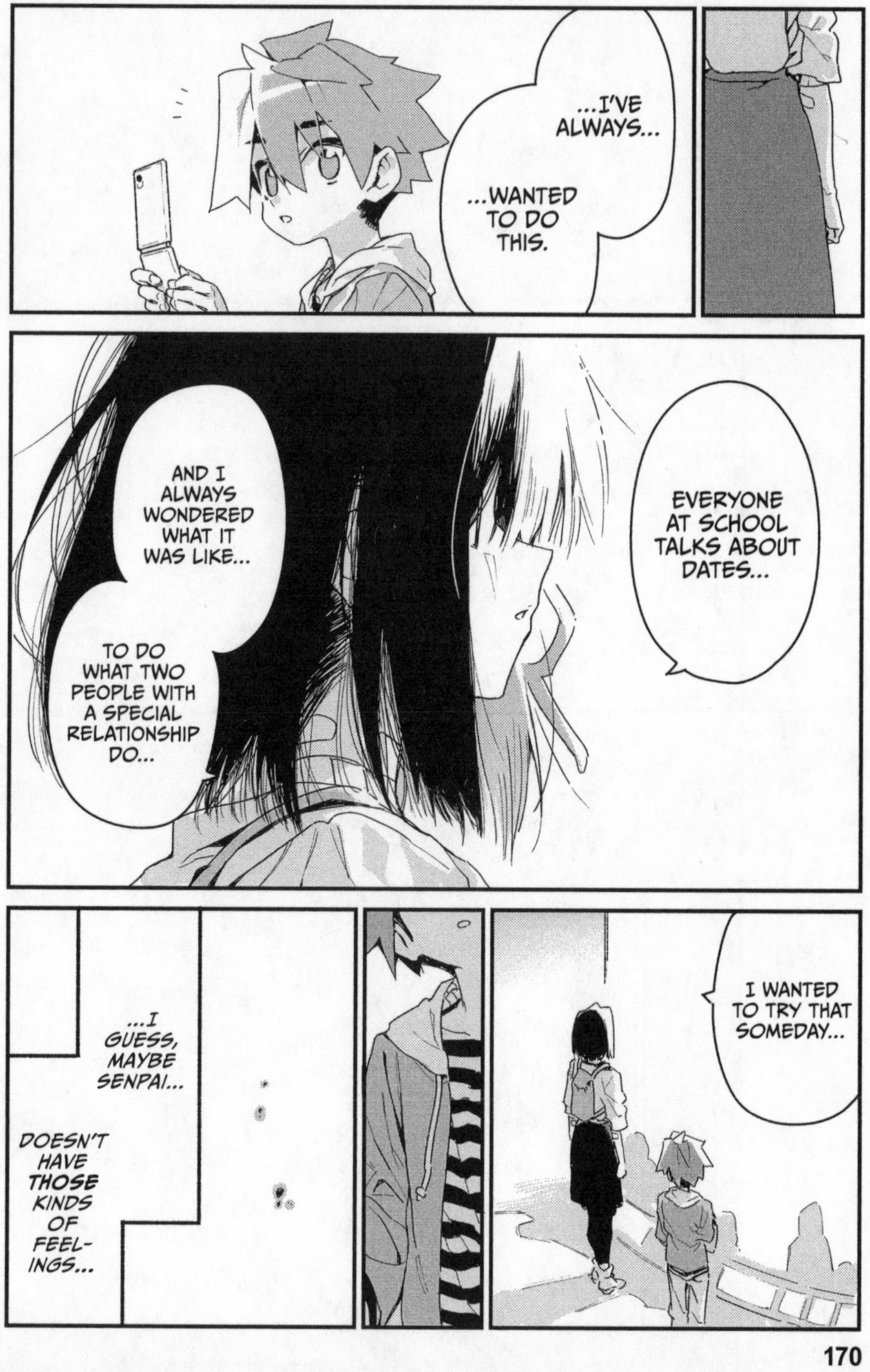
...I'VE ALWAYS...
...WANTED TO DO THIS.
EVERYONE AT SCHOOL TALKS ABOUT DATES...
AND I ALWAYS WONDERED WHAT IT WAS LIKE...
TO DO WHAT TWO PEOPLE WITH A SPECIAL RELATIONSHIP DO...
I WANTED TO TRY THAT SOMEDAY...
...I GUESS, MAYBE SENPAI...
DOESN'T HAVE THOSE KINDS OF FEEL- INGS...

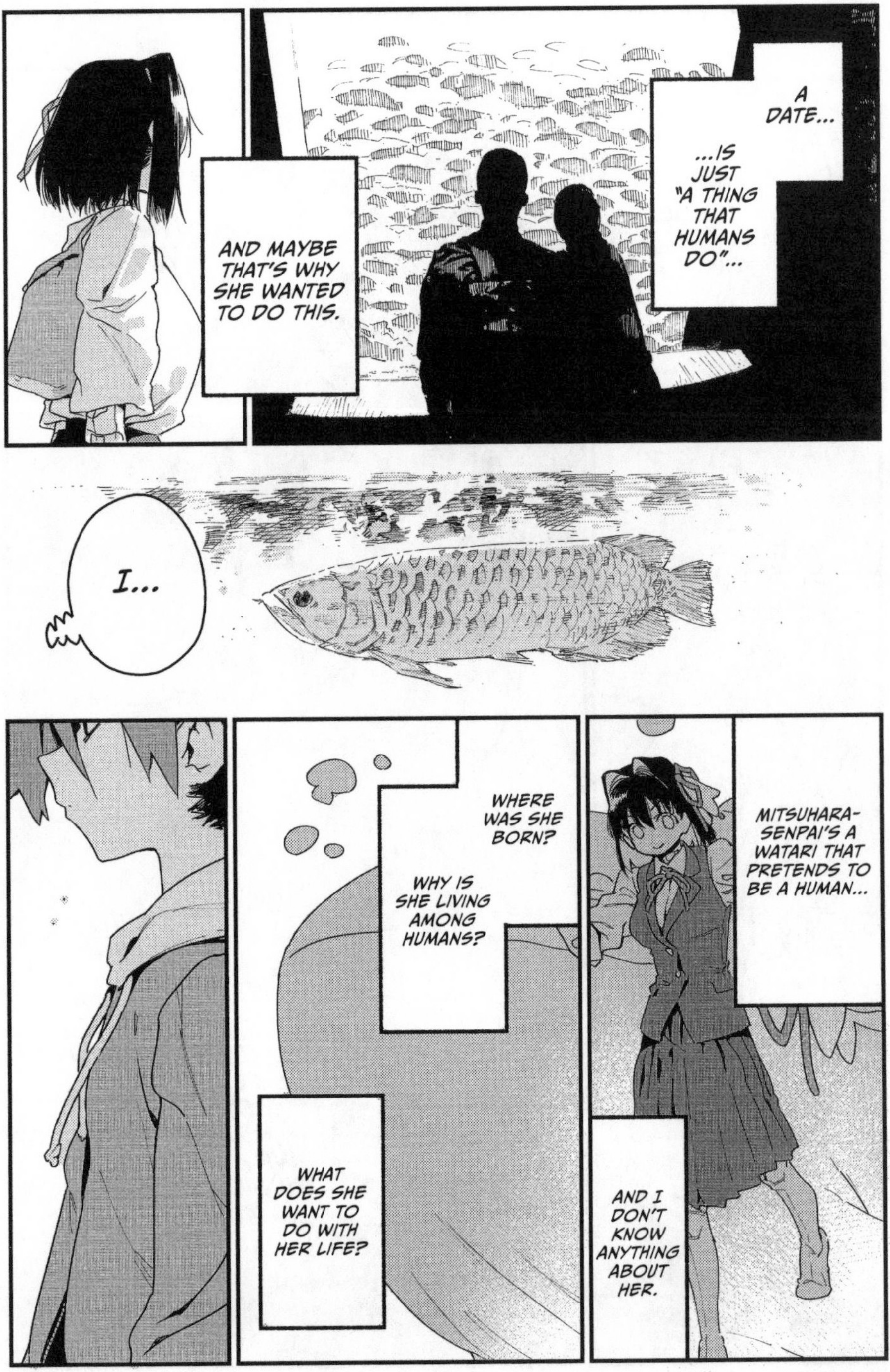
A DATE...
...IS JUST "A THING THAT HUMANS DO"...
AND MAYBE THAT'S WHY SHE WANTED TO DO THIS.
I...
MITSUHARA-SENPAI'S A WATARI THAT PRETENDS TO BE A HUMAN...
AND I DON'T KNOW ANYTHING ABOUT HER.
WHERE WAS SHE BORN?
WHY IS SHE LIVING AMONG HUMANS?
WHAT DOES SHE WANT TO DO WITH HER LIFE?

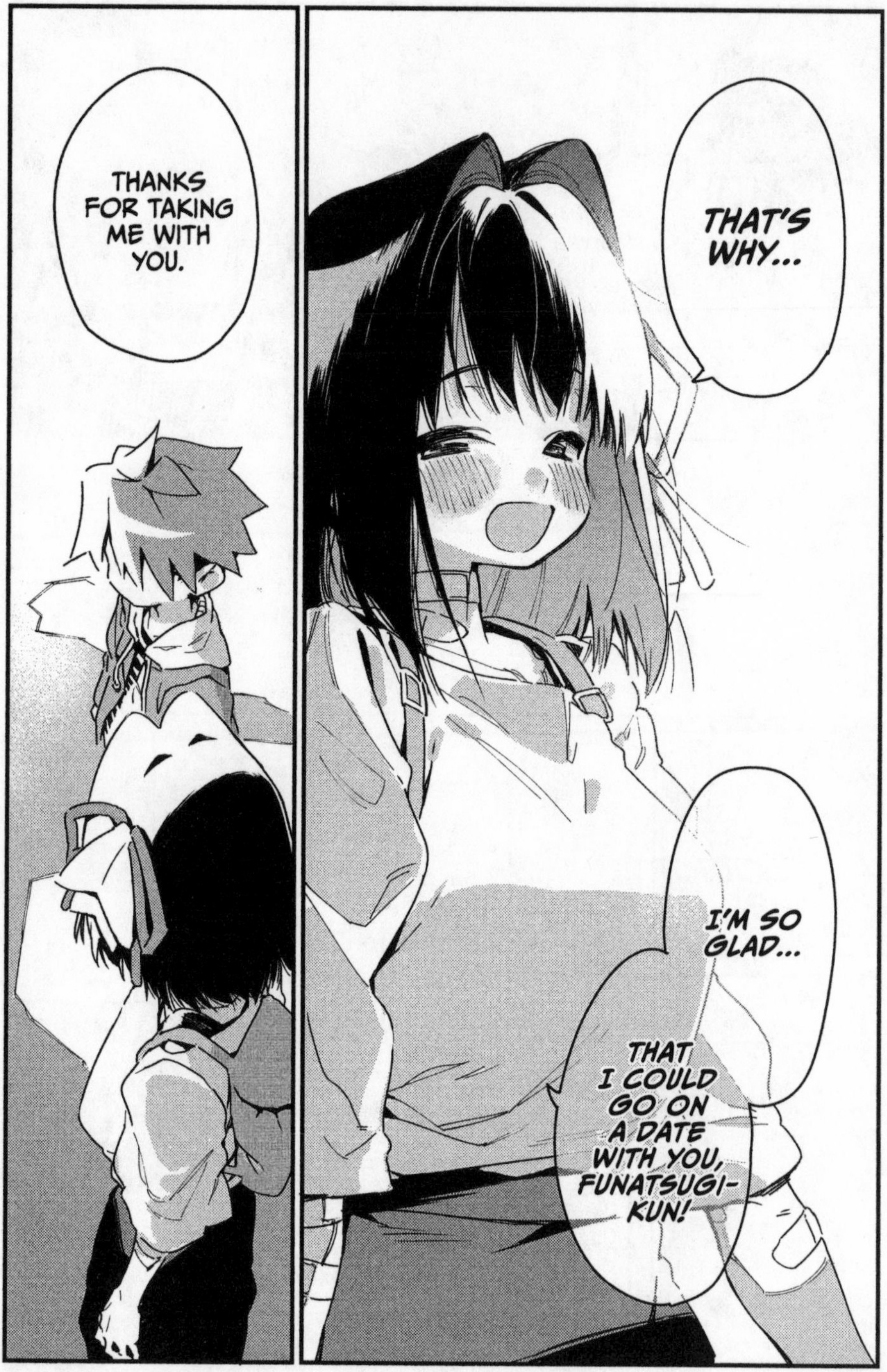
THAT'S WHY...
I'M SO GLAD...
THAT I COULD GO ON A DATE WITH YOU, FUNATSUGI-KUN!
THANKS FOR TAKING ME WITH YOU.

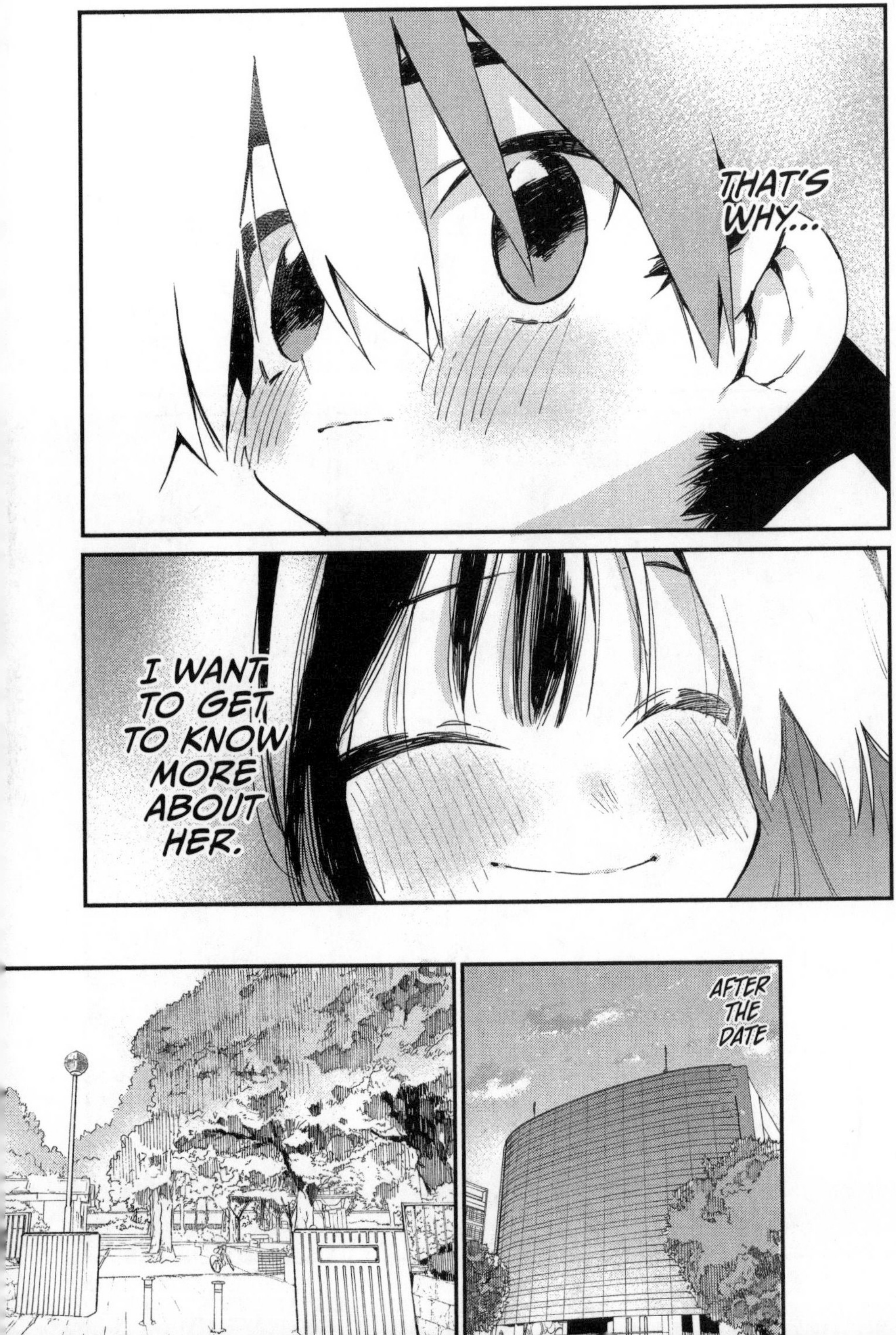
THAT'S WHY...
I WANT TO GET TO KNOW MORE ABOUT HER.
AFTER THE DATE

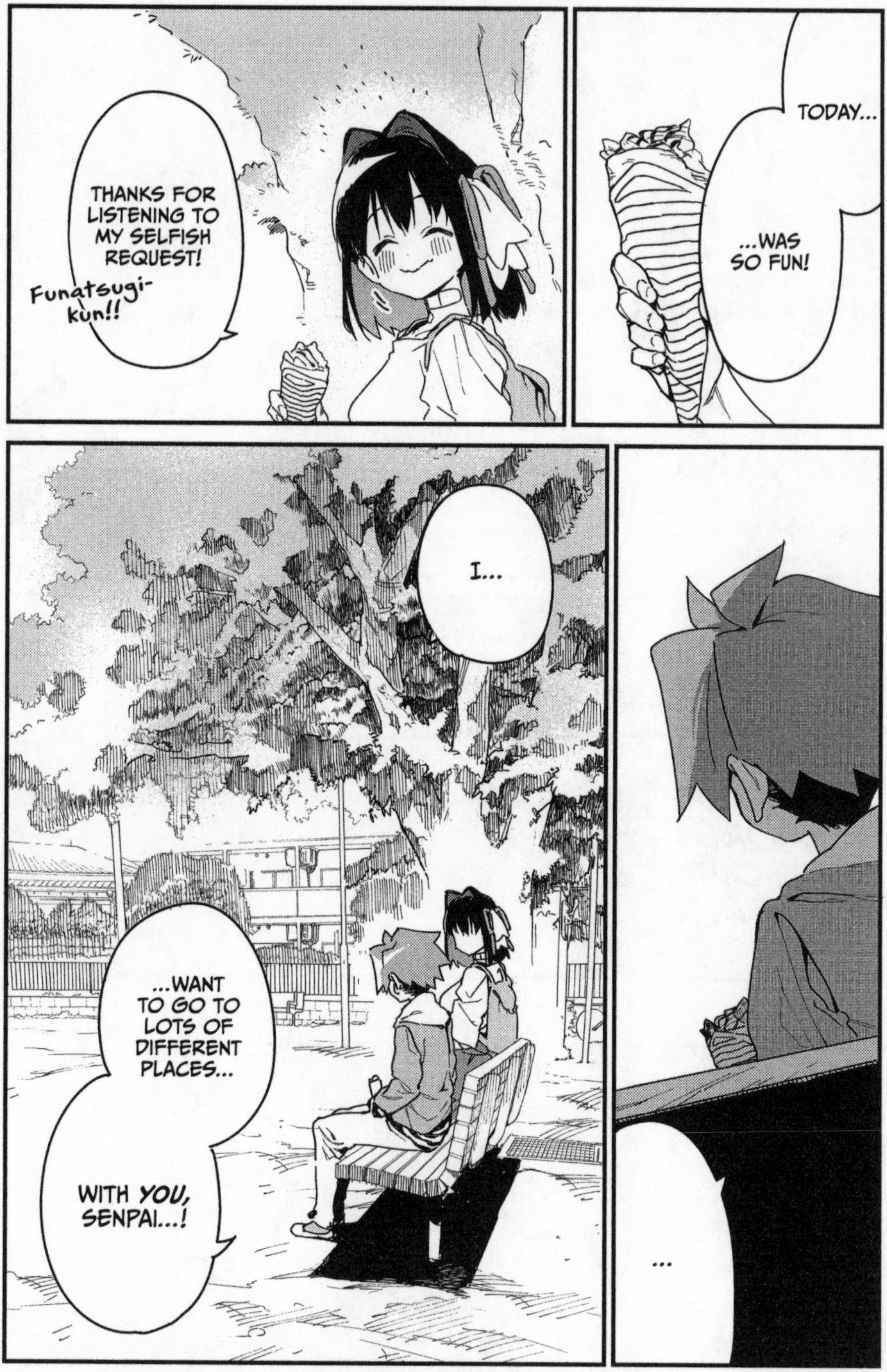
TODAY...
...WAS SO FUN!
THANKS FOR LISTENING TO MY SELFISH REQUEST!
Funatsugi-kun!!
...
I...
...WANT TO GO TO LOTS OF DIFFERENT PLACES...
WITH *YOU*, SENPAI...!

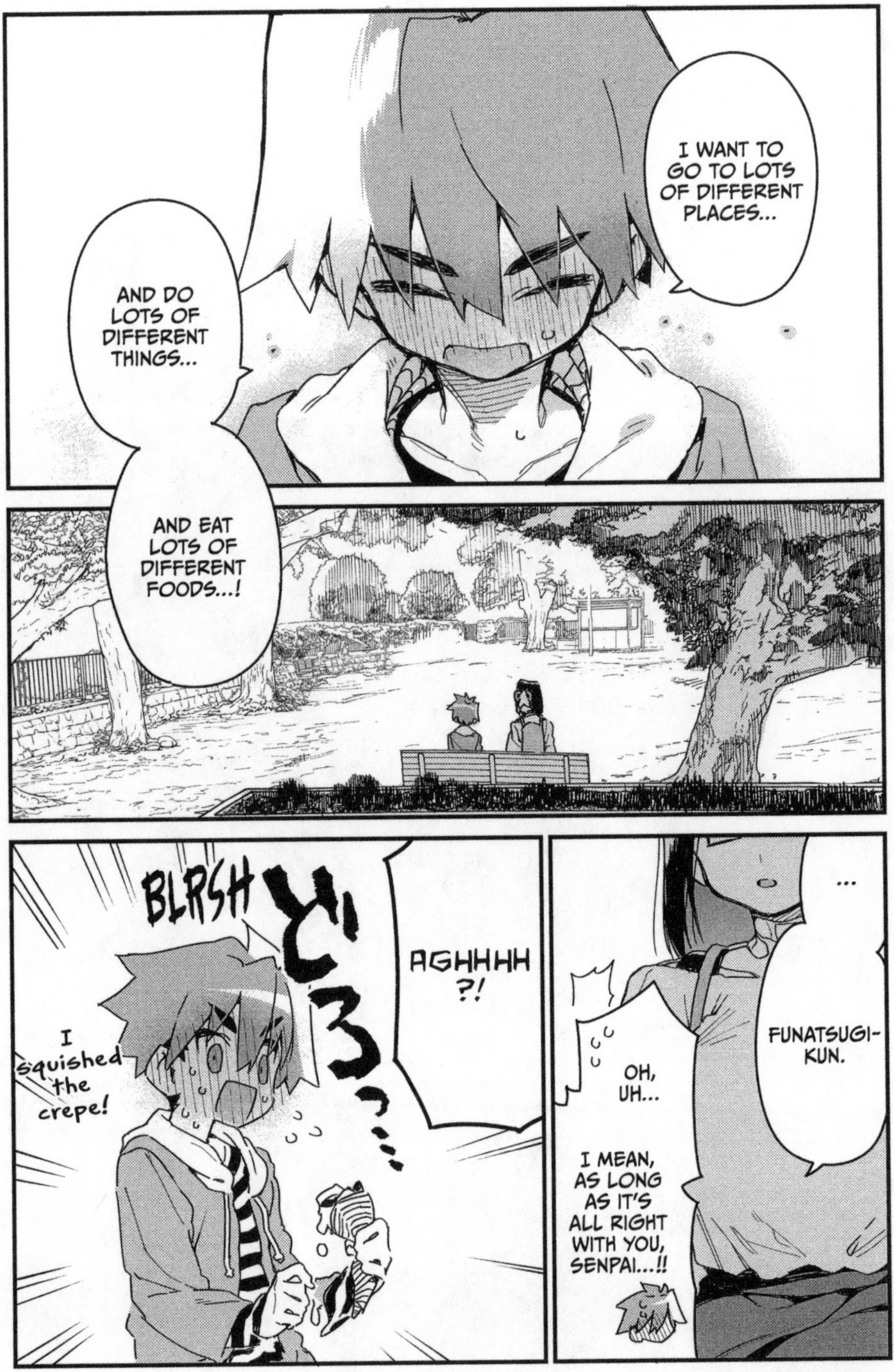
I WANT TO GO TO LOTS OF DIFFERENT PLACES...
AND DO LOTS OF DIFFERENT THINGS...
AND EAT LOTS OF DIFFERENT FOODS...!
...
FUNATSUGI-KUN.
OH, UH...
I MEAN, AS LONG AS IT'S ALL RIGHT WITH YOU, SENPAI...!!
BLRSH
どろっ
AGHHHH ?!
I squished the crepe!

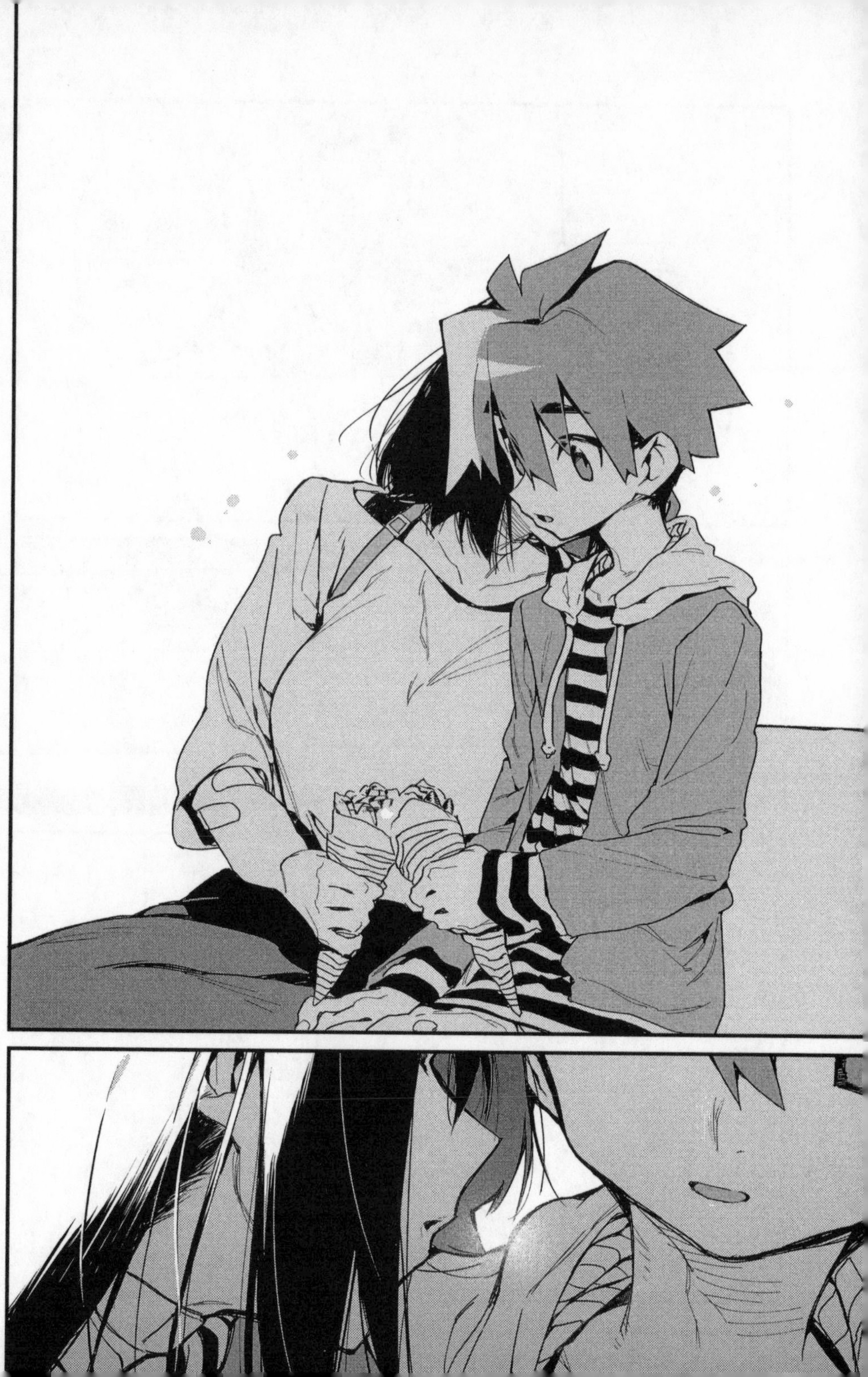

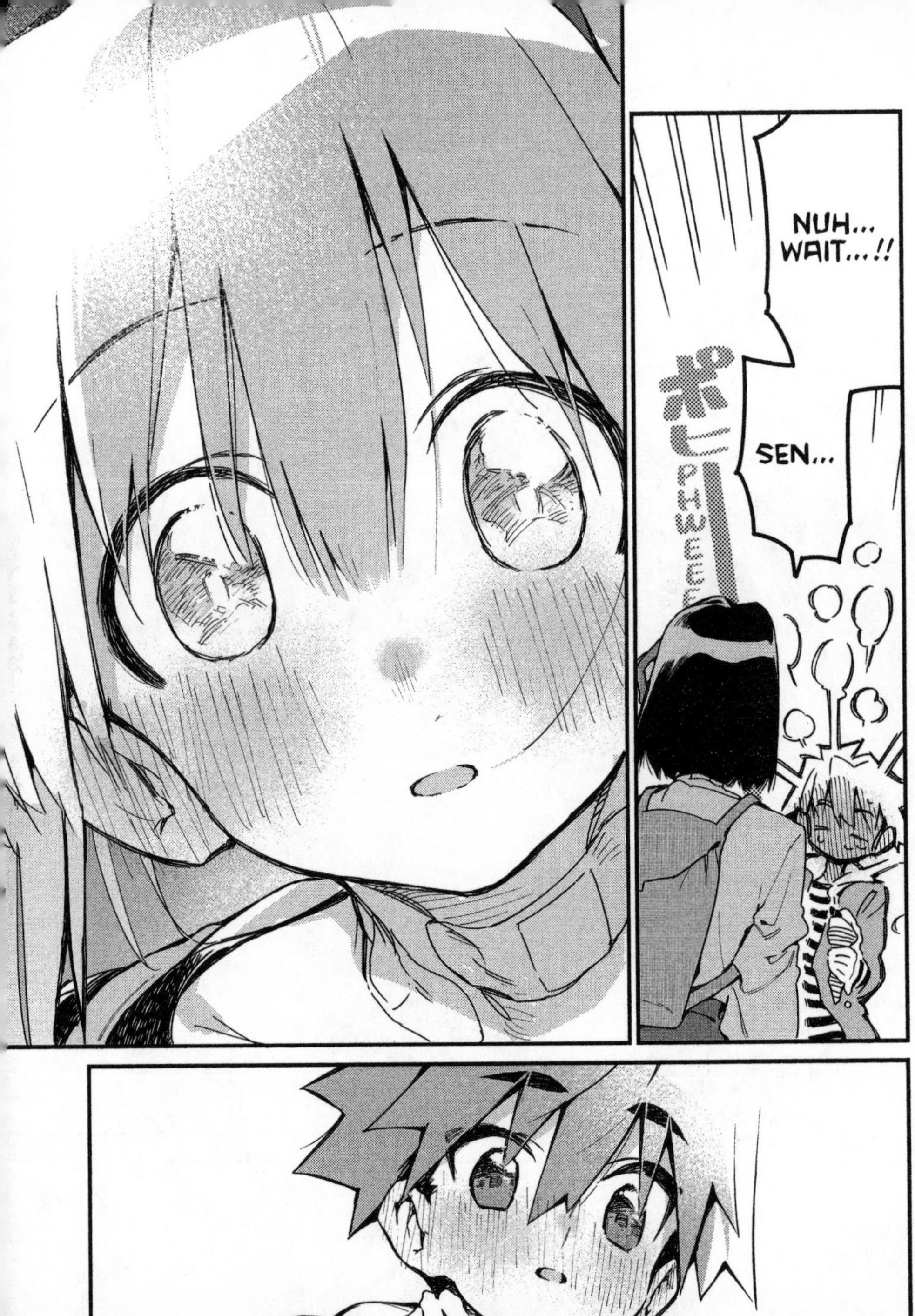
NUH... WAIT...!!
SEN...
ポピ
PHWEE

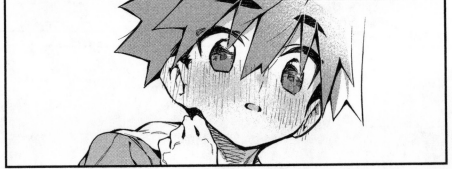

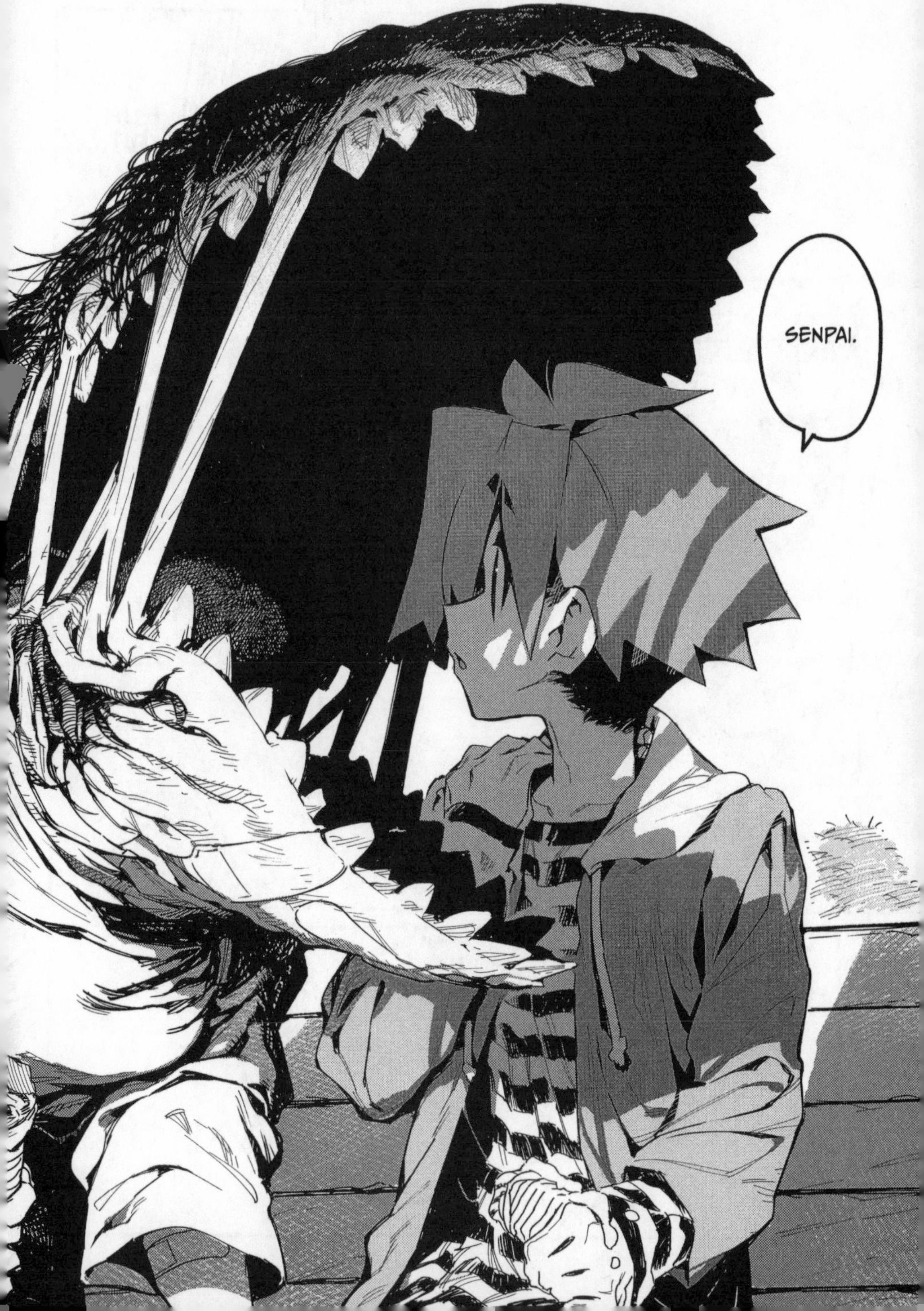
SENPAI.

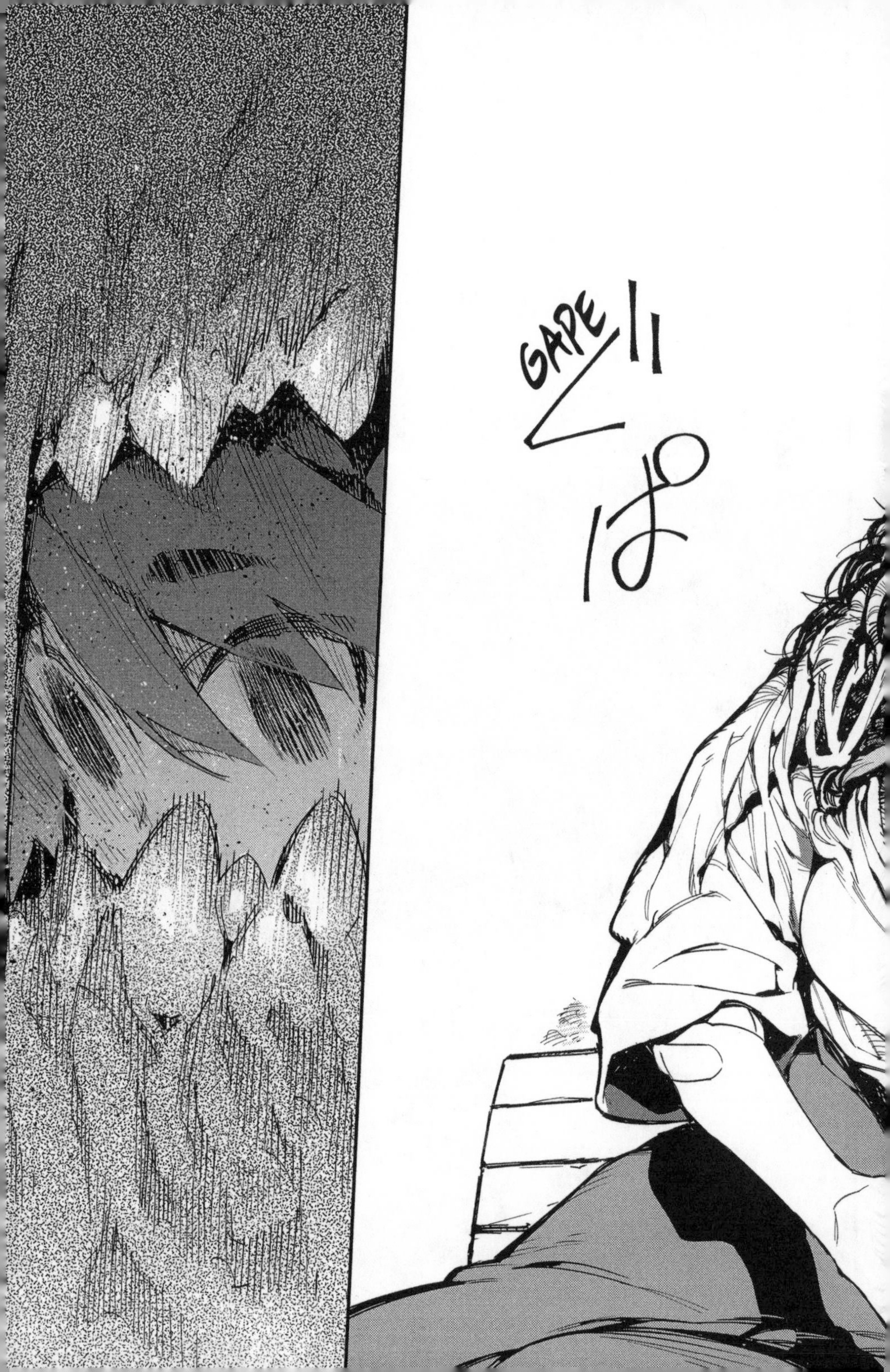
GAPE
ぱ

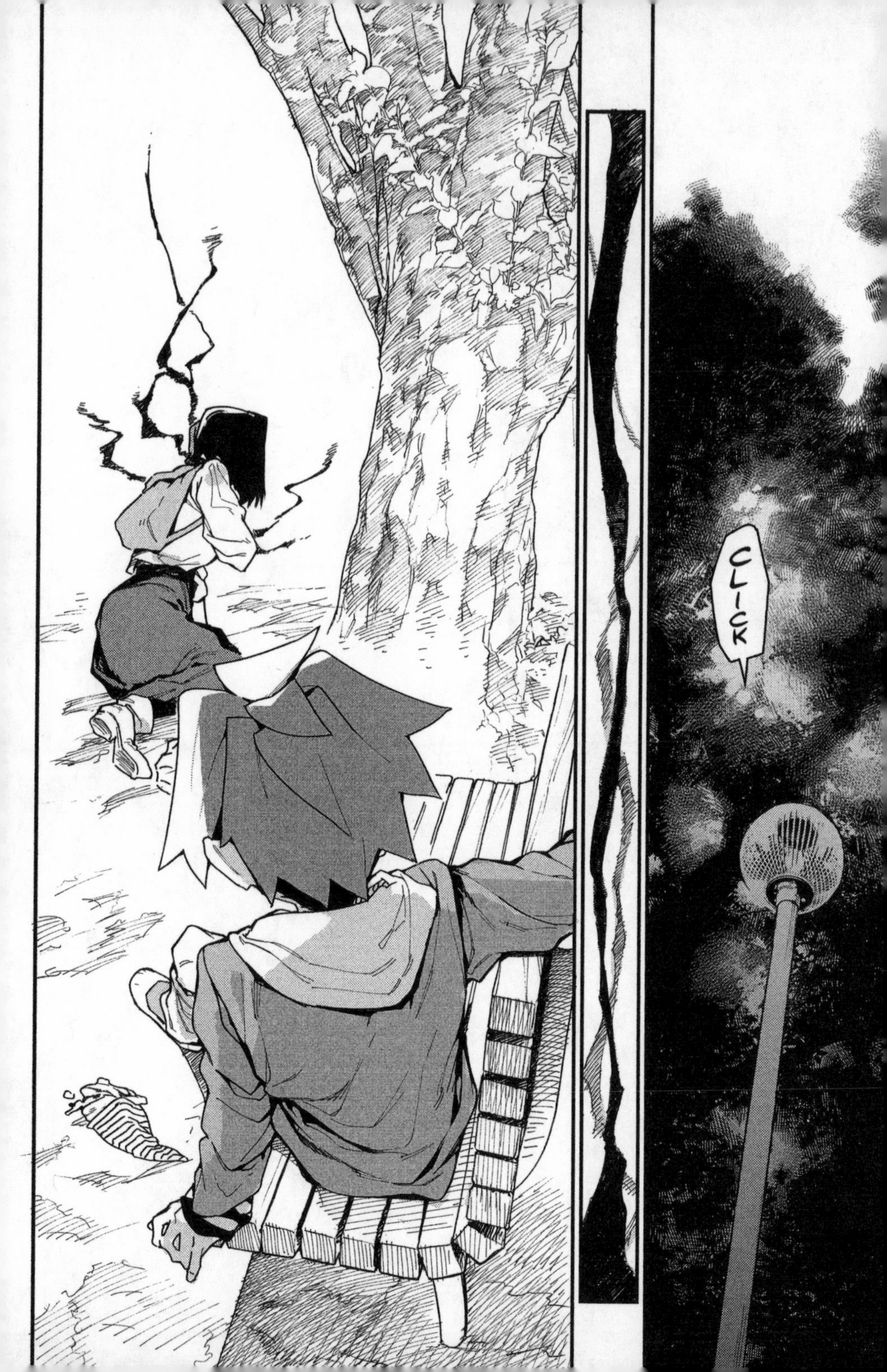
CLICK

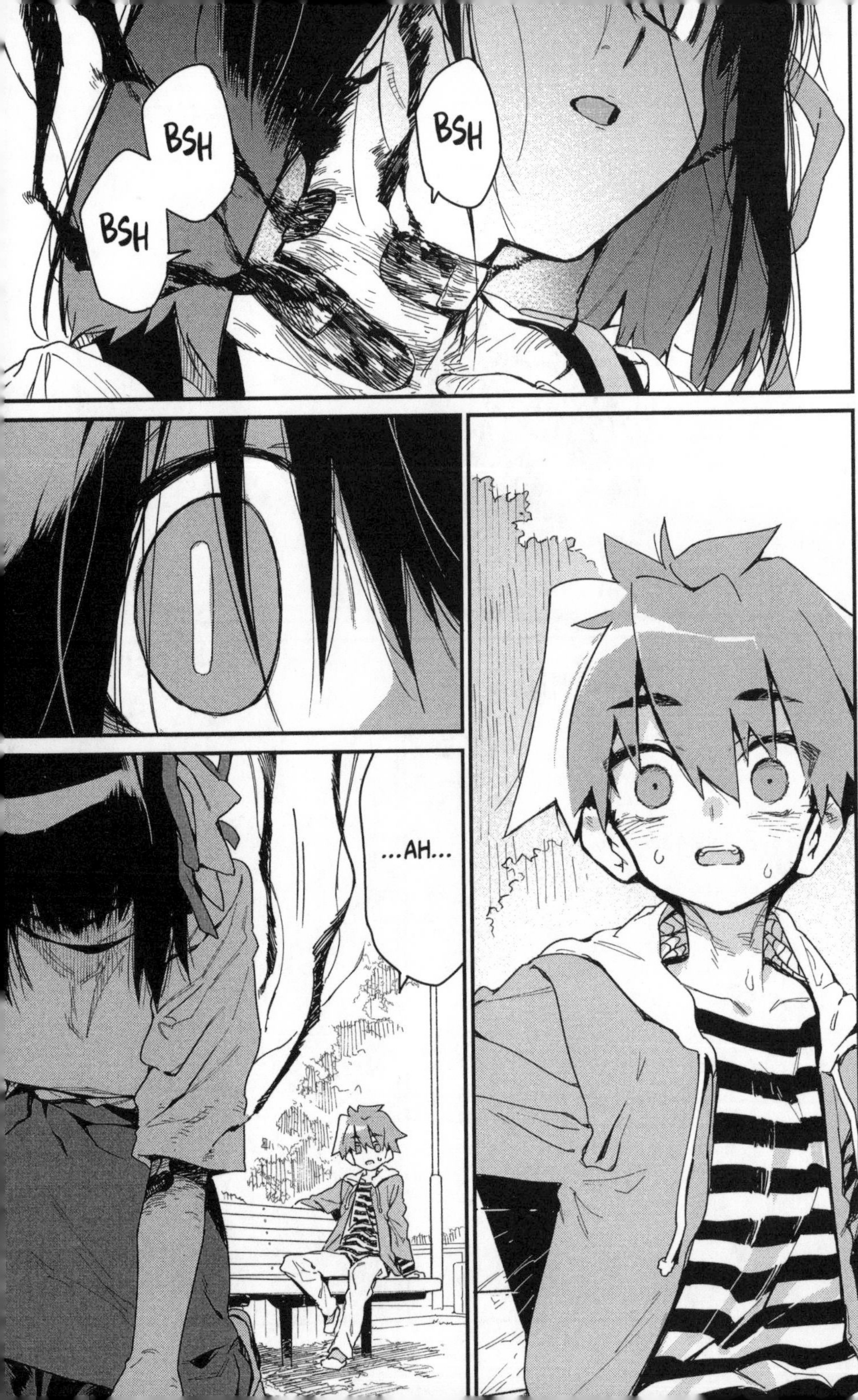
BSH
BSH
BSH
...AH...

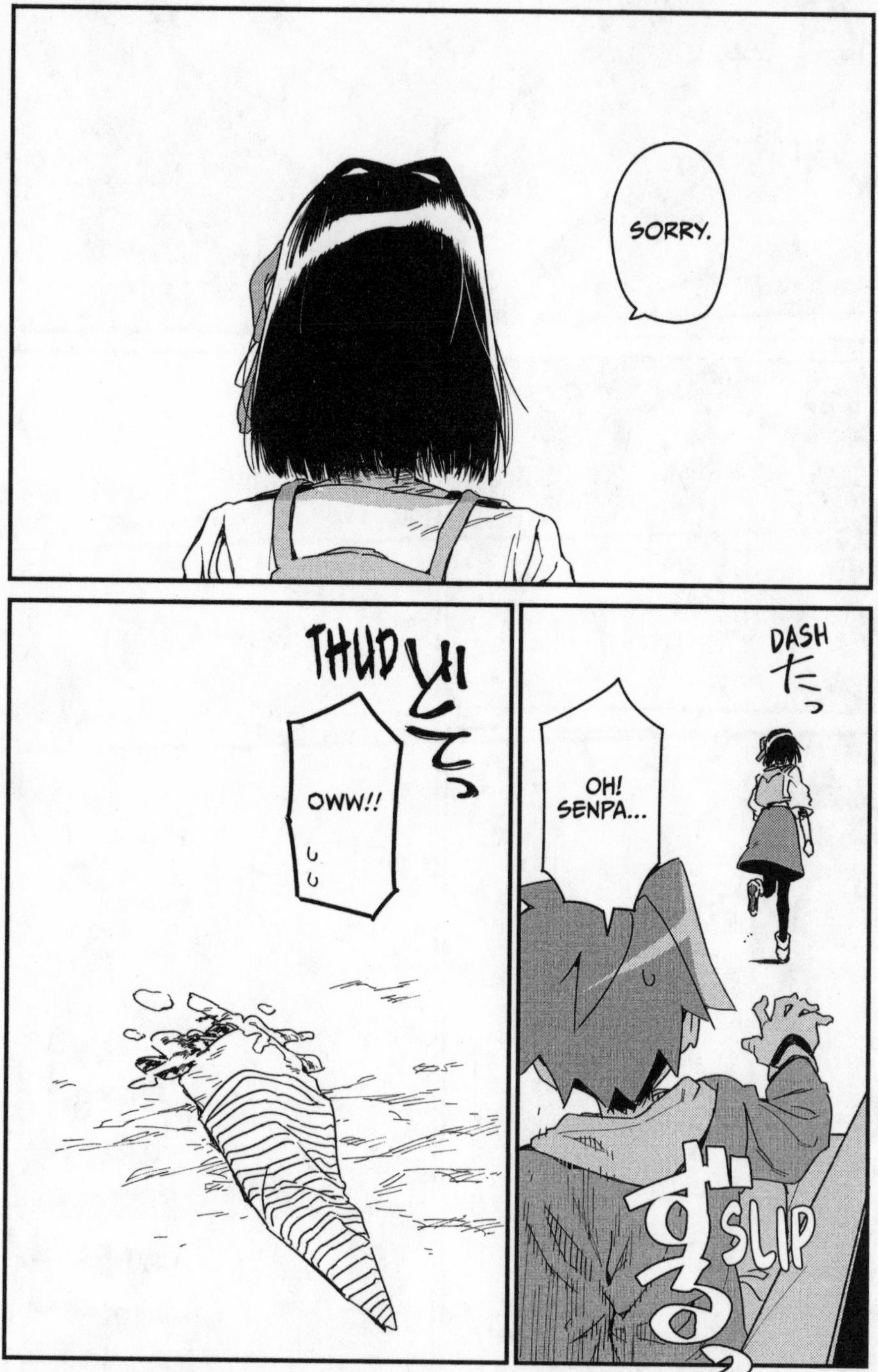
SORRY.
DASH
たっ
OH! SENPA...
ずるっ
SLIP
THUD
どてっ
OWW!!

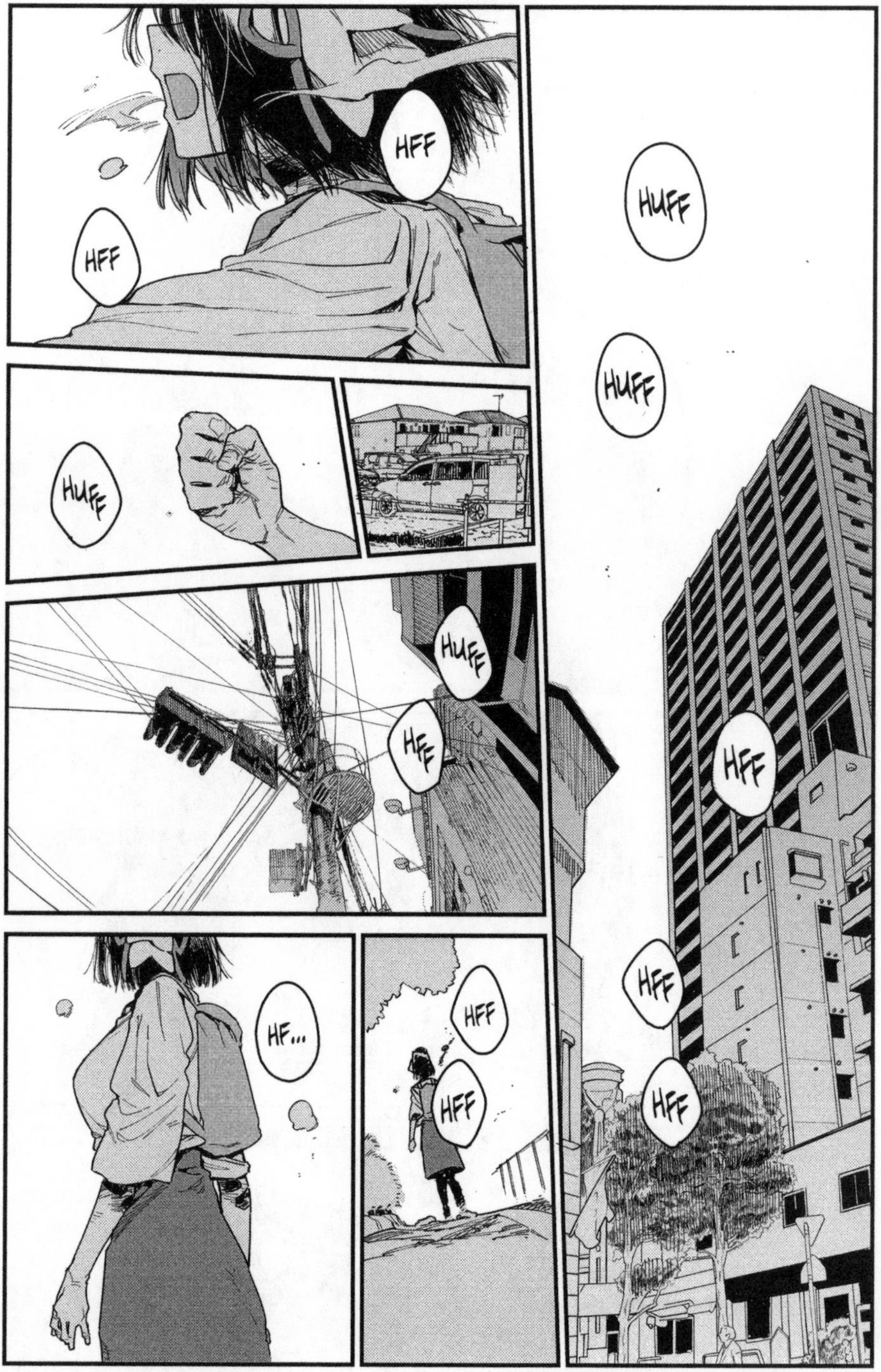
HUFF
HUFF
HFF
HFF
HFF
HFF
HFF
HUFF
HUFF
HFF
HFF
HFF
HF...

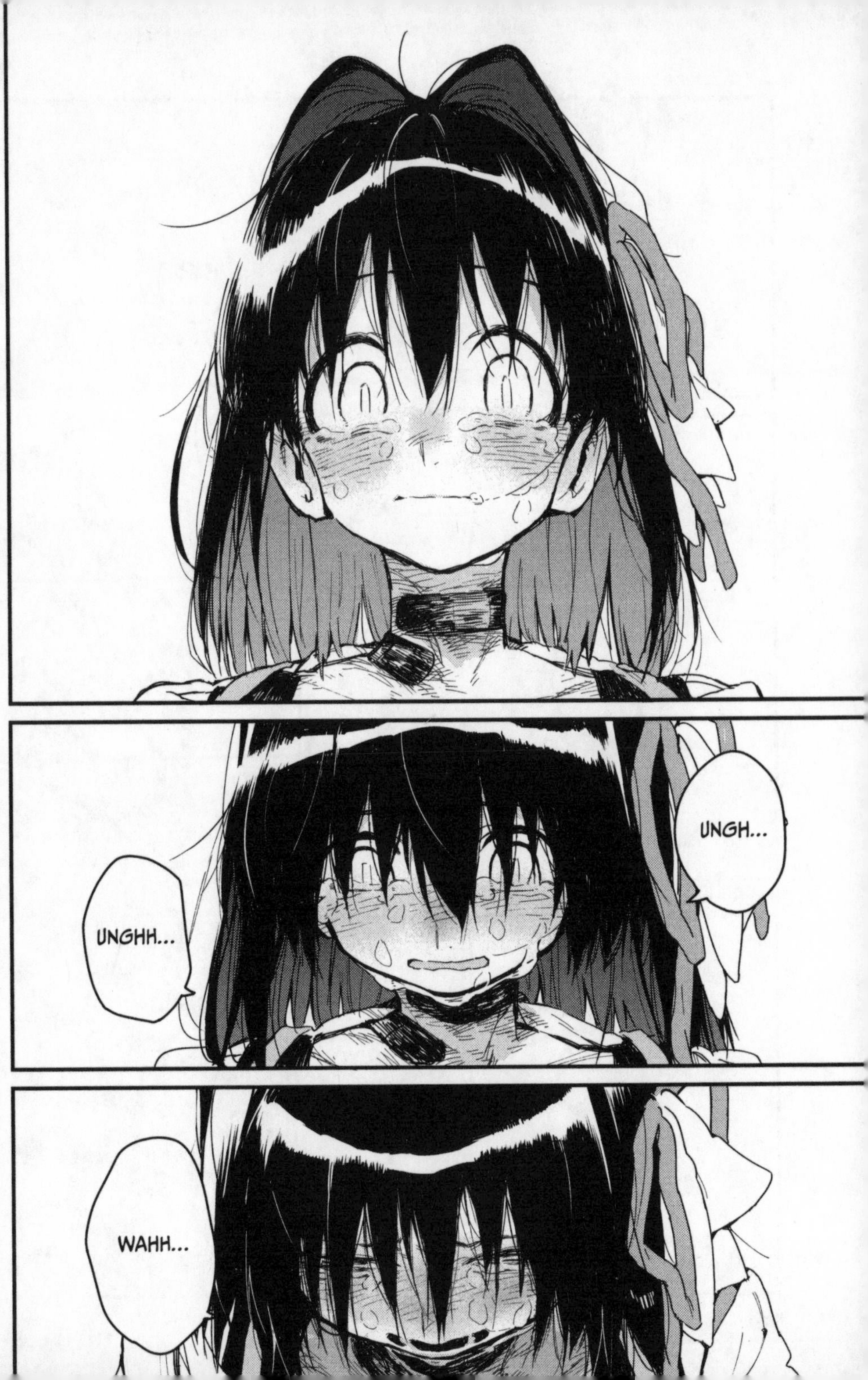
UNGH...
UNGHH...
WAHH...

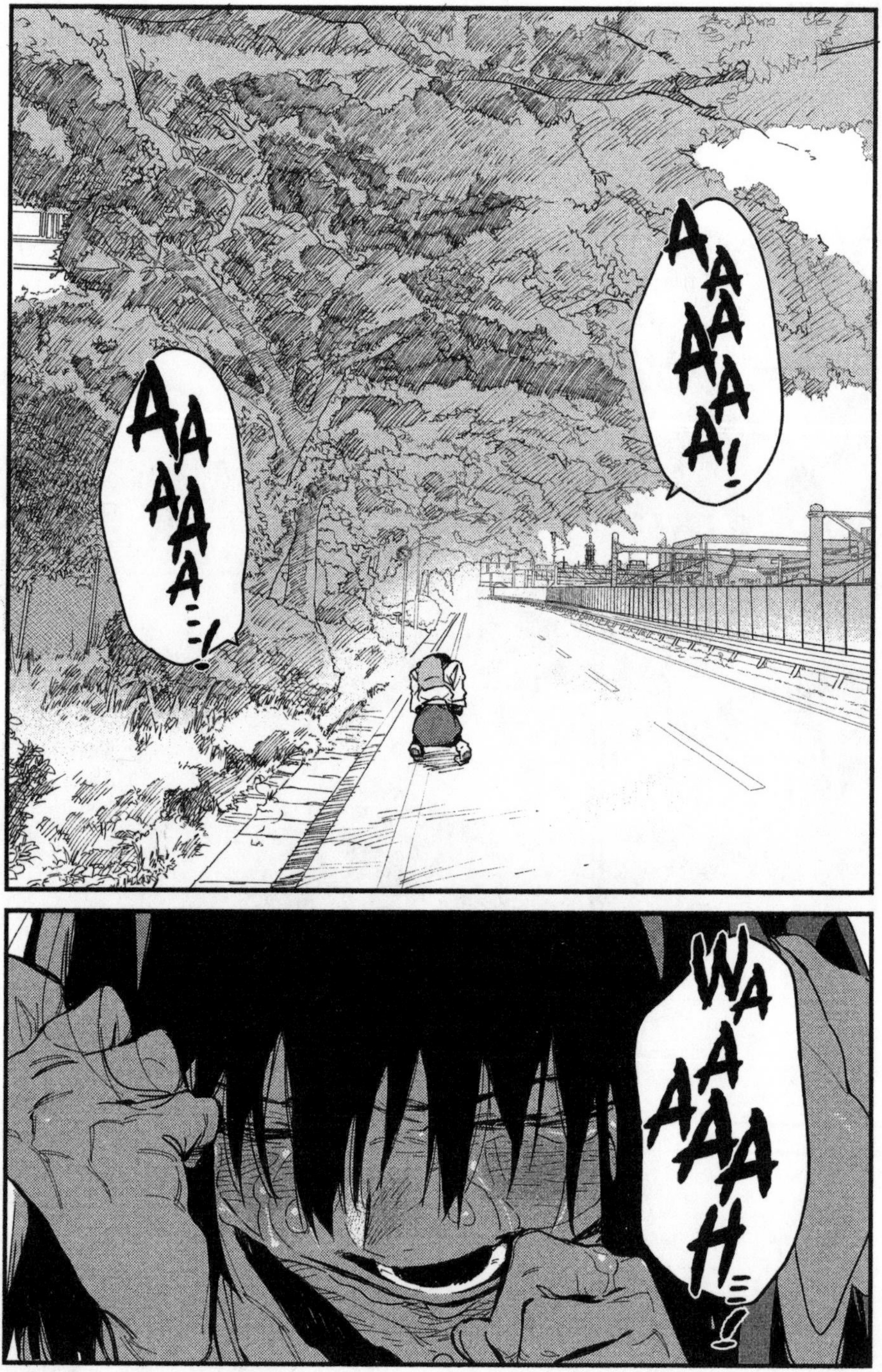
AAAAAA!
AAAAA...!
WAAAAAH...!

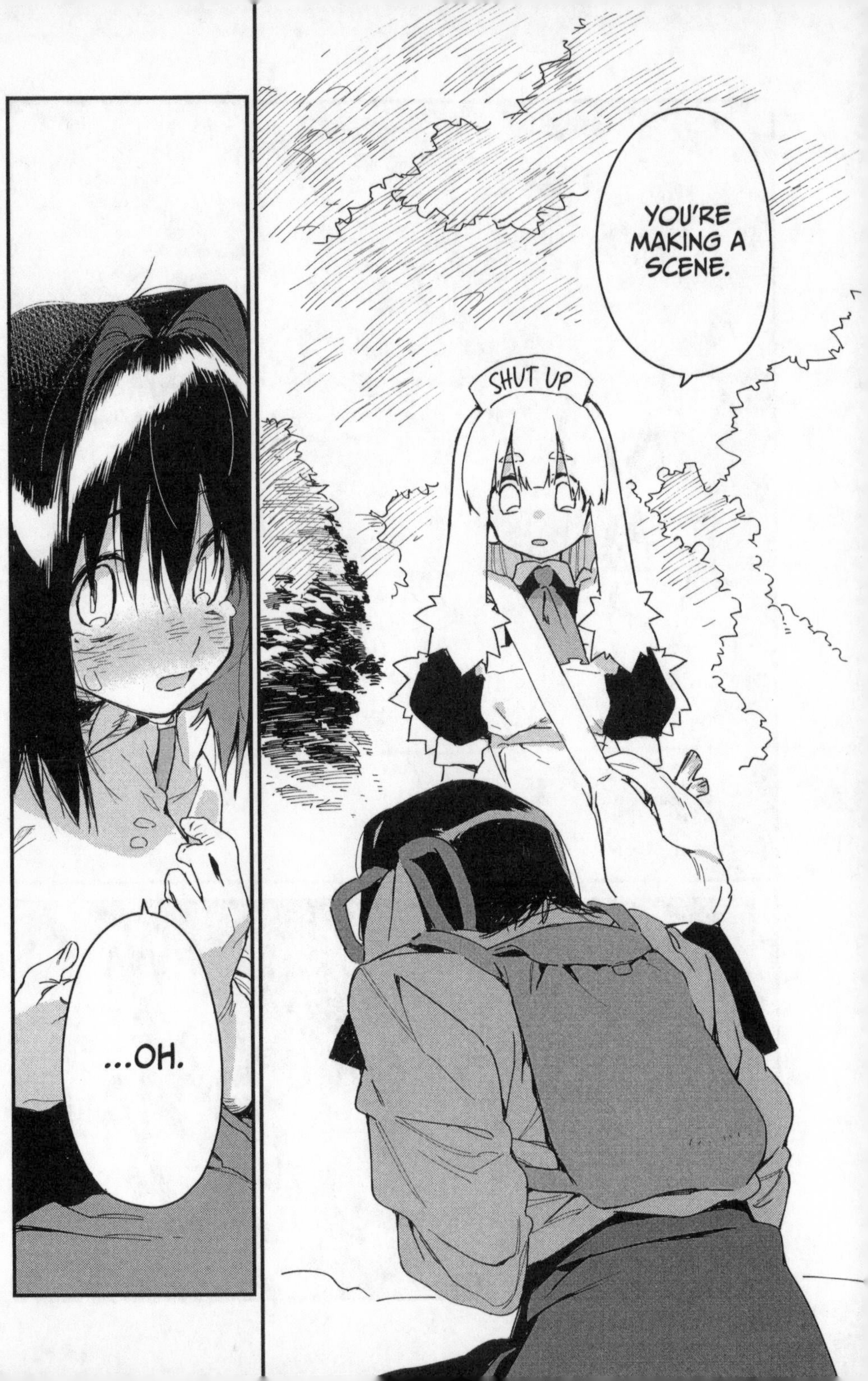
YOU'RE MAKING A SCENE.
SHUT UP
...OH.

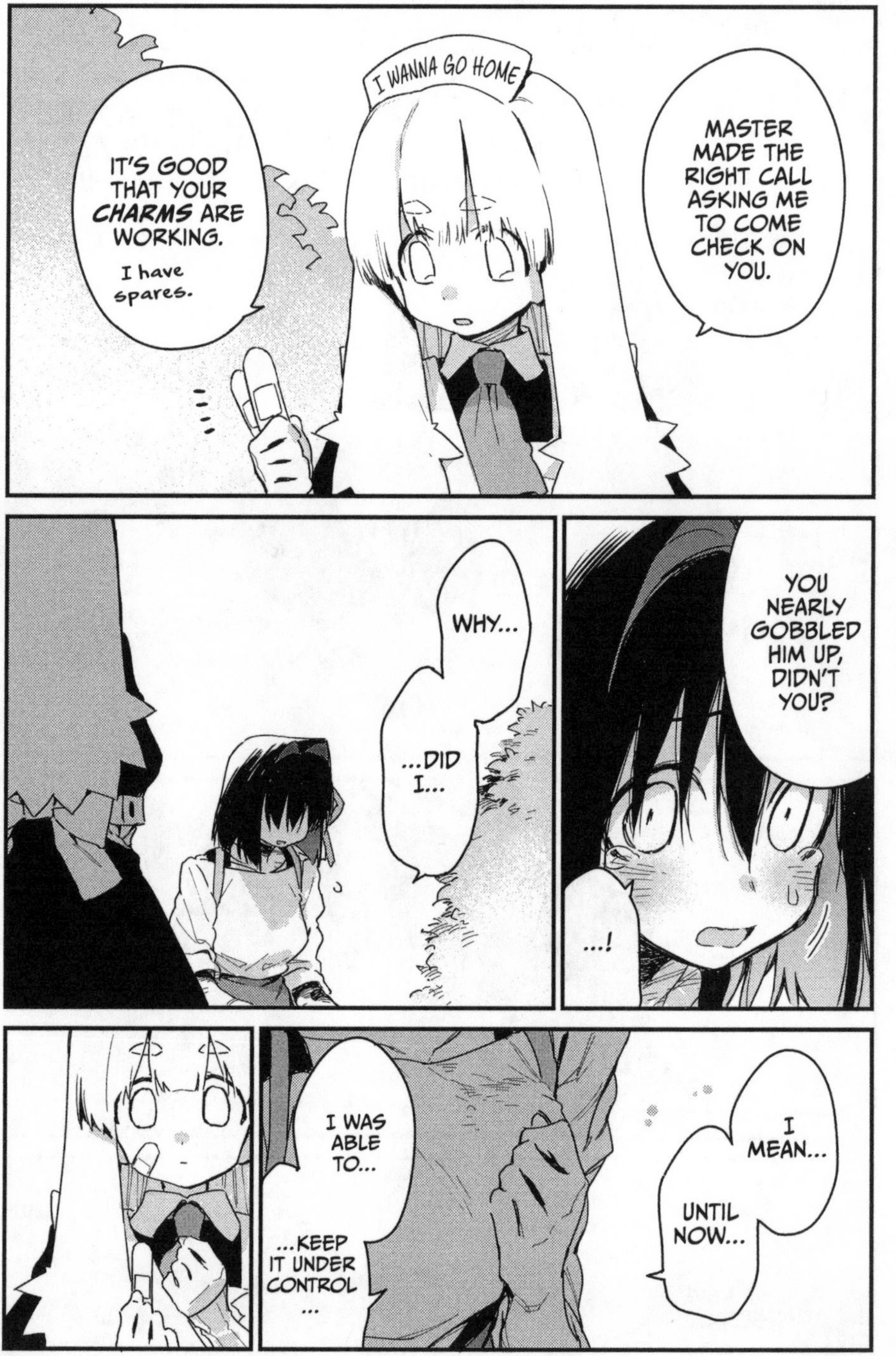
MASTER MADE THE RIGHT CALL ASKING ME TO COME CHECK ON YOU.
I WANNA GO HOME
IT'S GOOD THAT YOUR CHARMS ARE WORKING.
I have spares.
YOU NEARLY GOBBLED HIM UP, DIDN'T YOU?
...!
WHY...
...DID I...
I MEAN...
UNTIL NOW...
I WAS ABLE TO...
...KEEP IT UNDER CONTROL ...

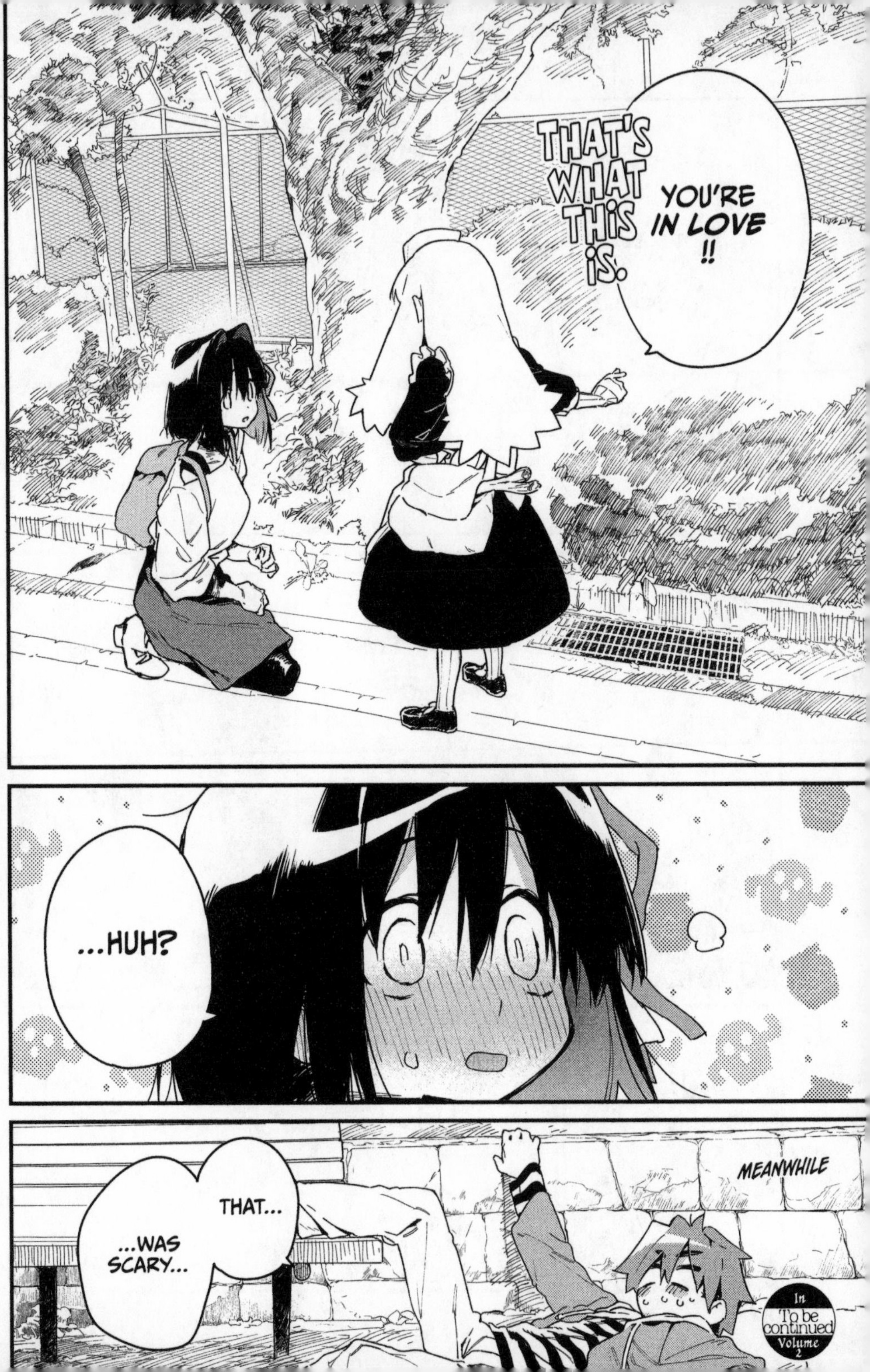
YOU'RE IN LOVE !!
THAT'S WHAT THIS IS.
...HUH?
MEANWHILE
THAT... ...WAS SCARY...
To be continued In Volume 2

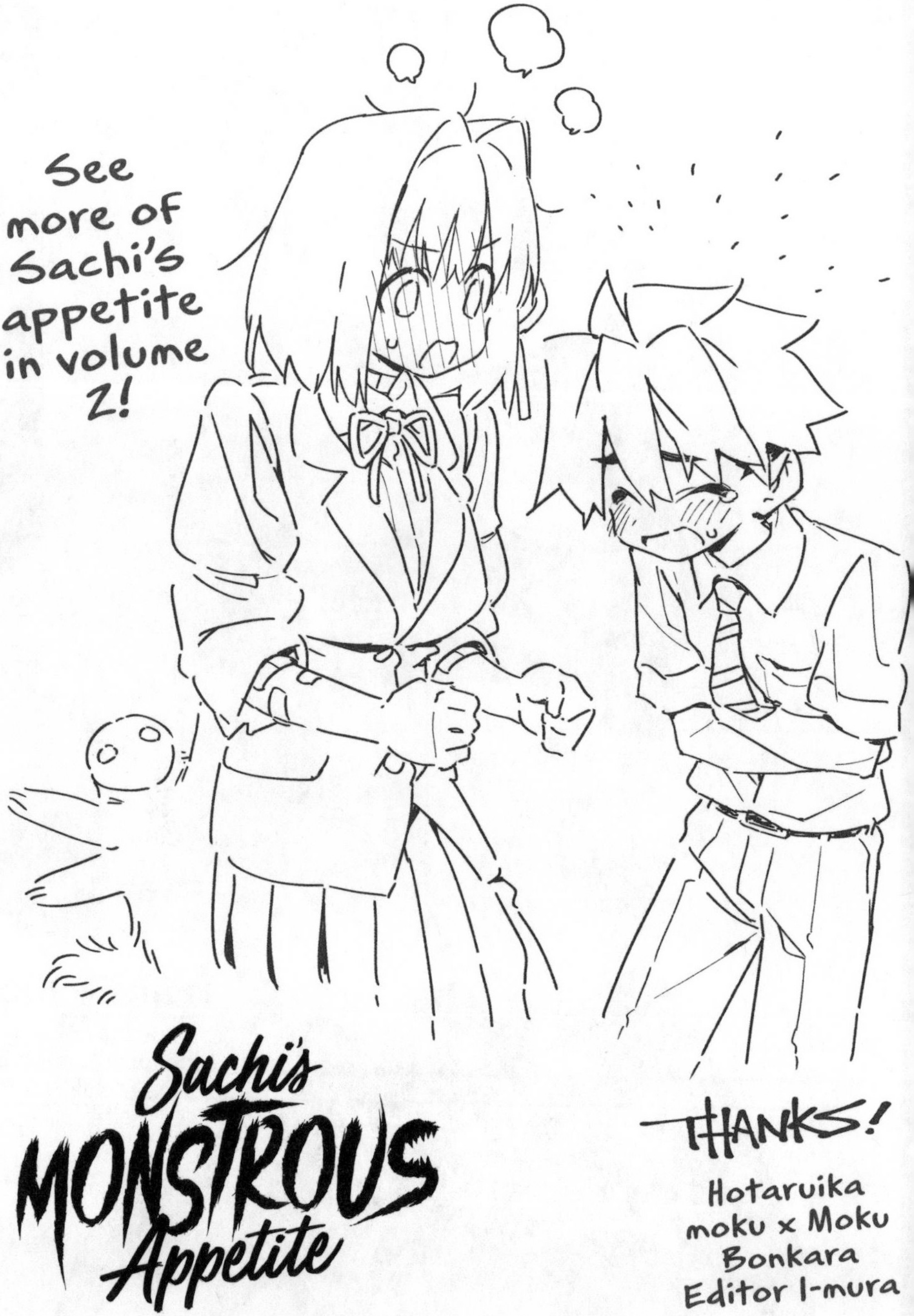
See more of Sachi's appetite in volume 2!

Sachi's MONSTROUS Appetite

THANKS!

Hotaruika
moku x Moku
Bonkara
Editor I-mura

Continued in Volume 2

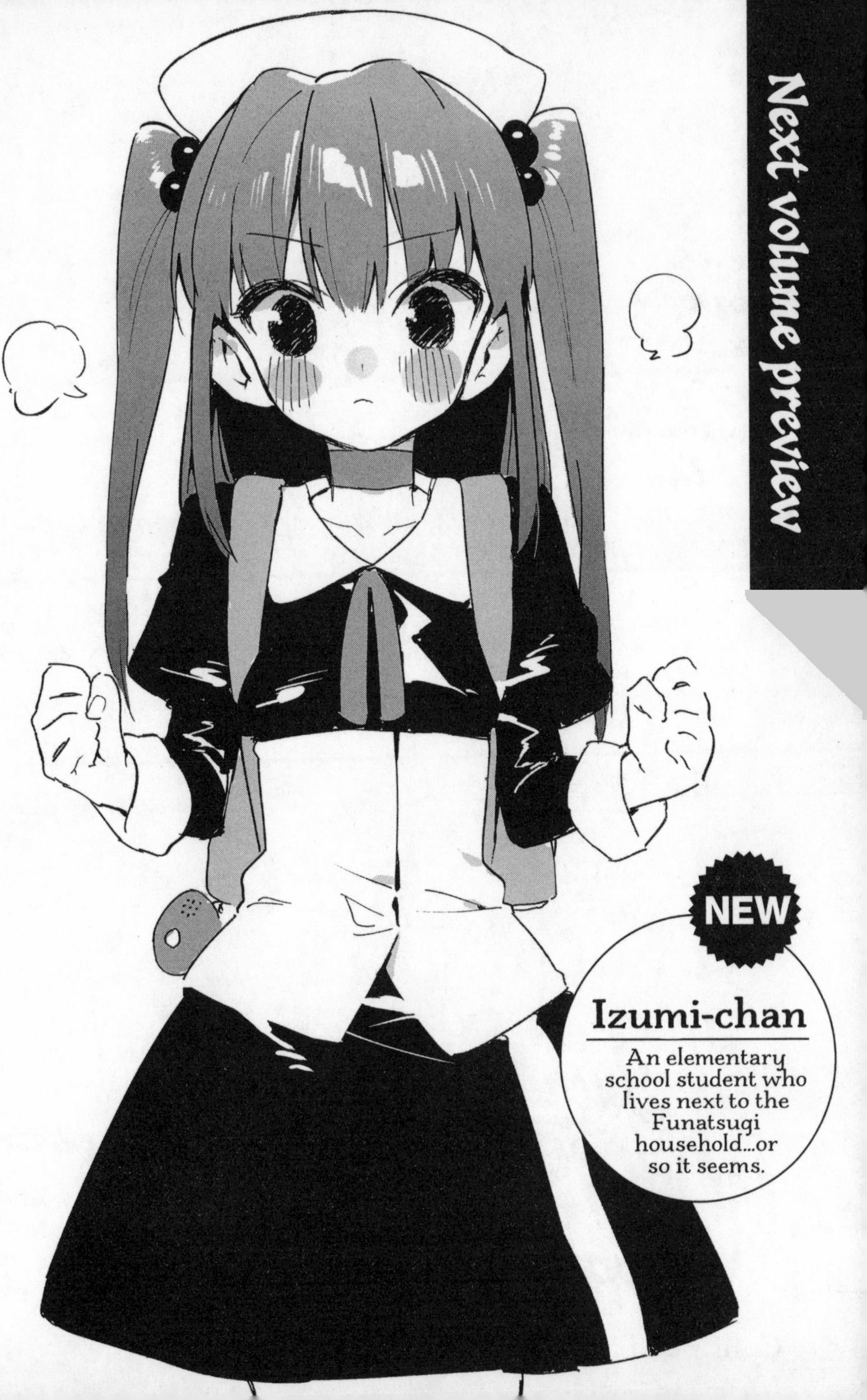
Next volume preview
NEW
Izumi-chan
An elementary school student who lives next to the Funatsugi household...or so it seems.

Translation Notes

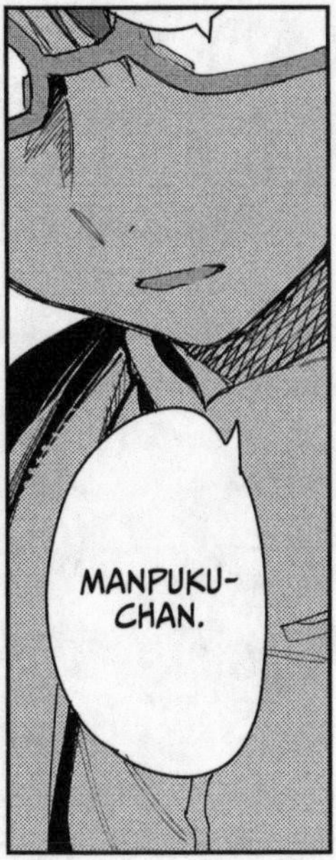
MANPUKU-CHAN.

Manpuku-chan, page 89

Sachi's nickname is an alternative reading for her last name, Mitsuhara. Without seeing it written out, Sachi's last name sounds somewhat standard, but as written, her name literally means "full stomach." The usual reading for the characters in Sachi's last name is "*manpuku*," which is an apt nickname for someone with such a voracious appetite.

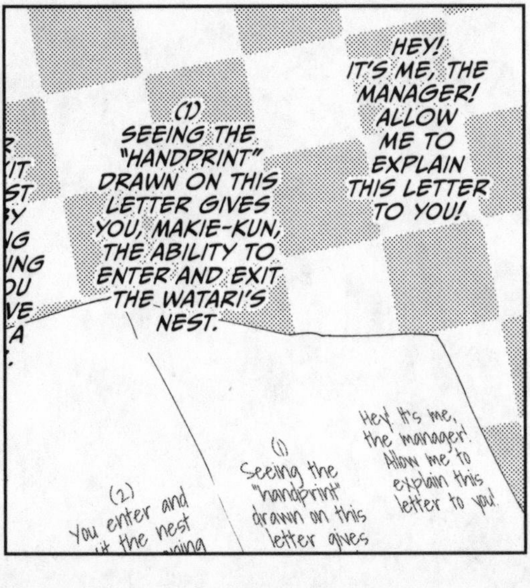
HEY! IT'S ME, THE MANAGER! ALLOW ME TO EXPLAIN THIS LETTER TO YOU!
(1) SEEING THE "HANDPRINT" DRAWN ON THIS LETTER GIVES YOU, MAKIE-KUN, THE ABILITY TO ENTER AND EXIT THE WATARI'S NEST.
Hey! It's me, the manager! Allow me to explain this letter to you!
(1) Seeing the "handprint" drawn on this letter gives
(2) You enter and

Hey! It's me, the manager, page 131

In Japanese, this line was an instantly recognizable reference to a catchphrase said by Goku of Akira Toriyama's *Dragon Ball* series. In the Japanese version of the series, the previews for upcoming episodes were narrated by Goku, who would start off by saying "Hey! It's me, Goku!"

Sachi's
MONSTROUS
Appetite

A dark and sexy body-horror action manga perfect for fans of *Prison School* and *High School of the Dead*!

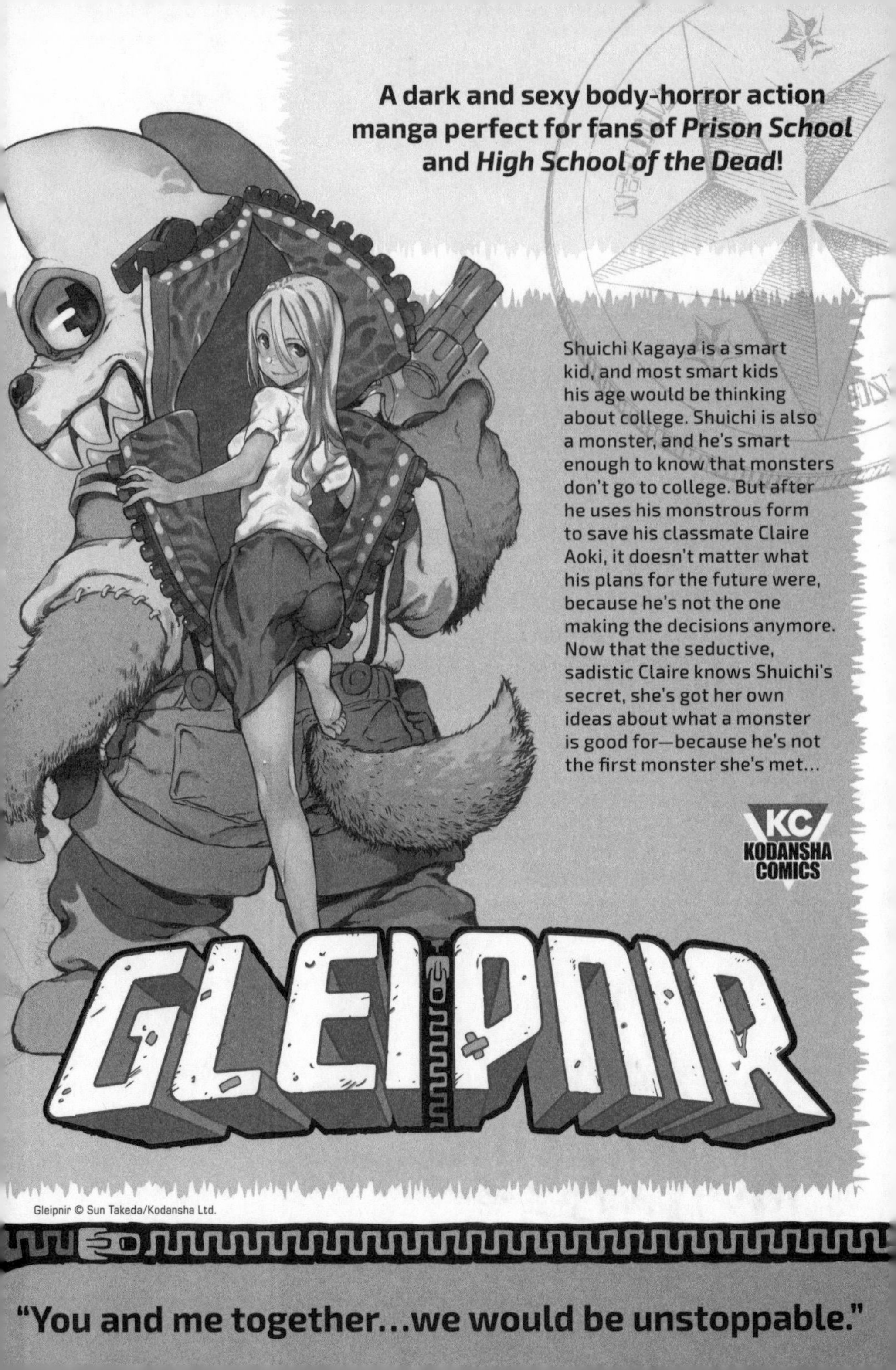

Shuichi Kagaya is a smart kid, and most smart kids his age would be thinking about college. Shuichi is also a monster, and he's smart enough to know that monsters don't go to college. But after he uses his monstrous form to save his classmate Claire Aoki, it doesn't matter what his plans for the future were, because he's not the one making the decisions anymore. Now that the seductive, sadistic Claire knows Shuichi's secret, she's got her own ideas about what a monster is good for—because he's not the first monster she's met...

KC KODANSHA COMICS

GLEIPNIR

"You and me together...we would be unstoppable."

THE SWEET SCENT OF LOVE IS IN THE AIR! FOR FANS OF OFFBEAT ROMANCES LIKE *WOTAKOI*

VOL. 1

SWEAT AND SOAP

KINTETSU YAMADA

Sweat and Soap © Kintetsu Yamada / Kodansha Ltd.

In an office romance, there's a fine line between sexy and awkward... and that line is where Asako — a woman who sweats copiously — meets Koutarou — a perfume developer who can't get enough of Asako's, er, scent. Don't miss a romcom manga like no other!

KC
KODANSHA
COMICS

Japan's most powerful spirit medium delves into the ghost world's greatest mysteries!

Story by Kyo Shirodaira, famed author of mystery fiction and creator of *Spiral*, *Blast of Tempest*, and *The Record of a Fallen Vampire*.

Both touched by spirits called yôkai, Kotoko and Kurô have gained unique superhuman powers. But to gain her powers Kotoko has given up an eye and a leg, and Kurô's personal life is in shambles. So when Kotoko suggests they team up to deal with renegades from the spirit world, Kurô doesn't have many other choices, but Kotoko might just have a few ulterior motives...

IN/SPECTRE

STORY BY KYO SHIRODAIRA
ART BY CHASHIBA KATASE

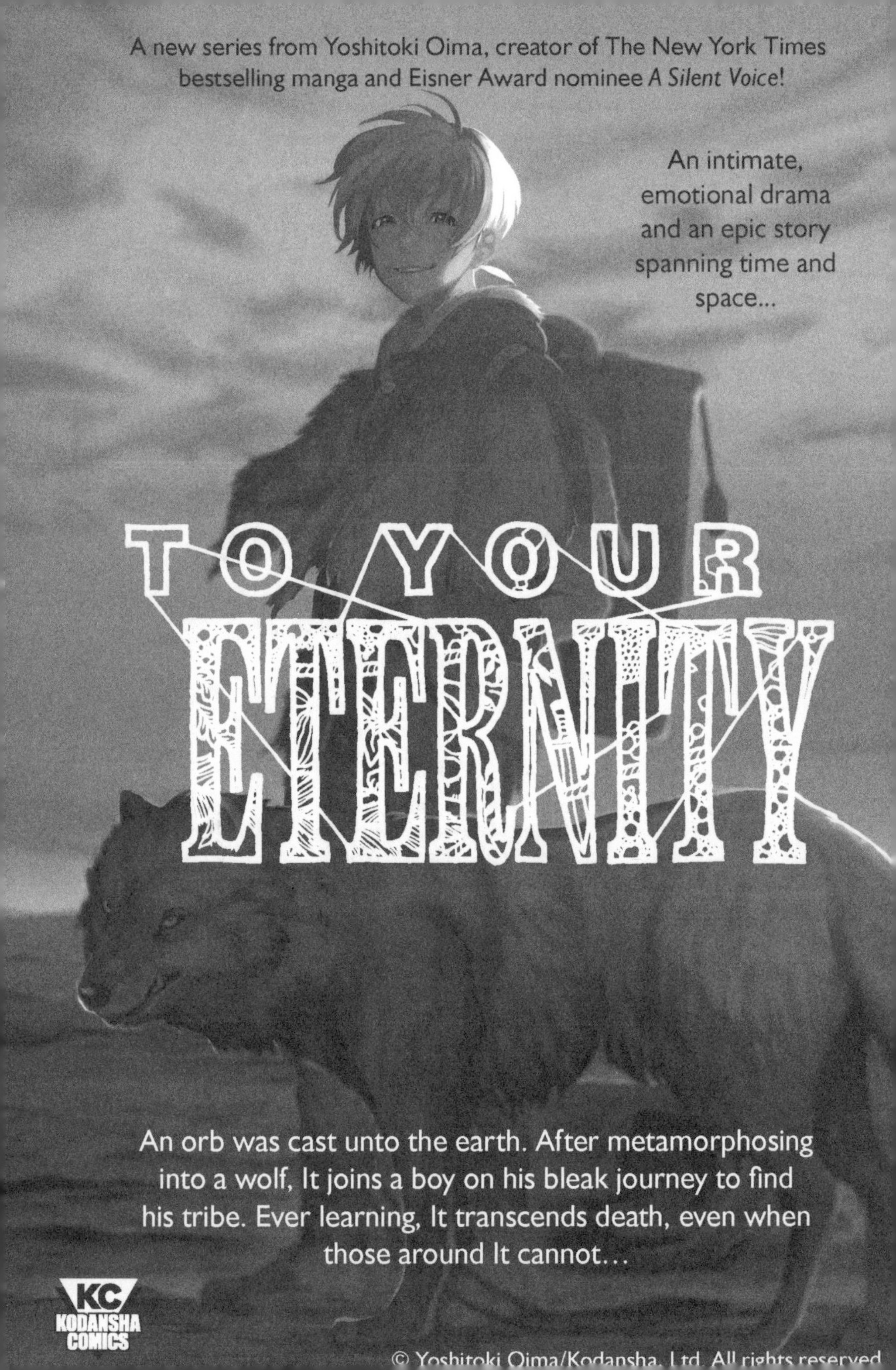
A new series from Yoshitoki Oima, creator of The New York Times bestselling manga and Eisner Award nominee *A Silent Voice*!
An intimate, emotional drama and an epic story spanning time and space...
TO YOUR ETERNITY
An orb was cast unto the earth. After metamorphosing into a wolf, It joins a boy on his bleak journey to find his tribe. Ever learning, It transcends death, even when those around It cannot...
KC KODANSHA COMICS
© Yoshitoki Oima/Kodansha, Ltd. All rights reserved.

A Kodansha Comics Trade Paperback Original
Sachi's Monstrous Appetite 1 copyright © 2018 Chomoran
English translation copyright © 2020 Chomoran

Published in the United States by Kodansha Comics, an imprint of Kodansha USA Publishing, LLC, New York.

Publication rights for this English edition arranged through Kodansha Ltd., Tokyo.

First published in Japan in 2018 by Kodansha Ltd., Tokyo.

ISBN 978-1-64651-173-0

Original cover design by imagejack danyumi

Printed in the United States of America.

www.kodanshacomics.com

9 8 7 6 5 4 3 2 1
Translation: Ajani Oloye
Lettering: Brandon Bovia
Editing: Haruko Hashimoto
Kodansha Comics edition cover design by Adam Del Re

Publisher: Kiichiro Sugawara

Director of publishing services: Ben Applegate
Associate director of operations: Stephen Pakula
Publishing services managing editor: Noelle Webster
Assistant production manager: Emi Lotto, Angela Zurlo
Logo and character art ©Kodansha USA Publishing, LLC